Franciscan Theology
of the
Environment:

AN INTRODUCTORY READER

Franciscan Theology
of the
Environment:

AN INTRODUCTORY READER

EDITED BY

Dawn M. Nothwehr, OSF

Franciscan Press
Quincy University

Franciscan Theology of the Environment: An Introductory Reader
edited by Dawn M. Nothwehr

Franciscan Press
Quincy University
1800 College Avenue
Quincy, IL 62301
PH 217.228.5670
FAX 217.228.5672
http://www.qufranciscanpress.com

© 2002 Franciscan Press

Book design and typesetting by Laurel Fitch, Chicago, IL.
Cover design by Soraya Jimenez, Bogotá, Colombia, S.A.

Printed in the United States of America
First Edition: November 2002
First Printing: November 2002
1 2 3 4 5 6 7 8 9 0

Library of Congress Cataloguing-in-Publication Data
Franciscan theology of the environment : an introductory reader / edited by
    Dawn M. Nothwehr
        p. cm.
    Includes bibliographical references.
    ISBN 0-8199-1007-4
    1. Human ecology -- Religious aspects--Catholic Church. 2. Franciscans--
    Theology. I. Nothwehr, Dawn M., 1951-

    BX1795.H82 F73 2002
    261.8'362--dc21   2002035304

Dedication

I dedicate this work to the memory of Marie Nord, OSF (July 2, 1945–April 9, 2001), who was a member of my religious community, the Sisters of St. Francis, Congregation of Our Lady of Lourdes, Rochester, MN.

Marie was a farmer, social justice activist, poet, artist, biologist, teacher, mentor, and friend. From a true believer in the way of St. Francis of Assisi, Marie's poems express the wonder, delight, playfulness and joy she found in creation. Through this dynamism Marie was drawn in and she invited others to accompany her into the very heart of God. Those of us who knew her were blessed, indeed!

Bosque del Apache[1]
November 19, 1994

ASTONISHING BEAUTY!

Breath and heartbeat
collide in my throat
tears sting my eyes—
    i watch

blizzards of snow geese
frozen in gold
against blackening sky
brilliance on dark velvet.

Elegant sandhill
steel grey wings
caress steel grey waters
a graceful two-step landing
as near to me as you.

Endless sweep of land and sky
    marsh and mountain
held for eternity
as fingers of the gods
press sun into the horizon
squishing golden magic
E V E R Y W H E R E!

      — Marie Nord 11-20-94

HOME[1]

I came home to a place
    I had not been before.

I return to a place that
    may not recognize me.

What mystery is this
    placed before me?

Is there no place that is "home?"
    Or are all places home?

      — Marie Nord 10-23-94

RACES[1]

This afternoon there was
    a leaf regatta at the pond.
Colorful sails flagged
    a playful breeze,
Tension was in the air.
    A close race —
Pin Oak and Sugar Maple lead early,
    but Tulip Tree won the cup.

      — Marie Nord 10-21-94

Contents

Commendatory Foreword

"Praise be to you, my Lord, with all your creatures..."
(*The Canticle*, St. Francis of Assisi)

For generations, the awe-inspiring, joy-filled words of Francis of Assisi have touched the hearts of people and moved them to contemplation, reverence, prayer, and action. The simple truth that is so poignantly articulated in Francis' song of universal praise has affected believers and non-believers alike. For Francis, Jesus Christ stands at the heart of all theology and spirituality. Through his Incarnation the magnificence of all creation and its relationship to God is revealed. Francis' unconditional love of Christ was manifest in his love for the entire created world. Franciscan theology is firmly grounded in the values that moved Francis and guided his spiritual journey. In our world today there is great need for this wisdom as we face the environmental issues that challenge our global society.

In this important text, *Franciscan Theology of the Environment: An Introductory Reader,* Dawn M. Nothwehr, OSF, gathers together for the first time, the contributions of significant Franciscan scholars who offer their insightful interpretations of the primary Franciscan sources as they speak to today's environmental concerns. The structure of this work invites the reader to walk the path of cosmic discovery as environmental issues are viewed through the lens of Franciscan tradition. Beginning with Sacred Scripture and proceeding to the classical Franciscan texts the reader is immersed in the rich heritage of Franciscan thought that probes the heights and depths of God's relationship to the cosmos.

Dr. Nothwehr's well-developed pedagogical style is apparent in the introductory remarks she provides for each of the major sections of the book. A valuable source for the student reader, her comments link the sources, introduce pertinent terminology and theological concepts while highlighting the essential elements contained in each successive essay. The questions for discussion and reflection that appear at the end of each section prompt the individual or group examining the work to see the relationship between and among the ideas raised, to think more deeply about these concerns, and to consider their relevance to themselves and the global community. Dr. Nothwher's teaching philosophy is further in evidence through the supplemental materials she provides for the reader including: a list of resources and action organizations, a glossary of essential terms, journal exercises, and suggestions for research and reflection papers. This book is an invaluable resource for study and reflection that students from all walks of life can return to again and again. Following in the footsteps of Francis and Clare of Assisi, Dr. Nothwehr, in service to all God's creatures, has heralded a strong Franciscan voice in the ongoing environmental conversation.

Shannon Schrein, OSF
Professor of Religious Studies
Lourdes College

Acknowledgements

The articles, chapters, and essays reprinted in *Franciscan Theology of the Environment: An Introductory Reader* first appeared in the following publications and are reprinted with permission: Zachary Hayes, OFM, "A New Reading of the Sources," in *A Window to the Divine: A Study of Christian Creation Theology*, Quincy, IL: Franciscan Press, 17–30; Jeanne Kay, "Concepts of Nature in the Hebrew Bible," *Environmental Ethics* 10 (Winter 1988): 309–327; Susan Power Bratton, "Christian Ecotheology and the Old Testament," *Environmental Ethics*, 6 (Fall 1984): 195–209; Robert J. Karris, OFM, "Colossians 1:15–20—Christ Jesus as Cosmic Lord and Peacemaker," in *A Symphony of New Testament Hymns*, Collegeville: The Liturgical Press, 1996, 63–91; William Short, OFM, "The Franciscan Spirit," in *The Franciscans*, Wilmington DE: Michael Glazier, 1989, 104–121; Elizabeth A. Dreyer, "'[God] Whose Beauty the Sun and Moon Admire': Clare and Ecology," *The Way*, Supplement 80 (Summer 1994):76–86; Thomas Murtagh, OFM, "St. Francis and Ecology," *The Cord* 39/4 (April 1989): 99–109; Eric Doyle, OFM, "'The Canticle of Brother Sun' and the Value of Creation," in *St. Francis and the Song of Brotherhood and Sisterhood*, [reprint of New York: The Seabury Press, 1981] St. Bonaventure, NY: The Franciscan Institute, 1997, 41–59; 219–20.(page citations are to the reprint edition); Thomas A. Nairn, OFM, "St. Francis of Assisi's *Canticle of the Creatures* as an Exercise of the Moral Imagination," in Kathleen Hughes, ed. *Finding a Voice to Give God Praise: Essays in the Many Languages of the Liturgy*, Collegeville, MN: The Liturgical Press, 1998; Zachary Hayes, OFM. "Bonaventure: Mystery of the Triune God," in Kenan B. Osborne, OFM, ed., *The History of Franciscan Theology*, St. Bonaventure NY: The Franciscan Institute, 1994, 43–93; Phil Hobbing, OFM, "St. Bonaventure and Ecology," *The Cord*, 40/11 (December 1990): 336–345; Philotheus Boehner, OFM, "The Franciscan Doctor," *The Cord*, 45/3 (May–June 1995):37–38;

Kenan B. Osborne, OFM, "Incarnation, Individuality and Diversity,"*The Cord*, 45/3 (May–June 1995):19–26; Séamus Mulholland, OFM, "Christ: The Haecceitas of God," *The Cord* 40/6 (June 1990): 165–72; William Short, OFM, "Pied Beauty: Gerard Manley Hopkins and the Scotistic View of Nature," *The Cord* 45/3. (May–June 1995): 27–36; Mary Beth Ingham, CSJ, "A Certain Affection for Justice,"*The Cord* 45/3 (May–June 1995):11–18; Michael J. Himes & Kenneth R. Himes, OFM, "The Sacrament of Creation," *Commonweal* 117 (Jan. 26, 1990): 42–9; James F. Edmiston, OFM, "How to Love a Worm? Biodiversity: Franciscan Spirituality and Praxis," in John E. Carroll and Keith Warner, OFM eds., *Ecology and Religion: Scientists Speak*: Quincy, IL: Franciscan Press, 1998, 289–301; Margaret Pirkl, OSF, "Care of Creation: Working With the United Nations," *The Cord* 40/8 (September, 1991): 238–48.

This volume would not have come into existence without the encouragement and advice of my friend and classmate, Shannon Schrein, OSF, Ph.D., Professor of Religious Studies and the 2000 recipient of the Lourdes College Teaching Excellence Award (Sylvania, Ohio). I am indebted to Ramona Miller who read and critiqued some of the earliest drafts of this work and Ingrid Peterson who encouraged me along the way. A particular note of thanks is due to Eileen Haugh, OSF, who proofread the final proofs of the book. Last but not least, I am grateful to my colleagues in the Department of Historical and Doctrinal Studies at Catholic Theological Union, especially Tom Nairn and Zachary Hayes for helping me bring this work to publication.

Preface

The seminal thoughts leading to the compilation of this volume came from several directions. Initial conversations with my Franciscan sisters—Margaret Pirkl, Ingrid Peterson, and Ramona Miller at Tau Center in Winona, MN, stirred my curiosity about the potential for a unique contribution by Franciscan theology to conversations on the present environmental crisis. I later discovered that current theological reflection was also turning to the Franciscan school—long neglected by the Roman Catholic tradition, particularly after the promulgation of *Aeterni Patris* by Leo XIII (August 4, 1879)—for some unplumbed wisdom to guide the people of God attempting to resolve environmental issues in our ecologically threatened age.

One outstanding event that piqued my awareness was Elizabeth A. Johnson's 1996 Presidential Address to the Catholic Theological Society of America in San Diego, California. Johnson cited St. Bonaventure among those who had integrated the cosmos into theology in an exemplary manner:

> Bonaventure instructs the soul journeying toward God to see the universe as a wonderful work of art in which one recognizes traces of its maker:
>
> "Whoever is not enlightened by the splendor of created things is blind; whoever is not aroused by the sound of their voice is deaf; whoever does not praise God for all creatures is mute; whoever after so much evidence does not recognize the First Principle is a fool [*stultus est* = an idiot]."[1]

She further challenged theologians: "What is needed now, I am convinced, is yet one more turn, a fully inclusive turn to the heavens and the earth, a return to cosmology, in order to restore fullness of vision and get theology back on the track from which it fell off a few hundred years ago."[2]

At about that same time, I was invited to teach an upper level undergraduate theology course, designed with the particular needs of the environmental studies and theology majors in mind. The course came to be known as *Franciscan Theology of the Environment*. When creating the course, I quickly discovered that while the Franciscan tradition is indeed rich with material that would provide fertile sources of reflection for these students, there was very little (beyond the primary sources) from which I could draw in order to make that wealth of information accessible to them.

In recent years numerous undergraduate resources on ecotheology had become available. But it was confirmed in conversations among Franciscan educators at the *Earth Conference '98: Canticle of Creation*, September 26–27, 1998, in Sylvania, OH, at Lourdes College, that there was yet no single volume that focused exclusively on Franciscan sources and which is directed to the undergraduate audience. While clearly there was a movement among Franciscan educators toward placing the sciences and Franciscan theology in conversation with one another, James F. Edmiston, OFM, Phil Hoebing, OFM, and I at Quincy University were among the few who had actually engaged this enterprise in an established curriculum. These realizations sparked the idea to publish a reader for undergraduates, based on the materials I had utilized for the *Franciscan Theology of the Environment* course.

The articles for this collection were selected with an eye toward discovering what Franciscans are saying about the appropriation of their own charism to the various issues of the environmental crisis. The works included here are recognized by the Franciscan family as those of fine scholars who have appropriated the charism in a fitting manner. Although several of the authors are not formal members of the Franciscan community, their work is accepted among Franciscans as being consistent with the widely-recognized interpretive framework of the Franciscan intellectual tradition.

A word must be said about three sets of terms used in the introductory pieces to each section of this book. *Franciscan theology of creation* or *creation theology* addresses the Franciscan appropriation of the Christian doctrine of creation and the correlative Christian response of wonder and worship. *Franciscan theology of the environment* stresses the notion that one context is shared by all in the cosmos—human and non-human, animate and inanimate alike. Franciscan ecotheology distinguishes the facticity and the ontological status of the relatedness of all beings, and the ethical norms of love, justice and mutuality that flow from that reality.

Several of the articles in this reader were written prior to the publication of the 1999–2001, three-volume critical edition of the Franciscan sources, *Francis of Assisi: Early Documents*, edited by Regis J. Armstrong, J. A. Wayne Hellmann, and William J. Short. Readers will discover that some of the early Franciscan sources are given a different title in the new critical edition than in the common 1973 *Omnibus of Sources* edited by Marion A. Habig. A list of abbreviations for the titles used in the older *Omnibus* is included with the Glossary at the back of this volume for the reader's convenience. Readers should be aware that all notes in this volume that refer to an article, essay, lecture, paper, or chapter reprinted here, cite the pagination of the original source in which the selection appeared.

This volume is divided into five major sections. The first section provides discourse on some of the essential texts from the Hebrew and Christian scriptures which form the unity of the creation/redemption schema distinctly present in Franciscan theology, and which are frequently referred to in Franciscan discussion and understanding of environmental issues. The second section treats the significant notions central to the Franciscan charism raised in the primary works of Francis and Clare, and formative of their particular spiritualities. Part three unfolds the significant contributions of Bonaventure and shows how his theology and philosophy bring systematic form to the mystical intuitions of Francis of Assisi concerning the essential kinship of creation. The notions of the primacy of Christ, *haecceitas*, and mutuality are among the significant contributions from the work of John Duns Scotus that have provided great insight for a modern Franciscan understanding of environmental issues. The final section provides some insights into the direction of Franciscan praxis and work on behalf of peace, justice and the integrity of creation. A list of key resources and organizations that may be useful to those seeking to work for environmental justice and the integrity of creation from a Franciscan perspective is also included. Some ideas for journal work and research and reflection papers are given in the final pages before the Glossary.

It is my hope that this work will make the Franciscan contribution to ecotheology accessible to a wider audience, and ultimately, contribute in some small way to an increase in reverence for all creation and a more healthy environment.

Notes

1. Elizabeth A. Johnson, "Presidential Address: Turn to the Heavens and the Earth: Retrieval of the Cosmos in Theology," *Proceedings of the Catholic Theological Society of America* 51 (1996):3. Johnson cites Bonaventure, *Intinerarium mentis in Deum*, c.1, no.15; adapted from *The Mind's Journey to God*, trans. Lawrence Cunningham, (Chicago: Franciscan Herald Press, 1979).
2. Johnson, "Presidential Address," 5.

Cosmic Mysticism, Cosmic Christ, Cosmic Mutuality

Dawn M. Nothwehr, OSF

INTRODUCTION

There is perhaps no better illustration of the relationship between ecology, theology, spirituality, and the meaning of human life than the way of the Kogi of the Sierra Nevada de Santa Marta mountain range in Northern Colombia.[1] Their entire worldview and self-understanding has deep theological roots. The profound sense of relationship with all beings known by this people is rooted in the narrative of their distinct and intentional creation by the god Aluna to inhabit and care for "the heart of the earth," their particular region in northern Colombia. Theirs is a life connected to the land upon which Aluna placed them, giving them the ways and the knowledge they needed in order to not only sustain and flourish themselves, but also the means by which the rest of the world would be sustained and enabled to flourish. Theirs is a world view that sees everything and everyone interconnected from the moment of creation. The interrelationships set by Aluna, which form and shape the patterns of daily life, will, if heeded, enable all to flourish. To violate Aluna's trust by stepping away from the spiritual understanding of their role in the world is to invite disaster, not only for themselves, but also for the entire world. The role of the Kogi is to maintain the harmony between themselves and the natural world and to banish from their life all that would destroy it. The world is a sacred place because the source of all is the same Whole and Holy One.

There is no such thing as poverty within this Kogi community.

They believe the world was created as a plentiful habitat and it has been maintained generation after generation in rhythm with the original patterns of plenty that Aluna established. Sadly, over the past five hundred years, forces that willfully violate the harmony Aluna set in place, have encroached ever more deeply on this way of life. The Kogi have observed the growth of the nearby city of Santa Marta. There, pollution and abuse of land by "civilization" brought with the Spanish conquest has increasingly broken the patterns Aluna set in place. Unless this violation stops, as the Kogi see it, the world will come to an end! Sadly, this prediction of the Kogi, based on their religious and spiritual understandings, is also substantiated by science and ecology! In 1995, the Kogi allowed the BBC to film their message to the polluting, destructive, and abusive "civilized world," those they term the "Younger Brother." The basic message of the Kogi, who call themselves "the Elder Brother" is: "Open your eyes! You must stop what you are doing or the world will come to an end!"

But what does all this have to do with a Franciscan theology of the environment? At first blush, the answer seems quite simple. The Kogi have a story that provides them with an identity and a way of life. They see themselves as particular creatures among all the others, charged with a role of preserving creation. However, to be simple is not necessarily to be simplistic. Christianity, too, is heir to a story that tells us that the Earth is first and foremost "habitat earth," the natural content and context within which the *homosapiens (demens)* must live and, hopefully, thrive. It declares that the human is fundamentally social; everyone and everything in this world is interdependent with all else for surviving and thriving. Further, Judaism[2] and Christianity[3] have understood that the inner secret of the interdependent world which is creation is the *indwelling of God*. Indeed, the overall message of Judaism and Christianity indicates that "God is 'home' here, as are we."[4] It is because of this indwelling that the world is indeed habitable and sacred. The earth is in fact a vast household of life—productive land, potable water, a hospitable atmosphere, and innumerable creations brought forth by *homosapiens (demens)* such as artistic expressions, forms of education, and spiritualities. Yet we find ourselves in a world that is on the brink of ecological disaster, even though it has been dominated by the Christian West for centuries. How can this be? What if anything can be retrieved from the Christian tradition that can contribute to staving off an ecological calamity?

In her 1996 Presidential Address to the Catholic Theological Society of America in San Diego, California, Elizabeth A. Johnson challenged theologians: "What is needed now, I am convinced, is yet one more turn, a fully inclusive turn to the heavens and the earth, a return to cosmology, in order to restore fullness of vision and get theology back on the track from which it fell off a few hundred years ago."[5] She cited the Franciscan theologian, St. Bonaventure, among those who had integrated the cosmos into theology in an exemplary manner. Bonaventure instructs the soul journeying toward God to see the universe as a wonderful work of art in which one recognizes traces of its maker:

> Whoever is not enlightened by the splendor of created things is blind; whoever is not aroused by the sound of their voice is deaf; whoever does not praise God for all creatures is mute; whoever after so much evidence does not recognize the First Principle is a fool [*stultus est* = an idiot].[6]

But to begin with Bonaventure is to enter the history of Franciscan theology at a rather late point. If we are to understand what drew him to view the world as he did, we need to know the founders of the Franciscan orders. In many ways like the Kogi, the stories of Francis and Clare of Assisi follow rather simple lines; yet it is in the simplicity that their most powerful challenges lie. What follows attempts to uncover just what it is about a Franciscan method of doing Christian theology that can enable us to respond positively to "the Elder Brother's warning."

COSMIC MYSTICISM —FOUNDATIONAL INTUITIONS FOR A THEOLOGICAL METHOD

Francis of Assisi was a nature mystic, and Clare was a mystic in her own right. Neither were scholars or theologians as we define these roles in the classical sense. (For example, the Roman Catholic Congregation for the Doctrine of the Faith defines a theologian as one who "pursues in a particular way an ever deeper understanding of the word of God found in the inspired scriptures and handed on by the living tradition of the Church."[7]) Interestingly enough, in 1989 the U.S. Catholic Bishops included the following in their definition of a theologian: "The Catholic who seeks to mediate through the discipline of scholarship between a living faith and the culture it is called to transform."[8] It is in this sense that I consider Francis and Clare of Assisi to be theologians.

Over the centuries, as Christian theology developed, a real dichotomy took shape between "thinking about God"—the *sacra paginia*[9] of the monks, who stressed *lectio divina*[10] and *comtemplatio*,[11] and coming to know God and know about God through "doing" ministry and actually living the apostolic life. One classical text that influenced theology around the time of Francis and Clare and which is often used to illustrate this difference is *The Ladder of the Monks* by Guigo II.[12] In that text, we find a synthesis of the predominant Western Christian idea of the way to perfection and to knowing God. One begins by reading and meditating on a sacred text, then one moves to prayer, and finally one is caught up in contemplation. What is significant about this method is that it requires the person to become increasingly separated from the world. Indeed, Guigo and his followers considered the created world an obstacle and distraction from the Christian life.

By contrast, Francis and Clare came to know God and know about God through an integrated life of contemplation and action, choosing to live the Gospel and to follow in the footprints of Jesus. By doing so, they gave us both a method for doing theology and a content (topics or subject matter) of theology that is very "earth-friendly." In what follows, we will first examine the theological method and then highlight the content of the theology given us by Francis and Clare. Later we will feature two of the early Franciscan theologians and some of their central ideas, which built on the founders' insights in a more formal sense. All through this discussion we will be concerned to notice how the knowledge and experiences of these forebears can assist us in facing the environmental crisis the Kogi warn against.

PENANCE, POVERTY, AND PRAYER

Regis J. Armstrong has selected three starting points which, taken together, most adequately frame Francis of Assisi's theological method, namely: penance, poverty, and prayer.[13] These three prisms are also evident in Clare's method of doing theology. The *Testament* of Francis and that of Clare, each in its own distinct way, bear witness to the call to do penance.[14] To do penance meant to embrace a life of loving relationship with God, to see the world as an expression of the Creator's goodness, and to live in hope of the fulfillment of the Reign of God. Both Francis and Clare show us that a life of penance is a journey of faith which climaxes in conversion, a new way of knowing, and a greater sensitivity to the voice of God. Most importantly, this conversion leads to action.

In Francis' *Testament*, Chapters 1 and 2, he describes his experience of embracing a leper, a moment of true conversion in his life. In that moment, he became conscious of God's unconditional largess, and he responded by embracing the leper "with a heart sensitive to misery."[15] When Bonaventure tells of this experience of the leper, he also talks about Francis' encounter with a beggar and a poor knight, and he calls Francis' responses acts of *pietas*—"an act of devotion to God and compassion."[16] Penance is a process of engaging in a spirit-filled life which draws one, in the fullest sense, into the very heart of God—the goal of all theology. Living the lifestyle of a penitent readily leads one to an attitude of poverty, Armstrong's second prism of a Franciscan theological method.

Once one has caught a glimpse of the infinitely loving and gracious God, by contrast, one is confronted with one's human limitations of sin, arrogant self-centeredness, or an unhealthy lack of self-confidence and the deceptions of our restrictive biases and prejudices. In this moment of recognition it is possible to comprehend the necessity of choosing to face the world with open head, heart, and hands—not clinging to anything as exclusively one's own. As Francis pointed out in his *Second Admonition*,[17] the fall of humanity into sin had everything to do with the human desire to grasp things and use them in an arrogant and selfish manner. This grab for power and security is the injustice of appropriating for ourselves what is rightfully the Creator's.

Another aspect of poverty is material poverty. There is a sense in which material poverty is sacramental for Franciscans: "It is an outward sign of an inner reality, spiritual poverty, and, more importantly, an outward sign that leads to a deeper reality."[18] As we embrace material poverty more seriously, we are prompted to identify more honestly our other appropriations until, when we are bereft of everything, God alone becomes our treasure which we can both cherish and give away.

According to Francis' *Seventh Admonition*, the virtue of poverty is most important for anyone who is a theologian because it affects how she or he does theology.[19] The true theologian is not reliant on the power and prestige of scholarship. Rather than being focused on the letter of the law, the authentic theologian is centered on others and has a self-deprecating attitude[20] concerning her or his gifts.

Francis' letter to Brother Anthony of Padua,[21] the first Franciscan "lector" in theology, indicates how integrated an approach to theological reflection Francis promoted. Francis wrote: "I am pleased that you teach sacred theology to the brothers providing that, as is contained in the Rule, you 'do not extinguish the Spirit of prayer and devotion' during study of this kind."[22] Typically, Francis insisted that the brothers attend to the prompting of the Spirit in all things. This kind of dependence comes through a consciousness of one's own poverty—sinfulness and limitations—and utter reliance on God's ever-abiding love and goodness.

Prayer, Armstrong's third prism of the Franciscan theological method, can be described as the process of attending to one's relationship with the divine. As Francis recognized, there is no relationship within the Trinity without the mysterious energy of love, which is the Holy Spirit, who enables the Father and Son to see and know each other. Humans, Francis reminds us, are empowered by the same Spirit to see, know, and believe. Indeed, it is the Spirit who enables one to recognize the human Jesus as the Christ, and the bread and wine of the Eucharist as the Body and Blood of Our Lord Jesus Christ. Beyond the Eucharist, the Spirit enables one to perceive ordinary earthly things as reflections of God, not as objects of one's egotistical self-aggrandizing grasp for power.[23]

When describing Francis' capacity to grasp and know things beyond what he could see, Bonaventure used an interesting and unusual Latin verb, *contuere*. When one knows something through the Holy Spirit, one "co-intuits" (*conituita*) not only the contingent particulars, but also the eternal reasons in those particulars. So, Bonaventure explains concerning Francis' perception of the world:

> In beautiful things he contuited Beauty itself and through the footprints impressed in things he followed his Beloved everywhere, out of them all making himself a ladder through which he could climb up to lay a hold of him who is utterly desirable. With an intensity of unheard devotion he savored in each and every creature—as in so many rivulets—that fontal Goodness, and discerned an almost celestial choir in the chords of power given to them by God, and like the prophet David, he sweetly encouraged them to praise the Lord.[24]

The more deeply Francis lived in the life of the Spirit, the more he grew in his capacity as a "contuitive," delighting in the world as a revelation of the divine. Indeed, "Prayer, then, a principal activity of the Spirit, must be the starting point of our theologizing, but it must also be its culmination. For the contuitive theologian, one who gazes upon the world with the eyes of the Spirit, every moment becomes, to borrow Thomas Merton's words, "a seed of contemplation."[25]

COSMIC MYSTICISM—FOUNDATIONAL INTUITIONS FOR A THEOLOGY

Having briefly reviewed Armstrong's three prisms for a Franciscan theological method—penance, poverty, and prayer—we now turn to the content of Franciscan theology. Michael Blastic has gleaned several significant insights about the content of Franciscan theology from Thomas of Celano's two biographies of Francis of Assisi.

The first insight is the strong intuition that *the world is good and it will provide for every authentic human need.* The vast variety and abundance in creation is, for Francis, ample evidence of the nature of God. His usual ways of identifying God in superlative terms shows he understood God to be both powerful and profoundly intimate, loving and generous. One of many examples of his naming God this way may be found in *The Earlier Rule*, Chapter twenty-three.[26]

A second insight concerns the meaning of the human Christ. This insight both flows from and suggests a positive world view. Francis' reading of creation was that *creation manifests Christ.*[27] Everything—flowers, lambs, worms, lepers, poor women—are all recognized in the incarnate Christ, the human "babe from Bethlehem," portrayed at Greccio.[28] Clearly, because Christ chose human form and the limits of time and space of *this* world, the goodness of this world is affirmed. Indeed, as humans and as followers of this Christ, our place, too, is in *this* world. We don't have to escape this world to be in the presence of Christ.

The third intuition that reveals Francis of Assisi's theology is found in Celano's account of Francis receiving the stigmata.[29] When the Crucified One gave Francis "a kind and gracious look," Francis was frightened because he also saw the pain and suffering of Christ. From this experience Francis drew insight into the meaning of the human person. People are fragile, limited, and vulnerable. Yet it is this very condition of fragility, limitedness, and vulnerability that reveals human creatureliness and the wondrous love of God. *Authentic humanness is revealed in relationship with Christ.*

In short, what is uncovered in Celano's *Life of Francis* is a pattern of conversion, action, and contemplation through which one is transformed and converted, and then repeatedly recycled through the process, moving ever more deeply into the heart of God. This is the pattern of the Franciscan evangelical life—living the Gospel and following in the footprints of Jesus. Celano and the first generations of Franciscan theologians understood Francis and Clare to be the embodiment of a Franciscan evangelical theology. This theology understood God as a compassionate Lover, made manifest in the Incarnation and revealed in all of creation. Though marred by sin and finitude, the world is a good place. As God in Christ looks lovingly upon humanity in its vulnerability, so too must humans reach out to the lepers of our day—the poor, the oppressed and forgotten, the polluted environment, and threatened species. The world is good because the Creator is good and because of the Incarnation. We must value it and cherish its every member in its particularity for its own sake, and in so far as each reveals something of God.

COSMIC CHRIST—ST. BONAVENTURE

That God is "Good" was Francis of Assisi's byword. This goodness of God is most perfectly manifest in the Incarnation. In his *The Soul's Journey into God*, Bonaventure elaborates how humans experience God. Looking to the scripture, he cites Ex. 3:14 ("I am who am") and the story of Jesus and the Rich Young Ruler (Mk 10: 18 and Lk 18:19) where Jesus tells the young man that God alone is good.[30] From this, Bonaventure concludes that God's truest name is "Good." But within the context of the development of theology in the thirteenth century at the University of Paris, Bonaventure took things a step further. When discussing questions of Trinitarian processions and relations, and using the thought of Pseudo-Dionysius, he reasoned that because goodness is naturally self-diffusive, this happens immanently within God's-self and extends outside of God toward creation. This external expression of God's goodness takes place in terms of the union of "God and man in the unity of the Person of Christ."[31] Bonaventure continues:

> Wonder that in him there is joined the First Principle with the last, God with man, who was formed on the sixth day; the eternal is joined with the temporal man, born of the Virgin in the fullness of time, the most simple with the most composite, the most actual

> with the one who suffered most supremely and died, the most powerful and immense with the lowly, the supreme and all-inclusive one with a composite individual distinct from others, that is, the man Jesus Christ.[32]

This understanding of Christ, which places Him at the center, certainly has vast implications for how we view and treat our environment. What if we really integrated a belief that God is Good, that we are good, that the world is good and that all in creation, in some way, is an image of Christ? Would we ever find ourselves in a position to strike out at another? Would we tolerate poverty and oppression? Would we abuse our earth by stripping the land of its verdancy and capacity to rejuvenate itself? The theology of Bonaventure that can assist in answering these questions will be treated in readings in Part III of this volume.

COSMIC MUTUALITY—JOHN DUNS SCOTUS

John Duns Scotus applied the understanding of God's goodness to a different question that was part of the theological discussions of the late thirteenth and early fourteenth centuries. He firmly held that God's action could never be controlled by human sinfulness. On the contrary, from the very beginning God's plan was to create one who could love God perfectly. God is motivated by love, and that love is most clearly and distinctively embodied in the created world in the person of Jesus Christ. So, creation exists for the sake of the Incarnation. Because of the goodness of creation, there is in all of creation a natural affection for justice.[33] The lot of each person is bound up with everyone else's. There is a mutuality that defines all the relationships within the community of creation. Scotus also understood the uniqueness (*haeccietas*) of every particular element of creation as an expression of the great variety that is in God. There cannot be community without particularity. Authentic particularity is well-defined individuality; yet it is able to reform and renew itself in ever-changing contexts. True community is formed and shaped in the exchange and conversations that uncover common ground and common goals among persons who are social beings. When the boundaries of relationship are negotiated together, true harmony can exist. Scotus' approach to Christology and creation helps define meaning that is expressed in terms of valuing the unique and diverse, and which make mutual relations possible.

What might Scotus' understanding of *haeccietas* mean in our day when we discuss concerns about endangered species and biodiversity? What if we followed the good instincts of our natural affection for justice? How might we understand our human life if we view ourselves in mutual relationship with God, ourselves, one another, other living beings, the earth itself, and the entire cosmos? The answers to these questions lead to a reassessment of our deepest values and elicit from us the possibility of transformation. The essays in Part IV of this reader address the theology of John Duns Scotus in greater detail and suggest some possible responses to these questions, and more.

COSMIC MYSTICISM, COSMIC CHRIST, COSMIC MUTUALITY— TRANSFORMATIVE POTENTIAL

The habitat that is *oikos*, this earth that is our home, is a closed space; sunlight is the only life form that comes to it from outside. Thus, for better or for worse, we are all forever and always united in one household (*eco-*). Earth beings are one family who must find the laws or rules (*nomos*) that will make possible the surviving and thriving of the entire family, if indeed any one being would live to its fullest. This twenty-first century observation finds common voice with Francis of Assisi's understanding of the kinship of creation.

Even the most casual observer will notice that the global economy does not operate as if the Earth and its inhabitants is an interdependent unit. In fact, the prevailing economic theories view the earth as a series of interchangeable parts and machine-like rather than as an organic and communitarian whole. The general attitude toward the natural world has been that it has no intrinsic value, but is like a refrigerator to be treated in a utilitarian manner—raided and depleted, only to be refilled with the better, tastier food of a new discovery. Ever new discoveries make the discoverer satiated and rich, enable her/him to move from place to place, and entitle her/him to limit the access of all others to the even the most basic nutrition. In the meantime the "garbage" of all meals is randomly thrown (to that illusive place) "away"—which means, fundamentally, thrown into (another illusive place) "*someone else's* backyard." The rise of the global corporation further alienates the household and community by shifting the goal and purpose of human activity from maximizing the quality of life for all the members of the household to making the greatest profit and market-share for a few elite stockholders and owners. Most recently technology and science has made it possible to shift wealth and resources from place to place and owner to owner electronically, within seconds, leaving no time for the "victim" to seek out other means of survival.

The modern economy operates on the presumption of scarcity (often artificially created) rather than abundance. It refuses to recognize the wholeness of any one place (or the Earth itself) and the internal harmonies that sustain it, but rather views all things and beings as separate parts to be assembled interchangeably at will and for the benefit of some. Unlike Francis, who through doing penance knew the authentic reality of sin and finitude but also understood God's largess and the goodness of the world, the modern economy views limits as negative and restrictive to maximizing profit. Such an attitude is increasingly being proven a false perception of reality. As Guy Beney has shown, it is no longer possible to flee to yet another place to escape the closed nature that is our *oikos* (earth-home).[34] The long pattern of neglecting limits and not respecting the cyclical patterns through which the natural world renews itself is reaching its breaking point. We now find our world in a condition of ecological crisis and vulnerability. We have violated the goodness of God and the integrity of creation which required that we recognize each member as having intrinsic value and thus, moral status. We now are reaping the results:

> Between 1500 and 1850 one species was eliminated every ten years. Between 1850 and 1950 the rate was one a year. In 1990 ten species a day were disappearing. By the year 2000 one species [was] vanishing every hour. The species mortality rate is speeding up constantly. Between 1975 and 2000, 20% of all living species will have disappeared.[35]

The human species is not excluded from this sad picture. According to the United Nations Development Program, if the world population is divided into quintiles according to income, the richest 20% of the population receives 82% of the total income; the second 20% of the population receives 11.2% of the total income; the middle 20% receives 2.3% of the total income; the fourth 20% receives 1.9% of the income; and, the poorest 20% receives 1.4% of the income.[36] Globalization has become the force of exploitation and among the most threatened are the human poor, especially indigenous peoples.

To be human as Francis knew humans, to be created in God's image and likeness, loved and redeemed by the Lord Jesus, and poor seems to be an oxymoron. There is precious little goodness in being forced into dehumanizing poverty. To be poor is to have survival as the primary task every waking moment; it is to not sleep well when you do sleep either from exhaustion or to escape from reality. The question of how to get a daily minimum amount of food and water drives millions through their day. How and where to hide to get through the night and safeguard one's meager personal possessions stands behind each action. How to prevent chronically sick children from dying; how to have a family life; how to remain sane; how to remain hopeful; how to remain? To be poor is to be displaced and disoriented from all that befits an understanding of "home": adequate food, clothing, shelter, basic education, rest, peace and security.

In the case of many indigenous peoples, today (and in the not far distant past) to be poor is/was to be absolutely powerless in the face of government and corporate collusion to exploit the only home you knew: food, clothing, shelter, land, the entire way of life taken by a bulldozer, a drill, or the pollution of industry and technology. Such is the case of the Kogi of Sierra Nevada De Santa Marta of Northern Colombia. One who has experienced a similar kind of poverty among the indigenous peoples of the Brazilian Amazon region is Leonardo Boff. He has some important insights that can help us understand the relationship between issues of economic poverty and ecological issues.

Following his Franciscan roots, Leonardo Boff argues that liberation theology and ecology must become partners in light of the current state of affairs of the poor. He recalls that very soon after Ernest Haeckel first formulated the notion of ecology in 1866, a significant further development occurred. Ecology was soon understood as the unity of three ecologies.[37] *Environmental ecology* is concerned with the environment and relations that various societies have with it in history and how human beings are integrated into it. *Social ecology* is primarily concerned with social relations as belonging to ecological relations; that is, because human beings (who are personal and social) are part of the natural world, their relationship with nature passes through the social relationship of exploitation, collaboration, or respect and reverence. "Hence social justice, the right relationship with persons, roles, and institutions, implies some achievement of ecological justice, which is the right relationship with nature, easy access to its resources, and assurance of quality of life."[38] *Mental ecology* starts from the recognition that nature is not outside human beings but within them, in their minds, in the form of psychic energy, symbols, archetypes, and behavior patterns that embody attitudes of aggression or of respect and acceptance of nature.

As classical liberation theologies claim, the human person stands in need of a threefold liberation: of the human person as earth creature (self-actualization), social being (political, economic, etc.), and spiritual person. The three levels of liberation align well with the three ecologies (above). They also find a correlative in the three-fold Franciscan method of doing theology by engaging in penance, poverty and prayer. The human person thrives when s/he is at home, in a place where s/he is at peace with her/himself, in right relationship with God and neighbor, and respectful of the integrity of creation. Boff rightly contends that when these relationships are broken, we also see the emergence of dehumanizing poverty, oppression, and injustice of all sorts.

The truth of Boff's claim is reinforced concretely by the multitudinous public statements by the Parliament of World Religions, World Council of Churches, Roman Catholic Bishops, and numerous others around the globe. Perhaps the most striking thing about all of these statements is the return to the Jewish and Christian narrative of creation that names this Earth as "good." The role of the human is to nurture and care for creation as one who has a special relationship with God, but who remains yet a creature of God. To not fulfill this role is not only to risk our own life and the lives of other humans, but it is to risk the very destruction of the harmonious good God created, the Earth itself. Such destruction is, ultimately, idolatry—as Francis knew long ago—to put our "knowledge" above divine wisdom concerning the meaning of this life. This Earth and the entire cosmos were created with generosity and superfluity, not selfishness and paucity.

These statements also sing in harmony with what Boff calls "the permanent message from the original peoples" of the Earth.[39] These documents call us to harken back to the wisdom of our ancestors which shows us how we are connected to the Earth and one another. The sacredness of nature must be given due importance; we must face the reality that science taken to its depths brings us to mystery, and mystery brought to intelligibility moves to concreteness. The issue of work and the proper understanding of the created world as God's are intimately linked as Francis implied in the *Rule* and in *The Canticle of the Creatures*.[40] Indeed, Mother Earth nourishes and sustains all. So too, in the modern world of work, which has removed itself from the Earth into concrete jungles and cyberspace, we must find ways to touch the Earth from which we came. There needs to be a return to the experience of celebration, for there is much to celebrate. Like the original peoples, we need to stand in the truth of awe and wonder, dance to the thousand names of God, and know ourselves for who we truly are, *adam*, "earth creature," again for the first time. It is in the intimacy of this dance, which is in fact prayer, attuning body, mind, and spirit to the rhythms of this Earth which reveals God the Good Creator, that we also will come home to the heart of God.

Our Earth is ill. It has been infected in many ways over time. We, as Boff rightly concludes, stand at a crossroads of three possible paths: To continue the deepening of separation and competition of the 1990's fostered by the forces of globalization and neoliberalism; to choose to attempt to minimize the effects of modernity by supporting "sustainable development" of our Earth; or, to make a radical turn to the Earth, choosing to do penance as Francis did, and making the deep conversion required to live *with* nature, not *from* nature.[41] This will require that we take seriously the foundational moral experience that Francis knew so well— reverence for persons and their environment. It is this last alternative that Boff claims is the only real choice, if indeed we are to avoid the fate of the dinosaurs. To that end, Boff outlines a "pedagogy for globalization."[42]

> We must bring about a great revolution that grounds the new cosmology.... We are the sons and daughters of the earth.... we are the earth itself become self-aware.... Time must be extended to global dimensions.... we must become aware of the dimensions that evoke in us the sacredness of the universe and the wonder of our own existence.... The space where we are must be understood comprehensively.... The vastness of the universe that boggles the mind.... Each of us needs to realize how astonishing it is that we exist at all.... All human beings must discover themselves as members of the species *homosapiens (demens)*, in communion and solidarity with all other species that make up the community of living beings.... We must always remain aware of our uniqueness as a species.... It is crucially important human beings become aware of our role within the

overall direction of the universe that has been established over the course of fifteen billion years of evolution.... We are late-comers to the earth; it existed before us, and it likely can exist after us.

Notice how these exercises have a Franciscan flavor about them. These are the concrete actions we must take if we are to heed the advice of the Kogi elders to "Open your eyes" and "...stop what [we] are doing!" In fact, they might be a twenty-first century equivalent of the reasoning Francis expressed before he composed his *Canticle of the Creatures*. He realized how humans had abused creation and failed to honor the Creator. He is said to have given this reason for writing as he did:

> So, to God's praise, for our own comfort, and to edify our neighbors, I want to compose a new *Praise of the Lord in His Creatures*; for we daily make use of them and cannot live without them, and through them the human race greatly offends their Creator. For we are always ungrateful for God's many graces and blessings, and do not praise the Lord, the Creator and Giver of all good gifts, as we should.[43]

May we who are the heirs of this wisdom, choose to do theology in a way that enabled Francis to have such an insight. Let us open ourselves to the pattern of conversion, action, and contemplation through which one is transformed and converted, and then repeatedly recycled through the process, moving ever more deeply into the heart of God. To do so is to be a theologian and a Franciscan. The essays of this volume are intended as a tool to aid this process.

Notes

1. See Michael J. Farrell, "Warning from the Heart of the World," *National Catholic Reporter* (October 27, 1995). An excellent video presentation of a visit to the Kogi by the BBC's Alan Ereira, "From the Heart of the World: The Elder Brother's Warning," is available from Mystic Fire Video, call 1-800-292-9001.
2. The Jewish way of speaking of God's indwelling was *Shekinah*. See Ex. 25:22; Lev. 16:2; II Sam. 6:2; II Kgs. 19:14; Ps. 80:1; Is. 37:16; Ezek. 9:3, 10:18.

3. The ancient Christian way of speaking about the redemptive transformation of the earth for its fulfillment was *oikonomia tou Theou* (the economy of God).

4. Larry L. Rasmussen, *Earth Community, Earth Ethics*, (Maryknoll, NY: Orbis Books, 1996), 90.

5. Elizabeth A. Johnson, "Presidential Address: Turn to the Heavens and the Earth: Retrieval of the Cosmos in Theology," *Proceedings of the Catholic Theological Society of America* 51 (1996): 5.

6. Johnson, "Presidential Address," 3. Johnson cites Bonaventure, *Intinerarium mentis in Deum*, c.1, no.15; adapted from *The Mind's Journey to God*, trans. Lawrence Cunningham, (Chicago: Franciscan Herald Press, 1979).

7. Congregation for the Doctrine of the Faith, "Instruction on the Ecclesial Vocation of the Theologian," *Origins*: 20/8 (July 5, 1990): 119.

8. United States Conference of Catholic Bishops, "Doctrinal Responsibilities: Approaches to Promoting Cooperation and Resolving Misunderstandings Between Bishops and Theologians," *Origins* 19/7 (June 29, 1989): 101.

9. *sacra paginia* referred to the sacred page; Sacred Scriptures.

10. *lectio divina* referred to holy readings or the Divine Office.

11. *comtemplatio* means to be attentive to or look eagerly at something; to contemplate it.

12. Guigo II was a monk of the late 12th century who became the second prior of the monastery of the Grande Chartreuse in France.

13. See Regis J. Armstrong, "Francis of Assisi and the Prisms of Theologizing," *Greyfriars Review* 10/2 (1996): 179–206. See also Giovanni Iammerrone, "Franciscan Theology Today: Its Possibility, Necessity, and Values," *Greyfriars Review* 8/1 (1994): 103–26.

14. For Francis' *Testament* 1–3, see Regis J. Armstrong, J. A. Wayne Hellmann, and William J. Short, eds., *Francis of Assisi Early Documents*, Volume I - The Saint, (New York: New City Press, 1999), 124. For Clare's *Testament* see *Clare of Assisi: Early Documents*, Revised and Expanded Edition, trans. and ed., Regis J. Armstrong, (St. Bonaventure, NY: The Franciscan Institute, 1994), 24–25. Sadly, not many works of Clare or records of the thought and action of other women of the Franciscan Family exist. Thus, it is difficult to continue to illustrate their contribution to the development of Franciscan theology. An important explanation of this state of affairs is given in Margaret Carney, "Franciscan Women and the Theological Enterprise," in Kenan B. Osborne, ed., *The History of Franciscan Theology*, (St. Bonaventure, NY: The Franciscan Institute, 1994), 331–45.

15. Armstrong, "Francis of Assisi and the Prisms of Theologizing," 185.

16. See Bonaventure, *The Major Legend of Saint Francis* (1260–1263), 1: 5–6, in Regis J. Armstrong, J. A. Wayne Hellmann, and William J. Short, eds., *Francis of Assisi Early Documents*, Volume II - The Founder, (New York: New City Press, 2000), 533–35.

17. Francis of Assisi, *Admonitions* 2:1–2, in Armstrong, Hellmann, and Short, eds., *Francis of Assisi Early Documents*, Volume I - The Saint, 129.

18. Armstrong, "Francis of Assisi and the Prisms of Theologizing," 189.

19. Francis of Assisi, *Admonitions* 7: 1–4, in Armstrong, Hellmann, and Short, eds., *Francis of Assisi Early Documents*, Volume I - The Saint, 132.

20. The theologian, though gifted, does not boast of her or his talents, but recognizes those gifts are freely given to her or him by God. Thus, she or he will play down her or his personal involvement in what is achieved, giving full honor and glory to God.

21. Francis of Assisi, *A Letter to Brother Anthony of Padua* in Ibid., 107.

22. Ibid.

23. See Francis of Assisi, *Admonitions* 6, in Ibid., 131.

24. Bonaventure, *The Major Legend of Saint Francis*, 9:1, in Armstrong, Hellmann, and Short, eds., *Francis of Assisi Early Documents*, Volume II - The Founder, 596–97.

25. Armstrong, "Francis of Assisi and the Prisms of Theologizing," 199.

26. Francis of Assisi, *The Earlier Rule (1209/10–1221)*, Chapter XXIII, in Armstrong, Hellmann, and Short, eds., *Francis of Assisi Early Documents*, Volume I - The Saint, 81–86.

27. Thomas of Celano, *The Life of Saint Francis*, Book I 28:77, in Armstrong, Hellmann, and Short, eds., *Francis of Assisi Early Documents*, Volume I - The Saint, 248.

28. Thomas of Celano, *The Life of Saint Francis*, Book I 30:84, in Ibid., 254–57. It is an understatement to say that Francis was deeply moved by the great love of God who came to this world as a meek human child, Jesus. Christmas was for Francis the most important day of the year. In order to make clear what it meant for God to come to us in the form of a baby, Francis gathered people in the Italian city of Greccio to enact the nativity of Our Lord. Today this tradition lives on in the numerous Christmas plays and crib displays around the globe.

29. Thomas of Celano, *The Life of Saint Francis*, Book II 3:94, in Ibid., 263–64.

30. Bonaventure, *The Soul's Journey into God*, 5: 1–2, in Ewert Cousins, trans and intro., *Bonaventure*, The Classics in Western Spirituality, (New York: Paulist Press, 1978), 94–95.

31. Bonaventure, *The Soul's Journey into God*, 6: 4, Ibid., 106.

32. Bonaventure, *The Soul's Journey into God*, 6: 5, Ibid., 107.

33. See Mary Beth Ingham, *Harmony of Goodness: Mutuality and Moral Living According to John Duns Scotus*, (Quincy, IL: Franciscan Press, 1996), 47–72.

34. Guy Beney, in *Global Ecology*, ed., by Wolfgang Sachs (London: Zed Books, 1993), 181–82, cited by Larry Rasmussen, *Earth Community, Earth Ethics*, (Maryknoll: Orbis Books, 1996), 91–92.

35. U.S. Worldwatch Institute cited in Leonardo Boff, *Ecology and Liberation: A New Paradigm*, (Maryknoll: Orbis Books, 1995), 15.

36. The United Nations Development Project cited in Daniel C. Maguire, *Sacred Energies*, (Minneapolis: Augsburg Fortress, 2000), 27.

37. F. Guattari, *As Três Ecologias* (Campinas: Papirus, 1988).

38. Leonardo Boff, *Cry of the Earth, Cry of the Poor*, (Maryknoll: Orbis Books, 1997), 105.

39. Boff, *Cry of the Earth, Cry of the Poor*, 123–27.

40. See *The Later Rule*, 10: 8–9, in Armstrong, Hellmann, and Short, eds., *Francis of Assisi Early Documents*, Volume I - The Saint, 105. See also *The Canticle of the Creatures*, 9, in Ibid., 114.

41. Boff, *Cry of the Earth, Cry of the Poor*, 128.

42. Ibid., 119–22.

43. *The Mirror of Perfection*, 100, in Marion A. Habig, ed., *Francis of Assisi: Writings and Early Biographies — English Omnibus of Sources*, Third Revised Edition, (Chicago: Franciscan Herald Press, 1973), 1236. See also Regis J. Armstrong, J. A. Wayne Hellmann, and William J. Short, eds., *Francis of Assisi Early Documents*, Volume III - The Prophet, (New York: New City Press, 2001), 346–48.

PART ONE

Scripture:
Creation and the Word

One need not look far to realize the importance of the scripture in the life of St. Francis and St. Clare.[1] It is in the spirit of Francis and Clare of Assisi that this study begins with an examination of use of the Hebrew and Christian scriptures in the current discussions about ecotheology and the present threats to the world environment. Clearly, for Francis the sacred texts revealed Jesus Christ, the Incarnate Word in whose footprints all must follow.[2] It is said that Francis had such great reverence for the scriptures that he would pick up pieces of paper that contained any lettering on them from the ground, because those letters were the same means of writing the Word of God.[3] This reverence is also evident in Clare's *Second Letter to Blessed Agnes of Prague*, where we find that the contemplation of scripture was very important for the Poor Ladies as a means to "[hold] fast to the footprints (1 Pt 2:21) of Him to Whom you have merited to be joined as a Spouse."[4]

Another way we know of Francis' deep regard for the scriptures is through his *Testament* and the fact that he regarded the Gospel itself as the center of the Rule for the Friars and the Poor Ladies.[5] Clare and the Poor Ladies of Assisi joined Francis in espousing a life in pursuit of Gospel perfection.[6] The Poor Ladies embraced a way of life that included daily common meditation on scripture and pausing to integrate into their lives the Word that had grasped their heart.[7]

Finally, in the writings of Francis and Clare it is rare to find a text which fails to at least paraphrase some portion of a biblical text. Given the thirteenth century context in which Francis and Clare lived, we find that their use of scripture lacks the sophistication brought to the biblical texts by modern scripture scholars. Instead, we find they use scripture as a narrative of faith, in a literal or analogical sense, and as a means of providing authority to what they say concerning the topic at hand.[8] Both Francis and Clare are "at home" with scripture as one is comfortable with a good friend.

Over all, the writings of Francis are far more numerous than those of Clare. Within the various works of Francis—his rules for the friars, prayers, poems—we find extensive use of scripture texts which show God as the Creator of the universe, and the reality of God revealed through the various elements of the natural world.[9] Intuitively, Francis wove this revelation from scripture together with his personal knowledge of Jesus the Christ Incarnate, the one who became part of the material world and through whom the world was brought into existence.

Today, we have the benefit of some eight hundred more years of scripture scholarship to assist us in discovering the relationship between biblical wisdom and questions of our day. As we seek to uncover a Franciscan theology of the environment, we need to follow Francis and Clare and utilize scripture as a major source. In "A New Reading of the Sources," from his book,[10] *A Window to the Divine: A Study of Christian Creation Theology*, Zachary Hayes, OFM, outlines important developments in biblical exegetical methodology. Contrary to some in the present day who promote a popular and more literal reading of Genesis exclusively as an actual historical event, Hayes shows that such a narrow approach is an anomaly and rare in Christian history.

The Fathers of the Church and the Scholastics drew the religious meaning of the Genesis creation accounts from the level of spiritual interpretation "using allegory and other techniques."[11] For them, not only did Genesis tell us how the world came to be, but it also disclosed a model for the interpretation of all of history.

More recent scripture scholars find a conjunction of the Hebrew creation and covenant traditions in the Hebrew Bible; the God who creates is the God who saves. "And this God creates not only Israel, but all other peoples and the whole world in which human history is enacted."[12] God's covenant with Israel has a particular end and purpose, namely to enter into a covenant relationship with humanity. The Hebrew Bible also shows God as the origin of goodness and life, while evil and sin originate in history where human beings have responded to God.[13] We find in the Hebrew Scriptures the grounding of "salvation hopes in the real order."[14] "It is clear, furthermore, that the expression of this religious faith employs symbols, stories, and a physical cosmology which manifest clear parallels with the accounts of origins in other religions of the ancient world, though these elements have been shaped and reformed by the confrontation with Israel's own religious experience."[15]

The Christian Scriptures build on the hope found in the Hebrew scriptures. For Christians, the mystery of Christ is added. The coming of Christ conditions the human experience of the Covenant. As Hayes points out, the preaching of Kingdom by Jesus in the Synoptic Gospels is consistent with the Hebrew Bible's view of the Covenant. But a shift in understanding takes place in the Johannine and Pauline literature, namely, the "conviction that God created the world in Christ."[16] Everything in history is now ordered to Christ including the destiny of humanity. This Johannine and Pauline contribution is particularly important for Franciscan theology. As we will see, beginning with the nature mysticism of Francis of Assisi, Franciscan spirituality and theology as developed by Bonaventure of Bagnoregio and John Duns Scotus is Christocentric.

Hayes concludes that:

> ...a reading of the biblical sources makes it clear that the doctrine of creation is not merely a question of interpreting the *Genesis* accounts that stand at the beginning of the Bible. It is a question of reading and interpreting the many texts that speak of the creation in terms of what seem clear facts in the historical development of the Bible. Viewed from this perspective, both the Hebrew and the Christian Scriptures reflect an actualistic understanding of the creation in which God's creative action is an abiding reality, and it is always the precondition for salvation. The doctrine of creation is primarily a religious confession, not a physical cosmology.[17]

Reading the theological sources requires that one follow a similar process as when dealing with the biblical texts. The texts of the Christian theological tradition tell the story of the encounter of the Christian faith and the numerous philosophical views of the world. Over the course of time, the Christian theology of creation *ex nihilo* (out of nothing) was developed as an alternative theological-metaphysical vision of the nature of the world. This theology holds in a very qualified way that it is God who brings about existence itself, being as such. Though many efforts have been made, no paradigm can adequately explain the reality of God creating from nothing; this remains a mystery of faith. In the later essays of this volume we will see how Franciscan theologians have grappled with the questions of how creation took place.

Theologians also wrestle with the question of why God created. Again, numerous explanations are advanced. As we shall see in the work of Bonaventure and Scotus particularly, Franciscan theology stressed the overflow of the abundant goodness of God as the reason for creation. In addition,

> If it is true to say that the destiny of created existence is realized in an anticipatory way in the destiny of the glorified Christ, then theology can conclude that the purpose or goal of created existence is the realization of the loving, transforming union of the creation with the Creator such as has been realized in the incarnation and glorification of Christ.[18]

While this is a long way from the exclusive discussion of the Genesis creation accounts, it is important to realize that some of the elements of that world-view do remain.

In our time of ecological crisis, the question is raised anew whether the Jewish and Christian scriptures and traditional Christian theological texts can illuminate the current situation. Just how valid is the frequently cited accusation of Lynn White, that Judaism and Christianity are to blame for the ecological crisis? White and other accusers who agree with him cite the interpretation of "dominion" in Gen 1:26–28 as basis for the anthropocentric belief that humans are to have power over all the earth. That belief about human superiority, in turn, it is claimed, has justified human abuse of the environment, leading to ecological disaster.

Jeanne Kay, a geographer, has engaged Lynn White's accusations in her article, "Concepts of Nature in the Hebrew Bible."[19] As Hayes has shown is necessary, Kay utilizes historical critical exegetical techniques to interpret the Hebrew Bible as a work of ancient literature. She shows that the lack of resolution in the debate about the Bible's environmental despotism or stewardship may be solved by more literary approaches. When the Bible is examined on its own terms rather than those of current environmentalism, the Bible's own perspectives on nature and human ecology emerge. The Hebrew Bible's principal environmental theme is of nature's assistance in divine retribution.[20] The Bible's frequent deployment of contradiction as a literary device, however, tempers this perspective to present a moral yet multi-sided view of nature.[21]

Susan Power Bratton is an ecologist and theologian. In her "Christian Ecotheology and the Hebrew Scriptures,"[22] we see how the presentation of creation theology in the Hebrew Bible is frequently misunderstood. This misunderstanding is often due to a failure to engage the entire corpus of relevant passages that are scattered throughout the Testament. Bratton utilizes the scholarship of Walter Eichrodt, Gerard von Rad, and Claus Westermann to uncover a theology of creation. Using the principles of Gerhard Hasel, she discusses how the Old Testament portrays God as acting in both the original creation and in the post-Genesis events. She is in agreement with Hayes that the role of God as creator is not independent from other Old Testament themes, such as God the savior.

In his article "Colossians 1:15–20—Christ Jesus as Cosmic Lord and Peacemaker," scripture scholar Robert J. Karris, OFM, unfolds one of the central texts utilized in Christocentric Franciscan creation theology.[23] He shows us an example of a scripture text that expresses the New Testament conviction that God created the world in Christ. Karris illustrates the relationship between the wisdom theology of the Hebrew Bible and the Johannine and Pauline traditions of the Christian Testament:

> ...[T]he composer takes us behind the scenes, before creation occurred, and struggles to express that in Jesus Christ God has manifested God's wisdom and plan of all creation. Just as wisdom represents God to the outside, that is, as God's image, so too does Jesus Christ, as God's image. And Jesus Christ has manifested that wisdom not just at the beginning of his earthly life, not just through his death and resurrection, but from the very beginning ([Jn]1:8b).[24]

So what might this mean for us in terms of the present day environmental crisis? It seems that the role of scripture for a Franciscan theology of the environment is first and foremost that it presents the story of God as the source, sustainer and savior of the created world. The focus of the texts is on the religious meaning of the acts of God and the response of humans to God. Beginning with the earliest texts of the Hebrew Scriptures, humans are to be the caretakers of creation, to live in right relationship with God, neighbor, and the earth. Failure to live in right relationship is to experience God's displeasure, often expressed through the natural elements. In the Christian Testament, we see that the created world bears the imprint of Christ, and we are reminded to treat our fellow beings with respect and care, for through the Incarnation they are, indeed, our sisters and brothers.

Notes

1. For works by Francis see Regis J. Armstrong, J. A. Wayne Hellmann, William J. Short, eds., *Francis of Assisi: Early Documents*, Volume I - The Saint, (New York: New City Press, 1999), 40–167. For works by Clare see Regis J. Armstrong, trans. and ed., *Clare of Assisi: Early Documents*, (St. Bonaventure, NY: Franciscan Institute Publications, 1993).

2. Francis of Assisi, "A Letter to Brother Leo," (1224-1226) in Armstrong, Hellmann, Short, eds., *Francis of Assisi: Early Documents*, Volume I - The Saint, 122–23.

3. Thomas of Celano, "The Life of Saint Francis," (1228-1229), Chapter 29:82, in Armstrong, Hellmann, Short, Eds., *Francis of Assisi: Early Documents*, Volume I - The Saint, 251–52.

4. Clare of Assisi, "Second Letter to Blessed Agnes of Prague" in Armstrong, trans. and ed., *Clare of Assisi: Early Documents*, 40.

5. See Francis of Assisi, "The Admonitions," VII, in Armstrong, Hellmann, Short, Eds., *Francis of Assisi: Early Documents*, Volume I - The Saint, 126. See also Francis of Assisi, "The Testament (1226)," 14–15, in Armstrong, Hellmann, Short, eds., *Francis of Assisi: Early Documents*, Volume I - The Saint, 124–27. In addition see Regis J. Armstrong and Ignatius C. Brady, trans. and eds., *Francis and Clare: The Complete Works*, (New York: Paulist Press, 1982) 4, 12,17-18, 108 n.2.

6. See Armstrong & Brady, *Francis and Clare*, 170, 172, 178.

7. See Ingrid J. Peterson, *Clare of Assisi: A Bibliographical Study* (Quincy, IL: Franciscan Press, 1993) 279, 283-84.

8. Thomas of Celano, "The Major Legend of St. Francis of Assisi," 1260–1263) Chapter 11:2, in Armstrong, Hellmann, William J. Short, Eds., *Francis of Assisi: Early Documents*, Volume II - The Founder, (New York: New City Press, 2000), 613.

9. For a small sampling of such texts, see: Francis of Assisi, "The Later Admonition and Exhortation to the Brothers and Sisters of Penance," 61;

Francis of Assisi, "Exhortation to the Praise of God," Francis of Assisi, "The Praises To Be Said at All the Hours," and Thomas of Celano, "The Life of Saint Francis," (1228-1229), Chapter 29:80–81, in Armstrong, Hellmann, Short, eds., *Francis of Assisi: Early Documents*, Volume I - The Saint, 49, 138, 161–62, 250–251. See also Thomas of Celano, "The Major Legend of St. Francis," (1260–1263), Chapter 8, in Armstrong, Hellmann, Short, eds., *Francis of Assisi: Early Documents*, Volume II - The Founder, 586–95.

10. See Zachary Hayes, *A Window to the Divine: A Study of Christian Creation Theology*, (Quincy, IL: Franciscan Press, 1997).

11. Ibid., 17.

12. Ibid., 18.

13. Ibid., 19.

14. Ibid., 20.

15. Ibid., 20–21.

16. Ibid., 21.

17. Ibid., 23.

18. Ibid., 28.

19. Jeanne Kay, "Concepts of Nature in the Hebrew Bible," *Environmental Ethics* 10 (Winter 1988): 309–27.

20. Ibid., 320–21.

21. Ibid., 326–27.

22. See Susan Power Bratton, "Christian Ecotheology and the Old Testament," *Environmental Ethics* 6 (Fall 1984): 195–209.

23. Robert J. Karris, "Colossians 1:15–20 — Christ Jesus as Cosmic Lord and Peacemaker," in *A Symphony of New Testament Hymns* (Collegeville, MN: The Liturgical Press, 1996), 63–91.

24. Ibid., 77-78.

A New Reading of the Sources

Zachary Hayes, OFM[*]

T he theology of creation has traditionally appealed to certain texts of Scripture for its basis and has worked itself out historically in dialogue with a number of alternate positions concerning the origin of the world. Textual criticism has made a fresh reading of the Scriptural sources both necessary and possible. A similar historical, critical method applied to later texts of the theological tradition opens up a new understanding of the later developments as well. Alerted by an analysis such as Gilkey's, we can read the basic texts in such a way as to distinguish the various levels of concern present in them.

SCRIPTURE

The Hebrew Scriptures

Familiar presentations of the theology of creation commonly appeal to the opening chapters of the book of Genesis as the basis for the church's doctrine on creation. All too often, at least at the popular level, it happens that these texts are understood to be, to some degree, an eyewitness account of the beginning of the universe and of the

* This article originally appeared as: "A New Reading of the Sources," in *A Window to the Divine: Creation Theology*, (Quincy, IL: Franciscan Press, 1998), 17–30. Reprinted with permission.

human race. The factual character of these events becomes all-important for the understanding of the faith, since all seems to stand or fall with these alleged facts.

It is interesting to discover that such an interpretation is of relatively recent origin and does not represent the much longer tradition of the Fathers and the Scholastics who, indeed, accepted a literal, historical level of meaning as self-evident, but for whom the true religious meaning was found only at the level of spiritual interpretation.[1] As this level of interpretation is unfolded by means of allegory and other techniques, the descriptions of the beginning of history commonly become a structure for interpreting what is happening throughout the whole of history, both in the life of the individual and in the life of the human race as such. Sermons and commentaries on the creation-accounts more often than not take the form of a theology of history which goes far beyond the understanding of *Genesis* as bald, historical accounts. Such an appeal to spiritual interpretation dominated Christian theology until it was gradually replaced by a one-dimensional understanding in various forms of fundamentalism which developed in the modern period by way of reaction to the growth of biblical criticism and the development of the modern positive sciences.

Recent historical, textual studies have led to the possibility of moving beyond this limited, positivistic approach to Scripture. It has become clear that the texts which now stand at the beginning of the Hebrew Scriptures do not represent the beginning of the literary history of the Bible.[2] They seem to be relatively late accounts of beginnings fashioned partly in the light of Israel's experience of Exodus and the Covenant of Sinai, and partly in the light of the experience of the Davidic and Solomonic kingship. The present redaction of the material probably comes from the post-Exilic period of Jewish history.

Viewpoints among exegetes differ as to whether the earlier creation-traditions were inserted into the later covenant-tradition, or whether the covenant-tradition was inserted into the creation-tradition. Regardless of how this question might be resolved, the conjunction of the two traditions in the present form of the texts effects the identification of the saving-God of the covenant with the creator-God of the world. The particular experience of the Hebrew people is seen within a universal context. What we now find at the beginning of the Bible may well be seen as a case of religious legitimation, that is, the experience of the presence of a saving God in the covenant-experience is grounded in the broadest possible way when the God of this particular people is identified with the Lord of the world and of history. The God who saves is the God who creates. And this God creates not only Israel, but all other peoples and the whole world in which human history is enacted.

Because of the elements drawn from the earlier tribal traditions, the first chapters of *Genesis* appear to reflect parallels with the cosmologies of other early Near Eastern religions; but because these traditions have been reshaped in the light of Israel's own religious experience, a close examination reveals many fundamental differences.

One of the implications of the historical development of biblical texts is the fact that, though the creation-accounts now stand at the beginning of our Bible, yet creation-theology in its present form was not the literary starting-point of the Hebrew Scriptures. One of the more influential attempts to formulate the theological significance of this is found in K. Barth: "Creation is the outer ground of covenant, and covenant is the inner ground of creation."[3] This formulation emphasizes the religious understanding of creation-theology rather than any form of physical cosmology. God creates for an end or purpose which becomes known in the history of the Hebrew people. God creates for the purpose of entering into covenant-relations with humanity. The doctrine of creation emphasizes the universal dimensions of the religious experience of a particular people.

The process of appropriating the mythical, tribal traditions in the light of later experiences has been described in detail by numerous exegetes.[4] From the viewpoint of the systematician, K. Rahner has highlighted the need for a proper means of interpreting the biblical texts in the light of their historical genesis and uses the term "historical aetiology" to underscore what is really happening in the history of these texts.[5] Conceived as an aetiology, the texts represent an attempt to locate and give expression to the basic causes of the present experience of the people, which includes the experience of goodness and promise as well as the experience of sin and evil. The goodness and promise of life are grounded in the theological fact of origins from a good, loving God, whereas the experience of sin and evil is grounded in the historical mode in which human beings have responded to God.

Such an approach to the texts makes it possible to recognize the distinction between the deep theological significance of the texts of *Genesis* on the one hand, and the mythical expression of this theological concern on the other hand. As often as the Hebrew Scriptures give expression to the religious vision involved in terms of the concrete world, this will take the form of the pre-scientific, mythical understanding available from the surrounding culture. Recognizing this distinction has the further effect of raising the challenge of expressing this religious concern in terms of a different concrete experience of the world. If the religious message is identified with the concrete imagery used to express it, we are inevitably condemned to conflict between the Bible and modern science. Recognizing the distinction as described here makes it possible to be fully serious about the religious concern and take up the challenge of expressing it in relation to the modern experience of the physical world.

It is clear, moreover, that the texts of *Genesis* are not the only texts of the Bible that speak of creation. In fact, if the present form of the *Genesis* texts is to be understood as coming from some form of backward projection, the reading of the prophetic literature indicates that the notion of creation is the object of a forward projection as well. In this case, the notion of creation points to the future when God will bring the divine work of creation to fulfillment. Thus, creation is related to the gradually emerging future-consciousness of the Hebrew people, and eschatological fulfillment is spoken of as a "new creation" or a "re-creation."[6] More and more, the term *creation* refers not simply to something that God did "in the beginning," but to something God is engaged in throughout history. The whole of history is initiated by God, who is present always in it, and who will bring to a victorious completion what was initiated "in the beginning." Protology is intimately related to eschatology. Theology of creation is bound up with theology of history.

These remarks on the present reading of the Hebrew creation-texts have been brief, but they should be sufficient to indicate some of the more significant reasons why theologians today are inclined to see the doctrine of creation in the Hebrew Scriptures primarily as a religious confession rather than as a physical cosmology. It seems sufficiently clear that creation-theology has a legitimating function in relation to covenant-faith which is a far more central religious category. Creation-theology as it appears in the Hebrew Scriptures functions to ground salvation hopes in the real order. It is clear, furthermore, that the expression of this religious faith employs symbols, stories, and a physical cosmology which manifest clear parallels with the accounts of origins in the other religions of the ancient world, though these elements have been shaped and reformed by the confrontation with Israel's own religious experience.

The Christian Scriptures

If the movement in the Hebrew Scriptures is from the hope of salvation to the grounding of this hope in creation, a similar movement can be perceived in the Christian Scriptures. The major shift involved here is the fact that, for Christians, the mystery of Christ must now be taken into consideration. As the Hebrew experience of God's saving presence centered largely around the Covenant, so the Christian experience of salvation centered around the experience that "God in Christ was reconciling the world to Himself" (2 Cor. 5, 19). If creation-theology in the Hebrew Scriptures appears largely as the condition for Covenant, so in the Christian Scriptures it will appear in a Christ-centered vision of God's relation to the world and to the human race.

This shift is not noticeably present in the Synoptic Gospels which, for the most part, reflect the Jewish tradition of creation as the context for the preaching of the Kingdom in the ministry of Jesus. The Kingdom-metaphor, which is basic to the preaching of Jesus, elicits an awareness of that goal which God intends "from the creation of the world" (Mt. 25, 34). It is particularly in the Pauline and Johannine literature that this shift can be seen clearly. It has been pointed out that the special Pauline contribution rests in the conviction that God creates the world in Christ.[7] The history of salvation, which is initiated by God's creative action, is ordered to the mystery of Christ, which, in turn, anticipates the destiny of the human race.

This understanding would provide the basis for a tradition of Christocentric creation-theology in later centuries. In this style of theology, the Father appears as the source and goal of creation. Christ is the mediator of creation, salvation, and consummation. This possibility of a universal mediatorship is rooted in the theological notion of the preexistent Son who is incarnate in Jesus of Nazareth. The fact that the person of the eternal Son is identical with the person of the incarnate Son provides the basis for affirming an inner, positive relation between the order of creation and the order of salvation through the one mediator. God creates for the sake of the final fulfillment accomplished in Christ.

It has been noted by O. Cullmann[8] that the prologue to the Gospel of John amounts to nothing less than a re-writing of the opening of the book of *Genesis* in the light of the Christ-mystery. In Jesus we are confronted with the eternal Word through whom God creates the world. He is the Word through whom God enlightens all who come into the world, bringing both light and life to those who receive him. He who has been operative in the world from the beginning now "sets up his tent" among us in the person of Jesus. The confluence of creation motifs and covenant motifs, and the mystery of Jesus Christ provides a strong impetus for affirming the fundamental unity of creation and salvation. Such a development may be seen to reflect the Christian conviction of the universal significance of the Christ-event, which is seen to be decisive in the world and in its history. If this is the case, it can hardly have been inserted into history as an after-thought. Only when the line of salvation is rooted at the origin of the line of creation can the universality of salvation be seriously affirmed.

Not only is the mystery of creation interpreted in the light of Christ, but the terminology of *creation* is used to express the effects of the Christ-event in human life and ultimately in eschatology. The goal of God's creative action is not merely the fact of existence, but a quality of life. The old order finds its goal in the quality of our life-in-Christ. Our historical share in the grace of salvation appears as a new, higher act of creation.[9] If the experience of the new creation is interpreted in the language of grace, then grace finds its fullest realization not in history but in eschatological fulfillment. What has happened in Christ is the anticipation of the collective future of the human race. The full realization of the new life in Christ will be found with Christ in the presence of the Father. Symbols of this in the Christian Scriptures are the Kingdom, the new heaven and the new earth, etc.

In this sense, the work of the first creation comes to its goal in the eschatological renewal of reality in the saving presence of God. Such a reading of the Christian creation-texts sees the mystery of creation not simply in terms of the beginnings of the physical universes, but pre-eminently in religious terms as the placing of the beginning of finite being which finds its consummation in the mystery of Christ and the eschatological dimension embodied in him. All flows from the creative action of God which, more specifically, flows from the Father and is mediated through the Son. The history of the world and of the human race hold together in the person of Christ.

It seems fair to conclude that, just as in the Hebrew Scriptures the account of origins is not an eyewitness reportage of the physical beginnings of the world but a faith-inspired grounding of salvation hopes of the Hebrew people in the ground of the universe, so the Christian creation-theology is the reflection on origins from the standpoint of the Christ-event. Its purpose is not to provide information about events in the physical history of the cosmos, but to provide the widest legitimation of the Christian religious experience of the saving presence of God in Christ.

In summary, such a reading of the biblical sources makes it clear that the doctrine of creation is not merely a question of interpreting the *Genesis* accounts that stand at the beginning of the Bible. It is a question of reading and interpreting the many texts that speak of creation in terms of what seem clear facts in the historical development of the Bible. Viewed from this perspective, both the Hebrew and the Christian Scriptures reflect an actualistic understanding of creation in which God's creative action is an abiding reality and is always the pre-condition for salvation. The doctrine of creation is primarily a religious confession, not a physical cosmology. Yet in relating this religious conviction to the world-experience available at the time, the writers of the Bible make use of the then current pre-scientific physical world-view.

Comparing the Hebrew Scriptures with the Christian Scriptures, we can conclude that the view of creation in the Christian texts is reshaped significantly in view of the person of Christ. Both protology and eschatology for Christian theology are deeply conditioned by Christ who functions as pre-existent Son, as incarnate Son, and as glorified Lord. Since he is the principle of unity between creation, grace, and consummation, he is intrinsic to God's plan from the beginning.

In brief, the theology of creation in both the Hebrew and Christian Scriptures appears as a theology of history deeply tied to the gradually emerging future-consciousness of the Jewish and the Christian communities. It is a theology which sees created being emerging from God's creative action in a temporal process which is ordered to a level of completion not possessed in history. In the Christian Scriptures, the decisive step to that consummation is realized in the mystery of Christ.

Brief though it is, this survey of the biblical theology of creation may serve to illustrate one of the major shifts of concern in the con-temporary theology of creation. In as far as we are talking about a Christian theology of creation, we cannot fail to take into account the texts of the

Christian Scriptures which, at certain levels, present the mystery of creation in deeply Christocentric terms. It becomes sufficiently clear that for a Christian theology of creation, regardless of how one may read the opening chapters of *Genesis*, it is not sufficient merely to recount the stories presented there.

There is, indeed, a history of biblical texts which must be taken into account, and that history reaches a significant level for Christian theology precisely at the level of Christological reflection. According to these later levels of inspired reflection, the cosmos is devoid of its most fundamental meaning without the person and destiny of Jesus Christ. What has happened in him is a new creation, a deeper, fuller level of being. Creation and redemption are not simply identical, but neither are they totally unrelated to one another. Creation is the placing of the beginning of that which finds its full consummation in the redemptive mystery of Christ. Redemption is the saving completion of the world of God's creation, which is intimately related to the history of grace and the history of Christ and the church. Christ is the Lord who, from eternity, is involved in God's creative intention; who has redeemed the world in the fullness of time; and who, as the glorified Lord, leads it on to communion with God.

THEOLOGICAL TRADITION

Such a reading of the biblical texts must be followed by a similar approach to the texts of the theological tradition. As an historical reading of the Bible helps to shed considerable light on the nature of the biblical faith and its relation to mythical expressions, so the historical readings of the later tradition will shed light on the confrontation of Christian faith with a variety of philosophical visions of the world. It is a fact which must be somehow explained that traditional theology does not simply repeat the world-view implicit in *Genesis*, though some elements of it do, in fact, remain. Christians throughout the centuries have had to confront the claims of a variety of pantheisms, dualisms, and monisms. Out of such confrontations emerged the characteristic Christian theology of creation.

In arguing against the Gnostic dualism of his day, Irenaeus of Lyons created an impressive form of Christocentric creation-theology which echoed many Pauline themes. Christ is seen as the fullness of time, the high point and decisive grace-filled moment of history. It is in him that the human race finds its Head. All of creation and its history is directed to him from the very beginning. Christ "recapitulates" humanity and the whole of creation together with its history. The incarnation is the beginning and the source of the unification of reality which takes place in the deification of humanity through grace; it is consummated in the general resurrection. In his own time and place, Irenaeus has carried on the biblical tradition of theological reflection on history.

Forms of this Christocentric, historically-oriented theology of creation were to become characteristic of Eastern patristic theology.[10] This style of theology would find its outstanding Western formulation much later in the thirteenth-century work of St. Bonaventure.[11] Perhaps no one in the history of Western thought has glimpsed the profound unity between the created world and Christ as consistently as did this great Franciscan for whom the whole of the world and its history constitutes a magnificent Christophany. Unfortunately, much of the grandeur of this deeply theological vision would be eclipsed by the more metaphysical style introduced into the West through the influence of Aristotle.

Another aspect of the theological tradition rests in the fact that in the confrontation with forms of dualism and monism, theology entered into dialogue with various philosophical world-views, elements of which would become building blocks of various styles of theology. Thus, much of Eastern patristic theology and Western theology from Augustine onward would employ fundamental notions of neo-Platonism in order to give a relatively coherent understanding of the world as a created reality. In a similar way, the Middle Ages wrestled with the problems raised by the philosophy of Aristotle, and gradually incorporated elements of Aristotelian metaphysics within Christian theology as basic structural elements. One of the implications of this is the fact that, while in the Hebrew Scriptures creation-theology expressed itself in terms of the pre-scientific world-view of the ancient world, now it expressed itself partly in those terms, but partly and even more decisively in terms of either Platonism or Aristotelianism. As world-view changes, the particular shape of the theology of creation changes as well. A comparison between Aquinas, Irenaeus, and the Hebrew Scriptures would demonstrate this with dramatic clarity.

The reading of the theological tradition in the light of the ongoing confrontation of faith with various philosophical view-points led to the possibility of singling out the central concerns of tradition and distinguishing them from the details of the physical cosmology which is clearly operative in the structure of theology. While some of the more general features of this cosmology such as the geocentric vision of the cosmos are familiar to us, many of its details have faded into oblivion in the popular mind even though they have left their impress on Christian religious language in many ways. In terms of this cosmology, theologians were accustomed to distinguish the ten heavenly spheres that surrounded the earth and the four spheres of elemental nature. Beginning at the lowest level, there were the basic elements of earth, water, air, and fire associated with the qualities of dryness, wetness, cold, and heat. Next were the seven planetary spheres which included five of the planets familiar to us together with the sun and the moon. Above this was the firmament of the stars, and then the crystalline heavens. At the summit was the empyrean sphere of fire or pure light. All this was seen to organized in supreme order and beauty, being in its own way an expression of the Creator.

Against the background of this cosmology and in dialogue with the various philosophical visions concerning the nature of the world and of the place of human beings in the world, Christian theology developed what might be called an alternate theological-metaphysical vision of the nature of the world which, to a great extent, is synthesized in the term *creation from nothing.*

In its most basic sense, this term is a theological attempt to express the conviction that God is the sole source of all existence.[12] God as Creator is the mystery of Absolute Origin; God is the ground of existence as such. Finite existence as we find it in the individual and multiple beings of the world derives not from some primal cataclysm, nor from some primeval conflict between opposed principles of good and evil, nor from some pre-historical rupture of primordial unity, but from the loving will of a Creator-God. To exist as a finite being and as an individual being in a world of multiplicity is not an evil but a gift and a responsibility given by a loving, creative God. In this theological-metaphysical conviction is grounded the Christian confidence in the goodness and the redeemability of life.

The *nothing* of which this formula speaks is not some pre-existent formless matter, nor the divine substance itself, but simply and absolutely non-existence. To say that God creates from nothing implies that there is no direct analogy from any human art that can be used to express the nature of God's creative act, for no finite act confers existence as such which is precisely what is said of God's creative act. Even the category of *cause* which is commonly used in this context must be carefully qualified. In Scholastic terms, God is a cause in a unique sense of the world. God is not a cause among causes, nor an extension of inner-worldly causes; God is not the first link in the chain of causes which are studied by the scientists. God is the cause of being as such (primary causality) while all those causes which we experience in space and time (secondary causes) are the causes of the concrete forms of being in individual existents. In terms of the category of causality, the Creator-God is not a cause within the world, nor a cause who stands at the first moment of the history of the world, but the abiding ground of inner-worldly being and causality at all times. Whether we choose to use the category of causality or any other category, there is no model which can adequately express the creative act of God as the conferral of existence after simple non-existence.

While we use a variety of models such as causality, making, or emanation to say something about how the world comes to be, these are of very limited usefulness and fade into the background in the face of what appears as a far more significant question namely, *why* does God create? This sort of question is more important because it is at this level that the real question of meaning arises. While one may come to no clear understanding of the purpose of created existence from the contemplation of the world alone, theology sees an answer to this question in the Scriptures, and most particularly in the mystery of Christ. If it is true to say that the destiny of created existence is realized in an anticipatory way in the destiny of the glorified Christ, then theology can conclude that the purpose or goal of created existence is the realization of loving, transforming union of the creature with the Creator such as has been realized in the incarnation and glorification of Christ.

To perceive the world in these terms is to perceive something about the nature of God as well. God creates for this purpose because the divine being is, in itself, a mystery of self-communicative love. Thus Irenaeus could write: "God creates so as to have someone on whom to confer the gift of goodness."[13] Augustine echoes this in his own way: "Because God is good, we exist."[14] God creates not in order to gain something for the divine being itself, but for the gain of creatures.

Viewed in this way, creation can be seen as a personal process flowing from a personal, loving God which results in personal creatures who are ordered to personal, loving union with the creative ground of their being. This personalistic understanding of created reality stands in striking contrast with most forms of monism and dualism for which personal, finite being is derived in some way from an impersonal Absolute. It is in this theological understanding of creation that the Christian hope in the fulfillment of individual and multiple existence is grounded. Fulfillment is seen to consist in a transforming union of love in which the individual and multiple are not absorbed into formless identity with the Absolute but are most fully defined in their individual existence as other than the Absolute.

The understanding of creation as purposive is further qualified by the understanding of God as one who is both intelligence and will. Finite existence, from this perspective, may be seen as a "being known and a being loved into existence" by the creative ground of all. Hence, meaning and purpose are not peripheral qualities of finite existence but are deeply rooted in the fact of existence as such. While the theology of creation recognizes the world as good in its basic reality, yet it sees this as a participated goodness. Therefore, neither the world as a whole nor any individual being within the world can be invested with absolute meaning.

As a theological concept, the notion of *creation from nothing* is an attempt to express the real ground of the Christian confidence in life. As an alternate metaphysical position, it involves the denial of ultimate irrationality which is replaced with faith in meaning and purpose. In as far as it sees value in the essential structure of the concrete existent, it opens to us the possibility that every dimension of our finite being is potentially meaningful and will be involved in the realization of human fulfillment. It offers a vision for liberating humanity from any impersonal, deterministic interpretation of the world and presents an understanding in which the free, creative work of humanity in history can be seen as ultimately meaningful.[15] As a vision of the world and of human life, it stands in striking contrast to all forms of nihilism and fatalism.

This theological vision can be distinguished from the physical image of the world described above as well as from the metaphysical visions of either Plato or Aristotle. While the development of this theological notion employed elements from both Plato and Aristotle, in both cases Christian theology had to make significant changes in the philosophical visions bequeathed to it from the world of antiquity.

The theological notion of creation may be seen as the fruit of the development of religious consciousness moving from its original religious experience and attempting to conceptualize the conditions that must obtain if that religious experience is to be taken as a genuine disclosure of saving-reality. If the religious experience is truly the opening of a saving, healing relation to the world and to God, then it must mean something about the nature of the world and of God. The theological concept of *creation from nothing* is an attempt to conceptualize those implications. It commits theology definitively to neither the physical cosmology nor to the metaphysical systems of antiquity.

From this sort of historical awareness there arises another shift in theological concern. Namely, if physical cosmology undergoes change, will this have any implications for theology? If theology will inevitably express the concerns of faith in terms of some scientific and philosophical world-view, and if there is no particular scientific or philosophical world-view that is binding as the content of revelation, what form will a creation-theology take if it should assume the task of speaking in terms of the twentieth-century experience of the world?

For many theologians this has come to mean asking about the possibility of constructing theology in reference to the modern experience of the history of the cosmos as perceived in the modern sciences. For many, it seems that the historical character of the modern experience of a world-in-process has a greater affinity with the vision of the Bible than does the physical and metaphysical view of Aristotle which has been the major dialogue partner of Christian theology for seven hundred years. What possibilities are there of retrieving the "forgotten truth" of a Christocentric history of creation and salvation and relating it to the historically-experienced world mediated to us not only by scientists and philosophers, but by television, movies, and popular news magazines on all sides? An honest and intelligent reading of the literary sources of our theological tradition will at least allow us to ask such a question with full seriousness and will encourage us in our attempt to deal with it.

Notes

1. H. De Lubac, *The Sources of Revelation*. (NY, 1968) p.11–72.

2. L. Scheffczyk, *Creation and Providence*. (NY, 1970) p.4–20.

3. K. Earth, *Die Kirchliche Dogmatik*, III/1 (Zurich,1957) p.103–258; *Mysterium Salutis: Grundriss heilsgeschichtlicher Dogmatik*, Ed. 1. Feiner, M. Lohrer, II (Einsiedeln, Zurich, Cologne, 1957) p.441–454.

4. H. Renckens, *Israel's Concept of the Beginning The Theology of Genesis* 1–3. (NY, 1964); E. Anderson, *Creation versus Chaos: The Reinterpretation of Mythical Symbolism in the Bible.(NY,* 1957); C. Westermann, *Creation*. tr. J.J. Scullion (Philadelphia, 1974).

5. K. Rahner, *Hominisation: The Evolutionary Origin of Man as a Theological Problem*. (NY, 1955) p.36–44. This English text is the translation of Rahner's contribution to an earlier German work: K. Rahner & P. Overhage, *Das Problem der Hominisation*. (Freiburg, 1958).

6. *Ps.* 102,26–28; *Jer.* 31,22; *Jer.* 43,14–21; *Is.* 51,27ff; 65,17;66,22.

7. *1 Cor.* 8,6; *Eph.* 1,3–14, *Col.1,15–20*.

8. *The Christology of the New Testament*. tr. S. Guthrie & C. Hall (Philadelphia, 1959) p.247–248; 262–269.

9. *Rm.* 5,12–21; *1 Cor.* 15,45; *Gal.* 6, 15; *2 Cor.* 5, 17; *Rm.* 6,4; *Eph.* 2,15; 4,24; *Col.* 3, 10.

10. J. Meyendorff, *Christ in Eastern Christian Thought*. (Washington, 1969).

11. This is clearly expressed in two important works of Bonaventure: the *Itinerarium* and the *Hexaemeron* in: *Works of Bonaventure*, tr. J. De Vinck (Paterson, NJ., 1960–69) vol. I & V. (Now available through Franciscan Press, Quincy University, Quincy, IL).

12. L. Gilkey, *Maker of Heaven and Earth: The Doctrine of Creation in the Light of Modern Knowledge,*(Garden City: Doubleday, 1965), p. 49.

13. *Adversus haereses*, IV, 14.

14. *De doctrina Christiana*, I, 32, 35.

15. Gilkey, *op. cit.*, p. 178–200.

Concepts of Nature in the Hebrew Bible[1]

Jeanne Kay[*]

T he lack of resolution in the debate about the Bible's environmental despotism or stewardship may be resolved by more literal and literary approaches. When the Bible is examined in its own terms, rather than in those of current environmentalism, the Bible's own perspectives on nature and human ecology emerge. The Hebrew Bible's principal environmental theme is of nature's assistance in divine retribution. The Bible's frequent deployment of contradiction as a literary device, however, tempers this perspective to present a moral yet multi-sided view of nature.

INTRODUCTION

Fresh analyses of environmental thought in the Hebrew Bible (Christian Old Testament) seem long overdue.[2] Many authors have reiterated the same few verses from Genesis and the Psalms to demonstrate either the Bible's antagonistic attitude toward nature or paradoxically its protective approach toward the environment. Most scholars additionally have studied the Bible as only part of a broader problem, such as Christian or even Western environmental attitudes, and they typically view the problem through the perspectives of the modern environmen-

[*] This article originally appeared as: "Concepts of Nature in the Hebrew Bible," *Environmental Ethics*, 10 (Winter 1988): 309–27. Reprinted with permission.

talist movement.[3] In this paper I have different purposes: (1) to interpret the Hebrew Bible synchronically,[4] that is, in its entirety as a work of ancient literature and (2) to interpret the Bible geosophically,[5] in terms of its own Iron Age and Near Eastern perspectives. I apply these interpretations to the Bible's depiction of plants and animals as well as to the biota's relationship with humanity and develop an argument that is very different from either side of the standard despot-stewardship debate. I demonstrate similarities with key elements of ancient pagan religions, with ecological realities of the ancient Middle East, and with the currently unfashionable retribution theology, and in doing so set the Lynn White-initiated debate about the Bible on a different and hopefully more productive footing.

THE "LYNN WHITE DEBATE": PROBLEMS AND PROSPECTS

The argument proposed by Lynn White, Jr., that the root of current environmental problems is Judeo-Christian arrogance toward nature,[6] promptly encouraged two competing groups of scholars to examine religious attitudes toward the environment. These two opposing camps largely shaped the outlines of discussion about nature, Judaism, and Christianity during the subsequent twenty years. One group might be termed the despotism school because it views Gen. 1:26–28 and subsequent Christian writers as mandating tyrannical human control over nature. The competing stewardship tradition interprets the identical verses and other early Christian writings as assigning humans a caretaker role.[7]

This lively and long-lived debate has frustrated attempts at reconciliation between the two camps. The reason may lie in some of the debate's basic assumptions. Three basic challenges have so far criticized the logic of the polarized despot/steward debate. First, the assumption that the entity to blame for the modern environmental crisis is in fact "Judeo-Christian" has been challenged. Passmore has argued that the tradition in question was not Judeo-Christian, but rather Graeco-Christian.[8] He sees little evidence that the Hebrew Bible was anti-environment, and additional evidence that the Bible constrained human use of nature. Ehrenfeld and Bentley as well as Helfand have pointed out that Judaism and Christianity are two separate religions, and have examined Jewish beliefs alone in support of a stewardship position.[9] Schwarzschild has also examined Jewish beliefs independently in order to support the despot model.[10]

Second, Tuan and Kay, in contrast, have questioned the assumption that religious beliefs have such influence over human environmental impact,[11] arguing that a variety of cultural and ecological factors moderate the impact of beliefs on nature. Third, Glacken and Attfield have argued that the Bible's environmental attitudes should be understood through their own ancient perspectives rather than through the hindsight and potential ethnocentric bias of the modern environmentalist movement.[12] Bratton has promoted a historical approach that focuses specifically on the Christian Old Testament rather than on the Bible as interpreted through related or subsequent traditions.[13]

In addition to questions about the existence of a Judeo-Christian tradition, the effects of environmental beliefs on environments, and the enormous potential bias in viewing Iron Age beliefs through modern environmentalist lenses, there are other problems. The first concerns the wisdom of considering any intellectual tradition over several millennia without first ensuring that each individual period, critical source, and important author are first understood. For example, of the many studies of Western religion and nature, relatively few recent ones look exclusively at the fundamental reference, the Bible, before moving on to later periods or modern environmentalist concerns.

The second is the problem of identifying biblical beliefs, let alone a "Judeo-Christian tradition," in studies which at most examine a handful of verses in *Genesis* and *Psalms* and perhaps a few additional verses from the Wisdom Literature. The rest of the biblical books should be systematically investigated for environmental messages which perhaps do not refer to White's concerns.

The third concerns the problem of translation. The Jewish Bible *cum* Old Testament was written in the ancient Hebrew language, whereas most English-speaking participants in the despotism/stewardship debate apparently read it only, or at least primarily, in English translation. Students of ancient Middle Eastern languages devote entire careers to debating the meanings of single biblical Hebrew words, an occupation which should give pause to Anglophones who claim to understand the Bible's environmental thought based solely on English translations. Examples of the translation problem for Anglo-American environmentalists abound. The names of many plant and animal species are misidentified in the King James version—and in fact many identifications have been lost since the early centuries C.E.[14] The Hebrew Bible does not even have an equivalent term for the generalized

English word wilderness, but rather has several terms for specific types of Near Eastern habitats, such as the seasonally arid pastureland *midbar*. Although much good scholarship has come out of the Lynn White debate, some fundamental concerns remain about its underlying assumptions, regardless of an individual author's side in the matter.

Each of the challenges sketched above could form the basis of an entire paper. In this paper, however, I contribute a more detailed look at the Jewish Bible and its attitudes toward nature through a more literary, synchronic approach to the Bible and a more literal, geosophical interpretation.[15] Although several literary approaches are current in biblical scholarship, I work the rich vein struck by Robert Alter.[16] Of particular relevance to biblical environmental studies are Alter's examination of the modes of biblical communication (e.g., reticence, binary opposition) and of motifs and themes extending within and across narrative cycles. If the Bible's environmentalism seems rather thin to modern environmentalists, the reason may be that standard historical or philosophical approaches are less suitable for the Bible's mode of expression. The geosophical approach attempts to understand a culture's geographical beliefs in its own terms, rather than through an unflattering comparison with the researcher's own ethnocentric biases.[17] Geosophy, rather than blaming the Bible for a harmful environmental stance, might reconstruct the world view of Israelite society and its environment to determine what conditions made a given attitude a rational response to their environmental relationships.

I specifically examine biblical concepts of plants and animals both as independent entities and as entities whose fate depends on human behavior. The model of nature as God's instrument of divine reward and retribution may be out of favor with theologians and environmentalists today, but it clearly fits better the scope of biblical texts than do the despot or stewardship models, which are more recent innovations. Once nature is understood through the Bible's moral concerns with reward and punishment, ancient Judaism's proscriptions against both arrogance toward nature and nature worship can be better understood.

THE STATUS OF PLANTS AND ANIMALS IN THE HEBREW BIBLE

The Bible's discrete distinctions between God, nature, and humanity form a core of current scholarly thought on biblical attitudes toward nature.[18] Because God is distinct from his creation, nature is effectively secularized. Stewardship proponents would add to this typology their biblical evidence of God's continuing care for and participation in nature. An extreme view within the despotism school, however, holds that since monotheism does not deify nature or equate its deity with nature, monotheism therefore perceives nature as mere matter, devoid of independent integrity and completely subjugated to human will. If whatever is not deified is spiritless matter, however, this logic places humanity itself in a peculiar position.

The Bible actually describes an intermediate level of being somewhere between God and potter's clay, in which *both* living nature and humanity exist: that of the "living soul" or "living creature" (*nefesh chayah*). The Bible in fact characterizes animals and sometimes plants in ways very reminiscent of the pantheistic nature religions which Judaism is supposed to disparage. For example, the Carmodys state in their environmentally-oriented survey of world religions that Eskimos regard all nature as living; both animals and people have true souls: "The basic image for those souls was either a shadow or a breath."[19] The Hebrew word *nefesh* is used in the Bible both as the human spirit and also for animal spirits. English translations usually call animals "living creatures," rather than "souls," but compare *nefesh* in Gen. 1:20 ("Let the earth bring forth the *living creature*") with Ps. 42:2–3 ("My *soul* thirsteth for God"): the Hebrew word is *nefesh* in both cases.

Ruach, meaning wind, spirit, or breath, is the force through which God animates all life (see Ps, 104:30).[20] Ecclesiastes (3:19,21) states, "For that which befalleth the sons of men befalleth beasts... yea, they have all one *breath*; so that man hath no preeminence above a beast; ...Who knoweth the *spirit* of man whether it goeth upward, and the *spirit* of the beast whether it goeth downward to the earth?" Ecclesiastes uses the same Hebrew term, *ruach*, in all three cases. This use of the same terms for both human and animal souls, combined with our joint creation on the sixth day (Gen. 1:24–26), suggests more similarities in biblical human and animal conditions than is generally recognized.

The biblical concept of nature is strongly anthropomorphic. Nature has its own commandments. In *Genesis*, God commands animals to be fruitful and multiply, along with Adam and Noah (Gen. 1:22,8:17). God creates plants simultaneously with their reproductive potentials (Gen. 1:11–12,9:3). Domesticated animals are to observe the Sabbath (Deut. 5:14) and refrain from murder (Gen. 9:7).

Creation has a covenantal relationship with the Creator. Animals share with Noah's family in God's covenant to sustain the earth and its seasonal cycle (Gen. 8:21–22, 9:10–17). Creation enters into the Mosaic covenant in its role as witness to the Israelites' observance of the *mitzvot* (commandments) (see Deut. 30:10). In the millennium, God promises a new covenant with animals, birds, and creeping things so that they will no longer fear destruction and will live amicably with humans and among themselves: carnivory is to be abolished (Isa. 11:6–9, 65:25; Hos. 2:20). Nature, like man, is to praise the Creator and to rejoice:

> Praise ye Him, sun and moon;
> Praise Him, all ye stars of light...
> Praise Him, ye heaven of heavens,
> And ye waters that are above the heavens...
> Praise the Lord from the earth,
> Ye sea-monsters, and all deeps;
> Fire and hail, snow and vapor,
> Stormy wind, fulfilling his word;
> Mountains and all hills,
> Fruitful trees and all cedars;
> Beasts and all cattle,
> Creeping things and winged fowl.... (Ps. 148:3–4, 7–10)

In the Psalms, hills are girdled with joy, valleys shout for joy (65:13–14), floods clap their hands, the whole earth worships God and sings praises to His name (66:1–4, 89:6). In I Chron. 16:23–33, the fields exult and the trees of the wood sing for joy. Like man, nature also fears God (Ps. 68:9) and trembles at His presence. Nature's *mitzvot* (commandments) of worshipping God and rejoicing are to become much easier in the millennium, however, when nature will no longer suffer for human transgressions.

MAN'S DOMINION OVER NATURE, NATURE'S DOMINION OVER MAN

Most of the debate about humanity's dominion over nature has been too simplistic. The despot arid stewardship schools actually both agree that Genesis 1:26–28 sets humanity in a separate and superordinate position over nature, they only disagree about whether this dominion is to be arrogant or responsible. The Bible's portrayal of the dominion issue is actually more detailed and complex than most studies have indicated. The Bible indicates a variety of ways in which nature is subservient to man, but also ways in which man is subservient to nature.

To be sure, Genesis 1:26 and 2:19 tell Adam to rule over the biota, but biblical writers of the ancient Middle East probably had no experience of an egalitarian society. The Bible depicts few relationships among equals of any kind. In the biblical world, Adam rules Eve, patriarchs rule their extended families and servants, kings rule their nations. The sun rules the day and the moon rules the night (Gen. 1:16). Leviathan apparently rules the sea (Job 40:25–32, 41:1–26) and Behemoth, the world of land animals (Job 40:15–24). God rules the whole. Nor can we rule out the historical possibility that the book which explains the origins of rainbows, place names, and musical instruments merely intended to describe, rather than prescribe, this ranking in explaining the observed activities of hunting, fishing, and plant and animal domestication, presumably all invented in the Neolithic period before the Bible was written.

Although the relationship between man and nature in the Bible is unequivocally homocentric, the Bible depicts additional relationships within nature in which humans do not figure, and which center upon the needs of other living beings. Man's use of plants and animals for his own comfort is only part of what the Bible has to say about nature. Animals are more than just meat for the table or traction for the plow; plants are more than firewood or bread. Glacken advances the idea that various elements of the environment are created in their respective forms in order to serve one another—a biblical concept of symbiosis (Ps. 104:14–20. See also Gen. 1:30; Ps. 145:16, 147:8–9; Job 38:39–41, 39:1–8, 28). Glacken notes that God's care for nature is without reference to utilitarianism: At times the Bible mocks man's inability to comprehend, let alone to use or dominate the wild nature which exists outside of his own cultural landscape (Job 38:25–27,39:9–12; Eccles. 11:5).[21]

Where nature is subservient to humanity, its relationship can be helpful and empathetic. Nature sorrows and rejoices with the fortunes of the Israelites (Joel 1:12; Amos 1:2; Jonah 3:7–9; Isa. 14:7–8). Fruit trees and vines willingly serve man in his ritual observance by providing oil, fruit, and wine:

> The trees went forth on a time to anoint a king over them;
> and they said unto the olive-tree: Reign thou over us. But the olive-
> tree said unto them: Should I leave my fastness, seeing that by me

they honor God and man, and go to hold sway over the trees? And the trees said to the fig-tree: Come thou, and reign over us. But the fig-tree said unto them: Should I leave my sweetness, and my good fruitage, and go to hold sway over the trees? And the trees said unto the vine: Come thou, and reign over us. And the vine said unto them: Should I leave my wine, which cheereth God and man, and go to hold sway over the trees? (Judg. 9:8–13)

Although Jotham's parable refers to political maneuverings for the kingship of Shechem, the text clearly shows the idea of the service of trees in religious ritual.[22] For trees, at any rate, to serve man ultimately is to serve God (see Deut. 8:7–10, 26:10–11).

But nature has another, less cheerful relationship with mankind. Plants and animals actually ascend in the Bible's moral landscape and dominate people who misbehave. The Bible describes nature's dominion over man in the straightforward realm of divine punishment: God sends wild beasts to destroy people, or strikes agricultural fields with insect pests. Plant and animal dominion over man, however, has other literal meanings. When God delivers the Israelites into the hands of their enemies, who reduce their walled cities to rubble and destroy their agriculture, these devastated sites are invaded by bird and mammal scavengers (see Jer. 15:3, 35:20). "Thorns and thistles," ruderals even today of Israel's derelict lands, invade former habitations as a pioneer stage of ecological succession. In the final humiliation, corpses of the slain are consumed by worms and maggots, and man indeed returns to the dust from which he was taken (Hos. 13:8; Joel 1:4; I Kings 21:23–24; Isa. 13:17–22, 14:11).

Isaiah 34–35 provides a representative example of the themes of nature's dominion over humans and of nature's empathy for them. Because of its peoples' wickedness (in this instance against Israel) God will totally devastate the land of Edom, leaving it as the domain of predators, weeds, and scavengers:[23]

And the streams thereof shall be turned into pitch,
And the dust thereof into brimstone,
And the land thereof shall become burning pitch. (34:9)

...the pelican and the bittern shall possess it,
And the owl and the raven shall dwell therein; (34:11)

And thorns shall come up in her palaces,
Nettles and thistles in the fortresses thereof; (34:13)

And it shall be a habitation of wild-dogs...
And the wild-cats shall meet with the jackals... (34:14)
Yea, there shall the kites be gathered, Everyone with her mate (34:15)

During Israel's future salvation, however,

The wilderness and the parched land shall be glad;
And the desert shall rejoice, and blossom as the rose.

It shall blossom abundantly and rejoice
Even with joy and singing (35:1–2)

Springs of water are to break out in the thirsty ground, domesticated animals are to replace the wildlife endemic to war-demolished cities, and predators are to disappear (35:6–10).

Similar patterns echo throughout the other prophets: the environment of sinful countries, both of Israel and of neighboring lands, is to deteriorate and nature is to make a mockery of "man's dominion" over nature. In the future, whether following the Jews' return from exile or in the millennium, a harmonious and joyful nature is to sustain the commonweal of Israel and her allies. Nature is God's tool of reward and punishment, and its beneficence depends on human morality.

In another variation of the theme of animal dominion over humans, a few righteous people gain ascendancy over animals by virtue of their wholeheartedness toward God.[24] The "beasts of the field" are not to multiply against the Israelites under Joshua. The shepherd David overcomes the lion, ravens feed Elijah, King Solomon gains unprecedented knowledge about nature and its ways (I Sam. 17:34–36; I Kings 5:13, 17:6). In contrast, Baalam's ass prevents him from cursing the Israelites, and bears come out of the forest to kill Elisha's tormentors (Num. 22:23–33; II Kings 2:24). The great fish swallows the errant Jonah, but delivers the prophet safely to shore when he repents.

The theme of the negative correlation between human and animal power crystallizes in the book of Daniel. The righteous Daniel is unharmed in the lions' den (Dan. 6:21–23), while his false accusers are torn to bits (Dan. 7:23). Even more striking is Nebuchadnezzar's metamorphosis. God made Nebuchadnezzar great and delivered into his hand "the children of men, the beasts of the field, and the fowls of heaven" (Dan. 2:38). In a dream, the king is compared to a mighty tree in which all the birds and animals find refuge. The king's dream then predicts that the king's glory is near an end: "Let his portion be with the beasts in the grass of the earth; Let his heart be changed from man's, And let a beast's heart be given unto him" (Dan. 4:15–16). Because of the king's hubris, God deprives him of his kingdom, and in his descent from power, Nebuchadnezzar takes on animal characteristics. "He was driven from men, and did eat grass as oxen, and his body was wet with the dew of heaven, till his hair was grown like eagles' feathers, and his nails like birds' claws" (Dan. 4:33). When the king learns to praise God, his animal features disappear, and his royal stature returns to him.

Discussions of animal dominion over people are foreign to most modern commentaries on *Genesis*, which stress humanity's role as either despot or steward. However, the ideal of nature's ascendancy over erring humans definitely made sense to rabbinical commentators of late Roman times.[25] In the Bible, human kingship over nature is a conditional post, based upon moral fitness.

The biblical theme of humans created in the divine image (Gen. 1:26–27; Ps. 8) also relates to humanity's conditional dominion over nature. In Genesis 1:26 the concepts are grammatically conjunctive. Anthropomorphisms aside, what does it mean to be created in the Creator's image? Most environmentalist commentators have explained this theme as mandating either human despotism or stewardship over nature, apparently authorizing man to wield godlike power over human fertility and the environment. Conversely, the rest of the Bible abounds in narratives of ungodly behavior and the ecological punishment it accrues. A geosophical interpretation of man's formulation in the divine image would hold that humans who deliberately sin bestialize their divine image, thus necessarily diminishing their authority over nature and their own fertility. By behaving "worse than animals," the ungodly set into motion animal control over human destiny. In contrast, lordship over nature and progeny result when humans behave according to their divine image. The concept of evil as an affront to man's divine image is most clearly articulated to Noah in Genesis 9:7: "Whosoever sheddeth man's blood, by man shall his blood be shed; for in the image of God made He man." Following this verse is a repetition of the command to multiply, suggesting that, just as murder diminishes the divine image, procreation magnifies the divine image.

Readers familiar with the Bible may at this point argue that the Bible is inconclusive or contradictory: The commandment to subdue nature is followed by many accounts of nature controlling man. The role of nature as reward and punishment is contradicted by Job and

Ecclesiastes who assert that reward and punishment do not correlate with moral and immoral behavior. These are but examples, however, of the biblical mode of communication in thesis and anti-thesis, which Alter describes as one of the Bible's grand themes: divine plan in conflict with human failing.[26] The ability to interpret seemingly contradictory verses as part of a literary theme, rather than as textual flaws, is a strength of the synchronic literary approach to the Bible.

THE BIBLE ON HUMAN ARROGANCE TOWARD NATURE

Regarding the issue of whether the Bible entitles an arrogant humanity to destroy nature, one should notice that biblical images of God's punitive blighting of the landscape, whether described or predicted, appear far worse than any ecological deterioration which ancient peoples could have expected simply from their technologically unsophisticated mismanagement of resources. The Bible's frequent reminders of the absolute destruction of the landscape surrounding Sodom and Gomorrah are a case in point (see Deut. 29:22; Zeph.1:9). While the Bible unquestionably develops the belief in God's continuous care for the environment, that theme is also contrasted, in characteristic biblical fashion, to passages of God's destruction of the natural world. However, this dilemma points out what may be the Bible's most relevant position for modern environmentalists. In the Bible, premeditated decimation of nature is not man's prerogative, but God's.

God's prerogative is to sustain or to destroy the Bible's most exalted wild species, the cedars of Lebanon:

> The voice of the Lord breaks the cedars;
> Yea, the Lord breaks in pieces the cedars of Lebanon.
> He makes them also to skip like a calf;
> Lebanon and Sirion like a young wild ox...
> The voice of the Lord makes the hinds to calve
> And strips the forests bare.... (Ps. 29:5–6, 9; cf. also Zech. 11:1–3;
>   Hab. 3:5–8)

In contrast, proud mortals who usurp God's role in Lebanon's wilderness forests are humiliated. Arrogance against nature is blasphemous arrogance toward God. Isaiah prophesies against King Sennacherib of Assyria:

> By thy messengers thou hast taunted the Lord,

And hast said: With the multitude of my chariots
Am I come up to the height of the mountains,
To the innermost parts of Lebanon;
And I have cut down the tall cedars thereof;
And the choice cypresses thereof:
And I have entered into his farthest lodge,
The forest of his fruitful field
I have digged and drunk strange waters.
And with the sole of my feet have I dried up
All the rivers of Egypt. (II Kings 19:23–24)

In images evoking man's subjugation of animals, God promises Sennacherib to "put My hook in thy nose, And My bridle in thy lips" (II Kings 19:28; see also Isa. 9:9–11, 10:13–19, 14:24). Thus, the king who boasted of his ascent over nature is to descend to the level of a beast of burden. (Sennacherib is subsequently slain by his own sons.)

In similar examples, Habakkuk (Hab. 2:17) predicts humiliation for wanton destroyers of nature: "For the violence done to Lebanon shall cover you, And the destruction of the beasts, which make them afraid; Because of men's blood and the violence done to the land...." In Judges 6:3–6 the pagan Midianites and Amalekites overpopulate the land of Israel with their livestock and destroy the pasturage, but are beaten by the Israelites under their righteous leader Gideon (cf. also Ezek. 29:3–5,9; 31:3–14).

Boastful destruction of resources apparently was common testimonial to the might of kings in the ancient Middle East.[27] The biblical condemnation of deforestation for self-aggrandizement may be contrasted with the Mesopotamian Epic of Gilgamesh (third millennium B.C.E), in which the heroic king destroys a cedar forest to "establish his name."[28] To be sure, Joshua urges the tribe of Joseph to clear hillside forests for their allotment, but it is because of an insufficiency of previously cleared land necessary to secure subsistence, not a demonstration of the tribe's power (Josh. 17:14–18). The Bible credits Solomon and Hiram with a massive joint lumbering project, but whatever the environmental outcome, the two undertake it to glorify God rather than Solomon.

In the Bible, humans indirectly bring about environmental destruction as the outcome of sin, or do so directly through foolish arrogance. These analyses scarcely support the theory that the roots of the modern environmental crisis rest in perspectives intrinsic to the Bible.

THE MORAL LANDSCAPE OF THE BIBLE

The foregoing discussion raises a troublesome question about the Bible's concept of the immoral destruction of nature. Why should innocent nature deteriorate on account of human transgressions in seemingly unrelated areas of life? Regarding nature as victim, the Torah clearly considers that crimes against God or society are simultaneously crimes against the landscape in which they are committed. After Cain murders Abel in the field, God charges, "The blood of your brother cries out to Me from the ground: Therefore you are cursed from the ground which opened her mouth to receive your brother's blood from your hand" (Gen. 4:10). Concerning the Canaanites, Leviticus 18:25 states: "And the land was defiled, therefore did I visit the iniquity thereof upon it, and the land vomited out her inhabitants" (cf. also Ezek. 12:19; Hos. 1:1–3). The Bible prescribes not only reward and punishment, but *reciprocal* justice. This concept is crucial for understanding why the Bible threatens to punish misdemeanors in business or interpersonal relations with drought or eviction from the land. In the Bible, all moral and immoral deeds have positive or negative impacts on the land on which they are perpetrated, and the land responds accordingly.

Biblical justice implies enormous injustice for innocent bystanders who happen to be present when the punishment descends. Humans do not commit evil in isolation without repercussions for the community. In the biblical narratives, the people are punished for the sins of the king, the sins of the fathers are visited upon the children, and a landscape suffers for the crimes of its inhabitants (for the antithetical view, see Ezek. 18.).

The idea that God punishes evil committed in a given place through ecological deterioration of that place seems to leave nature at a major disadvantage. At times, the Bible itself appears to question this philosophy of nature; ("Is it, O Lord, that against the rivers, Is it that Thine anger is kindled against the rivers, Or Thy wrath against the sea?" [Hab. 3:8].) Rabbis in late Roman times were also perplexed as to why the earth should be punished for human transgressions. Some suggested that the earth and its creatures were themselves culpable, such as through carnivory (shedding blood) or otherwise failing to obey God's commandments to them in the beginning. Other sages argued that the "Mother Earth" was chastised for the sins of her human children, for whom she, as parent, was responsible.[29]

The Bible's concept of divine punishment is that the masses may suffer for the crimes of a few. The moral implication is a tremendous burden of responsibility upon each individual. Each must behave uprightly to protect the innocent within one's own nation, as well as to preserve the environment upon which all depend. This responsibility extends far beyond one's direct impact upon specific people or sites and calls for their sustenance through exemplary behavior in all realms of religious and interpersonal life. If these biblical concepts were carried to their logical conclusion, we would have to recognize the entire set of commandments as set forth in the Torah as a comprehensive guidebook for environmental maintenance. (Moses does as much in the last chapters of Deuteronomy). In a belief system that postulates environmental repercussions for the entire range of human actions, humans indeed "hold nature in jeopardy."[30] The belief that all human offenses potentially imperil nature is the Bible's strongest statement about human dominion over the environment.

WORSHIPPING IN NATURE AND WITH NATURE

An additional problem of the Bible in the eyes of some environmentalists is its condemnation of animism and nature worship. Despite the efforts of Tuan and others, many environmentalists still presume that nature-worshipping societies are more ecologically beneficent than either Judaism or Christianity.[31] A further elaboration of biblical attitudes toward plants and animals and of nature as reward and punishment may help to explain the Bible's attitudes toward nature worship, the obverse of human dominion over the environment.

One should first note that the Bible makes few direct attacks against the worship of natural features per se, whether in the context of neighboring polytheistic cultures or within Judaism itself. On occasion, the Bible condemns the worship of celestial bodies, stones, or the Egyptian animal deities (see Deut. 4:16–19; Ezek. 8:16). Biblical scholars currently debate whether sacred trees were worshipped in ancient Israel: for example, backsliding Israelites venerated objects called *asherim*, but researchers are uncertain as to whether these were sacred trees, pillars, or carved idols.[32] The literal worship of natural features is not a preoccupation of the Bible, perhaps because of the ancient Middle East's elaborate anthropomorphic pantheons. The Bible does strongly and persistently condemn the veneration of manufactured images of these deities, which have been excavated in great numbers from archaeological sites in the region.

Natural features, nevertheless, provided both Jews and polytheists with milieus in which supernatural visitations were expected. With both kinds of religions, adherents often do not worship the literal natural object itself, but rather deem it sacred because of a spirit which they believe to live within or nearby it. The spirit, rather than its ecological housing, is actually the object of deification.[33] Thus, the prophets typically condemned Israel for worshipping pagan gods "under every leafy tree," not for worshipping the trees themselves. The Bible depicts both Israelites and heathens as sanctifying specific types of environments. The former do so without condemnation when they worship God: The Bible, however, denounces both groups when nature becomes the setting for worship of Baal, Asherah, or other deities (cf. Jer. 2:20–23, 3:13; Ezek. 20:28).

Although Judaism eventually relinquished worship in outdoor settings in favor of worship in the Jerusalem temple, the Bible obliquely depicts an Israelite religion with a strong sense of nature as sacred space. Mountain tops, such as Mount Sinai and Mount Zion were sites of divine manifestations to both Jews and non-Jews. The Bible mentions terebinths (*Pistacia atlantica*) as identifying sites where God appears to Abram/Abraham (Gen. 12:6–8, 18:1–3), and an angel to Gideon (Judg. 6:11). Joshua sets up a monument under a terebinth (oak in some translations, Josh. 24:26) (cf. also Gen. 35:4, 8; I Chron. 10:12). The Hebrew root *el*, or god, appears in both *elah*, the terebinth, and in *elan* or *alan*, the oak, implying that these trees had divine associations for the ancient Israelites and their neighbors.[34] (The same root is in *Elohim*, the Creator name among Hebrew names for God; and in *El*, the Canaanite father-creator deity.) Haruveini and Schaffer discuss the role of the plant species essential to the ritual observance of the biblical festivals of Succot (Tabernacles) and Shavuot (Weeks), a role verging on sympathetic magic.[35]

Jewish literature, codified in post-biblical times, though probably originating during the late biblical period, suggests that ancient Jews believed in other spirits animating nature, such as angels. The apocryphal I Enoch of the third to first centuries B.C.E. identifies specific angels responsible for governing various types of weather and seasons.[36]

The natural aspects of the biblical God Himself are often overlooked, perhaps because they relate so strongly to the cultural ecology of the ancient Near East. The Bible describes God as living in heaven, today considered an abstract or spiritual state entirely separate from creation. This distinction was not an ancient Mediterranean one: the biblical Hebrew term *shmayim* means both sky and heaven. It is occupied by God, the all-important dispenser of rainfall, upon whom all life depends in Israel's seasonally arid Mediterranean and hot desert environments, Israel's spiritual and agricultural dependency on God as the God of rainfall is explicitly described in the convenanted gift of Israel (Deut. 11:10–17) and in a variety of other situations (see Deut. 28:22–24; Jer. 14:1–6). (Compare with the competing Canaanite rainfall deity Baal.) God as the ruler of heaven was thus not simply a spiritual abstraction for ancient Israelites, but a way of portraying their crucial dependence on precipitation:

> He sends forth His word to the earth;
> His command runs swiftly.
> He lays down snow like fleece,
> scatters frost like ashes.
> He tosses down hail like crumbs—
> Who can endure His icy cold?
> He issues a command—it melts them;
> He breathes—the waters flow. (Ps. 147:15–18)

In the context of the biblical God as the sky-dwelling ruler of rainfall, we can also understand the Bible's apparent dislike of arid wildlands like the southern Negev and Sinai deserts. If God rewards with rainfall and punishes with drought, a true desert may be interpreted as cursed. Rain in the desert, one of the Bible's most powerful ecological metaphors, symbolizes both a belief in God's blessing and forgiveness for the landscape, and by extension symbolizes Israel's hoped for transition to a state of harmony with God and nature.

God in the Bible manifests Himself in a variety of natural settings. God is also often described as the God of earthquakes and volcanoes (see Ps. 18:29). In the Bible, Moses fears the God who speaks through the burning bush and its precinct of sacred ground. Jonah senses his need to submit to the God who acts through an ocean storm, a great fish, and a vine, and Job to the God who speaks out of the whirlwind. David praises a God manifested in thunder (Ps. 29). Such natural theophanies, especially considered with God's action through climate, suggest a more nature-oriented Bible than is generally recognized.

LIFE AND DEATH, BLESSING AND CURSE: REINTERPRETING GENESIS 1:28

The Bible develops a pervasive theology of nature: it sanctifies certain aspects of the environment and its characters are very concerned about environmental well-being. Yet they do not worship nature. To see why they do not, we need to consider not only the biblical concepts of the ultimate governance of nature, but also Judaism's emphasis on life rather than on death or life after death.

At the conclusion of the giving of the law at Mount Sinai, Moses tells the assembled Israelites:

> See, I have set before you this day life and good, death and evil, in that I command you this day to love the Lord thy God, to walk in His ways, and to keep His commandments and His statutes and His ordinances: then you shall live and multiply.... But if your heart turns away, you shall surely perish.... I call heaven and earth to witness against you this day, that I have set before you life and death, the blessing and the curse; therefore choose life, that you may live, you and your seed: to love the Lord your God... for that is your life and the length of your days.... (Deut. 30:15–20)

The Bible's preoccupation with life versus death is at the heart of the ancient Jews' relationship with nature. What does it mean to choose life? Or to put the question in operational terms, what does one do as one chooses life? The survival instinct is strong in most living souls, presumably even in those Israelites who disobeyed God and invoked the curses upon their compatriots' heads. By "choose life" the Bible must mean something more than mere survival instinct. In this passage from Deuteronomy, choosing life is also held to be synonymous with keeping the *mitzvot*.

Apart from biblical exegesis, what does it mean to choose life? At the most individual level, it means having enough to eat and the ways to produce it, protection from extremes of moisture and temperature, freedom from life-shortening events like war, murder, or disease. At the level of a population, it means reproduction at numbers sufficient to ensure continuity. To the religious mind, choosing life may also mean aligning oneself with that which provides the means of preparing food and shelter and of escaping from life-threatening events. That which empowers nature, the source of food and shelter, may be envisioned as spiritual forces within plants, animals, and physical features, or as the spiritual force which created them. To choose death must mean the opposite. The Bible speaks of individual decisions to choose life or death in these terms. For example, despite the negative association of carnivores and scavengers with death as the outcome of sin, the Bible does not actually express dislike for these creatures. The lion and the eagle are also admired as powerful symbols of freedom and strength (Prov. 30:18–19,30–31; Isa. 40:31). Nor does the Bible actually despise wilderness. In another example of unfortunate English translations, Hebrew terms like *Arava, Negev,* and *Midbar,* which refer to specific places or kinds of habitats, have been translated broadly as "wilderness" or "desert" in English Bibles. When the prophets threaten that the Jews' fruitful landscape will turn into the *Arava,* the prophecy must be understood as meaning a specific portion of the Jordan Rift Valley which receives less than five inches of precipitation per year and has insufficient vegetation for year-round pasturage, not as a blanket dislike of wild places. Compare, after all, the powerfully positive images of the wild mountains of Lebanon (see Hos. 14:6–7). The negative association of lions and deserts in the Bible simply reflects the fact that they were inimical to the "life" of an ancient pastoral-agricultural people. Lions are known to attack humans and livestock. The Arava desert of the Jordan Rift Valley and the neighboring Negev are beautiful but arid and could support few people. The *midba*r apparently means a rugged land of seasonal pasturage unfit for cultivation.[37] For a people absolutely and precariously dependent on crops and livestock for survival, choosing a course of behavior believed to incur lion attacks and desertification would indeed be to choose death.

Part of what is necessary for life also includes the troublesome concepts of Genesis 1:28, to multiply and to subjugate the earth. To produce children and to "live to see [one's] children's children" must indeed have seemed a course toward choosing life in ancient Israel. The Hebrew Bible does not promise people an eternal afterlife of the soul: that concept belongs to post-biblical Judaism and to Christianity. Progeny were the Israelite parents' best hope for immortality. Manipulating the earth, such as the gift of the land of Canaan, may also be seen as choosing life: Both land and the ability to utilize it were necessary to provide subsistence for a pastoral-agricultural economy. To lose one's homeland or the right to use it for life's necessities would indeed be to choose death.

The Bible's horror of idolatry and nature worship can be interpreted in terms of the Mosaic concepts of life and death, blessing and curse. The Bible's most extensive passages on idolatry mock idols as insensate, powerless manufactures of wood and stone, incapable of sustaining human life (see Isa. 46). In ancient times, some idols apparently "demanded" child sacrifice of their worshippers.[38] In this sense, to worship an idol would indeed be to choose death. Even natural features, such as trees or animals could not be venerated according to the Torah's view of life and death. A tree itself is mortal and dependent on the Creator for its life. Animals also are fellow travelers on earth, *nefeshot chayot*. The physical environment is awesome and powerful, but it too is a dependent variable.

Ancient Judaism differs from pantheism not in any inability to perceive spirits in animals and plants, but because it does not deify the spirits which it sees. Animate nature has a *nefesh* or *ruach* as do people. But just as the Hebrew Bible does not deify human beings, it cannot deify nature. Nature in the Bible may be loved for its beauty, its utility, or its unfathomable ways, but the Bible portrays it as incapable in itself of sustaining life. Like humankind, nature depends upon the Creator for its existence. God may speak through thunder, earthquake, and the burning bush, but His presence within them is never taken for the natural phenomena themselves, nor for their anthropomorphized traits. Judaism's belief in nature dependent upon a single Creator-God is therefore a belief in the fundamental unity of nature rather than in its fragmentation under different powers as depicted by some forms of pantheism.

To "choose life," as the concept probably seemed to ancient Jews, therefore, required use of nature for human purposes. Indeed all societies, whether biocentric or homocentric in their world view, must extensively use nature in order to survive. But there is no textual or archaeological evidence that ancient Jews believed that God commanded humanity to deplete the environment to such an extent that its life-supporting capabilities would deteriorate. In contrast, a life-sustaining environment, with sufficient rainfall and fertile soil is considered among the most desirable of God's gifts. It is a principal reward for the demands of a Jewish life (Deut. 11:14–17).

CONCLUSIONS

In this paper I present an alternative interpretation to the current stewardship and despot models of the Jewish Bible's environmental ethics. However, I ultimately side with those who disagree with the idea that the

Bible is ecologically arrogant, because the Bible in fact condemns the ruthless despoliation of nature, or any choice of "death" rather than life for humanity, the earth, and its creatures. The Bible upholds as its millennial ideal a symbiosis of animals and people in which all living creatures dwell in peace. However, the Bible views observance of its commandments, rather than specific attitudes toward nature or techniques of resource protection, as the prerequisite of a sound environment.

Because the interpretation of biblical environmental ethics described here is so different from modern environmentalist thought, the Bible may be less relevant to modern environmental issues than the stewardship school has claimed. A society which explains destruction of pasturage as the result of God's anger over idolatry or insincerity in Temple sacrifices rather than as the direct outcome of climatic fluctuations or overgrazing may have little to offer modern resource management. Few environmentalists today believe that environmental deterioration results from oppression of widows and orphans. Moreover, the Bible's environmental imagery, blessings, and curses refer specifically to one small piece of Middle Eastern territory with its own unique ecological geography. Biblical environmental messages may be very difficult to translate to other places where the climate and agricultural economy are quite different.

Yet an environmentalism based upon biblical commandments can discourage coveting one's neighbor's property and exploiting the poor as steppingstones to wealth and power: greed has long been blamed as a root of the current environmental crisis. An environmentalism based in biblical poetry can encourage us to see in nature living souls who praise their Creator and shout for joy. A belief that the entire range of human actions has environmental repercussions can add a new dimension to ecological awareness. A biblically-based environmentalism can function compatibly alongside a deeply sensitive care for nature and with modern principles of resource management.

Notes

1. This work was supported in part by a Fulbright Fellowship (Israel, 1985–86) and by a University of Utah Faculty Fellow Award. Thanks are due to Robin Doughty, Temi Goldwasser, Paul A. Kay, and Aharon Kellerman for their comments on earlier drafts of this paper.

2. Numerous English translations and commentaries on the Masoretic (traditional) text of the Jewish Bible were consulted for this study, most frequently the Jewish Publication Society's standard 1917 translation and the 1945–50 multivolume Soncino edition. In some biblical quotations, the author has emended the English of the standard translation in favor of current English.

3. This literature is now too voluminous to review in full. For some recent overviews, see Robin Doughty, "Environmental Theology: Trends and Prospects in Christian Thought," *Progress in Human Geography* 5 (1981): 234–48; Richard Hiers, "Ecology, Biblical Theology, and Methodology," *Zygon* 19 (1984): 43–60; and Nigel Pollard, "The Israelites and Their Environment," *The Ecologist* 14 (1984): 125–33. More recent papers and book reviews on the topic are regularly published in *Environmental Ethics* and *Environmental Review.*

4. Robert Alter, *The Art of Biblical Narrative* (New York: Basic Books, 1981); Robert Alter and Frank Kermode, eds., *The Literary Guide to the Bible* (Cambridge: The Belknap Press of Harvard University Press, 1987).

5. John K. Wright, "Terrae Incognitae: The Place of Imagination in Geography," *Annals of the Association of American Geographers* 37 (1945): 1–15.

6. Lynn White, Jr., "The Historical Roots of Our Ecologic Crisis," *Science* 155 (1967): 1203–07. For a critique of this debate, see the preface to Eugene C. Hargrove, ed., *Religion and Environmental Crisis* (Athens and London: University of Georgia Press, 1986), pp. xv–xvii.

7. Robin Attfield, *The Ethics of Environmental Concern* (New York: Columbia University Press, 1983), pp. 4–20.

8. John Passmore, *Man's Responsibility for Nature: Ecological Problems and Western Traditions* (New York: Charles Scribner and Sons, 1974).

9. David Ehrenfeld and Philip J. Bentley, "Judaism and the Practice of Stewardship," *Judaism* 34 (1985): 301–11; Jonathan Helfand, "The Earth is the

Lord's: Judaism and Environmental Ethics," in Hargrove, *Religion and Environmental Crisis*, pp. 38–52.

10. Steven S. Schwarzschild, "The Unnatural Jew," *Environmental Ethics* 6 (1984): 347–62.

11. Yi-Fu Tuan, "Treatment of the Environment in Ideal and Actuality," *American Scientist* 58 (1970): 244–49; Jeanne Kay, "Preconditions of Natural Resource Conservation," *Agricultural History* 59 (1985): 124–35.

12. Clarence J. Glacken, *Traces on the Rhodian Shore: Nature and Culture in Western Thought from Ancient Times to the End of the Eighteenth Century* (Berkeley: University of California Press, 1967), p. 166; see Attfield, *Ethics of Environmental Concern*, p. 25.

13. Susan Power Bratton, "Christian Ecotheology and the Old Testament," *Environmental Ethics* 6 (1984): 195–209.

14. Fortunately, Israeli botanists and biblical scholars have contributed much research in this direction. Yehuda Feliks, *Nature and Man in the Bible: Chapters in Biblical Ecology* (London: The Soncino Press, 1981); Nogah Haruveini, *Nature in Our Biblical Heritage* (1980) and *Tree and Shrub in Our Biblical Heritage* (1984), both published by Kiryat Ono, Israel: Neot Kedumim Ltd.); Michael Zohary, *Plants of the Bible* (Cambridge: Cambridge University Press, 1982).

15. Wright, "Terrae Incognitae"; Luis J. Stadelmann, *The Hebrew Concept of the World: A Philological and Literary Study* (Rome: Pontifical Biblical Institute, 1980); Analecta Biblica 39:8.

16. Alter, *The Art of Biblical Narrative*.

17. Wright, "Terrae Incognitae."

18. Passmore, *Man's Responsibility for Nature*, pp. 10–12.

19. Denise Carmody and John Carmody, *Ways to the Center: An Introduction to World Religions*. 20 ed. (Belmont, Calif.: Wadsworth Publishing Co., 1984), pp. 32, 35.

20. Bratton, "Christian Ecotheology."

21. Glacken, *Traces on the Rhodian Shore*.

22. Tuan. "Treatment of the Environment."

23. Feliks (*Nature and Man in the Bible*, pp. 100–04) and others have suggested that these species are incorrectly identified in English translations, based on the species' autecology. He suggests that most of the birds listed in Isa. 34 are various species of owls.

24. This ascendancy in a few instances applies to surface waters, as in the examples of Moses and the Israelites' crossing of the Red Sea, and Joshua and the Israelites crossing of the Jordan River (Josh. 3:15–17).

25. H. Freedman and M. Simon, ed., *Genesis Rabbah* (London: Soncino Press, 1961), 8:12, pp. 62–63. See also Ehrenfeld and Bentley. "Judaism and the Practice of Stewardship."

26. Alter, *The Art of Biblical Narrative*, pp. 33–34.

27. Marvin W. Mikesell, "The Deforestation of Mount Lebanon," *The Geographical Review* 59 (1969): 1–28.

28. N. K. Sandars, ed., *The Epic of Gilgamesh* (Hannondsworth, England: Penguin Books, 1972), pp. 70–84.

29. Freedman and Simon, *Genesis Robbah*, 9:39–40.

30. Stadelmann, *The Hebrew Conception of the World*, 8.

31. Tuan, "Treatment of the Environment."

32. Andre Lemaire, "Who or What Was Yahweh's Asherah?" *Biblical Archaeology Review* 10, no. 6 (1984): 42–51; William G. Dever, "Asherah, Consort of Yahweh? New Evidence from Kuntillet Ajrud," *Bulletin of the American School of Oriental Research* 255 (1984): 21–37.

33. Mircea Eliade, *The Sacred and the Profane: The Nature of Religion* (New York: Harper and Row Publishers. 1961), pp. 11–12. 20–28.

34. Zohary, *Plants of the Bible*, pp. 108–11.

35. The olive, fig, and grape are three of the seven pieces offered at the "first fruits" festival of Shevout. Haruveini (*Nature in Our Biblical Heritage*, pp. 30–42) and Schaffer ("The Agricultural and Ecological Symbolism of the Four Species of Sukkot," *Tradition* 209 [1982]: 128–140) stress the connection of ritually important plant species with Israel's annual weather cycles. Thus the plants' assistance in ritual has a secondary meaning akin to sympathetic magic.

36. I Enoch, chaps. 60.69, 82 (H. F. D. Sparks, ed., *The Apocryphal Old Testament* [Oxford: Clarendon Press, 1984]).

37. Stadelmann, *The Hebrew Conception of the World*, pp. 133–39.

38. Lawrence E. Stager and Samuel R. Wolff, "Child Sacrifice at Carthage: Religious Rite or Population Control?" *Biblical Archaeology Review* 10, no. 1 (1984): 30–51.

Christian Ecotheology and the Hebrew Scriptures*

Susan Power Bratton**

Because of its theocentric nature and the dispersion of relevant passages, the Hebrew Scriptures' presentation of creation theology is frequently misunderstood. I investigate the works of modern Old Testament scholars, particularly Walther Eichrodt, Gerhard von Rad, and Claus Westermann, in regard to the theology of creation. Using principles of analysis suggested by Gerhard Hasel, I discuss how the Hebrew Scriptures portray God as acting in both the original creation and post-Genesis events. The role of God as creator is not independent of other major Biblical themes, such as God the savior. God's care for creation continues as does God's blessing.

INTRODUCTION

The role of Jewish and Christian theology in developing environmental ethics has often been portrayed as negative or inadequate to modern problems. Historians such as Lynn White, Jr. and Roderick Nash have blamed either the Church or Biblical writings for encourag-

* This article originally appeared as: "Christian Ecotheology and the Old Testament," *Environmental Ethics* 6 (Fall 1984): 195–209. This revised version is reprinted with the author's permission.
** The author thanks Gene Hargrove for his encouragement and Gerald Wilson for advice and additional assistance.

ing abuse of nature.[1] Even modern theologians from the Christian tradition, such as John B. Cobb, Jr., find the traditional Jewish and
Christian view inadequate and have suggested we must seek new theological or philosophical alternatives.[2] The question is a complex one,
however, because the Western Church has, through the centuries,
neglected the study of creation.[3] Interest in creation theology has been
minor compared to other doctrinal issues such soteriology and
Christology, and many Christian scholars have a better understanding
of the Greek texts than of the older Hebrew writings. The attitude of
the Church may, therefore, not have been based on a thorough analysis
of Scripture. Further, the recognition of a global environmental crisis is
a recent phenomenon; our current scientific understanding of the
processes of environmental change was not available at the time the
scriptures were written.

One possible way to develop a sound Christian ecotheology, and to
determine a proper Christian approach to environmental ethics, is first
to analyze scriptural texts concerning God-creation and human-creation
relationships. We can then draw an accurate picture of what the Biblical
writers originally meant when discussing creation. My purpose in this
paper is to look at the works of modern Christian Old Testament scholars, particularly Walther Eichrodt, Gerhard von Rad, and Claus Westermann, who have made substantial contributions to our current understanding of Hebrew theology, including theology of creation. I begin
with an overview of important components of ancient Hebrew thought
on both creation and God as creator, and discuss these ideas in relation
to the development of a viable Christian ecotheology. Most of the references for this paper, other than those by Jewish authors, were written at
a time when Christians almost exclusively referred to the pre-Christian
portion of the Bible as the Old Testament. I presently prefer the term
Hebrew scriptures, because it avoids the notion that these books are out-
dated or have somehow been replaced, and forwards shared Jewish and
Christian discussion about the intent of their original authors, and the
full meaning of their content. Following the sources, however, both the
terms Hebrew scriptures and Old Testament (OT) will be utilized in this
essay.

It should be pointed out at the beginning that modern Old Testament critics are not in agreement regarding the best methodology for
analysis, nor do they all handle the question of the historical content of

the texts in the same way. Some critics treat the Hebrew scriptures as if they had one central theme; others see them as presenting several themes. Some authors, such as Gerhard von Rad and Brevard Childs, attempt to include the entire canon in their work, or at least hold that all the books must be considered, while others, such as Claus Westermann, do not see all the books as equally important or interpretable in terms of central themes. (Westermann omits the wisdom literature from consideration in developing Old Testament theology.) Writers also differ greatly in how they relate the Hebrew scriptures to the New Testament: some disregard the New Testament entirely; others attempt to integrate the two sets of works, even though they are the products of different historical and cultural environments and were composed in different languages.[4] Although these disagreements among scholars are important to the detailed study of this diverse collection of texts, they are generally beyond the scope of this paper. I attempt to avoid these conflicts by using the principles for a Christian theology of the Hebrew scriptures outlined by Hasel.[5] These are (in edited form):

(1) Biblical theology is to be treated as a historical-theological discipline,[6] and (2) the method must be historical and theological from the starting point.[7] These are quite different from many attempts at constructing ecotheologies or at evaluating the potential success of a Jewish and Christian ecotheology, in that most such efforts are either historical or theological, but not both.

(3) The only appropriate source for theology of the Hebrew scriptures or the Old Testament is the works themselves, not related literatures and traditions.[8] This principle is important to ecotheologies where authors have seen passages such as the Genesis accounts only as versions of myths derived from other sources. Hasel would reject this treatment as inadequate.

(4) An analysis need not follow the order of books in the canon, but should be based, as best can be determined, on the dates of the writings.[9]

(5) "An OT [Old Testament] theology not only seeks to know the theology of the various books, or groups of writings; it also attempts to draw together and present the major themes of the OT.... OT theology must allow its themes, motifs, and concepts to be formed for it by the OT itself."[10] We must, therefore, be careful not to do what many environmental writers have done and see the Hebrew scriptures largely from

the point of view of our own current philosophical interests and cultural environment. If we are to evaluate ancient Hebrew thought, we must do this with a recognition both of the writer's original intentions and the Hebrew worldview. Christian theology of the Hebrew scriptures must be based on what the Hebrew scriptures themselves actually say about something. Further, we must discriminate between those concepts, events, or practices merely recorded or described in the texts and those which are affirmed or condoned. Since any discussion of creation theology must attempt to be eclectic, care must be taken not to replace the priorities of the ancient Hebrews with our own.

(6) "As the OT is interrogated for its theology, it answers first of all by yielding various theologies, namely those of the individual books and groups of writings, and then by yielding the theologies of various longitudinal themes. But the name of our discipline as theology of the OT is not only concerned to present and explicate the variety of different theologies. The concept foreshadowed by the name of the discipline has one theology in view. namely, the theology of the OT."[11] For our purposes, this implies that in analyzing creation theology of the Hebrew scriptures, one has to look both at individual books and at the overall presentation of all the books. In light of Hasel's remarks, creation theology might be better termed the "creation theme" and seen as one of many theological strands, intimately connected to the other themes that combine to make Christian Old Testament theology. In pursuing the creation theme one cannot depend solely on the first few chapters of Genesis, nor can one ignore the wisdom literature. Many writers who have tackled the question of the adequacy of Jewish and Christian environmental ethics, have relied on one or two passages of Scripture and may thus have misunderstood the total thrust of the scriptural texts.[12]

(7) "The name 'theology of the Old Testament' implies the larger context of the Bible of which the New Testament is the other part. An integral OT theology must demonstrate its basic relationship to the NT or to NT theology."[13] This is, of course, critical in determining how the Old Testament should relate to Christian ecotheology.

Within this theological framework then, I attempt to develop an overview of the creation theology of the Hebrew scriptures, and try to avoid both excessive cultural distortion of their meaning and incomplete analysis of the Hebrew position.

The reader should note that a proper grasp of God's role in Creation is rooted in the understanding that the Bible utilizes both masculine and feminine metaphors for God. Since the references for this essay employ only masculine pronouns, I continue this convention for consistency. The pronouns, however, should remind us of the personal nature of God, rather than declaring God to be an exclusively male deity.

THE CREATOR GOD

Although many environmental commentators begin the discussion of Jewish and Christian ecotheology with the question of human dominion, most Biblical scholars begin the discussion of creation theology with an investigation of God as creator. The modern reader tends to look for passages explaining human relationship to nature, but this is of itself a poor way to start analyzing Hebrew texts, which are very theocentric. Westermann, for example, states: "A theology of the Old Testament has the task of summarizing and viewing together what the Old Testament as a whole, in all its sections, says about God."[14]

In order to answer our first question—how do the Hebrew scriptures present God as acting in the original creation?—we can begin by comparing the Hebrew presentation to those of neighboring cultures. The Hebrew scriptures present some striking parallels to Babylonian creation accounts[15] and were, of course, developed in an environment where there was considerable threat of syncretism with Canaanite and Egyptian cultures. Despite some borrowing of imagery, the Hebrew picture of God as creator was quite distinct. In the Babylonian accounts, the god Marduk fights chaos and in the process creates life and order. In the Genesis accounts chaos is mentioned, but is conceptually different. The "Enuma Elish" epic of the Babylonians describes a watery chaos that is not only living matter, but is part of the first two principles, Apsu and Tiamat, "in whom all elements of the future universe were commingled."[16] Thus, in the Babylonian epic the universe is preexisting. In Genesis, God creates all matter and imparts life to His creatures via His divine breath.[17] The gods of the Babylonians arise out of the primeval chaos and are, therefore, merely deified natural forces. In the Hebrew accounts, even when Yahweh confronts chaos, "creation does not draw the deity into the flux of the world process...,"[18] much less generate God or the godly. The Hebrew scriptures present the universe as a creation of God, which God transcends. This is in marked contrast to both

Babylonian and Canaanite religions, where heavenly bodies, trees, and other natural objects were credited with supernatural power and thereby deified.

From the very beginning Yahweh is seen as acting spiritually and personally to create order. In the Genesis account and in the prophets, Yahweh creates through His word. These accounts provide us "with an idea of the absolute effortlessness of the divine creative action..." and also make clear that "if the world is the product of the creative word, it is therefore ...sharply separated in nature from God, himself—it is neither an emanation nor a mythically understood manifestation of the divine nature and power."[19] This has a number of implications for the relationship between God and creation. As Langdon Gilkey observes, no part of creation shares "divinity in any of its aspects, as if the being or substance of God had separated itself into many pieces to become the being of each creature."[20] Furthermore, the difference between God and His creation "is the result of God's creative act, not of a 'fall' or turning away from God..." and God's transcendence is itself a source of the "alienation" of creation from God.[21]

The spirit, or in Hebrew "Ruah" (breath of God), is instrumental in the original creative act, and is held throughout the Hebrew scriptures to be the very principle of life. Both humans and animals come to life through this breath of God. If God withdraws His spirit, then "every creature must sink down in death."[22] It should be noted that this spirit is also seen as "the instrument of God in salvation history,"[23] "the consummating power of the new age,"[24] and "the power behind the life of the people of God."[25] Neither the spirit nor the creation event are independent of other major themes in the Hebrew scriptures. As Claus Westermann points out:

> ...only he who is active in everything could be savior. Since God is One, the savior must also be the creator. It follows that in the Old Testament the history established by God's saving deed was expanded to include the beginning of everything that happens. The savior of Israel is the creator; the creator is the savior of Israel. What began in creation issues into Israel's history.[26]

Environmental commentators who restrict their reading to Genesis often miss the complex interweaving of the Hebrew concept of creation with other themes. Von Rad even proposes "that Israel was interested in creation not because of nature and its problems, but because of history."[27]

The "history only" point of view is extreme, but a careful reading of the entire Hebrew scriptures shows creation as relating to history, salvation, the people of Israel, wisdom, and eschatological events. The references are scattered throughout the Hebrew texts, but are most numerous in Psalms, the Prophets, and the wisdom literature.

In the middle section of the Book of Isaiah[28] (chaps. 40–55), for example, the author combines two major Hebrew traditions, that of God the creator and of Yahweh of the Exodus as God active in history.[29] As von Rad suggests:

> A special feature in Deutero-Isaiah's thought about creation is, of course, that he does not regard creation as a work by itself, something additional to Yahweh's historical acts.... [F]or him creation is the first of Yahweh's miraculous historical acts and a remarkable witness to his will to save. The conclusive evidence for this 'soteriological' conception of creation is the fact that Deutero-Isaiah can at one time speak of Yahweh, the creator of the world and at another of Yahweh, the creator of Israel.[30]

In Isaiah 40–55, the original act of creation and the creation of the people of Israel through the Exodus become types for a "new saving event" and thus are integrated into eschatology. Yahweh can, through the power of His word and His spirit, create a new kingdom of Israel. Deutero-Isaiah makes frequent use of the word *bara*, which is also used in the first chapters of Genesis to imply a creative act, such as the creation of Adam, which only God can perform. *Bara* is used not only to refer to the first creation, but also in establishing God's loving kindness toward Israel. Since both the original creation and the new saving event are accomplished by the Word and the Spirit of God, these deeds of creation are "personal, responsible" acts of God.

Having established that God the creator is transcendent and that God's creative acts include not only the creation of the universe via His word, but also the creation and salvation of his people, we now can ask, what are the characteristics, according to the Old Testament, of creation itself? Returning to the Genesis account we find that after the earth is separated from the seas "God saw that it was good...,"[31] and that at the very end of the creation effort, "God saw everything that he had made, and behold, it was very good."[32] The English translation misses the full meaning of the Hebraic adjective *tob*, which can mean good and beautiful:

In the concluding sentence the listener can thus also hear the echo: "Behold, it was very beautiful." The beauty of creation has its foundation in the will of the creator; beauty belongs to God's works. Whoever speaks about the work of the creator also speaks about what is beautiful.[33]

The creation accounts include a judgment by God and it is a highly favorable one. A second characteristic of creation is that it is blessed by God. When God said, "Be fruitful and multiply...," he gave a blessing that continues outside of the events of salvation history.[34] Although many environmental critiques mention this statement only in regard to humankind, or actually treat the statement as if it were a curse, the original intent was both universal and beneficial. A third characteristic of creation is that it praises or glorifies God. In Psalm 148:3–10, for example, all creation is called on to praise God:

Praise him, sun and moon,
    praise him, all you shining stars!
Praise him you highest heavens,
    and you waters above the heavens!....

Praise the Lord from the earth,
    you sea monsters and all deeps,
fire, hail, snow and frost,
    stormy wind fulfilling his command!

Mountains and all hills,
    fruit trees and all cedars!
Beasts and all cattle,
    creeping things and flying birds!

The same type of imagery is found in other books such as Job and Isaiah. Isaiah 55:12 reads:

For you shall go out in joy,
    and be led forth in peace:
the mountains and the hills before you
    shall break forth into singing,
and all the trees of the field shall
    clap their hands.

Creation may also act as a party in a covenant lawsuit concerning the sins of the people of Israel, as in Micah 6:1–2:

Hear what the Lord says:
Arise, plead your case before the mountains
and let the hills hear your voice.
Hear, you mountains, the controversy of the Lord,
and you enduring foundations of the earth;
for the Lord has a controversy with his people;
and he will contend with Israel.

All this implies that God has a continuing concern for creation and that creation is continually able to respond to God. Further, in Deutero-Isaiah, creation is described as participating in the new saving event.

It should be noted that the Hebrew scriptures usually deal with creation in its entirety and there is no divine hierarchy within the whole. All is good and beautiful, while none is in any way God. For the ancient Hebrew, evil is not a necessary element in creation, and the evil now operating on and through creation will ultimately be defeated by the "new saving event," which will also be a new creative act.

ADAM IN CREATION

Having looked at the role of God, we now need to analyze how humankind relates to God in the midst of creation, and thereby relates to creation. The first problem concerns the statement in Genesis 1:26: "Then God said: 'Let us make man in our image, after our likeness....'" This has been interpreted by some authors as simply setting man above creation, but it might be better interpreted as setting humans in an especially close relationship to God. Von Rad states in his commentary on the passage that "God participates more intimately and intensively in this than in the earlier works of creation."[35] Westermann goes further and suggests that "this is not primarily a statement about human life, but about the creation of human life by God. The creature God is now planning is to stand in relationship to the divine; humans are to correspond to God so that something can happen between them and God, so that God can speak to them and they can answer."[36]

In the same verse, immediately after God declares that Adam is to be made in the divine image, we find the controversial passage: "...and let them have dominion over the fish of the sea, and over the birds of the air, and over cattle, and over all the earth and over every creeping thing that creeps upon the earth." Many environmental commentators have taken this as a presentation of earth to human beings as a gift to them, when in reality it is a more complex matter of setting humans to work under the continuing authority of God. Even the creation in the image of God is not a gift or a declaration of simple superiority but a necessity required before Adam can rule. As Von Rad suggests:

> This commission to rule is not considered as belonging to the definition of God's image; but is its consequence, i.e., that for which man is capable because of it.... Just as powerful earthly kings, to indicate their claim to dominion, erect an image of themselves in the provinces of their empire where they do not personally appear, so man is placed upon earth in God's image as God's sovereign emblem. He is really only God's representative, summoned to maintain and enforce God's claim to dominion over the earth.[37]

Eichrodt basically concurs when he writes:

> The connection between Man's creation in the image of God and his dominant position within the world of creatures is... indeed associated with the declaration of God's intention to create Man, being mentioned as a consequence of the especially close relationship of this creature to his Creator; but in the detailed exposition of the divine plan it is then quite clearly distinguished from this relationship as a separate item which has to be promised by a special creative act of blessing. Subjugation of the earth and dominion over its creatures bestows on the human race a common universal task, and in the execution of this task Man's special nature is to become visibly effective in that he is hereby made the responsible representative of the divine cosmic Lord.[38]

The command to take dominion was necessary for humans to assume their special responsibility. That is, the command was both enabling and differentiating. Human dominion was not a simple transfer of civil power, but was actually a spiritual transfer of authority centered in a special creative act.

After giving humanity dominion, God repeats the blessing given to the creatures and applies it to humankind: "And God blessed them, and God said multiply, and fill the earth and subdue it; and have dominion over the fish of the sea and over the birds of the air and over every living thing that moves upon the earth."[39] Again, environmental commentators have tended to emphasize the dominion aspect and have neglected the fact that God gives mankind exactly the same blessing as the rest of creation and that God requires that humans assume the responsibility of representing God's interests. As Westermann states:

> These verses sum up what it means to be a human being; man is what he is precisely as a creature of God; his creature-state determines his capability and the meaning of his existence. What man is capable of is bestowed on him by the blessing. The blessing seen as controlling the power of fertility is a gift which man shares with the animals. It is something that binds man and beasts together.[40]

Thus, we have in this short text humans set in the image of God and therefore in special relationship to the divine. Humans are set above creation, but because they are given the same blessing as creation, they are therefore insured of creatureliness.

In Genesis 2, which scholars hold to be a second separate creation account combined with Genesis 1, "The Lord God took the man and put him in the garden of Eden to till it and keep it."[41] This passage does not give a portrait of humans called to be despots, but presents humans as called to serve. The verb *abad* translated as "to till" has the connotation not only of work, but of service, and can be translated as "to serve" or "to be a slave to." The word *shamar* "to keep" might also be translated "to watch" or "to preserve."[42] It is important that God's power placed humans in Eden to serve and preserve the earth. God then allowed humans to eat the fruits of the garden. Nowhere is it implied humans have a right to do this, or that the earth is humanity's servant to be done with as he pleases.

Some authors have pointed out that the command "to take dominion" uses the Hebrew words *rada* and *kabas*, which are very strong and imply treading down or trampling.[43] All relevant texts need to be interpreted in a compatible fashion, however, and in this context some form of ravishing the earth is clearly not intended in Genesis 2:15. James Barr has suggested that nothing more is to be read into the Hebrew words of the dominion passage than "the basic needs of settlement and agriculture," including tilling the ground, and this interpretation is satisfactorily within the limits imposed by the passage on the keeping of Eden.[44]

Following Adam's placement in Eden comes the temptation and spread of sin in Genesis 3. Humans, having been given a special relationship to God and a position of power over creation, break their relationship with God, who then reacts to the "increasingly grave violation of his order."[45] Adam's power is limited, and these limitations affect his ability to understand and know God. Adam also ceases to comprehend godly matters, such as executing dominion and receiving the blessings of Genesis 2.[46]

In the course of rebuking Adam and Eve for the transgression in Eden, God pronounces divine punishment via a curse, which includes a curse of the ground. This curse puts a stumbling block in front of Adam who is still under the commission to work given in Genesis 2:15. Henceforth, "man's work is always in some way tied up with toil and effort; every area of work throws up its thorns and thistles which cannot be avoided...."[47] In basic recognition that what humans need must come from creation, the passage declares that the barriers to humans' successfully completing their tasks are found in their broken relationship with creation itself. Although theologians disagree as to whether all creation fell with Adam, nature is at the very least an innocent victim, under a curse because of human sin and does not now fully produce its full fruits because of it.[48] From this it can be inferred that proper dominion is not an easy matter for humans, who are struggling because of the effects of sin to relate not only to God, but also to other humans and all of nature. The breaking of the relationship with God and the expulsion from the garden also imply that dominion, as God intended it, can only be carried out with careful attention to the will of God and a tremendous effort. If dominion originally required God as both a lord and cooperator, God becomes even more necessary after the curse, because only God can lift it.

It should be recognized that much of the remainder of the Hebrew scriptures deal directly with the character of God, human relationship to God, and other issues relevant to God's expectations of humanity. The establishment of covenant relationships, such as those made with Abraham or with Moses, present humans with an opportunity to reestablish open communication with Yahweh. In the process of describing the expected human-God relationships the Prophets, for example, used a theology that included God as creator. Creation had "opened up the dimension of history and saving history" for Israel and therefore is repeatedly mentioned in her sacred texts.[49]

One last series of passages deserve analysis in regard to humanity's relationship to nature, and these are the references to creation and wisdom in the wisdom literature. This literature is relatively late and is the beginning of an attempt to seek out the mysteries of nature. It presents wisdom as preexisting before the rest of creation and as immanent in the world. God gave an order to the divine works at the very beginning and this order is separate from the activities of men. Unlike the modern who considers wisdom and knowledge to be solely the product of human endeavor, the scholars who wrote the wisdom literature considered wisdom something created by God which existed in creation, whether humans were there or not. This literature also held that the way to wisdom was through fear (not literally fear, perhaps respect or awe is a better term) of Yahweh. If someone cares to pursue it, therefore, wisdom, the key not only to order in the universe but also the key to correct behavior or proper action before God, is available.[50] A characteristic of the wisdom literature is "the determined effort to relate the phenomenon of the world, of 'nature' with its secrets of creation, to the saving revelation addressed to man."[51] These concerns are rarely discussed in the environmental literature, yet they represent an extensive block of "how to" texts which have parallels in other religions, including those of the Far East.

GOD'S CONTINUING INTERACTION WITH CREATION

Rather than stop with the Genesis accounts, we can now pose the question: Does God continue to interact in creation and if so, how? Since there are relatively few direct references to creation in the New Testament and the references in the Hebrew scriptures are scattered, it is easy to concentrate on the Genesis passages and to begin to take a deist view, that is, to see God as creator only at the beginning of time. In the Hebrew scriptures God continues as creator throughout.

As mentioned previously, God acts in creation by both blessing and saving. Blessing is different from saving in that the continuing blessing of God "is a quiet, continuous, flowing, and unnoticed working... which can not be captured in moments or dates.... Evening and morning songs speak about the activity of a blessing God."[52] In addition, God also saves individuals and communities and will ultimately redeem creation as a whole. "The entire Old Testament thus speaks of God's continuous action in addition to the acts which occur once in his saving and judging deeds."[53]

Heschel makes the point that "the fundamental thought in the Bible is not creation, but God's care for his creation."[54] On one hand, we have what modern theologians call providence: the very ordering of nature is "a revelation of God's goodness, particularly his mercy and long suffering,"[55] and on the other hand, we have God working to bring about salvation. This includes miracles (or in Hebrew terms, God's mighty deeds) which may be regarded as creative acts. The Exodus, for example, was marked by a series of miraculous events, each of which may be viewed independently as a move of God the creator exercising divine prerogatives with God's own handiwork. One may also see the entire Exodus, however, as a single new creative act of Yahweh.[56]

THE HEBREW SCRIPTURES AND CHRISTIAN ECOTHEOLOGY

In the preceding discussion of the Hebrew scriptures, I showed that creation theology was more to the ancient Hebrew than a theology of original creative acts; it was a theology of God's continuing interaction with both humankind and nature. The concept of an ecotheology based on relationships between God and humankind, God and nature, and humankind and nature, therefore, has a foundation in the ancient writings and is by scriptural precedent a legitimate Christian concern.

In developing a sound Christian ecotheology, we have to accept the fact that the majority of scriptural texts directly mentioning creation are in the Hebrew scriptures, and that any dependable theology of creation must be founded on extensive Hebrew scholarship.[57] We also have to accept the fact that some common criticisms of Jewish and Christian thinking—that it desacredizes nature and that it sets humankind in a special position—are basically correct interpretations of ancient Hebrew theology. Concluding that these theological attributes of Jewish and Christian thinking produce an inadequate view of nature is an oversimplification, however.

Although the Hebrew scriptures clearly and purposefully remove any trace of divinity from nature, its discussions of creation are so spiritualized that they are difficult for the modern secular reader to comprehend fully. The very fact that nature praises God gives nature continuing intrinsic value. The Hebrew scriptures stress the spiritual and aesthetic, neither of which can be given the definite material values our modern minds would prefer. We may actually be more comfortable with the sacred groves of the Baal worshipers, because they give individual natural features a special value and avoid the problem of having to grasp the entirety of creation as the work of God remaining under divine care. The holism of the Hebrew scriptures in regard to nature presents an ironic stumbling block to categorized, materialistic modern thinking.

A second area of weakness in modern Christian interpretation concerns the ideas of "man in the image of God" and of "dominion." Many people remove these from their proper spiritual context and simply assume that the earth was placed here for the benefit of humankind. This is not, however, what the texts say. What the Genesis passages and much of the rest of the Hebrew scriptures speak for is a servitude of humans to God, and as a result, to God's interests. The Hebrew scriptures record many failures in this regard, and humankind's inability to see their responsibilities begins when Cain asks: "Am I my brother's keeper?"[58]

The themes of servitude and of covenant relationships requiring responsibility to God are woven into the entire corpus of Hebrew scriptures. In the poetic crown of the Prophets, the second half of Isaiah, we find the "suffering servant" of Yahweh, and "might see in this description of one 'despised and rejected by men' the increasingly familiar pattern... dominion is servitude."[59] The Hebrew scriptures also make clear that to serve God adequately one must be faithful, diligent, self disciplined, giving, forgiving, etc. Dominion is not an easy task and can only be executed by continuing hard labor and overcoming major obstacles. The effort must be under God's direction and must be accomplished for God, not for personal gain.

In the United States, concepts of God and nature have had a variety of cultural associations. Barbara Novak claims that in the nineteenth century, for example, "Ideas of God's nature and of God in nature became hopelessly entangled, and only the most scrupulous theologians even tried to separate them."[60] Further, Americans have often seen the natural bounty of the continent as a special blessing, and have often extended their patriotism into a perceived divine appointment as the New Jerusalem.[61] The intent of the ancient Hebrews not withstanding, the romantic tendency to equate nature with God on one hand, and the conservative tendency to promote civil religion as part of the national destiny on the other, are likely to perpetuate the confusion and misinterpretation surrounding the "dominion passage."

Since the theme of creation in the Hebrew scriptures is not independent of other themes, current Christian attitudes about creation cannot be independent of other related issues such as salvation. The attitude that "the Lord will fix it all in the end" is escatologically correct but ignores God's continuing care and blessing via God's own servants. Christ's parables of the householder who returns to check on the tenants working his estate and of the king who returns to see what his servants have done with the money they have been given are good models, since God has given us both a responsibility and a blessing.

If God created the cosmos as *tob*, humankind should help to maintain it as such and preserve its aesthetic values. Unfortunately, modern English translations miss the impact of the Hebrew word, and the modern reader may secularize the passage: "And God saw that it was good for something" or "And God saw that it was full of material value." In "taking dominion" the Hebrew scriptures shows a concern both for the maintenance of the aesthetic values of creation and, in the Pentateuch and the writings of the prophets, for the just distribution of the resources available.

The Hebrew scriptures provide numerous texts on how one can serve God and the entire wisdom literature is dedicated to the topic of righteous action. The idea that the ancient writings are too weak and their view of the environment too primitive to be of much help today comes from superficial analysis or actual ignorance of the texts. The ancient Hebrew attitude toward creation is so strongly spiritualized that it is hard for us to understand it. Moreover, the standards set on service to God are so high that most people, as the Hebrew scriptures so candidly illustrates in the case of the nation Israel, have no inclination to even try to meet them. Passages written centuries ago can be both difficult to understand and difficult to set in a meaningful modern context. It is important, however, that we avoid hasty judgments on one of the central roots of the Western spiritual heritage and that our approach to the Hebrew scriptures be both thoughtful and scholarly. Those interested in developing a Christian ecotheology should not be too cursory in their treatment of the Hebrew texts or too glib in their assumptions concerning the will of God for creation. In-depth studies of specific writings and literatures, i.e., the psalms or the wisdom literature, and a search for more strands in the creation theme, will produce a better formed and sounder ecotheology and may also help to compensate for any past Christian theological neglect of God's role as creator.

Notes

1. Lynn White, Jr., "The Historical Roots of Our Ecological Crisis," *Science* 155 (1967): 1203–07; Roderick Nash, *Wilderness and the American Mind* (New Haven: Yale University Press, 1970).

2. John B. Cobb, Jr., *Is It Too Late? A Theology of Ecology* (Beverly Hills, CA: Bruce, 1972).

3. James B. Packer, "The Gospel: Its Content and Communication," in John Stott and Robert Coote, eds., *Down to Earth: Studies in Christianity and Culture* (Grand Rapids: William B. Eerdmans, 1980), pp. 97–114.

4. Gerhard Hasel, *Old Testament Theology: Basic Issues in the Current Debate* (Grand Rapids: William B. Eerdmans, 1972).

5. Ibid., pp. 169–83.

6. Ibid., p. 169.

7. Ibid., p. 171.

8. Ibid., p. 177.

9. Ibid., p. 179.

10. Ibid., p. 180.

11. Ibid., p. 181.

12. Discussions of some of the cultural results of this sort of limited interpretation may be found in Clarence Glacken, *Traces on the Rhodian Shore* (Berkley: University of California Press, 1967) and in Keith Thomas, *Man and the Natural World: A History of Modern Sensibility* (New York: Pantheon Books, 1983).

13. Gerhard Hasel, *Old Testament Theology*, p. 183.

14. Claus Westermann, *Elements of Old Testament Theology* (Atlanta: John Knox Press, 1982), p. 9. Hereafter cited as Westermann, OTT.

15. Bernhard W. Anderson, *Creation Versus Chaos: The Reinterpretation of Mythical Symbolism in the Bible* (New York: Association Press, 1967).

16. Alexander Heidel, *The Babylonian Genesis* (Chicago: University of Chicago Press, 1951), p. 97.

17. Biblical scholars disagree on the question of whether the first chapter of Genesis really describes creation from nothing. Genesis 1:1 could also imply there was something present before creation, even if it were "chaos." Gerald Wilson has pointed out to me this is a semantic question, and alternate readings are possible.

18. Walther Eichrodt, *Theology of the Old Testament*, vol. 2 (Philadelphia: Westminster Press, 1967), p. 98.

19. Gerhard von Rad, *Old Testament Theology*, vol. I (New York: Harper and Row, 1962), p. 142 (hereafter cited as von Rad, OTT). This tradition is not without parallels in other cultures. The Egyptian god, Ptah, also creates by his word.

20. Langdon Gilkey, *Maker of Heaven and Earth* (New York: Doubleday and Co., 1959), p.86.

21. Ibid., p. 87.

22. Eichrodt, *Theology*, p 48.

23. Ibid., p. 50.

24. Ibid., p. 57.

25. Ibid., p. 60.

26. Westermann, OTT, p. 86.

27. Gerhard von Rad, *God at Work in Israel* (Nashville: Abingdon, 1980), p. 99.

28. There is some scholarly disagreement over the number of authors of the Book of Isaiah. Conservatives hold to one author. Some critics propose three or more. The term Deutero-Isaiah is used both for chapters 40–55 and the supposed author of this section.

29. Carroll Stuhlmueller, *The Prophets and the Word of God* (Notre Dame: Fides Publishers, 1964), p. 200.

30. Gerhard von Rad, *The Message of the Prophets* (New York: Harper & Row, 1962), p. 208.

31. Gen. 1:10: all translations are from *The New Oxford Annotated Bible* (New York: Oxford University Press, 1973).

32. Gen. 1:31.

33. Westermann, OTT, p. 93.

34. Gen. 1:22; Westermann, OTT, pp. 102–04.

35. Gerhard von Rad, *Genesis* (Philadelphia: Westminster Press, 1972), p. 57.

36. Westermann, OTT, p. 97.

37. Gerhard von Rad, *Genesis*, p. 57–58.

38. Eichrodt, *Theology*, p. 127.

39. Gen. 1:28.

40. Claus Westermann, *Creation* (Philadelphia: Fortress Press, 1974), p. 49.

41. Gen. 2:15.

42. Loren Wilkinson, ed., *Earth Keeping: Christian Stewardship of Natural Resources* (Grand Rapids: Eerdmans, 1980), p. 209.

43. von Rad, *Genesis*, p. 59.

44. James Barr, "Man and Nature: The Ecological Controversy and the Old Testament," in David and Ellen Spring, eds., *Ecology and Religion in History* (New York: Harper and Row, 1974), pp. 63–64.

45. von Rad, *Genesis*, p. 155.

46. Claus Westermann, *Creation*, pp. 89, 112.

47. Ibid., p. 102.

48. Paul Santmire, *Brother Earth: Nature God and Ecology in Time of Crisis* (New York: Thomas Nelson, 1970), pp. 163–68.

49. von Rad, OTT, p. 450.

50. Gerhard von Rad, *Wisdom in Israel* (Nashville: Abingdon, 1972), pp. 144–76.

51. von Rad, OTT, p. 449.

52. Westermann, OTT, p. 103.

53. Ibid.

54. Abraham Heschel, *The Prophets*, vol. 2 (New York: Harper & Row, 1962), p. 264.

55. William Dyrness, *Themes in Old Testament Theology* (Downers Grove: InterVarsity Press, 1979), p. 76.

56. Ibid. p. 77.

57. David Ehrenfeld justly criticized a draft of this paper for its lack of references to Jewish exegetes such as Rashi. Jewish interpretation of the Old Testament could not, of course, be based on Hasel's principles since Hasel accepts the New Testament as canonical. At the time this paper was originally written in the early 1980s, a thorough overview of Jewish scholarship on creation was not available. A number of Jewish authors have since, provided up-to date commentaries on Jewish thought about the Torah and other relevant texts.

58. Gen. 4:9; Wilkinson, *Earthkeeping*, p. 212.

59. Ibid., p. 214.

60. Barbara Novak, *Nature and Culture: American Landscape Painting*, 1825–1875 (New York: Oxford University Press, 1980), p. 3.

61. See, for example, Robert Linder and Richard Pierard, *Twilight of the Saints: Biblical Christianity and Civil Religion in America* (Downers Grove, IL.: InterVarsity Press, 1978).

Colossians 1:15-20—
Christ Jesus as Cosmic Lord and Peacemaker

Robert J. Karris, OFM*

A. TRANSLATION AND STRUCTURAL ANALYSIS

15a   ...Who is the image of the invisible God,

15b   the firstborn of *all* creation.

16a   For **in him** were created *all* things

16b   in heaven and on earth,

16c   the visible and the invisible,

16d   whether thrones or dominions

16e   whether principalities or powers;

16f   *all* things were created **through him** and **for him**.

17a   And he is before *all* things,

17b   and *all* things **in him** hold together.

18a   And he is the head of the body, the church.

18b   Who is the beginning, the firstborn from the dead,

18c   that in *all* things he himself might be preeminent.

19   For **in him** *all* the fullness was pleased to dwell,

20a   and **through him** to reconcile *all* things **for him**,

*   This article originally appeared as: "Colossians 1:15–20: Christ the Cosmic Lord and Peacemaker," in Robert Karris, A Symphony of New Testament Hymns, (Collegeville, MN: The Liturgical Press, 1996) 63–91. Reprinted with permission.

20b   making peace through the blood of his cross, **through him,**
20c   whether those on earth or those in heaven (italics mine, NAB
adapted).

Before commencing my analysis of this majestic hymn, I offer two
observations: one short and one lengthy. First, the scholarly literature on
this hymn concerning its relationship to the polemic of Colossians 2 and
its contemporary applications is massive. To do justice to the hymn and
to its ancient and contemporary contexts, I will have to sample much
scholarly literature and bring in technical arguments from time to time.
Readers not interested in such discussions are advised to skip these
scrumptious side dishes and to feast straightaway on the savory and suc-
culent entree. In passing, I note that Eduard Norden in 1913 was the first
scholar in modern times to identify "the undoubtedly old traditional
material" of Colossians 1:15–20 (Martin 1973,61).

Second, I must forewarn you that in my analysis of Colossians
1:15–20 I will be parting company with the scholarly consensus. Thus, I
will not teach you that the author of Colossians redacted (corrected?) a
hymn, highly regarded by him and the Colossians, by adding such
words as "the church" in 1:18a and "through the blood of his cross" in
1:20b. But why would scholars see a redactor's pen at work at all? I enlist
Ernst Käsemann as spokesperson for the scholarly majority. First, he
argues that the hymn is composed of two parallel and antithetic stanzas
(the same two stanzas I have proposed in my translation above), one dealing with creation and one with re-creation. Then he argues that the
expression "the church" in 1:18a does not belong to the content of the
first stanza which deals with creation seen almost from an a historical
perspective, for "the church" is a theological term stemming from re-
creation and is used to root creation in history. Next, Käsemann detects
an exegetical stumbling block in 1:20b, for the "connexion of creation and
eschatological new creation is broken by the reference to the event of the
Cross—a reference for which the way is totally unprepared and which
has immediately an anachronistic effect" (1964, 152). The reference to the
cross also roots the theology of the hymn in everyday human existence.
Käsemann provides some additional observations (1964,150–52), but his
main arguments are based on an analysis of style (two parallel and antithetic stanzas) and content (creation/re-creation).

How does one evaluate Käsemann's analysis and those like his? I make two methodological points. One is my own, and one is that of N. T. Wright. To me Käsemann's study of Colossians 1:15–20 is excellent in a New Testament classroom where philosophical and narrative logic reigns and dictates that creation must be separated from re-creation and the event of Jesus' death on the cross must be mentioned before the event of his resurrection from the dead. But hymns, and poetry in general, have a logic of their own, as our culture manifests in the phrase "poetic license," which the 1992 edition of *Random House Webster's College Dictionary* defines as "deviating from conventional form, logic, fact, etc., to produce a desired effect." Perhaps we scholars had better check our presuppositions about New Testament hymns: Do we assume that they must say everything about God and Jesus Christ and do so in the order of "salvation history"? Do we suppose that the New Testament hymns must follow the order we have detected, with the result that words like "the church" are seen as deviating from our order and therefore are additions?

If you press me for another example of New Testament "poetic license" in a hymn, I point to 1 Timothy 3:16:

> Who was manifested in the flesh,
> vindicated in the spirit,
> seen by angels,
> proclaimed to the Gentiles,
> believed in throughout the world,
>   taken up in glory *(NAB)*.

I refer my readers to my chapter on 1 Timothy 3:16 for a full treatment of this hymn about the universality of salvation. For our purposes, it is sufficient to note that the hymn almost defies the logic of the temporal sequence of salvation history to sing its Christology, for how can proclamation to the Gentiles and belief throughout the world occur before Jesus has ascended ("taken up in glory")? To my knowledge no scholar has seriously suggested that we eliminate a word from or add a word to 1 Timothy 3:16 so that it makes better chronological sense. Interpreters try their best to make sense of the hymn as it stands and do not resort to the speculation that an original hymn was redacted by the author of 1 Timothy. Interested readers can also check 1 Peter 3:22, which occurs at the end of a hymn which I discuss in another chapter of this book. This verse defies logic when its Greek text states that Jesus

Christ sits at the right hand of God, has gone into heaven, with angels, authorities, and powers subject to him. In our way of thinking, first you enter a place and then you sit down. But that's not the logic of the author of this hymn.

N. T. Wright finds fault with analyses like that of Käsemann on another level of method, as he employs a modern version of the *reductio ad absurdum* argument. If Käsemann can argue that the redactor added words to the hymn to have it make better theological sense, why can't some scholar argue that the redactor omitted words to have the hymn make better sense? Wright writes: "...if insertions are to be allowed omissions should be as well, making the task of reconstruction virtually impossible..." (1990,445). I am in accord with Wright's conclusion: "The best way to proceed is to treat the passage, in the first instance, as it stands, and to see if it will yield satisfactory sense" (1990,445). It will be the responsibility of my readers to see whether I have made satisfactory sense of the unredacted, integral hymn of Colossians 1:15–20.

Having completed my two initial observations, I turn to an analysis of the structure of Colossians 1:15–20, and do so by following the schema of Jean-Noël Aletti, who argues that it is composed of two stanzas and is unredacted. N. T. Wright has much the same schema, although he detects a chiasm (cross pattern) of A (1:15a–16f), B (1:17ab), B' (1:18a), and A' (1:18b–20c). Wright's chiastic structure may be an over-refinement. What is important is that Aletti, Wright, and I are members of a minority who maintain that Colossians 1:15–20 is composed of two stanzas; and what is even more important is that we maintain that the author of Colossians has not wielded a redactor's pen on this traditional hymn of two stanzas.

In the translation as I present it, I have highlighted other poetic features. I have italicized *all*, which occurs a total of eight times. There is a ninth time if you include 1:20c: "whether those on earth or those in heaven." As we will see later on, the hymn sings of the universal lordship and absolute primacy of Jesus Christ over all. No creature is excluded from his power.

I have put in boldfaced print the eight prepositional phrases where the composer of the hymn may have drawn upon popular philosophical tradition to indicate the primacy of Jesus Christ. In his power, through his power, and for the purpose God set forth through him is Jesus Christ supreme and preeminent. Eduard Lohse quotes Seneca to support his contention that "the final unity of all that exists is expressed by this succession of prepositions, which appears almost a play on words" (1971, 49 and no.121). In *Epistle* 65,8 Seneca writes: "Accordingly, there are five causes, as Plato says: the one 'from which' (material), the one 'by which' (agent), the one 'in which' (formal), the one 'according to which' (exemplary), and the one 'for which' (final). Last comes the result of all these. Just as in the case of the statue... the one 'from which' is the bronze, the one 'by which' is the artist, the one 'in which' is the form which is adapted to it, the one 'according to which' is the pattern imitated by the maker, the one 'for which' is the purpose in the maker's mind, and finally the result of all this is the statue itself." This same philosophical tradition is no stranger to the Pauline epistles, for it is also evidenced in 1 Corinthians 8:6: "..yet for us there is one God, the Father, from whom all things are and for whom we exist, and one Lord, Jesus Christ, through whom all things are and through whom we exist." Jesus Christ is not just one of five possible causes. He is all the causes.

Also, the composer has used various artistic parallels to construct the hymn. See, for example, how "the firstborn of all creation" (1:15b) of the first stanza corresponds to "the firstborn from the dead" (1:18b) at the beginning of the second stanza. As a matter of fact, this parallelism is one of the main reasons for separating Colossians 1:15–20 into two stanzas. Further, there is the clear parallelism, which is also chiastic, between 1:16b and 1:20c: heaven/earth—earth/heaven. More subtle is the chiastic parallel between 1:16a and 1:16f: "in him were created all things" (prepositional phrase, verb, *all things*) and "all things were created through him and for him" (*all things*, verb, prepositional phrases). There is also the less than perfect chiastic parallel between 1:17a and 1:17b: "And he is before all things" (personal pronoun, verb, *all things*) and "and all things in him hold together" (*all things*, personal pronoun, verb).

Finally, I refer my readers to the experience of everyone who wants to read serious poetry. You need to dust off your dictionary, for you must finger-walk incessantly through its pages as you try to figure out the uncommon vocabulary of serious poetry. I give a few examples of how this experience applies to Colossians 1:15–20. The adjective "visible" (Greek: *horatos*) in 1:16c, the verb "to be preeminent" (Greek: *proteuein*) in 1:18c, the verb "to make peace" (Greek: *eirenopoiein*) in 1:20b, and the phrase "the blood of his cross": (Greek: *haima tou staurou autou*) in 1:20b are found nowhere else in the New Testament. Also, the only occurrence

in the Pauline letters of the noun "thrones" (Greek: *thronoi*) is found in
1:16d.

Why such a density of uncommon words in six verses? My answer
is twofold. We are dealing with poetry. Also, we are pondering traditional material, formulated in a vocabulary different from that ordinari-
ly used by the author. For those who doubt the veracity of my second
answer, I refer them to a common experience. As you read through a
term paper you gain a fairly good grasp of the author's vocabulary and
style. Then at a certain point in the paper you come across pages written in a different, perhaps more elegant and clear style. Then you return
again to the regular style of the author of the term paper. It took me
one reading of term papers to detect this type of borrowing. In a similar
sense, the author of Colossians flattered the composer of the hymn
found in 1:15–20 by quoting it in its entirety with its uncommon vocabulary at the beginning of his letter.

By means of special vocabulary, parallelisms within and between the
two stanzas, artistic repetition of prepositions, and the refrain "all
things," the composer of Colossians 1:15–20 has created a wondrous
hymn to draw attention to the one who is absolute in every way—Jesus
Christ.

Perhaps we can tune into the composer's artistic wavelength by
reflecting upon another two-stanza religious poem, whose deepest focus
is Christ the Lord. I refer to the sonnet, "The Windhover: To Christ our
Lord," by the Jesuit Gerard Manley Hopkins, who was born in England
in 1844 and died in Ireland in 1889. In struggling to understand Hopkins'
sonnet, we will find ourselves soaring within our religious imaginations
under the power of language fashioned by an expert wordsmith, and
we'll find numerous interpretive challenges analogous to those we'll face
in Colossians 1:15–20.

The Windhover: To Christ our Lord

I caught this morning morning's minion, kingdom of daylight's
    dauphin, dapple-dawn-drawn Falcon, in his riding
Of the rolling level underneath him steady air, and striding
High there, how he rung upon the rein of a wimpling wing
In his ecstasy! then off, off forth on swing,
As a skate's heel sweeps smooth on a bow-bend: the hurl and gliding
Rebuffed the big wind. My heart in hiding
Stirred for a bird,—the achieve of, the mastery of the thing!

Brute beauty and valor and act, oh, air, pride, plume, here
Buckle! AND the fire that breaks from thee, then, a billion
Times told lovelier, more dangerous, O my chevalier!

No wonder of it: sheer plod makes plough down sillion
Shine, and blue-bleak embers, ah my dear,
Fall, gall themselves, and gash gold-vermilion.

My comments on this marvelous poem will be brief and will parallel what I have said above about the poem in Colossians. First, both
Colossians 1:15–20 and "The Windhover" have two stanzas. In its sonnet
form the first stanza of "The Windhover" has eight lines while its second stanza has six lines. Second, with regard to content, the first stanza
of "The Windhover" largely focuses on the achievements of the material
creature, the falcon, whereas its second stanza accentuates the deeper,
spiritual, Christ-like meaning of the falcon's accomplishments. Recall
the scholarly opinion about the two stanzas of Colossians 1:15–20: the
first stanza deals with creation while the second stanza focuses on re-
creation. Yet just as there is tension between the goodness of all creation
in the first stanza and the need for all creation to be reconciled in the
second stanza... so too is there tension between the two stanzas of "The
Windhover." While there is admiration for the falcon in stanza one,
there is apprehension about the pain inherent in getting involved with
the "lovelier, more dangerous" fire of Jesus Christ and being the subject
or object of "fall, gall, and gash."

Third, there is rhythm and rhyme galore in "The Windhover."
Take, for example, "riding," "striding," "gliding," and "hiding" in the first
stanza. And "here," "chevalier," and "dear" in the second stanza paralleled
by "billion," "sillion," and "vermilion."

Fourth, there is strange vocabulary. Hopkins has taken three terms
from the world of knighthood: "minion" (servile follower); "dauphin"
(crown prince); "chevalier" (knight). And I would wager that "dapple"
(marked with spots) is not part of your common vocabulary. And would
you believe it? Although we have millions of words in the English language, Hopkins coined a new one in "sillion," which probably means
"furrow." Needless to say, "sillion" doesn't bear the theological weight of
the verb "making peace" in Colossians 1:20b, but it has this in common
with it: both are very rare or even neologisms (technically and in Greek:
hapax legomena).

Fifth, I build upon my previous point by highlighting vocabulary which is key to the meaning of "The Windhover," but which is patient of multiple meanings. I refer to line ten: "Buckle!—AND." Hopkins wrote the exclamation point and put the word "and" in capitals. Is "buckle" an imperative? Does "buckle" refer to "buckle up" your seat belts or the walls and floor "buckled under" the heat of the fire or some other meaning of "buckle"? And then what about "AND"? I prefer the meaning of the buckling which opens up solid materials and reveals the fire deep within. For me, the second stanza reveals the falcon as Christ, "my chevalier," whose fire of life is far more lovely and dangerous than that of any grand predator bird performing according to its nature. Again the parallels between important and multi-layered vocabulary in "The Windhover" and Colossians 1:15–20 are telling. The Arian controversy revolved around the meaning of Colossians 1:15b: "the firstborn of all creation." That is, did this mean that Jesus Christ is the supreme creature or the one who is before all creation? What does "the fullness" in 1:19 mean? All the heavenly aeons, as in Gnosticism? Or all God's power for goodness? Finally, are the terms "principalities and powers" used in the same meaning in 1:16e, 2:10, and 2:15? Happily, linguistic and theological investigations have settled the issue of the meaning of 1:15b, "the first-born of all creation," and of 1:19, "the fullness." In our third section on key concepts and images we will return to the unsettled issue of the meaning of "principalities and powers."

I conclude this section by referring to the deep Christology which underlies Hopkins' poem, a Christology based on the interpretation of Colossians 1:15–18 championed by the Franciscan theologian, Blessed John Duns Scotus (ca. 1265–1308). As Elizabeth Jennings observes: "Duns Scotus was an important influence since his theology included the belief that God the Son would have become man even if Adam had not fallen from grace. This unusual attitude towards the Incarnation, not shared, for example, by Aquinas, had a powerful effect on Hopkins' poetry in that it enabled him to see the Incarnation as more than simply the means of man's redemption. For him, such a doctrine glorified the material world and was, perhaps, largely responsible for the lovely, care-free poems of praise such as... 'The Windhover'..." (1975, 195). Jennings' point about the influence of Duns Scotus' Christology on Hopkins' poetry is perhaps best seen in the final lines of his sonnet, "As kingfishers catch fire":

Christ—for Christ plays in ten thousand places,
Lovely in limbs, and lovely in eyes not his
To the Father through the features of men's faces.

In the final section of this chapter I will return to the question of
the relevance of Duns Scotus' interpretation of Colossians 1:15–20 for
today's ecological concerns.

B. THE CONTEXT

Before treating the immediate and broader context of Colossians
1:15–20, I want to make explicit what has been implicit in my discussions
so far. That is, in my opinion the author of Colossians was not Paul, but
a trusted Pauline disciple writing in the 60's to a church which Paul did
not found, but which was perceived as needing further instruction in
faith because of the threats posed by some opponents. I will provide
more information about these opponents in the section below on broader
context.

Also, I want to remind my readers of the cultural context within
which Colossians was written and which I've called "an age of anxiety"
in my previous chapter on backgrounds. In his excellent commentary on
Colossians, Eduard Schweizer gives the following description of the
Hellenistic world at the time of the writing of Colossians: "The stability
of the world has become problematic. The struggle of the elements of
nature (water, air, earth, and fire) against one another expresses itself in
catastrophes and threatens to lead to a complete breakdown of the universe. The fragile nature of the world and its order is experienced everywhere, and the individual seems like a prisoner of nature, a nature at
war with itself" (1982, 80). In all fairness to this cultural context, however,
I must observe, along with Richard E. DeMaris (1994, 94–96), that
Schweizer may have painted too pessimistic a picture. There were some
philosophers and divines who sometimes detected order or reason or
logos in the way the elements of nature normally operate. Incidentally,
"elements of nature/universe" is a translation of the Greek phrase which
occurs in Colossians 2:8 and 2:20. In Greek the phrase is *stoicheia tou kos-
mou*. The NAB translation is "elemental powers of the world."

Commentators have noted that the *immediate context* of Colossians
1:14 and 1:22 underlines the truth that it is through Christ and his cross
that believers have "forgiveness of sins" and are "reconciled." Thus, by

means of the brackets of 1:14 and 1:22 the author endeavors to eliminate any possible interpretation that the reconciliation sung about in 1:20a was merely cosmic, automatic, and did not require Christ's salvific action or any moral response from believers.

Further, the immediate context of 2:2–3 makes clear on what grounds the author of Colossians will face the "philosophers" who threaten the community's faith. The author knows and understands the "mystery of God, Christ, in whom are hidden all the treasures of wisdom and knowledge." Implied is that these errorists lack such knowledge and understanding. The author makes this claim explicit in 2:8: The errorists proclaim a philosophy "according to human tradition, according to the elemental powers of the world, and not according to Christ."

In dealing with the *broader context* for 1:15–20, I will give special attention to 2:4–3:12. I begin with 2:8,16–23, which Richard DeMaris has termed "the polemical core in Colossians." Granted all the methodological hazards of trying to reconstruct the viewpoint(s) of the "errorists" from the author's attack on their tenets, DeMaris quite plausibly maintains that the major issue between the author and the "errorists" involved the pursuit and acquisition of divine knowledge. The "philosophers" at Colossae pursued their wisdom in multiple ways. First, they relied on the "elemental powers of the universe," whose harmony and proportion reflected a divine ordering. And since Jesus Christ had established peace among all things (all elements) once and for all (see 1:20b), they had, assurance that ordering and balance among the elements were secured. Second, through ascetical practices of fasting, abstinence, and observance of special days they tried to liberate their minds from distractions and prepare themselves to receive and comprehend revelatory insight from above. Third, like thousands of their compatriots they reverenced demons/angels, who acted as messengers between heaven and earth (DeMaris 1994, 131–32, 142).

In 2:8, 16–23, the author vigorously argues that the three avenues just described do not lead one to divine knowledge. Repeating in different ways his foundational point that only in Christ is there wisdom (2:3), the author maintains that dying with Christ in baptism liberated the Colossians from (the study or control of) the elemental powers of the universe (2:20). That is, no divine knowledge will come from study of what we today would call first principles, natural law, and the elements by which all reality is held together. Further, fastings and such may well have an effect contrary to the ecstatic experience anticipated, for they may set into motion drives to gratify "the flesh" (2:23). Moreover, seeking revelation from angels and engaging in profound investigations of visionary experiences will not lead to humility, but to pride and community-destroying elitism (2:18). In brief, the author insists that the Colossians stick close to Christ, the head (2:19), that is, they must adhere to the wisdom of the hymn and not wander down avenues which might be heralded as passages to divine wisdom, but which in reality are dead ends.

It seems that the goal of the author's polemic against the errorists is to prompt his readers to hasten back to the wisdom of Colossians 1:15–20 and abandon any inkling they might have had to find divine knowledge in any other place than in Christ. But the author does not want his readers to hasten back too fast to the traditional material of 1:15–20. First, they must learn how he has interpreted it by the teaching of 2:9–15, which he has inserted right into the middle of the polemical core of 2:8, 16–23. To 2:9–15 I now turn.

For our purposes I limit our discussion of 2:9–15 to what the author says about Christ and the principalities and powers in 2:10 and 2:15. Recall that the principalities and powers were positively mentioned in 1:16e of the hymn as having been created in Jesus Christ and in 1:20a as having been reconciled. 2:9 says that Christ is head, that is, lord, of every principality and power. That's about the same thing the hymn itself implied, although when the specific word "head" is mentioned in 1:18a, reference is made to the body, the Church. So far, so good. In 2:15, however, the author goes beyond what the hymn said in 1:20a and 1:20b about "reconciliation" and "peacemaking" and says that through his cross Christ has despoiled the principalities and powers. This imagery is derived from the Roman triumphal procession, the highest honor Rome could bestow on its conquering heroes, and graphically shows how God has publicly shamed the principalities and powers and exposed them in his triumphal procession through Christ's cross. With studied understatement Wayne A. Meeks observes that the metaphor (of triumph over the cosmic powers "betrays a rather more negative evaluation of them than does the reconciliation metaphor of the hymn" (1979, 211). Why this negative evaluation of the principalities and powers? Perhaps they are conceived as the divine powers which "stand behind the elements and move them" (Schweizer 1982, 81). And since the author has such a low regard of these elements, he paints the principalities and powers in the same negative light. Would that the author had been more clear about what the errorists said about the relationship between the elemental powers of the universe and the principalities and powers! In any case, we know that the author viewed both negatively, whereas the hymn of 1:15–20 had a more positive regard for the principalities and powers.

Finally, I call to your attention briefly the significance of 3:11 in the broader context of 1:15–20. Meeks makes the excellent point that the hymn of 1:15–20 praises Jesus Christ as the one who restores a created but lost unity. And if we look at the unification formula in 3:11, we begin to glimpse that baptism was a ritual actualization among humankind of that universal and cosmic restoration to unity. 3:11 reads: "Here there is not Greek and Jew, circumcision, and uncircumcision, barbarian, Scythian, slave, free; but Christ is all and in all." Thus, in the Church and through baptism exist all stripes of humanity, whose restoration and reconciliation have been effected through Jesus Christ. Put another way, when we read 1:18a, "and Jesus Christ is the head of the body, the church," we are made aware of the profound truth that the One who holds all things together (1:17b) has also put them back together again— in the Church. In terms of content and style 1:18a not only concludes the first stanza of the hymn about creation, but it also leads into the second stanza about restoration and reconciliation.

After this extensive discussion of the context of Colossians 1:15–20, I need to review where we've been and what we've seen. It seems clear that the author of Colossians and the philosophers belonged to the people of their time who were searching for a deeper meaning in life, who were investigating the teachings and practices of various philosophies and religions to achieve unity between themselves and God, between themselves and peoples of other nations, and between themselves and nature/the cosmos. Both the author of Colossians and the philosophers accepted the truth of the hymn of Colossians 1:15–20, but they differed in how this hymn was to be interpreted.

The philosophers had a high regard for the knowledge to be derived from the study of the elemental principles of the universe whereas the author of Colossians degrades such knowledge, preferring exclusively the wisdom of Jesus Christ. The author of Colossians viewed the principalities and powers as bringers of evil, who had to be despoiled and humbled by the death of Jesus Christ on the cross. It would seem that the philosophers had a higher regard for these powerful creatures.

Having shown how the immediate and broader contexts of the hymn of Colossians 1:15–20 have aided its interpretation, I want to turn next to its key concepts and images. We may well find that the hymn used concepts and images which were open to the various interpretations we have found in the polemical core of Colossians 2:8, 16–23, and in the author's theology and Christology of 2:9–15.

C. KEY CONCEPTS AND IMAGES

I want to consider four key concepts and images, all of which are interrelated: (1) the Old Testament background of Colossians 1:15–20; (2) the absolute primacy of Jesus Christ; (3) the principalities and powers; and (4) reconciliation and peacemaking.

In talking about *the Old Testament background* of Colossians 1:15–20, I do not mean to say that there are not some Gnostic and philosophical parallels which provide helpful interpretive back-ground to our hymn. Such do exist. For example, recall the philosophical background I noted earlier about the prepositions in, for, and through. I also recall the fleeting reference I made earlier to a possible Gnostic background for understanding "fullness" (Greek: *pleroma)* in 1:19. In stressing the Old Testament back-ground, I advise my readers that it provides the most explanatory parallels. Pragmatically stated, the Old Testament background, especially that of the wisdom literature, gives me the most interpretation for my exegetical dollar.

There is considerable truth in the claim which N. T. Wright makes that the wisdom literature is not the total answer to the background for Colossians 1:15–20. Rather, both stanzas of this hymn should be interpreted from the Jewish worldview, of which the wisdom literature is merely one facet. That is, the Old Testament assumes that the redeeming/electing God is also the creator God and vice versa. In Wright's own words: "For this worldview, there is one God; he made the world, and is neither identified with it (as in pantheism and its various pagan cousins) nor detached from it (as in dualism); he is in covenant with Israel; and he will, in fulfilling that covenant, reclaim and redeem his whole creation from that which at present corrupts and threatens it" (1990, 453).

Granted the overall merit of Wright's observations, I still think it helpful to rehearse the wisdom background of Colossians 1:15–20, bearing in mind that these wisdom parallels only help explicate the hymn's first stanza. That is, we'll have to find a different background for the second stanza. I follow Mary Rose D'Angelo's list of parallels between wisdom (in Greek: the feminine noun *sophia*) and Colossians 1:15–20 (1994, 318):

Colossians 1:15a: "the image of the invisible God"

Wisdom 7:26:   "[Wisdom] is the refulgence of eternal light, the spotless mirror of God, the image of God's goodness."

Colossians 1:15b: "the firstborn of all creation"

Proverbs 8:22:   "The Lord begot me [Wisdom], the firstborn of his ways, the forerunner of his prodigies of long ago.

Sirach 24:9:   "Before all ages, in the beginning, he created me [Wisdom] , and through the ages I shall not cease to be."

Colossians 1:16ab: "For in him were created all things in heaven and on earth."

Wisdom 7:22:   "For Wisdom, the artificer of all, taught me."

Proverbs 3:19–20:   "The Lord by wisdom founded the earth, established the heavens by understanding; by his knowledge the depths break open, and the clouds drop dew."

Proverbs 8:23, 30:   "From of old I [Wisdom] was poured forth, at the first, before the earth....Then [at creation] was I beside God as God's master worker, and I was God's delight day by day, playing before God all the while."

By means of Jewish wisdom theology the composer of Colossians 1:15–20 created one of Christianity's first and loftiest Christologies. As commentators continually remind us, this hymn is being sung in praise of someone who was executed as a criminal in a remote part of the Roman Empire some thirty years earlier. Yet this hymn mentions the human life of Jesus Christ only once, and that by means of the theologically freighted expression, "blood of his cross" (1:20b). This is not the narrative Christology of the four gospels, although John's Gospel, especially through its hymnic prologue about God's Logos, provides some parallels to the Christology of Colossians 1:15–20. We are viewing protology at work, as the composer takes us behind the scenes, before creation occurred, and struggles to express that in Jesus Christ God has manifested God's wisdom and plan for all of creation. Just as wisdom represents God to the outside, that is, as God's image, so too does Jesus Christ, as God's image. And Jesus Christ has manifested that wisdom not just at the beginning of his earthly life, not just through his death and resurrection, but indeed from the very beginning (see 1:18b).

Let me put the wisdom Christology of the Colossians in other terms. God is not so transcendent that God is not immanent to creation. That immanence might be seen through the eyes of Genesis 1:26: God created human beings in God's image. That immanence might be seen in the wisdom of God, the image of God. But now the composer of 1:15–20 says: God has become immanent in Jesus Christ, God's all-encompassing and perfect image. Or as N. T. Wright expresses this mystery: "The pre-existent lord of the world has become the human lord of the world, and in so doing has reflected fully, for the eyes of the world to see, the God whose human image he has now come to bear." This explains, among other things, the nature of the language often used to describe him: As in 2 Cor 8.9, the preexistent one, who (strictly speaking) had not yet 'become' Jesus of Nazareth, can be referred to by that name in advance, much as we might say 'the Queen was born in 1925'" (1990, 461). If I replace "Queen" with "President," citizens of the United States might more readily appreciate the force of Wright's analogy: How can one say that the President was born in 1925 when she didn't become President until her inauguration in 1996?

My second key concept—*the absolute primacy of Jesus Christ*—builds upon the point just mentioned regarding the lordship of Jesus Christ. Perhaps "the absolute primacy of Jesus Christ" is unfamiliar terminology to some of my readers, for it comes from a centuries-old Roman Catholic tradition, brought to full articulation by the Franciscan medieval theologian John Duns Scotus, and insists on the absolute priority of God's will and grace and on the secondary role of human sin. Put another way, even if women and men had not sinned, God would still have expressed his love for humanity through the self-communication of the Incarnation. I turn, however, to a Jesuit New Testament scholar rather than a Franciscan one, to find words to express what Colossians 1:15–20 says about Jesus Christ's primacy.

Jean-Noël Aletti, S.J., has detailed six ways in which Colossians 1:15–20 expresses the primacy of Christ (1981, 93–94). It should be noted that each one of the six ways finds expression in both stanzas of the hymn and lends weight to Aletti's argument that the composer is a consummate artist and theologian.

The first way is that of *eminence*. In the first stanza eminence is found in the expressions "firstborn" (1:15b) and "image" (1:15a). In the second stanza 1:18c gives voice to this notion: "he himself might be *preeminent.*"

The second way is that of *universality.* I would refer my readers to my translation of 1:15–20 at the beginning of this chapter where I italicized the eight references to "all things." Here I merely mention the references given by Aletti. In stanza one we have: "all creation" (1:15b); "all things" (1:16a, f, 17b); "before all things" (1:17a plus the list in 1:16b–e). In the second stanza we find: "all things" in 1:20a and "whether those on earth or those in heaven" in 1:20c.

The third way is that of *uniqueness* or the insistence that it is solely and uniquely Jesus Christ who is and does what the hymn says. The easiest way to perceive this point is to review my translation of 1:15–20 at the beginning of this chapter where I have highlighted the prepositional phrases with boldfaced print. In stanza one you will see "in him" in 1:16a, and "through him" and "for him" in 1:16f, and "in him" in 1:17b. In the second stanza there is "he himself" in 1:18c, "in him" in 1:19, "through him" and "for him" in 1:20a and "through him" in 1:20b. For those who know Greek I call your attention to the fact that 1:17a and 1:18a use *autos* to make it explicit that it is Christ only who is the subject of the verb that follows.

Aletti's fourth way is a little subtle and is a variation of the second way of universality. The fourth way of primacy is that of *totality* (on all levels). In the first stanza this way finds expression on the level of creation: "were created" (1:16a, f). Also on the level of modality this way is found in the prepositions: "in" (1:16a and 1:17b); "through" (1:16f); "for" (1:16f). Moreover, the level of "being held together" or "being sustained in existence" (1:17b) is part of the fourth way. In the second stanza "in all things" shows Christ's primacy on every level of being. And finally 1:20a is rich as it sings of the reconciliation of all through Christ and for Christ.

The fifth way is that of *priority.* "Firstborn" (1:15b) and "before all things" are the means by which the first stanza sings of Christ's primacy in this regard. In the second stanza "the beginning" and "firstborn of the dead" (1:18b) proclaim loudly this aspect of Christ's primacy.

The final way is that of *definitive accomplishment*. What is said of Christ in the two stanzas of the hymn is not the language of a commencement, but that of a jubilee celebration. That is, we do not sing congratulations about the future accomplishments of one embarking on a new career, but of things already accomplished by an individual, in this instance, Christ. Thus, Christ is already "the image of the invisible God" (1:15a) and "the firstborn of all creation" (1:15b). Christ is already "the beginning" and "the firstborn from the dead" (1:18b). Christ is already "the head of the body, the church" (1:18a). Christ is already the one in whom reconciliation and peace were accomplished (1:20a, b). Again note how these definitive accomplishments link together the two stanzas which make up our hymn.

Perhaps other Christian traditions have another way of articulating what Aletti and theologians centuries before him have termed the primacy of Christ in 1:15–20. In classroom discussions of my book these might surface. For the present I summarize my second key concept and image. In Christ and through Christ are eminence, universality, uniqueness, totality, priority, and definitive accomplishments. That is, Colossians 1:15–20 celebrates in song the absolute primacy of Jesus Christ.

In our discussion earlier in this chapter of the broader context of Colossians 1:15–20 I remarked that the author of Colossians seems to have a view of *principalities and powers* different from that of the composer of the hymn. In 2:15 the author states that through his cross Christ has despoiled the principalities and powers. This statement seems to stand in explicit contradiction to 1:16e which states that the same principalities and powers are good. On a certain level we might be tempted to dismiss this seeming contradiction as something contrived by scholars to keep them in the business of interpretation. But on a very serious level we are coming face to face with the problem of who is actually in control of our lives. We ourselves? We with Jesus Christ? We as driven hither and yon by fate? We as controlled by institutional power run amok? I will open a perspective on this very large and very real contemporary issue by using the insights of Walter Wink in his book *Naming the Powers* (1984).

Perhaps Wink's major contribution is to have investigated all the New Testament texts which talk about principalities and powers (Greek: *archai kai exousiai*) and related terms and not to have limited himself to texts from the Pauline letters. Two key Gospel passages are Luke 12:11

and 20:20. I adapt the NAB translation of Luke 12:11: "When they take you before synagogues and before principalities and powers (*archai kai exousiai*), do not worry about how or what your defense will be or about what you are to say." Surely, by principalities and powers, Jesus is not referring to good or bad angels. In Luke 20:20 the singular of principalities and powers is used and in clear reference to a human being in a governmental position of authority. Again I modify the NAB: "They watched Jesus closely, and sent agents pretending to be righteous who were to trap him in speech, in order to hand him over to the principality and power of the governor."

I think that it is justifiable to quote an entire paragraph from Wink's study in order to capture some of the revolutionary force of his analysis:

> These Powers are both heavenly and earthly, divine and human, spiritual and political, invisible and structural. The clearest statement of this is Col. 1:16, which should have been made the standard for all discussions of the Powers: "For in him [the Son] all things were created, in heaven and on earth, visible and invisible, whether thrones (*thronoi*) or dominions (*kyriotetes*) or principalities (*archai*) or authorities (*exousiai*)—all things were created through him and for him." The parallelism of the Greek, ably rendered here by the RSV, indicates that these Powers are themselves both earthly *and* heavenly, visible *and* invisible. We would expect them to include human agents, social structures and systems, and also divine powers. The reiteration of "whether on earth or in heaven" in v. 20 connects back to v. 16 and suggests that the cosmic reconciliation which God is bringing about through Christ will specifically include these powers, human and divine, and that no reconciliation would be complete without them (1984, 11).

What direct bearing does Wink's study have on the meaning of Colossians 1:16c–e? We should not put the "powers" in a negative light as the author of Colossians seems to have done in 2:15. If we follow the interpretation of the author of Colossians, we may miss the first century and contemporary meaning(s) of 1:16c–e. In my "Reflection Starters," I will return to this point as I look, through Wink's eyes and those of the composer of Colossians 1:15–20, at the good and the evil of government and other institutions.

My final key concept and image accentuates 1:20a and 1:20b and deals with *reconciliation and making peace*. From what I have said so far in this chapter, it is obvious that there is a tension between the *good* creation of the first stanza and the need for *bad* creation to be reconciled in the second stanza. The composer of the hymn does not tell us what went awry and necessitated that creation be re-created. While that is true, it will be helpful to seek for some background material which will help us interpret 1:20ab.

That background is not found in Israel's Wisdom literature, but in the philosophical-religious speculation of Philo of Alexandria, a contemporary of St. Paul, who used philosophical categories to make sense of his Jewish religious belief, first for himself and then for his fellow Jewish believers and interested non-Jews. Philo's works give us some indication of the human quest for peace. In Philo's *Special Laws*, 192 the word "peacemaker" occurs, but is nowhere else in Philo's voluminous writings. And this term is found in a context in which Philo describes the trumpet of the Jewish New Year festival as the signal for the end of war, "a cessation which God as founder and protector of peace, inaugurates; peace, that is, between the parts of the universe that are fighting against each other within the world of nature" (Schweizer 1982, 80). This parallel from Philo does not mean that Christ's death on the cross is the beginning of a New Year of peace. Rather, Philo's parallel gives evidence, in Jewish symbols, of the universal human and religious longing for peace, not just between humans but also between warring parties in the universe, be these fire, water, air, or earth in the form of brush fires, floods, cyclones, or earthquakes.

What Philo expressed in the Jewish symbol of New Year the composer of Colossians 1:20ab expresses through a fundamental Christian symbol, the Cross. That is, 1:20ab sings that the peace and reconciliation, universally longed for, has been achieved through Jesus Christ and his death on the cross. Earth and heaven are united. What was lost is restored. But such unification and such restoration are not automatic. They have a price: the shedding of Christ's blood on the cross. And as Wayne Meeks has reminded us, Christians must pay the price of baptismal commitment. For the cosmic drama of reconciliation is reenacted ritually in baptism where women and men must divest themselves of political, social, and ethnic ideologies and become one in the Church (see 3:11).

As we come to the conclusion of this section on key concepts and images, we might well ask what our four points have contributed to our comprehension of the Christologically rich hymn of Colossians 1:15–20. Christ, who lived, taught, and was crucified in an obscure part of the Roman Empire, was with God at the beginning of all things. He holds all things together. And as the firstborn from the dead, he is the conqueror of that power which holds all things in thralldom, death. Christ has primacy in everything and in every way. Through Christ and for Christ God has fulfilled the longings of the human heart for peace and a cessation of cosmic and human warfare.

D. RFLECTION STARTERS

Although I have sprinkled reflections throughout the previous three sections of this chapter, now is the time to give special attention to four reflections.

I begin with a reflection about one aspect of the Christology of Colossians 1:15–20 and do so by quoting an insight of Arnos N. Wilder: "Primitive Christian poetry is spoken, as it were, at the beginning of a world, indeed, at the beginning of the world. Its substance and forms are eloquent, then, of this hour, an hour, indeed, which ever renews itself for faith" (1971, 116). Yes, 1:15–20 invites us, challenges us to take flight in our religious imaginations back to the beginning, nay, before the beginning and to see Christ thoroughly enjoying creating and longing to become human to express tangibly God's unconditional love for all human and nonhuman creation.

A second reflection takes the following shape. During this era of ecological concern Colossians 1:15–20 reminds us of the solemn truths that creation is good and that reconciliation is for all. When Christians sing 1:15–20, as they do, for example, on Wednesdays at vespers, they are celebrating God's creative concern for all. Or as Eduard Schweizer phrases this truth: "They will therefore bring again and again before God everyone and everything, believers and nonbelievers, human and nonhuman creation, and demand his love for them" (1982, 300). Implied in the statement, "demand his love for them," is the fact that Christians themselves will display in their lives God's love for everyone and everything, believers and nonbelievers, human and nonhuman creation. Thus, reconciliation is not just for my part of the universe while I exploit other parts, thereby creating ecological chaos. Put another way, singing 1:15–20 in church is one thing. Living out its profound message in daily life is another. As the religious aphorism has it: You only know as much as you do.

Creation is not only good. It is Christic, for it bears the imprint of the one in whose image it was created—Christ. Perhaps it is easiest to try to see Christ in one's fellow human beings, be they rich or homeless, and to treat them reverently as Dorothy Day of the Catholic Worker did for decades. But how does one even begin to see Christ in nonhuman creatures? Earlier we saw how Gerard Manley Hopkins was able to see Christ the Lord behind and through the actions of a falcon in his poem, "The Windhover." I now suggest that St. Francis of Assisi provides many components of an answer in his "Canticle of Brother Sun," wherein he calls the elements of the universe "brother" and "sister." With such human terms of endearment Francis, perhaps too mystical for some, bridges the gap between human and inhuman, animate and inanimate and says volumes for today's world as the Patron of Ecologists, proclaimed such by Pope John Paul II in 1979. As I quote from Francis' canticle, I remind my readers that Sir William Walton has set this canticle to music under the title "Cantico del Sole" (available on CD from Chandos no.9222).

The Canticle of Brother Sun

Most high, all-powerful, all good, Lord!
All praise is yours, all glory, all honor
And all blessing.
To you, alone, Most High, do they belong.
 No mortal lips are worthy
To pronounce your name.
All praise be yours, my Lord, through all that you have made,
And first my lord Brother Sun,
Who brings the day; and light you give to us through him.
How beautiful is he, how radiant in all his splendor!
Of you, Most High, he bears the likeness.
All praise be yours, my Lord, through Sister Moon and Stars;
In the heavens you have made them, bright
And precious and fair.
All praise be yours, my Lord, through Brothers Wind and Air,
And fair and stormy, all the weather's moods,
By which you cherish all that you have made.
All praise be yours, my Lord, through Sister Water,

So useful, lowly, precious and pure.
All praise be yours, my Lord, through Brother Fire,
 Through whom you brighten up the night.
How beautiful is he, how joyful! Full of power and strength.
All praise be yours, my Lord, through Sister Earth, our mother,
Who feeds us in her sovereignty and produces
Various fruits with colored flowers and herbs.
All praise be yours, my Lord, through those who grant pardon
For love of you; through those who endure
Sickness and trial.
Happy those who endure in peace,
By you, Most High, they will be crowned.
All praise be yours, my Lord, through Sister Death,
From whose embrace no mortal can escape.
Woe to those who die in mortal sin!
Happy those She finds doing your will!
The second death can do no harm to them.
Praise and bless my Lord, and give him thanks,
And serve him with great humility (Habig 1973,130–31).

It should be noted that Francis' canticle, like Colossians 1:15–20, sings of creation and re-creation. For the latter term, Francis uses "pardon" and "peace." Rather, does not fear the potential chaos of the elements of the universe in earthquake, hurricane, forest fire, and flash flood. Rather he honors and praises the elements for all the good they are and do. They are brother and sister.

The focus of my third reflection is on a feminist critique of Colossians. The author of Colossians, who in Colossians 2 took issue with some tenets of the philosophers, might not be surprised that contemporary scholars are taking issue with some of his tenets and the way he may have been led in the controversy reflected in Colossians 2 to have stated things too narrowly. Let me be more specific.

In her commentary on Colossians, Mary Rose D'Angelo is highly critical of the author's use of the household codes in 3:18–4:1 wherein wives are instructed to be subordinate to their husbands and slaves are directed to obey their human masters in everything. In her feminist critique of 3:18–4:1, D'Angelo not only finds fault with the household codes themselves, but also and especially with their theological underpinning: "Despite its brevity and simplicity, Colossians' code is not merely conventional exhortation but the integral consequence of Christ's universal lordship. If that universal lordship liberates from the heavenly powers and authorities, it nevertheless affirms the patriarchal rule of the masters of this world" (1994,322).

While D'Angelo may be right that the author of Colossians "affirms the patriarchal rule of the masters of this world," she has overstated her case that "Colossians' code is...the integral consequence of Christ's universal lordship." How one author, even be he the author of the canonical Colossians, views Christ's universal lordship does not determine that this view is the only one or "the integral consequence of Christ's universal lordship." As I have stated frequently in my section above on the broader context of 1:15–20, the author of Colossians has a view of the principalities and powers and even of the elements of the universe which is different from that of the hymn itself. Expressed differently, in the canonical Colossians there are two views of the meaning of Christ's universal lordship: that of the author of Colossians and that of 1:15–20. In interpreting 1:15–20 as Walter Wink has done (see reflection four following), we may find a way, from within Colossians itself, to attend to D'Angelo's critique.

While we await the insights of Wink in reflection four, I mention that Meeks calls our attention to the apologetic nature of the household codes, which answered the "common Roman complaint that foreign cults disrupted households and thus eventually the public order" (1979,220, no.33). In Colossians the household code "assures that the basic structure of the Christian household will resemble that which is insisted upon by society at large." If Meeks is correct, and I believe that he is, then we have one way of answering D'Angelo's critique. That is, let's give shape to a basic structure of Christian household today which will resemble that which society today enjoins upon its people. Of course, giving shape to such a basic structure is not an easy endeavor. Nor is it facile to ascertain the household structure which society today requires of its people. But the components are at hand to prevent the present and future generations from reading Colossians 3:18–4: 1 as eternal and unalterable law. In brief, D'Angelo has alerted our attention to the fact that Scripture is not a museum piece nor something to be mouthed at the Church's liturgy, but lays awesome responsibilities upon preachers and teachers who must help believers to assimilate its demanding meanings for daily life.

Walter Wink's trilogy on the "powers" leads us into my fourth reflection on the social justice implications of Colossians 1:15–20. For the powers are not just spiritual powers, but can also be today's institutions, systems, and structures which have a compelling force for good or evil which goes beyond anyone individual or individual manifestation of the force. Take as one example the institution of "the old boys' club," which can and has taken on a life of its own to exclude women and other people of lesser station in life. In order to try on Walter Wink's thought processes about the social justice implications of the powers, I want to repeat part of an earlier quotation. In talking about 1:16, Wink writes: "We would expect them (the Powers) to include human agents, social structures and systems, and also divine powers"(1984, 11). Wink goes on to say that reconciliation through Christ is also for the sake of these powers (see 1:20). Put another way, according to the theology of the composer of the hymn the powers are good, have fallen, and are in need of reconciliation. As we have seen time and time again, that is not necessarily the total view of the author of Colossians in 2:9, 15. So far, so good.

Wink's next step is to take with utmost seriousness the wisdom background of 1:15–20, especially as it applies to 1:20b: "through the blood of his cross." Wisdom personified in Christ has been crucified. Again, so far, so good.

Wink's final step consists in interpreting 1:15–20, especially 1:20b by means of the Pauline statement in 1 Corinthians 2:6–8: "Yet we do speak a wisdom to those who are mature, but not a wisdom of this age, nor of the rulers of this age who are passing away. Rather we speak God's wisdom, mysterious, hidden, which God predetermined before the ages for our glory, and which none of the rulers of this age knew for, if they had known it, they would not have crucified the Lord of glory." Without entering into a lengthy interpretation of 1 Corinthians 2:6–8, we can make the following assumptions: (1) Christ is God's wisdom; (2) "rulers of this age" refer to both human and demonic powers (Wink 1984, 44–45). With the aforementioned notions in mind, we can begin tentative, but very serious reflection upon the powers and the implications of their reality for social justice in today's world.

At this point I refer back to D'Angelo's critique of the patriarchy of Colossians 3:18–4:1. Indeed, 1:16 sings that the powers are good and 1:20 sings that the powers have been reconciled tough the blood of the Cross. But does that mean that in singing of such goodness and reconciliation, the worshipping community receives instantaneous communication about the nature of the powers that afflict them and about the necessary steps to take to neutralize them? At the time when Colossians was written, believers may have been primarily concerned with the power of fate and magic, gained insight from the Christian community on how to neutralize them, and praised Christ for liberation from their clutches. Today socially enlightened Christians may name as powers for their fellow believers some of the ideologies inherent in the socialization processes by which we become men and women and relate to one another as such in our society. Such ideologies may truly be the powers today, for us.

I conclude my reflection upon the social justice dimension of Colossians 1:15–20 with a challenge to myself and to my readers: How do we name the powers in their goodness and in their need for reconciliation? How do we ritualize that the powers are good, but need reconciliation? Finally, how do we actualize our praying of 1:15–20, our song to Christ our Cosmic Peacemaker?

For my final remark on the vastly complicated, but immensely fruitful Christological hymn of Colossians, I want to quote from another writing by Walter Wink. Readers must aver the fact that in this quotation Wink is talking about good powers that need much reconciliation: "...I remember hearing of a Native American woman who rejected an offer of companionship on her lonely walk home in the dead of night: 'No, I won't be afraid. We have songs for this.' There is another story, as well, of a man being crucified, crying out an old Israelite hymn sung by his people under duress: 'My God, my God why hast thou forsaken me?' That hymn, sung to its close, ends in an affirmation of God's steadfast love.... The Jew, too, could say, 'we have songs for this.' We, too, even today—however evil the Powers may be, however resistant to change and violence they may be in their self-defense, however nimble and crafty they are in crushing opposition—we, too, thanks to the Colossians Christ-hymn, can say, 'We have songs for this'" (Wink 1990, 242–43).

Praise the Lord for the songster artist who composed Colossians 1:15–20!

ANNOTATED BIBLIOGRAPHY

Aletti, Jean-Nöel. *Colossiens 1,15–20; Genre et exégèse du texte; Fonction de la thèmatique sapientelle.* Analecta Biblical 91. Rome: Biblical Institute Press,

1981. Aletti argues for the integral, nonredacted nature of the hymn of Colossians 1:15–20 and for its wisdom background.

D'Angelo, Mary Rose. "Colossians." *Searching the Scriptures. Volume Two; A Feminist Commentary.* Ed. Elisabeth Schussler Fiorenza, 313–24. New York: Crossroad, 1994. Presents a challenging feminist critique of the theology and ethics of Colossians.

DeMaris, Richard E. *The Colossian Controversy: Wisdom in Dispute at Colossae.* Journal for the Study of the New Testament Supplement Series 96. Sheffield, England: JSOT Press, 1994. Surveys previous scholarship on the opponents of Colossians and investigates the "polemical core." (Col 2:8, 16–23) of Colossians by utilizing philosophical and archaeological backgrounds.

Habig, Marion A., ed. *St. Francis of Assisi: Writings and Early Biographies, English Omnibus of the Sources for the Life of St. Francis.* Chicago: Franciscan Herald Press, 1973.

Jennings, Elizabeth. "The Unity of Incarnation." *Gerard Manley Hopkins: Poems.* Casebook Series. Ed. Margaret Bottrall. London: Macmillan Press, 1975.

Käsemann, Emst. "A Primitive Christian Baptismal Liturgy," in a book of his collected essays, *Essays on New Testament Themes,* 149–68. Naperville: Allenson, 1964. With his characteristic brilliance Käsemann sharpened the focus on the meaning of Colossians 1:15–20. Few scholars today accept his view that a Gnostic myth lies behind Colossians 1:15–20.

Lohse, Eduard. *Colossians and Philemon: A Commentary on the Epistles to the Colossians and to Philemon.* Hermeneia Commentary Series. Philadelphia: Fortress, 1971. Rich in background materials from various sources.

Martin, Ralph P. *Colossians and Philemon.* New Century Bible Commentary. Grand Rapids: Eerdmans, 1973. His interpretive thrust is captured in his comment on Colossians 1:20b: "This is his (Paul's) counterblow to gnostic redemption and reconciliation which works by non-moral fiat and automatic process" (p. 61).

Meeks, Wayne A. "In One Body: The Unity of Humankind in Colossians and Ephesians." *God's Christ and His People: Studies in Honour of Nils Alstrup Dahl.* Eds. Jacob Jervell and Wayne A. Meeks, 209–21. Oslo, Norway: Universitetsforlaget, 1979. Meeks offers this fertile insight: "That baptism dramatized a cosmic, not merely a human, restoration of unity is shown clearly by the liturgical composition quoted in Col 1:15–20" (p. 211).

Pokomy, Petr. *Colossians: A Commentary.* Peabody: Hendrickson, 1991. Pokomy notes the tension that exists between the hymn's view that the "superhuman powers" are good and the letter writer's view in Colossians 2 that they are defeated opponents and instruments of sin: "The theology of Colossians is not a systematic work" (p. 142).

Schweizer, Eduard. *The Letter to the Colossians: A Commentary*. Minneapolis: Augsburg, 1982. A superb, faith-filled commentary which explores Colossians 1:15–20 primarily from a philosophical perspective.

Schweizer, Eduard. *Jesus Christ: The Man from Nazareth and the Exalted Lord* Macon: Mercer University Press, 1987. Schweizer's chapter, "The Hymns in the New Testament," has a particular emphasis on Colossians 1:15–20 (pp. 24–25).

Vawter, Bruce. "The Colossians Hymn and the Principle of Redaction." *Catholic Biblical Quarterly* 33 (1971) 62–81. Vawter makes the good point that the author of Colossians cited the hymn of Colossians 1:15–20 because he agreed with its theological content.

Wedderburn, A.J.M. "The Theology of Colossians." *The Theology of the Later Pauline Letters*. New Testament Theology Series. Cambridge: Cambridge University Press, 1993. (See pp. 1–71, esp. 64–71, on "The Continuing Influence of Colossians.")

Wilder, Amos N. *Early Christian Rhetoric: The Language of the Gospel*. Cambridge: Harvard University Press, 1971. A revolutionary book which highlights the wealth of insight to be gained from a literary rather than an historical approach to the New Testament.

Wink, Walter. *Naming the Powers: The Language of Power in the New Testament*. Philadelphia: Fortress,1984. This is volume one in Wink's three-volume series on "The Powers" and contains excellent linguistic studies which lay the foundations for the interpretations he expounds in volume two, *Unmasking the Powers* (1986), and volume three, *Engaging the Powers* (1992), also published by Fortress. The first volume was largely written in reaction to the monograph of Wesley Carr, in which Carr argued that the author of Colossians views "the principalities and powers" in Colossians 2:10 and 2:15 as good. See Wesley Carr, *Angels and Principalities: The Background, Meaning and Development of the Pauline Phrase HAI ARCHAI KAI HAI EXOUSIAI*. Society of New Testament Studies Monograph Series 42. Cambridge, England: Cambridge University Press, 1981.

Wink, Walter. "The Hymn of the Cosmic Christ." *The Conversation Continues: Studies in Paul & John In Honor off Louis Martyn*. Eds. Robert T. Fortna and Beverly R. Gaventa, 235–45; Nashville: Abingdon, 1990. Explores the parallels between Colossians 1:15–20 and the *Tripartite Tractate* from Nag Hammadi. More importantly, Wink ends with some challenging contemporary reflections on Colossians 1:15–20.

Wright, N. T. "Poetry and Theology in Colossians 1:15–20." *New Testament Studies* 36 (1990) 444–68. I agree with Wright about the integral, nonredacted nature of Colossians 1:15–20 and have benefited from the richness of his Christological reflections.

Yates, Roy. *The Epistle to the Colossians.* Epworth Commentaries. London: Epworth, 1993. In this popular work, Yates often offers solid commentary, but agrees with the view of Wesley Carr that the author of Colossians views "the powers and principalities" of Colossians 2:10 and 2:15 as good. See above under Wink, *Naming the Powers.*

Discussion Questions

1. How does the Hebrew Bible present God as acting in the original creation? Is this presence different or the same, today?

2. In the Hebrew Bible, what characteristics are attributed to creation itself? Does this make a difference for your understanding of the created world? If so, how?

3. According to the Hebrew Bible, how is humankind to relate to God and the whole creation? What significance does this hold for you personally? For your future career?

4. What is the status of plants and animals in the Hebrew Bible? Can we say that status is the same today? What implications does this hold for your daily activity?

5. Have you ever experienced how humans "have dominion over" nature and how nature "has dominion over" humans according to accounts in the Hebrew Bible? Is this the understanding you grew up with? How does the biblical understanding affect your daily life?

6. Consider the examples Jeanne Kay gives of how, according to the Hebrew Bible, personal morality/immorality of humans impacts the environment. Do you agree? What evidence is available? Have you experienced this personally?

7. Share your understanding of the distinction between how the Israelite people worshiped *in* nature and *with* nature, yet did *not* worship *nature itself*. How do you worship God? In what ways, if at all, is nature involved in your worship?

For Further Reading

Bergant, Dianne. *The Earth Is the Lord's: The Bible, Ecology, and Worship.* American Essays in Liturgy. Collegeville, MN: The Liturgical Press, 1998.

Bergant, Dianne. "Is the Biblical Worldview Anthropocentric?," *New Theology Review* 4 (1991): 5–14.

Bergant, Dianne. "Restoration and Recreation in Hosea," in Richard N. Fragomeni and John T. Pawlikowski, eds. *The Ecological Challenge: Ethical, Liturgical, and Spiritual.* Collegeville, MN: The Liturgical Press, 1994, 3–15.

Bergant, Dianne. *The World is a Prayerful Place.* Collegeville, MN: Michael Glazier, Inc., 1987.

Hayes, Zachary. *Window to the Divine: A Study of Christian Creation Theology.* Quincy, IL: Franciscan Press, 1997.

Reid, Barbara. "Paul for the Ecozoic Age," in Richard N. Fragomeni and John T. Pawlikowski, eds. *The Ecological Challenge: Ethical, Liturgical, and Spiritual.* Collegeville, MN: The Liturgical Press, 1994, 16–24.

PART TWO

Saint Francis and Saint Clare: Foundations

It is not without reason that on November 29, 1979 Pope John Paul II proclaimed St. Francis of Assisi the Patron Saint of Ecology. Sadly, too often the power of this patronage is lost amid the saccharine and romanticized likenesses of the saint that appear in flower gardens or statues of the servile Francis bearing a dish of water forming a birdbath. While these images are not entirely without meaning, they certainly miss the depth of the spirit of the Poverello and all that he can teach us about the cosmos and the God of All Creation.

As for St. Clare of Assisi, few environmentalists seem to even know who she is, let alone know anything about how her powerful spirituality can assist us in forming an ecotheology and an ecological ethic. Until recently, Clare and her spiritual writings have stood in the shadow of Francis.[1] Yet, as we shall see though her extant writings are far fewer in number than those of Francis, Clare is a powerful source for ecotheology in her own right, and we do well to hear her on her own terms.[2]

In order to understand the contributions of Francis and Clare of Assisi to environmental theology and ethics, we must be aware of their life stories and the profound depth of their conversion to Christ. Because the limits of this volume preclude a rehearsal of their spiritual biographies, any reader not familiar with the them is advised to seek out one of the several excellent accounts and study it before reading on. (See the "For Further Reading" list at the end of this section).

For our purposes, Francis of Assisi is best characterized as an ontological poet and a nature mystic who discovered the transformation of the universe and the interrelatedness of all beings through a spiritual journey of conversion, penance and praise. The journey to his conversion was arduous, and the subject of his entire life. In our ecologically threatened age, it is important for us to see the necessity of both the internal spiritual encounter and the external ecological effect of this spiritual journey in the life of Francis, for it points the way to our own conversion toward becoming sisters and brothers in the cosmos.

Three main explanations can be advanced for how Francis "arrived at sympathy and synergy with all things."[3] First, as a poet Francis was able to grasp the essence and sacredness in all of creation. As "The Troubadour of the Great King," he did not shy away from the erotic enchantment, wonder, fascination, and desire for and with all things in the universe.[4] Francis was captivated by the love of God seen in the Incarnation and demonstrated by Christ on the Cross. The depth of such passionate love disposed Francis to be free of possessiveness and to extend himself in relation to all of creation because he saw Christ's presence in everything and everyone, especially the poor and the lepers.

The second aspect of Francis' self-understanding that gave him insight into his kinship with all of creation, namely, his *religious experience* of the common origin of all things, is suggested in St. Bonaventure's *Major Life*, VIII, 6.[5] That all in the world comes from the same Creator was not a dry dogmatic tenet for St. Francis. Rather, it was more like a love song that drew everything and everyone to "the heart of the Father, through the Son in the enthusiasm of the Holy Spirit."[6] In light of this understanding, Leonardo Boff claims that it is more in the spirit of St. Francis to translate his famous "*Deus meus et omnia*," not as it is usually translated— "My God and my all,"—but, as "My God and all things."[7] Indeed, as Bonaventure recounts, Francis is most delighted to sing *with* the creatures: "Our sisters the birds are praising the Creator. We will go among them and sing God's praise, chanting the divine office."[8]

Francis' radical poverty is the third and final characteristic of his life that enabled him to be a kin to all of creation. Not holding on to anything, but rather meeting life with open hands and heart, Francis was able to set aside usual human tendencies toward subordination or domination and meet everything and everyone as one utterly available and completely focused on the need of the other. As Bonaventure claims, Francis was able to return to the state of "primeval innocence," a place of full mutuality in relationship with God and all creatures.[9] Indeed, Francis thoroughly understood his relationship to Jesus his brother and the entire family created by God, the Loving and Generous Creator and Great King.

Now few have come as close to living as a brother (or sister) to all of creation as Francis did, though thousands have tried, and many have written about it. In his essay, "The Franciscan Spirit," William Short, OFM unfolds some of the major theological themes of Franciscan theology which have their root in the life of St. Francis of Assisi.[10] Though traditional theologians have focused on the aspects of Francis' spirituality that fit the themes of classical theology Christology, ecclesiology, etc.—we also find themes that shape a Franciscan theology and an ethic of the environment.

As Short explains, Franciscan theology is an incarnational theology. At the heart of Franciscan theology stands Jesus, the Incarnate Word of God. From the goodness of God the Creator flows the entire created world. The crowning glory of creation is the Word, and all of the created world is modeled on it. Each being—living and non-living—in some way resembles the model, but humans bear the Divine image (*imago Dei*). The Incarnate Word, Jesus of Nazareth, is the "image of the invisible God..." through whom the entire universe has been created. Short explains how these amazing realities have led Franciscan Scholars and mystics to develop theological reflection on Christ's centrality. Short states: "Christ became the answer to the philosophical question, 'Why is there something and not nothing?'"[11] According to Short the early Franciscan theologians provided additional insights into just how Christocentric theology and spirituality is rooted in the New Testament and is relevant to Christian life. By approaching the Christian life in the light of these particular emphases—the goodness of God, Christ the Image of God, the Christocentric universe, the Imitation of Christ, and love—Franciscan living takes on a rather unique character.

The radical desire to live the *"full Gospel"* marks the distinctive Franciscan way as unique among the charisms of the Church's religious orders. Followers of Francis and Clare past and present stress the Gospel challenge to balance the active and the contemplative aspects of life. Such a balance of living enables Franciscans to hold a non-utilitarian attitude toward all of creation, to reverence it and nourish it, and to seek the optimal conditions of justice and mutual relationship among all creatures in the world and the cosmos. This attitude is all but absent from the dominant cultures in the modern world, particularly in the West.

Many scholars of both science and religion hold that it is the absence of an attitude of reverence for creation along with the human that is at the heart of the current ecological crisis.[12]

According to the Franciscan way, it is in prayer that we meet the Poor Christ who deified us and the material world by becoming part of it, and it is in the activity of daily living that we meet Christ in our neighbor. It is Christ, not humans and their desires for power or wealth, that stands at the center. Both the contemplative action of Francis and the active prayer and contemplation of Clare are necessary to bring justice and mutual relationship to reality for humans with all of creation.

St. Clare of Assisi and the Poor Ladies provide a superb model for a holy and ecologically friendly way of living. As Elizabeth A. Dreyer illustrates in her essay, "[God] Whose Beauty the Sun and the Moon Admire," Clare and the Poor Ladies exhibit a sense of self that is secured in a true understanding of the virtue of humility. Totally confident in the deep and abiding love of God for her and all others created in God's very own image and likeness, Clare shows us that such self-understanding "frees one to respect and raise up the 'other'—whether the other be a person, or a tree or a paper wasp—as also made and loved by God."[13]

Rooted in the love of God, the relationships of Clare with the Poor Ladies and the "trees, flowers, and bushes" went beyond mere acquaintance or a business-like association. As Dreyer points out, the sisters' relationships were marked by truly affectionate friendship. Not only were their ties friendly and rooted in humility, they were distinctively mutual. Though Clare was given the canonical title of "Abbess," she never used the title for herself and rarely exercised the full power over the sisters that the office technically provided. One might say that Clare chose to exercise her power *with* her sisters, rather than *over* them. In fact, she made provisions in her *Rule* for the Poor Ladies to participate fully in the governance of the community.[14]

While, like Francis, Clare knew a profound respect for human dignity which requires equal regard for all people, she did not neglect the particularities of relating to each of the Poor Ladies according to the requirements of her distinct personality or bodily needs. In addition to her loving deference for her sisters, Clare continued to nurture the relationship with the Friars Minor. Rather than discount those with whom relations were strained, Clare, rooted in the love of God, continued to reciprocate Francis' pledge to her and the Poor Ladies to give them love, care and solicitude, by extending her loving care and solicitude to the Friars.

Thus, we can glimpse the importance of Clare for ecotheology. In our world where the predominant paradigm of relationship is dominance and oppression of the less powerful by the more powerful, both human and non-human, Clare shows a way of engaged and respectful living. Beginning with the self confidence of one beloved of a God (who even cares for the birds of the air and the lilies of the field), and a respectful courtly bow to all of creation, Clare shows us a life marked by true deference, love, and equal regard, the fruits of which are sensitivity, unity and harmony. It is this kind of living that marks the paradigm to which our civilization must shift if, indeed, our planet is to survive.[15] By being mutually attuned to the "other"—human, non-human or divine—we can achieve the security of life and relationship that is often the goal of those who wield wealth and power, but which often eludes them.

Both Clare and Francis would certainly be the first to admit that it was through God's work of conversion in them that they were able to move beyond the promise of wealth and power that was within their grasp as children of the burgeoning merchant class in their day. We are left to wonder what it was exactly, that allowed Clare and Francis to be open to such a conversion. As Thomas Murtagh shows in his essay, "Francis and Ecology," some have speculated that Francis was simply born with the capacity to "foster nature" that made him stand out as as a model for ecologists today. Instead, the many sources show Francis' capacity for fostering nature developed as a part of his growth in the love of Our Lord. Referring to Thomas of Celano's *Life of Saint Francis*,[16] Murtaugh contends that Francis embraced a life of penance as a pathway to coming to know the love of God: "If Francis thought he could find direction for his own life through anything Christ did or said, he made use of it."[17] As we can see in the *Mirror of Perfection* 118,[18] Francis was quite a literalist in that he readily personalized and gave religious definition to objects from the natural world around him, associating them with scripture texts that spoke of those things or with liturgical and sacramental meanings associated with the articles. In addition, many observed a mutual bond of trust and affection between animals and Francis.

Lest we pass Francis off as a simple romantic or pietist, we can see evidence on the other side of Francis' struggle and human limitations in dealing with the natural world.[19] Murtaugh points out we see Francis, at times, annoyed by mice and flies just as we often are; and Francis was not a vegetarian. Thus, though Francis sought God in all things, there is evidence that he too had his limits! Indeed, Francis noted that though all creatures praise God, humans stand out in their refusal to praise God in a fitting way.[20]

Among all of the various ways Francis refers to creatures as objects of the natural world, his *Canticle of the Creatures* is unique. From the wide repertoire of creatures named in his other works, Francis includes only a few in the *Canticle*. According to Murtaugh, that the *Canticle* is built around the four classical elements earth, air, water and fire is of major import for discovering its meaning. At the time when Francis wrote the beginning part of the *Canticle*, Francis had received the gift of the stigmata, a sign of the profound intimacy of his identification with Jesus. He had recently been able to let go of his deep attachment to determining the future of the Order—realizing that it was not he, but God who would determine that. Near the end of his life, weak and suffering from a painful eye disease that left him sensitive to light and almost blind, Francis wrote the Canticle. Murtaugh concludes: "It is from this position of pain and peace that the Canticle makes sense; pain, because it can purify, clear away the dross and the unessential, and make clear the basics; peace because without peace of heart, how could anyone who was suffering at all compose such limpid, lyrical lines."[21]

Clearly, Francis' relationship with God is the governing factor in understanding his relationship with all creatures. There is little evidence that Francis had any unusual scientific understanding of the natural world. Yet, his insight into the three-dimensional relationship—humans and God, God and creatures, humans and creatures—was unique. The common relationship of both humans and the creatures with God makes humans and all other creatures sisters and brothers—and that makes all the difference!

While Murtaugh identifies the love of God as being at the core of Francis' ability to understand the kinship of all creation, in "'The Canticle of Brother Sun' and the Value of Creation," Eric Doyle shows us the process and the dynamics of Francis' journey toward this realization.[22] "The Canticle of Brother Sun" is the work of Francis the poet-mystic. As Doyle points out, poets use words in ways that point beyond the usual meanings assigned them. In the *Canticle* we not only have beautiful poetic praise of the God of all creation, but an "expression of the authentic Christian attitude toward creation which is to accept and love the creatures as they are."[23] As such, the creatures are not reflections of us nor objects over which we can claim power or control. Rather, the creatures, like us, are the expression of the goodness and love of God; in our creaturehood, we are equal with all other creatures. In fact, in the Covenant, God purposefully established a relationship not only with humans, but with *every living creature* (Gen 9:12-13). Each creature is a unique reflection of God and God's goodness. As God loves each creature uniquely, so too must we. Francis could know this way of the divine only because he first entered into a contemplative union with God; he knew God in and through all other beings and elements of creation. In union with God and all of the creatures, Francis found his uniqueness as one ever more original.

The realization of his uniqueness among the creatures, and yet his likeness to them as a recipient of the love of God was, in turn, a source of his great love of God's creation. To reflect on this emersion in love is to encounter Mystery, "the 'never-the-last-wordness' of our existence."[24] We are always seeking and searching for something more—yet, every human attempt to satisfy the "more" ends in more seeking. Francis' "heart sight" told him he had found the "more" in God; and God was ever present in the here and now and all around him.

The words of the *Canticle* express an integration in Francis' inner depths. As Doyle holds: "All beautiful words and music come from the mystery of personhood, welling up from the inner depths. It is not so remarkable that Francis, though blind, was able to write a song about the beauty and unity of creation. He was already one with himself and with the world, and the world was one in him."[25] This integration provided Francis with an inner confidence and a cure for alienation from any and all "others" that could pose a threat to him in any way. The path to such integration for Francis was a path of prayer that began with the first step of self- surrender.

The biography of Francis tells the story of his struggle toward embracing poverty as way of opening himself in freedom to God and all of creation. Through his relationship with God in prayer, he learned to love *as* and *what* God loves. To love authentically is to love and accept other humans and all creatures on their own terms. This is particularly significant for our ecologically threatened world that Francis was able to find himself, and true peace and harmony, not in warfare or wealth, but through spiritual means. In our own time when we are experiencing a spiritual malaise, prayer and spiritual practices are necessary to assist us in reversing the devastation of the planet.[26] This is not a call to escapism, but rather, to a move to the depths of our being to confront the deepest truth of being human, namely, that we are creatures who stand in relationship with both God and our fellow earth creatures. When we realize we are not alone, but rather surrounded with wondrous manifestations of God's love and care, personal integration can take place and alienation vanishes.

To understand one's relationship to all of creation through prayer and contemplation is also a political act. To be in a love relationship with all of creation is to risk being motivated to act in defense and protection of those we love. We cannot tolerate injustice nor abuse of the environment because all of creation is our sister and our brother. When one is motivated to defend another, one's focus shifts from self to the other. It is often risky to be so motivated; it is a move toward poverty, indeed, perhaps the ultimate poverty of losing one's own life for the sake of another. Quite significantly, Francis even called death "sister"; for he understood death as integral to life. Indeed, death is the ultimate journey into poverty, a letting go of all possessions including life itself. Having given his life completely to Christ, he had nothing to fear from death. Death was for Francis a passage into the fullness of life with Christ. In our day when fear of the "small deaths" of life such as personal limitations or the inability to achieve wealth or position are frequently the cause of discord, abuse, or other kinds of violence, we can learn much from Francis' embrace of "Sister Death" as a friend who opens the way to new life beyond imagination.

While Doyle's interpretation of the *Canticle* contributes important wisdom for Franciscan ecotheology, Thomas Nairn shows in his essay, "St. Francis of Assisi's *Canticle of the Creatures* as an Exercise of the Moral Imagination," that this classic is open to several other readings revealing yet additional insights pertinent to our discussion.[27] Nairn's own insight is that the *Canticle* can be understood as a call to moral conversion. Following the expositor of medieval popular culture, Aron Gurevich, Nairn places the references in the *Canticle* to the four cosmic elements—earth, air, water and fire—in their historical context. He shows how theologians, philosophers, troubadours and poets "saw the person not merely as part of the larger world, but rather as a 'microcosm' reflecting the larger 'macrocosm' and revealing a parallelism between the person and the world."[28] People of the Middle Ages understood the heavenly objects—sun, moon, stars—as powers which affected human destiny. Indeed, they believed that the four elements affected the very identity of the person. Thus, Nairn states, the goal of both medicine and natural philosophy was to restore the disease or temperamental problems caused by an imbalance among the four elements. With this in mind, Nairn engages us in an exercise of moral imagination.

Focusing on the verses that name the four elements, Nairn notes that this section differs from the rest of the *Canticle*. In each strophe there is both a movement towards God and a movement toward humanity. Francis shows the earth elements relating to God but also serving humanity. Nairn offers that perhaps Francis wishes to show us that when confronted with the cosmic elements, we must remember that they are *merely* creatures of God. Further, Nairn suggests, the terms "brother" and "sister" not only show the relationship of the elements to God and humans, but those terms are intended to serve "a relativizing function, as well."[29] Seen in the medieval context then, using the four elements as Francis does "bring[s] the cosmic elements, understood as elements which influence humanity, down to a human level."[30]

In the medieval context, nature was valuable in so far as it contributed to humanity's knowledge of God and drew humans to God. It was evil if it hindered humanity's quest for God. If the elements do not move humans to praise God, they are misused. "If the proper role of the elements points humanity to God, then God and not the elements is the true influencer of humanity... But as humanity accepts its place in the microcosm of this universe it must also appreciate its own vocation in serving God. It is in this calling that humanity finds true freedom."[31] Francis' *Canticle* understood in this way becomes a call to conversion to a freedom found only in God. Such freedom in God broadens humanity's vision and imagination to see the world as God sees it, and challenges humans to act in relationship to all of creation as God acts. In this way, the moral imagination is stimulated by and converted to the very mind of God. What a challenge the *Canticle* presents for environmental theology and ethics today!

Notes

1. See Ingrid J. Peterson, *Clare of Assisi: A Biographical Study*, (Quincy,IL: Franciscan Press, 1993).

2. See the essay that follows: Elizabeth A. Dreyer, "'[God] Whose Beauty the Sun and Moon Admire'," *The Way* Supplement 80 (Summer 1994): 76–86.

3. Leonardo Boff, *Cry of the Earth, Cry of the Poor*, trans. Phillip Berryman, (Maryknoll: Orbis Books, 1997), 213-16.

4. Boff cites the *Legend of Perugia*, 64. See "The Assisi Compilation," 99 in Regis J. Armstrong, J.A. Wayne Hellmann, William J. Short, eds., *Francis of Assisi: Early Documents*, Volume II - The Founder, (New York: New City Press, 2000), 202–03. See also, "The Beginning of the Mirror of Perfection of the Status of a Lesser Brother (Sabatier Edition)," 121, in Regis J. Armstrong, J.A. Wayne Hellmann, William J. Short, eds., *Francis of Assisi: Early Documents*, Volume III - The Prophet, (New York: New City Press, 2001), 369–79.

5. Boff, *Cry of the Earth, Cry of the Poor*, 214.

6. Ibid.

7. Ibid.

8. See Bonaventure, "Major Legend of St. Francis," VIII, 9, in Armstrong, Hellmann, Short, eds., *Francis of Assisi: Early Documents*, Volume II - The Founder, 592–93.

9. Ibid., VIII, 1, 586–87.

10. William Short, *The Franciscans*, (Wilmington, DE: Michael Glazier, 1989), 104–121.

11. Ibid., 112.

12. Boff, *Cry of the Earth, Cry of the Poor*, 1–34.

13. Dreyer, "'[God] Whose Beauty the Sun and Moon Admire'," 79.

14. Clare of Assisi, "The Form of Life of St. Clare of Assisi," 2: 15-18, 21-23; 3: 1-4; 7: 3-5, in Regis J. Armstrong, trans. and ed., *Clare of Assisi: Early Documents*, Revised Edition, (St. Bonaventure, NY: Franciscan Institute, 1993), 62 n. a, 66, 67, 73.

15. Boff, *Cry of the Earth, Cry of the Poor*, 31–34.

16. Thomas of Celano, "The Remembrance of the Desire of a Soul (1245–47)," 9:14, in Armstrong, Hellmann, Short, eds., *Francis of Assisi: Early Documents*, Volume II - The Founder, 253.

17. Thomas Murtagh, "St. Francis and Ecology," *The Cord* 39/4 (April 1989): 100.

18. *Mirror of Perfection*, 118 in Habig, ed., *Francis of Assisi: Writings and Early Biographies*, English Omnibus of Sources, 1256–57. See also, "The Beginning of the Mirror of Perfection of the Status of a Lesser Brother (Sabatier Edition)," 118, in Armstrong, Hellmann, Short, eds., *Francis of Assisi: Early Documents*, Volume III - The Prophet, 366.

19. Murtagh cites the *Legend of Perugia*, 43 and *2 Cel* 75. Cf. "The Assisi Compilation," 83, in Armstrong, Hellmann, Short, eds., *Francis of Assisi: Early Documents*, Volume II - The Founder, 184–87. Also see Thomas of Celano, "The Remembrance of the Desire of a Soul (1245–47)," 45:75, in Armstrong, Hellmann, Short, eds., *Francis of Assisi: Early Documents*, Volume II - The Founder, 297.

20. Francis of Assisi, "The Admonitions," 5, in Regis J. Armstrong, J.A. Wayne Hellmann, William J. Short, eds., *Francis of Assisi: Early Documents*, Volume I - The Saint, (New York: New City Press, 1999), 131.

21. Murtagh, "St. Francis and Ecology," 107.

22. Eric Doyle, "'The Canticle of Brother Sun' and the Value of Creation," in *St. Francis and the Song of Brotherhood and Sisterhood*, [reprint of *The Song of Brotherhood*, (New York: Seabury Press, 1981] (St. Bonaventure, NY: The Franciscan Institute, 1997), 40–59.

23. Ibid., 43.

24. Ibid., 47.

25. Ibid., 49.

26. Boff, *Cry of the Earth, Cry of the Poor*, 187–202.

27. Thomas A. Nairn, "St. Francis of Assisi's *Canticle of the Creatures* as an Exercise of the Moral Imagination," in Kathleen Hughs, ed., *Finding Voice to Give God Praise*, (Collegeville, MN: The Liturgical Press, 1998), 202–213.

28. Ibid., 207.

29. Ibid., 209.

30. Ibid.

31. Ibid., 210.

The Franciscan Spirit

William Short, OFM*

If this work can be considered in some way a biography of the Franciscan Family, a description of that family would be incomplete if nothing were said about the spiritual environment in which it lives and grows, and the climate it creates around itself. This chapter will describe characteristics, distinguishing features, special emphases of the family, and introduce the reader to some Franciscans who have helped to shape its spirit.

The Franciscans, in our great numbers and sometimes baffling diversity, hold in common a constellation of practices, ideas, devotions, and familiar images. All contribute to what may be called the "spirit" of Franciscans. In the following pages I will sketch outlines of this spiritual and intellectual topography.

A Poor Man's Theology

Francis was a theologian in the ancient sense, "one who speaks of God." Rarely expressed in dogmatic form, Francis' theology reveals itself in praises, letters, scraps of sermons, blessings, admonitions. Traits called characteristically and authentically Franciscan derive from this

---

* This article originally appeared as: "The Franciscan Spirit," in *The Franciscans*, (Wilmington DE: Michael Glazier, 1989), 104–121. Reprinted with permission.

source. Over the centuries Francis' theological vision has received more systematic presentation in the works of such disciples as Bonaventure and John Duns Scotus. Here we will interweave pieces from various parts of the Franciscan theological tradition, presenting a rapid and necessarily incomplete picture of the kind of theology Francis expressed and inspired.

THE GOD OF GENEROUS LOVE

God is good. Here is one possible beginning for Franciscan theology. God's goodness has special force because it is eminently real. The goodness of God the Creator (*fontalis plenitudo* for Bonaventure) is fully self-aware, this awareness being so real that it is personal, and is called "the Word" (*exemplar omnium*). The bond between the fullness and the exemplar is likewise eminently real and personal, and is the Spirit (*cogeneratus*). The very life of God is one of goodness expressing itself generously, fully. This divine goodness lives in personal communion. God is interpersonal and relational. This communion has at its center the Word, the core or middle of God's life as Trinity. Wishing to express overflowing goodness, God wishes to pour out an expression of the divine life. God's desire to share goodness is expressed as creation. But creation is not merely to receive some partial, limited sharing in God's goodness and life. God will actually give away even the very heart of the divine life, the Word. With this in mind, the will to give away the very core of divine life, God forms the world through the Word. Since the Word will be the crowning glory of the creation, God makes light and darkness, trees, stones and fish, all the creatures, according to the Word as model, or blueprint or form. The human person, man and woman, resembles most closely the model that God uses to create. Since the Word is to come among human beings, as one of them, they resemble the Word very exactly. In all this work of creation God shows one of the divine characteristics—outpouring of what is within, giving away all that is inside. This we may call the bowing over of God, the gesture typical of one who offers. We may also call this the humility of God, divine condescension. God gives away all, holds nothing back as property: this is the poverty of God, showing in the visible things of creation the invisible and constant self-giving which is the life of the Trinity. The world mirrors, now clearly, now obscurely, this inner, divine life of unending bowing over in generosity.

The universe and all creatures reflect God, speak of God, reveal God because they are made according to a pattern, the model of God's own heart, the core of the Trinity, the Word. The human person, coming at the completion of creation, gives voice to the praise of all creatures for the Creator.

The creation is fully understandable at the birth of Jesus. Here is the "missing link," always present, now visible. The core, the middle, the center of God's own inner communion comes, in order to be a creature. With the coming of the Word as one of them, creatures find their model enfleshed. Christ is no alien in a strange universe: he was from the beginning the reason and the Creator's blueprint for every particle of matter, for all things visible and invisible, for everything and everyone.

Whatever is beautiful reflects his beauty; whatever is living, lives because of him; whatever is true discloses him who is true; whatever is, is in him. "Everything was made in him, and without him was made nothing of that which was made" (John's Gospel, Prologue).

In his well-known love for creatures, Francis acts out this recognition of God's presence. He delights in the world of creation, and simply the touch of a creature can leave him enraptured. Francis continually exhorts every person and thing to "praise, bless and magnify the Creator." He treats them with deference and reverence, reminding his followers to be subject to every creature out of love for God. He calls every creature "brother" or "sister," and shows toward them, not simply curiosity or interest, but a tender affection.

Here is the full expression of God's identity: complete bowing over to offer the innermost reality of God as a gift. God's complete generosity is revealed in the Incarnation—nothing is held back, nothing is "property" to God, all is given away, God's true identity is communicated as poverty, holding on to nothing.

The religious world that humans developed cannot contain this mystery: God does not come as an angel, or as a burst of light, nor even as an idea or a vision—God comes as a baby. And the Word, incarnate, comes to a place and to people marked by poverty, because these are most fitting to express the mystery—the surprising revelation of who God really is.

These theological reflections were not systematized by Francis, yet they help us to understand the importance of certain gestures and phrases of his. The feast of Christmas recalls that great humility and self-giving of God. Francis celebrates the feast dramatically, composing a living scene of animals and people in a cave at Greccio—recreating in his gesture the mystery of God's poor love.

Jesus shows in his life this identity of God, in his choices, his words, his friends, his enemies, his gestures and signs. In the suffering he endures, and most fully in his Passion, Jesus—reveals the unexpected identity of a God bowing over to give away all.

Even as he prepares to leave his friends, at table with them, Jesus continues to reveal this identity, so hard for them to accept. According to John's Gospel, he removes his outer garments, binds himself with a towel and bows over to wash their feet. Here is the true image of God. In the Synoptics, he takes the work of peasants' hands and gives away his own life as a cup of wine and a piece of bread.

These gestures are anticipations of the great giving away, the bowing over of death. Stripped of everything, pouring out his own lifeblood, water and blood flowing from his opened side, breathing forth his spirit, completely broken and emptied, suffering physical agony and spiritual desolation, Jesus at the moment of his death gives away God's own life.

Francis speaks of the "crucified poor man," Christ, and knows that his death is the great act of God's loving graciousness. And in the Eucharist Francis recognizes the continuing gift—the Lord Jesus Christ gives himself fully as bread and wine. This divine life is given, eternally and irrevocably, for creatures.

The Trinitarian life of God, fully revealed and fully given away, shines with glorious joy in the Resurrection of Jesus, the glorification of Christ who becomes the first of creatures to be born into God. God's generosity now has opened the arms of the Trinity to every creature. Their full destiny is revealed—not only were they conformed to the Word in their origins, they are to be transformed in the Word as their fulfillment. All that God has given away begins its return to that personal and generous communion, glorified and transformed.

God's self giving is a gift, freely given. The very life of God is a continual giving of self in the Trinity. The divine gift of life and communion is poured out through the Word. The Word, born as a creature, a person, is the full gift of God's own self.

In the life of Jesus, in his death, and his being raised up, the creation can finally, fully return to God as a gift, the gift of the Word. This circle of giving, in which Creator and creatures give all and receive all, rests on a single premise: that one does not hold back what has been given. When this happens, the gracious circle is broken, the exchange of gifts is interrupted, the whole creation risks losing its meaning and its very life.

In Franciscan terminology, this is a definition of sin—the sin described in Genesis, and the sin that follows: refusing to give away the gifts one has received. For some Christian authors, the primary sin of Adam and Eve was pride, for others, it was disobedience. For Franciscans, it was the will to possess.

Reading the Genesis story in this light, we see the man and the woman are made "in the image and likeness of God." They receive all from God as a gift, and they give away all to God as praise and loving thanks. The serpent comes and proposes to offer them something, the fruit "that will make them like God." The offer is ludicrous: they are already like God. (The Father of Lies is at work, with a trick as old as civilization—selling you what is already yours). The difference, of course, is that this time it will not be given as a gift, it will be taken, grasped, held onto.

And in this moment, the circle of the gift is broken. Harmony in creation fails. The image of God is obscured.

We begin to see here the reason for the preeminence of poverty and gratitude in Francis' vision. They are the two faces of this holy exchange of gifts: gratitude acknowledges that everything has been given to us, and poverty gives it all away.

This rapid survey of a Franciscan theological insight helps us to interpret words, gestures, choices that Francis makes.

Francis marks the beginning of his new life with the sign of meeting the leper. Those suffering from leprosy in the thirteenth century lived a radical poverty. They were "dead," with funeral services celebrated over their still living bodies. Their property was confiscated; their family ties, friendship and social relations were broken. They lived by the gifts of others.

"The Lord led me among them"—Francis attributes this leading to the Lord. "What was bitter to me became sweet." Francis finds among the lepers a quality, "sweetness," which he usually attributes to God's presence.

And he wishes to stay among them, to be with "persons looked down upon, among the poor, the weak, the sick and the lepers, and those begging on the side of the road." Among these, the persons looked down upon, Francis wishes to live. They are like Jesus "who was poor, and a guest, and lived by begging, himself and holy Mary the blessed virgin, his mother."

In the poor, Francis sees the image of Christ, the Image of God. The Lord Jesus Christ is poor in his birth, poor in his life, and poor in his death. And he wants to be in the world as one "looked down upon, needy and poor."

Francis embraces the leper, and with that gesture embraces the "holy Lady Poverty," and her sister, "holy humility." He does this out of a profound intuition that, through giving away everything, he will share in a truly divine activity; he will be accepting his true identity as made in the image of the poor God. "God created and formed you to the image of his beloved Son according to the body," Francis said, "all spiritual and bodily things and ourselves were made to your image and likeness."

With his discovery of God's poverty, Francis knows his own identity as made in God's image, and recognizes his connection with all creatures—like him, they are images.

THE THEOLOGY OF IMAGE

To speak of images and their place in Franciscan devotion we may begin quite simply, with a mirror. This could be a plain, square, modern mirror with an even and exact reflection. Or it could be the slightly corroded and uneven reflection of an antique Venetian mirror. We may even think of the surface of an ordinary mud puddle on a clear, windless day. It too is a kind of mirror.

Think perhaps of this poetic image given us by T. S. Eliot. While riding in a train through the English countryside one evening at sunset, he looks through the window of his carriage onto the beauty of rolling hills lit by the sun's warm, reddish glow. As darkness falls, the lights in the carriage illuminate more strongly the interior, and in the window Eliot sees now his own face in the place of the darkened countryside. The transparent glass changes to a reflecting surface, a mirror.

With these examples I am trying to approach, from our everyday experience, the theology of image, perhaps the most fundamental component of the Franciscan understanding of God, Christ, the human person, and the world. The Second Letter to the Corinthians (3:18) speaks of mirrors and images, and for this reason has been a favorite text of Franciscan spiritual writers for centuries. As Paul writes, "We all reflect as in a mirror the splendor of the Lord; thus we are transfigured into his likeness, from splendor to splendor, such is the influence of the Lord who is Spirit."

The image of the mirror that Paul uses is only one kind of image, the photograph is another. Since Franciscans have always preferred the concrete to the abstract, the specific to the universal, let me mention a single photograph, one from my adopted home, California. The photographer, Ansel Adams, died recently; the photograph he took he later named "Moon and Halfdome." In many ways this is a very ordinary picture. The moon rises over the great granite cliff called Halfdome, located in Yosemite National Park.

The photograph records exactly what the lens of the camera projected onto the chemicals of the photographic plate: a big, dark mass and a light, round sphere. Yet I can look at that photograph with a sense of wonder and delight, realizing that Adams aimed the lens in such a way as to balance the mass of rock with the brilliance of the full moon. As I look more closely at the picture I am puzzled by the photograph itself. I can see the rocky cliff, and I know that it really exists in the way the photograph shows it. But it also shows the moon, which I can see only from thousands of miles away, on the same paper surface with the cliff. Beyond the moon, it shows me, in darkness, unbounded space beyond the moon. This darkness, in fact, makes up almost half of the photograph. The apparently infinite expanse of solar systems, galaxies, and emptiness sits in front of me, contained in an image that measures eight by fourteen inches. Infinity here fills a very small space. The paradox we observe in Adams' photography of cliff and moon puzzles us into admiration.

In a similar way, the mystery of the Incarnation has puzzled Franciscans into admiration.

Such a text as Colossians 1:15 has served as a source for profound meditation on that puzzle who is Jesus: "He is the image of the invisible God; his is the primacy over all created things. In him everything in heaven and on earth was created.... The whole universe has been created through him and for him."

The great paradox here consists, not in an infinity of space captured within the bounds of a photograph, but in the supreme power and glory of God contained in a human person, Jesus of Nazareth, a poor and suffering man.

Since Franciscan theology is unavoidably autobiographical, please allow me to add an image that is uniquely mine. On June 22, 1983, I was sitting in an Italian train traveling between Turin and Aosta, toward the Alps along the Italian-French border. As the slow local train passed the ancient town of Ivrea, rain began to fall very gently. From my window I noticed alongside the tracks a puddle of dirty water. A few drops of rain made its surface uneven, and it reflected only haphazardly what was above it. But even that uneven reflection showed me part of a dark, powerful storm cloud looming overhead, out of my line of vision; then, in a flash of light, I glimpsed a single, powerful ray of sunlight burning the edge of that cloud with an almost blinding brightness. For a moment glory and menace, brilliance and gloom, the height of sun and clouds were encompassed in that dirty, rainspotted face.

That mud puddle has become for me an icon of Franciscan devotion to the mystery of the Incarnation, the discovery of the mystery of God's unspeakable transcendence in a few cubic feet of human flesh. This discovery has led Franciscan mystics and scholars to develop a theological reflection on Christ's centrality and primacy, a reflection that has grown from an experience of Christ in creation, especially the experience of Francis himself.

SPIRITUALITY OF CHRIST AS CENTER

Wherever one turns in Franciscan spirituality, one finds Christ. He functions as the center of devotion, of ministry, of life together, of authority, of charity. It is a truism to say that such a spirituality is Christocentric. The word, so technical in appearance, in fact breathes and moves beneath every authentically Franciscan text and life.

Christ becomes the answer to the philosophical question, "Why is there something and not nothing?" The answer is, "Because of Christ." From the atom to the universe, and including every level and phase of life and love within that compass, the radiating life and presence of Christ hold all things together, as he vivifies and completes them.

While Christ must always be central to the faith of any Christian, there is a way in which we can speak of a special insistence on that centrality in the Franciscan tradition. We can speak of a "radical

Christocentrism," which willingly sees Christ within human psychology, social life, mathematics and physics, music and drama. Wherever something or someone is, there is Christ. He is the inescapable, though often unrecognized, meaning behind all things.

FRANCIS

The late Franciscan theologian, Fr. Eric Doyle, has written in this way about the importance of Christocentrism:

> If there is one word which does complete justice to Franciscan theology and spirituality it is "Christocentric," and they have this as their distinguishing feature, because the faith and holiness of St. Francis were totally centered on Christ. In Jesus Christ the revelation is made to us of what the world, as a whole and in all its parts, means to God.[1]

The doctrine of Christ as center can already be found in Francis' own writings, and has been developed by outstanding theologians, especially by Alexander of Hales and his student, Bonaventure. Later it takes on even greater importance in the teaching of John Duns Scotus. Francis contributes to the tradition with his own insight about the central role of Christ in the *Rule* of 1221, where he writes: "All things spiritual and corporal were created through the Son." In a long meditation of these few, simple words, Doyle remarks:

> ...his devout love of the humanity of Jesus Christ brought him to understand that everything in heaven and on earth has been reconciled with God through Christ (Letter to a General Chapter). Francis reminds us all to realize the dignity God has bestowed on us: our body he formed and created in the image of his Son, our soul he made in his own likeness (Admonition V) This reflection is one of the most profound and far-reaching in the writings of St. Francis. For it seems clear that he is asserting in it that the first Adam was created after thee Image of the second Adam, Jesus Christ. The body of the Incarnate Word, Jesus of, Nazareth, was the blueprint for the bodies of the first human beings. A little after the time of St. Francis, the learned doctor of the Order, Friar Alexander of Hales, explained that the image of God in whose likeness mankind was created, was the Saviour, who is the firstborn of all creatures.... For all their simplicity and clarity, these sentences

of Francis just quoted, have a rich theological content. Contained in embryo is the Christocentric vision of the Franciscan school and even the doctrine of Christ's absolute primacy as formulated and expounded by John Duns Scotus.[2]

BONAVENTURE

Francis' deep appreciation of the centrality of Christ within the work of creation found its most eloquent theological expression in the works of Bonaventure. Zachary Hayes has explained that in the growth of Bonaventure's theology Christ becomes more and more the central concern. In Hayes' words, "The core of the Christological mystery is the fact that in Jesus the center of all reality has become incarnate and has been made historically visible."[3]

Bonaventure's meditation on the theme of the image uses the notion of the "exemplar." We might say that the exemplar is the person standing in front of the mirror; and the reflection in the mirror is an image of the exemplar. As Bonaventure conceived it, using the beautiful metaphor of the artist at work: God is the exemplar of all things (the artist's interior concept); the humanity of Jesus is the expression of the exemplar (the artwork created by the artist); all creation is formed in Christ (artworks modeled on the original work). Bonaventure himself explains it in this way:

> One [exemplar] is interior, in the mind of the artist, as the cause according to which the artist produces his works. The other is exterior; it is that to which one who is ignorant of art looks and by which he is directed in a certain way, just as mechanical artists have certain forms external to themselves according to which they direct their works, as is clear in the case of shoemakers.[4]

This signified that Christ is the blueprint, the form, or the inspiring image that God uses as a model in molding every part of creation. The human person in a special way reveals that creative model. This theological understanding of Christ as image can be read as an extended meditation on a brief statement from Francis, his Fifth Admonition: "Consider... how excellent the Lord made you, for he created and formed you to the image of his beloved son according to the body and to his own likeness according to the spirit."[5]

That brief text may be read as the inspiration for many later developments in Franciscan theological tradition, containing in germ the essential components of later reflections on anthropology, Christology, and the theology of image.

A Franciscan named John Duns Scotus meditated earnestly on Bonaventure's figure of Christ as the center of all things. Before his untimely death, in 1308, at the age of thirty-four, John had developed his own expression of Christocentrism. Scotus built another level of the friars' intellectual tradition in his theological and philosophical works.

Scotus tried to resolve a difficulty he found in the works of many Christian theologians. To put it simply, the problem concerned this expression, "Christ came because Adam sinned." In Scotus' day, and in ours, many would not find any difficulty with that phrase. Christ came in order to repair the harm done by the sin of our first parents. No doubt, even Scotus would admit, the phrase expresses something quite true. Yet he remained unsatisfied—that phrase could not explain the fullest or best reason for the Incarnation of the Word. Why not? In his own technical language, Scotus argued, "It is not likely that the highest good in the whole of creation is something that merely happened by chance, and happened only because of some lesser good."[6]

In our words, we might explain this in the following way. The Incarnation of the Word is the highest good, the supreme expression of God's love. By comparison with the infinity of love revealed in the Incarnation, Adam's sin and correcting its effects appear as a lesser good. (To use a metaphor, why build the Taj Mahal to cover a pothole?) The solution is not in proportion to the problem to be solved. Furthermore, the theory refuted by Scotus implies that the Incarnation was an accident of sorts, that it happened by chance. If Adam had not sinned, there would be no need for the Incarnation. (An echo of this thinking can be heard in the *Exultet* of the Easter Vigil: *O felix culpa*, "O happy fault! O necessary sin of Adam!")

Scotus proposed his own reasons for the coming of Christ in this way: "I say that the incarnation of Christ was not foreseen as occasioned by sin, but was immediately foreseen from all eternity by God as a good more proximate to the end."[7] This statement, in technical medieval language, may need some translation. The end here refers to God's purpose or goal for the whole of creation. That goal, according to Scotus, is the sharing of God's own life, one so fruitful that it constantly seeks expression. The ultimate goal must be sharing the life of the Trinity itself. Within the Trinity, the Second Person, the Son or Word, is the center, or middle member. The Son may be called the heart of, or the way into the Trinity. As the self diffusive love of the Trinity is expressed in the act of creation, the Son is the Image or Form for everything God creates. Now, if God's ultimate goal for creation is participation in the divine life, the Incarnation of the Son is a "good" very close to the goal, or, in Scotus' words, "more proximate to the end." Why? Because Christ becomes the bridge, or the middle member, linking the creation, particularly humanity, to the inner life of God. Christ becomes the necessary gate or way into God's life, the ultimate goal intended for all creation.

IMITATION AND LOVE

This appreciation of the Incarnation underlies the Franciscan emphasis on repeating the actions of Jesus, the starting-point for devotional practices focused on the physical reconstruction of saving events, accessible to all, regardless of education or wealth, The origin of the Christmas creche, for example, shows Francis' insistence on reproducing in visible, tangible form the mystery of the Incarnation at Bethlehem, otherwise available only to a few privileged pilgrims to the East. Later Franciscan devotions, like that of the Way of the Cross in the eighteenth century, offered to the ordinary believer the opportunity to participate physically in a symbolic walk with Christ through the events of his passion and death, an opportunity otherwise restricted to those able to travel to Jerusalem.

The Franciscan way into the mysteries of the life of Christ does not move primarily through principles or ideals that can be abstracted from experience, but through learning by imitation, a reenacting of the life of Jesus in order to experience, from within, his reactions to children, lepers, the possessed, and the Pharisees.

The desire to be like Jesus has led Franciscans to emphasize the importance of imitation as a means of participation. One notices here an implicit trust in the value of giving a cup of cold water to the thirsty over abstracting a principle about the meaning of cold water in first-century Palestine. We could say that Franciscans have displayed a "sacramental consciousness," an awareness of the value of signs, gestures, actions as pedagogical tools in Christian life.

Following from the notion of imitation comes the supreme appreciation of the *form* of God's love for humanity. That love is a crucified love, or, in personal terms, it is Crucified Love.

Two major forms of approach to God may be summarized under the rubrics of "God as Truth," and "God as Love." These receive differing emphases in different Christian spiritual traditions, and there are undoubtedly other effective rubrics for explaining the way in which we approach God. The Franciscan tradition has consistently given greater emphasis to the rubric of love, of affectivity and the will in treating of our life of journeying toward God. Ultimately, for these masters of the spiritual life, the will and the affections lead a person most surely toward the heart of God, revealed as the burning love of the Crucified.

While respecting knowledge as a vehicle bearing believers toward union, this tradition emphasizes a wisdom wider than knowledge, one which takes the place of the heart seriously. We are, in fact, not only rational animals, but even more deeply, feeling animals. While this should not be construed as an open door to sentimentality in religious growth (it has sometimes degenerated into that), this tradition has at its core a wonderfully full and rich appreciation of the human person as a whole being, one in which the powers of thinking and feeling are not opposed but rather in which feeling complements and fulfills the functions of thinking.

Franciscan saints, mystics, theologians, poets and artists have never tired of the theme of the crucifixion of Love as the beginning and goal of all authentic union with God. There is for them no escape from the wounds of the Savior: there is no escape from the definitive act of self giving in Jesus' laying down his life for his friends.

In theological terms, Bonaventure tells us that in the journey of the soul into God the highest point of mystical union comes in embracing the Crucified. This is the way into the very life of God. There is no transcending or passing over the fact that the Risen Savior is risen from the Cross and bears in his glorified life the marks of human suffering and death. The story of the doubts of Thomas serves to underscore this truth for Franciscan authors.

The Word of God comes to us as a human being, Jesus of Nazareth. The Word also comes to us in the Scriptures of the Old and New Testaments, especially through the "Holy Gospel of our Lord Jesus Christ." The Word comes to us in a concrete, physical way in the form of bread and wine at the Eucharist. It is one and the same Word who comes to us in these different ways, the same one who came to Mary as her son.

This understanding will help us to grasp the interrelationship of three motifs in Franciscan devotion: devotion to the Scriptures, to the Eucharist, to Mary and the Church.

Mary is the dwelling place, the tabernacle of God's Word, which she treasures in her heart and offers to the world as her child. So Francis speaks of her in his "Salutation of the Virgin."[8]

So the Church serves as a bearer of the Word, after the example of the woman who gives the Word to the world. The Church, like Mary, is human, yet transformed by the gift of the Holy Spirit into the Spouse of the Spirit. She, the Church, is also tabernacle, dwelling-place of the Word. Therefore, Francis says with irrefutable logic, that Mary is "the virgin made Church."[9] Francis commands his brothers that they should show great respect for words written on even tiny scraps of paper. The letters written there may contain the name of the Lord. The simple, humble piece of paper becomes iconic, a sign of the Word to Francis. Respect for words, and our use of words, derives from his consuming love for the one who is God's Word to us.

In a similar manner Francis' respect for churches parallels his respect for bits of paper, or parchment. These buildings occupy an important place in Francis' biography as concrete, literally concrete, dwellings for the Word. Thus the friars are to show great respect for churches, since these are places wherein the Word dwells sacramentally in the Eucharist. Hence Francis' prayer, "We adore You, Lord Jesus Christ, in all Your churches throughout the world, and we bless You, for through Your holy cross You have redeemed the world."[10]

The Franciscan Way of Life and Its Purpose

It is all very well to have a theology, to develop a spirituality, and to have an impact on popular devotional life. But a spiritual tradition must do other things in order to survive and flourish within the Church. It must have a form of life, some system of relationships, structures and programs that help to translate the vision into lived experience, and to turn the lived experience constantly toward its founding vision.

The Franciscan "form" may be called the *vita evangelica*, the evangelical life, the Gospel life. That in itself would not seem to distinguish it from the ordinary life of dedication lived by any committed Christian. However, the reader may find, on closer analysis, that the specific meaning and interpretation of that term contains much that is distinctive.

First of all, Franciscans intend to live the whole Gospel. The question, as Bonaventure presents it, probably concerned others besides Francis. Clare lived as a "contemplative" (to use our modern categories); Sylvester, a priest, is known to us chiefly as a hermit, another contemplative. The question is directed to these two trusted advisors, and their answer is that Francis continue the "active" life of preaching.

Yet the terms "active" and "contemplative" are rather misleading when speaking of the early Franciscans. Neither Francis nor Clare use the word "contemplative." They do speak of "contemplation" in various ways, Clare more often than Francis, but it refers generally to "looking at" or "beholding."

Both Francis and Clare speak of the "spirit of prayer" as a guiding principle in the life of their brothers and sisters. And both expect that work will be an essential part of their lives.

The Brothers and Sisters of Penance, those who live in their own homes, have families and occupations in society, are called to a contemplative life of prayer in the circumstances of their lives.

Clare and her sisters give a special witness to the contemplative dimension of the Franciscan vocation. In solitude and communion as sisters, the Poor Sisters express this gift in complete poverty, mutual love, liturgical prayer, attentive listening to the Word of God, and in work.

This life is a form of preaching. Clare asks her sisters to live this evangelical life "in the sight of all," so that by their example people may be brought to Christ, to be "a mirror and example for all living in the world."

Francis writes a *Rule* especially for those brothers who live in hermitages, and in his own life witnesses to the importance of the contemplative foundation of his life of conversion. His biographers picture Francis spending as much as seven months a year living in the silence and solitude of the many early Franciscan hermitages. In these places (Greccio, Fonte Colombo, La Verna, among others) three or four brothers lead a contemplative life, alternating roles of "mothers" and "sons."

This easy exchange of roles which we would call active and contemplative, shows the difficulty of characterizing Francis' "form of life" as being *either* contemplative *or* active. It is quite simply, fully both.

Again, this may not seem surprising. But in fact most traditions within the Church claim to live one facet, or a couple of important dimensions of the Gospel. For example, one group may intend to imitate the hidden life of Jesus, while another models itself on Jesus the preacher during his public ministry A third may seek to model itself on the suffering of the Lord and a fourth on the glory of Christ's resurrection.

Franciscans have claimed from the very beginning that they wished to live every part of the Gospel, the "full Gospel." This desire to include all the many parts of the Gospel within its life has led the Franciscan family, in its many branches, to live with paradox, even seeming contradiction. The following pages will sketch some important features of the Franciscan way of life, showing how it includes many different parts of the "full Gospel."

THE HERMITAGE AND THE WORKPLACE

Because they wished to live all the Gospel, the new form of life Franciscans inaugurated fit neither the category of the contemplative nor the active life as these were being defined. They were classified as being of "mixed life," that is, both contemplative and active. This characteristic can help us to understand how the Franciscan family can include full-time contemplatives and missionaries, heads of families and hermits within its wide embrace. They all form a part of the whole, and the Gospel demands that wholeness.

Clare serves as a reminder that the Franciscan movement at its origins has no need to struggle with the issue of the importance and centrality of the contemplative life, but rather with the question of preaching and its place within a life dedicated to the spirit of "prayer and holy devotion."

In the *Major Life* of Francis by Bonaventure, Francis asks two people to help him discern the shape of his life. The two people are Sylvester, one of the brothers, and Clare. His question was this: Could he best serve God by living in a hermitage or by preaching? Clare and Sylvester prayed about this matter, and both replied that he should continue preaching.

Notes

1. "St. Francis of Assisi and the Christocentric Character of Franciscan Life and Doctrine," in Damian McElrath, ed., *Franciscan Christology* (St. Bonaventure, NY: Franciscan Institute Publications, 1980), p. 2.

2. *Ibid.,* p. 7.

3. "The Life and Christological Thought of St. Bonaventure," in McElrath, p. 63.

4. *Ibid.,* p. 79.

5. Quoted in Allan Wolter, "John Duns Scotus on the Primacy and Personality of Christ," in McElrath, p. 141.

6. *Ibid.,* pp. 150–1.

7. *Franciscan Christology.* p. 153.

8. Regis Armstrong and Ignatius Brady, trans. and intro., *Francis and Clare: The Complete* Works (Ramsey, NJ: Paulist Press, 1982), p. 149.

9. *Ibid.*

10. *Ibid.,* p. 154.

"[God] Whose Beauty the Sun and the Moon Admire":[1] Clare and Ecology

Elizabeth A. Dreyer*

I. Contemporary Concern for the Earth

In every age the human community has to deal with distinctive problems and crises. In the last quarter century, we have become increasingly alarmed at the growing threat to the ecosystem.[2] To find solutions, we employ a variety of resources—economic, educational, scientific, religious, literary, political, historical. Physicists articulate an awe-inspiring vision of the material universe and the interconnectedness of its parts—matter, energy, time. Chinese and Native American Indian cultures remind us of attitudes toward nature that have been allowed to atrophy in western culture. Feminists call for an end to relationships of domination, and a return to an appreciation and celebration of bodiliness and Mother Earth. Psychology views persons in their wholeness and in the context of the wider gestalt of history, geography and nature.

Also in every age, members of faith communities turn to the wellsprings of their particular religious traditions for ideas, behaviors, insights—anything that might provide a direction or be part of a solution to the crises at hand. For Christians, recovery of the tradition in the interest of ecological integrity involves particular ambiguity.

* This article originally appeared as: "'[God] Whose Beauty the Sun and Moon Admire.' Clare and Ecology," *The Way* Supplement 80 (Summer 1994): 76–86. Reprinted with permission.

Authors Thomas Berry[3] and Lynn White[4] lay some of the blame for our exploitative stance toward creation at the door of Christian tradition. Gregory Baum suggests that part of this blame resides in church teaching, legislation and practice that gave expression to the "sharp division between the Church as the fellowship of grace and the world as the place of God's absence."[5] The anti-matter, anti-worldly aspects of so much Christian literature have contributed to our inability to value matter in appropriate ways. And Christian ecofeminists connect the idea of the domination of nature with social domination starting with the basic relation between men and women.[6] Aware of these ambiguities we may find it worthwhile nevertheless to question, and plumb, the tradition with our concerns for the ecosystem in mind. Are there strains that can offer assistance across the centuries?

In particular, are there aspects of the life and spirituality of Clare of Assisi that can instruct us as we struggle to be more aware of, and responsible to, our environment? One must admit that a *direct* connection between Clare and ecology is difficult to establish. In spite of the recent and welcome research on Clare that highlights her gifts as an innovator in religious life for women in the thirteenth century,[7] Francis dominates the terrain when it comes to a theology of creation. His *Canticle of Brother Sun* expresses a positive relationship with the natural world that is virtually unprecedented in the tradition before his time.[8] Unlike the biblical reference in Matthew to the lilies of the field, which emphasizes human value, Francis' references to nature hold up the value of nature itself. Certainly, it is Francis who has inspired lovers of nature down through the centuries, leading to John Paul II's naming Francis the patron of ecology in 1980.

Clare's awareness of nature was quite different from that of Francis. Clare was more interested in speaking about God and human persons than about nature. In fact, she explicitly excludes creation as a vessel able to contain the Creator in the way a human soul can (45). Clare also often juxtaposes God and the world, emphasizing their differences. For her, the world is fleeting and filled with temptation whereas God is eternal and the source of our ultimate security.

But it is possible and legitimate to see in Clare certain qualities and dispositions that can, by extension, help us to reverence the natural world of creation. I would like to build on the feminist insight that domination in social relationships is related to domineering attitudes toward nature, and suggest that learning new pattenls of human relationships can enhance our ability to see ourselves as *part* of nature and to relate to the natural world in fresh and constructive ways. In particular, I examine the ways in which Clare related to those around her, and ask how we might appropriate her deferential ways of relating to others and extend them imaginatively to the cosmos.[9]

II. CLARE'S RELATIONSHIPS

A. The setting. Thirteenth-century Umbria, the setting for the founding of the Franciscans, provided the socio-political setting for a change in understanding of social relationships. The landowners *(maiores)* and the common people *(minores)* were locked in a struggle that led to the formation of a *commune*, in which economic factors gained prominence, over family line and feudal obligations.[10] And in her book, *The First Franciscan Woman*, Margaret Carney calls attention to the ways in which Francis and his companions developed similar patterns in their fraternal life. In contrast to the vertical, hierarchical patterns of medieval, feudal society ("power over"), the brothers emphasized the importance of horizontal relationships (humble "being-with").[11] In the Earlier Rule we read, "No one is to be called prior." And in *The Chronicles*, Jordan of Giano relates how early Franciscan superiors shared in menial household tasks and ruled as "a mother her sons and a hen her chicks."[12]

In significant ways, Clare was able to develop and maintain these new forms of relationship within the cloister more than the brothers, who soon became part of broader, ecclesial, hierarchical structures. As we examine the documents that give us clues to Clare's relationships, we should keep the following issues before us: What sense of self is revealed? How is this self-image reflected in dispositions and actions toward others? What qualities does Clare ascribe to the "other"? What are the fruits of her attitude toward others?[13]

B. Deference. When I first read Clare's letters to Agnes of Prague years ago, I was struck by Clare's deference to her sister. The letters reflect respectful awe, humility and the delight that accompanies friendship. It is true that Agnes is from a noble family, the daughter of a king, and therefore worthy more than others to be addressed with deference. It is also true that many expressions in the letters reflect epistolary literary conventions of the day. In addition, Clare lived in a culture alive with the language and imagery of courtly love. But for all this, one can suppose that there was a substantive reality behind the conventional language. Language does not exist in a vacuum. While the twentieth century seems far removed from the social canons of medieval knights and their ladies, some elements of the courtly tradition might serve us well in our relationships with others and with nature.

Clare addresses Agnes:

> Saint Agnes
> To the esteemed and most holy virgin, Lady Agnes
> Most beloved sister
> Lady, worthy of great respect
> Most noble Queen
> To the daughter of the King of kings, the servant of the Lord of lords, the most worthy Spouse of Jesus Christ, and
> therefore, the most noble Queen, Lady Agnes
> To the lady [who is] most respected in Christ and the sister loved more than all [other] human beings
> To her who is half of her soul and the special shrine of her heart's deepest love, to the illustrious Queen and Bride of the Lamb, the eternal King

If we imagine the effects of such salutations in modern terms, we might discover a sense of being loved; an invitation to self-esteem because of being called to a noble vocation; a call to courage for renewed dedication; perhaps the desire to treat others in like manner. Such language lifts one's spirits, reminds one of the *imago Dei* within. Clare's attitude is the opposite of domination, manipulation, utilitarianism, one-upmanship, objectification.

C. Model of humility. Clare's respectful address to Agnes is thrown into bold relief when juxtaposed with Clare's statement of her own self-image. These phrases include: "Clare, an unworthy servant of Jesus Christ and a *useless* servant of the enclosed Ladies of the Monastery of San Damiano, [Agnes'] subject and servant in all things, presents herself totally with a special reverence that she *attain the glory* of everlasting happiness." And again, "Clare *the useless* and unworthy servant of the Poor Ladies"; "Clare, the most lowly and unworthy handmaid of Christ and servant of the Poor Ladies." In the third letter, Clare says, "And I sigh with so much more exultation in the Lord as I have known and believe that you supply most wonderfully what is lacking both in me and in the other sisters in following the footprints of the poor and humble Jesus Christ." In the face of the lofty contemplation in which Agnes participates, Clare sees herself as "your poor little mother."

These words, properly understood, reveal a humble attitude toward self that flows out of an experience of strength and positive self-regard.[14] True humility develops in those who know and accept that they are made in God's image and that they are loved by God and by others. This knowledge and acceptance free one to respect and raise up the "other"—whether the other be a person, or a tree or a paper wasp—as also made and loved by God. To the extent that we are able to be at home with, and rest easy in love, we are able in all simplicity to face other persons, the animal and plant kingdoms and even rocks and twigs with a humble, awe-filled respect. With such a mind-set, it becomes unthinkable to treat others or nature with a flippant disregard or with an attitude of arrogance, indifference, utilitarianism or disdain. One's sense of deep connection with God can open us to experience the connections with all of reality—and vice versa.

In her Rule and letters, Clare's favorite virtues appear again and again—poverty, charity and humility (48, 49, 58, 59, 70). Humility is also one of the virtues used by others to describe Clare (123, 140, 151).

At San Damiano Clare lived as humble servant to others. In The Acts of the Process of Canonization, the witnesses repeatedly testified to Clare's humility and to her concern for the sick whose mattresses she washed. Perhaps the symbolic gesture most revelatory of her humble self-regard was foot washing. One time when Clare was washing the feet of one of the serving sisters, she turned to kiss her feet and when the sister pulled away, Clare was hit in the mouth with the sister's foot! Clare's response was to kiss the foot (140). While washing the feet of others is not a contemporary custom, it can serve as a symbol of humble reverence toward other people and things. One can speculate about possible modern ecological equivalents—growing one's own vegetables, contributing to clean-up efforts, caring for trees and shrubs, cleaning up beaches?

D. Affectionate friendship. Throughout her letters to Agnes, Clare names and celebrates Agnes' gifts and virtues, and is filled with joy because Agnes has become a diligent imitator of God. She wants Agnes to feel what God's friends feel as "they taste the hidden sweetness that

God has reserved for those who love." But Agnes also seems to elicit from Clare a personal affection. Clare laments that she has not written more often, saying, "Do not wonder or think that the fire of love for you glows with less delight in the heart of your mother." Clare ends her final letter to Agnes with a powerful expression of their intimate friendship and the resultant joy that Clare feels.

> ...I have inscribed the happy memory of you on the tablets of my heart, holding you dearer than all others. What more can I say? Let the tongue of the flesh be silent when I seek to express my love for you; and let the tongue of the Spirit speak, because the love that I have for you, O blessed daughter, can never be fully expressed by the tongue of the flesh, and even what I have written is an inadequate expression. (50)

At the least, Clare wants Agnes to receive her words as those of an "affectionate mother," but the letters reveal an even deeper and more egalitarian regard and affection.

As we have seen above, Clare explicitly excludes creation from this specific kind of intimate connection with God. Only the soul of the faithful person—not the heavens nor the rest of creation—can be adequate containers of God. On the other hand, at Clare's canonization proceedings, Sister Angeluccia testified that Clare told them that they should "praise God when they saw beautiful trees, flowers and bushes; and likewise, always to praise Him for and in all things when they saw all people and creatures" (160). Her focus on the eternal and the human did not prevent her from noticing and appreciating the beauties of God's creation.

In her Testament, Clare writes of personal remembrances, offering us a window onto the values she entrusts to the sisters to maintain after her death. It is filled with praise and thanksgiving for God's gifts and mercies. It contains a succinct and powerful statement about how the sisters were to care for each other in love.

> And loving one another with the charity of Christ, may the love you have in your hearts be shown outwardly in your deeds so that, compelled by such an example, the sisters may always grow in love of God and in charity for one another (58).

E. Equality among the Poor Ladies. As Francis transcended the times in which he lived in his attitude toward animals and the natural world, Clare transcended the mores of religious life in the way she set up her own community. In her Form of Life Clare described her vision of religious community. This "way" emphasizes horizontal rather than vertical relationships; concern for gentle, mutual care; power-sharing; compassion for sinners; special treatment for the ill; the Ladies' ability to live the rigors of religious life on a par with men.

Clare wanted a community that was as non-hierarchical in form as possible. Her models included sisterhood, maidservant/mistress and daughter/mother—"relationships characterized by emotional closeness, mutual responsibility, and common needs."[15] The "democratic" nature of Clare's community signaled a significant departure from the norm of organization in religious communities of women in the thirteenth century. In Clare's community, most important decisions were taken by all the sisters or by a special group of consultors. All the Ladies, including the leaders, confessed their faults and sought forgiveness. The sisters had the power to elect and to remove superiors. And while Clare accepted the title "Abbess" reluctantly and probably for political reasons, she never refers to herself in this way, but only to those who will succeed her (Rule 62, 66, 67, 73).

Life among the Poor Ladies was also filled with caring, deferential love. In The *Legend of Saint Clare* we read of Clare's love not only for the souls, but also for the bodies of her sisters. Clare nursed, kept warm and encouraged her sisters with the utmost kindness and compassion (224). Reverential love was the guiding spirit of Clare's Order. Like Francis, Clare had reached a deep understanding of human dignity, and from this understanding was born her love and respect for the personality of each member of her community.

Clare advocated this kind of respectful and careful mutual concern between the sisters and brothers as well. In the midst of ecclesial monitoring and ambiguity toward the women on the part of the males in the Franciscan movement, Clare was adamant in adhering to the Ladies' connection with Francis and the brothers. Till her death she clung to the words of the Form of Life received from Francis:

> Because by divine inspiration you have made yourselves daughters and servants to the Most High King... I resolve and promise for myself and for my brothers to always have that same loving care and solicitude for you as [I have] for them.

III. RELATIONSHIPS IN AN ECOLOGICAL AGE

What do these reflections on Clare's understanding of relationships contribute to a spirituality that has care for God's creation as an integral element? Unlike Christians in the thirteenth century, we have a new consciousness of the earth, its inhabitants and the ways in which it is threatened. In addition, we no longer embrace a Neoplatonic skepticism that disdains the goodness of matter and of the created universe. And yet we have much to learn from Clare's simple, deferential ways. She continues to teach us from her time and place in ways that can be beneficial to the quite different concerns of our time and place.

A. Deference. Clare invites us to nurture deferential ways towards others and by extension toward all of creation. As an exercise, one might reflect on experiences of deference. What persons do you know who stand out as being especially careful and respectful of others? When do you find *yourself* most deferential to others? And what has it felt like to be on the receiving end of someone's deference and care? Is it possible to begin to practice this kind of deference toward the universe?

One way to approach the meaning of deference is to think about the human gesture of "bowing." In her Testament, Clare herself makes this statement, "...on bended knee and bowing low with both [body and soul], I commend all my sisters..." (57). In its authentic forms, bowing symbolizes recognition of the beauty and dignity of human persons. Performers bow to their audiences, acknowledging their presence and their appreciation of the performers' service. Persons of oriental cultures bow routinely at introductions and leave-takings. And persons of many religious cultures bow at liturgical events. Clare's life might be described as a life of continual, reverential bowing to her God and to everyone in her world. In our time, we need to nurture our "bowing skills" towards others and extend them to the entire creation.

We can also develop deferential relationships with the scientific community. As Christians, we need to abandon our fear of scientific truth in order to find common ground with the scientific community. Physicist Werner Heisenberg reminds us:

> Science, we find, is now focused on the network of relationships between humans and nature, on the framework which makes us as living beings dependent parts of nature, and which we as human beings have simultaneously made the object of our thoughts and actions. Science no longer confronts nature as an objective observ-

er, but sees itself as an actor in this interplay between human persons and nature.[16]

Our base of critical discernment as Christians has to be *within* the community of humankind, not over against it. We need to guard against both pseudo-scientism, i.e. harmful technology fueled by greed, *and* an arrogant theology that tries to force the universe into narrow biblical categories or to reduce it to theological constructs.[17]

B. Humility. The humble, reverent way in which Clare interacted with others is a resource to the modern world as we struggle to overcome an exaggerated subject—object relationship with nature.[18] Clare invites us to a new kind of humility, to see ourselves as one among many species. As humans, our job is to provide a loving consciousness for the universe. As trees provide oxygen and the sun warmth, humans provide a loving consciousness of the universe's embodiment. It is not better than the functions of other species (without oxygen, there would be no one to know and love), but it is a sacred trust to which we must be humbly faithful.

The story of the universe provides the larger setting for the Christian story and also invites us to humility. Can we acknowledge the common myth of evolution as the all-inclusive story and allow it to lead us toward global communication and co-operation?[19] This story provides a needed perspective in which the arrival of *homo sapiens* is seen as the fruit of billions of years of intense activity on the part of the matter that preceded us. Before the earth, before human life, before Christianity, the universe was evolving and preparing for our arrival. To embrace such a cosmic perspective is humbling indeed.

C. Affectivity. Both Francis and Clare invite us to regard ourselves, each other and the natural world with a more intense and loving regard and to connect such regard with one's participation in the very life of God. Clare's passionate love affair with God can provide a way for us, as we entertain new ideas about the universe as God's body.

In her ground-breaking work, *Models of God*, Sallie McFague tries to think about the God-world relationship in an as-if fashion. She explores the metaphor of the world as God's body and wonders,

> What if, then, we did not have to go somewhere special (church) or somewhere else (another world) to be in the presence of God but could feel ourselves in that presence at all times and in all places?[20]

McFague reflects themes we meet in Clare: her experience of God as an intimate, generous lover; her affectionate attention to the bodies of her sisters,[21] her love of the body and blood or Christ in the Eucharist.

The metaphor of the world as God's body adds new ideas to our understanding of God's relationship to the world. It suggests that God knows and loves the world in an intrinsic, immediate way, as we know our own bodies. It points to God's acceptance of the vulnerability and risk of the cross in an inclusive, suffering love. "To trust in a God whose body is the world is to trust in a God who cares profoundly for the world."[22]

The metaphor of the world as God's "body" leads us to extend Clare's deep sense of loving interdependence with others and with God to the entire universe. It encourages us to relate to the vulnerable and oppressed in a non-hierarchical way with tenderness and care. Sin, then, becomes the refusal to acknowledge this interdependence, the refusal to take "responsibility for nurturing, loving, and befriending the body and all its parts."[23] It is the refusal to learn that we are always in God's loving presence and to nurture feelings of tender affection for all species and all elements.

D. Equality. Finally, we are called to a more democratized understanding of reality. As Clare respected and included all the sisters in the structures of their life together, we too must respect and include each person, and indeed all creation, in the decisions that affect our planet. Whom will we appoint to be the voice and advocate of the rain forests, the water and the air? We are not destined to be masters and mistresses of the universe, to rule over creation in utilitarian ways. Nature enjoys its own relationship to God so that its wanton destruction is an affront to God's very Self.[24]

We need to explore the moral implications or the ill-treatment of nature. Correction of destructive behavior toward the world cannot be considered merely in terms of prudence with regard to our own survival. Deliberate and unnecessary destruction of any aspect of the ecosystem infects one's very character and identity, distorting and warping it. One's attitude toward the non-human world directly affects our development and excellence as persons.

The cultivation of these dispositions can help us overcome dispositions of imperialism and support our struggle to save the cosmos from destruction. All of creation, as the cherished activity of God, deserves to be valued for itself as well as for its use to the human community. We who care genuinely for creation experience empathy with it rather than the need to control it. We eschew attitudes of domination in favor of those of interdependence. We avoid objectification in favor of identification. With a vision of cosmic harmony to lure us, we put ourselves at the service of the cosmos in a spirit of sacrificial love.

To live in hope as we face possible ecological disaster is a difficult and revolutionary activity. But the mandate of the gospel demands that we use the graces of the tradition—Clare of Assisi is one example—and the graces of our own commitment and creative imagination in the service of the universe.

Notes

1. Third Letter of Clare to Agnes of Prague in Regis J. Armstrong (ed.), *Clare of Assisi: Ear{y Documents* (New Jersey: Paulist Press, 1988), p 45. References in the text to early documents on Clare are from this volume.

2. In the United States, a well-known "marker" of this awareness was the publication in 1962 of Rachel Carson's *Silent Spring* (Boston, Houghton Mifflin).

3. Thomas Berry, "Classical Western spirituality and the American experience" (White Paper).

4. Lynn White, "The historical roots of our ecological crisis" in Ian G. Barbour (ed), *Western man and environmental ethics* (Reading MA: Addison-Wesley, 1973). For a critical response to this essay, see John B. Bennett, "On responding to Lynn White: ecology and Christianity" in *Ohio Journal of Religious Studies* 5 (April 1977), pp 71–77.

5. Gregory Baum, *Man becoming: God in secular language* (New York: Herder & Herder, 1970), p 25.

6. See Anne M. Clifford, "Feminist perspectives on science: implications for an ecological theology of creation," *Journal of Feminist Studies in Religion* 8/2 (Fall 1992), pp 65–90; and Rosemary Radford Ruether, *New woman - new earth: sexist ideologies and human liberation* (New York: Seabury Press, 1975), p 204.

7. In 1993 the Franciscan Press (Quincy IL) published the following studies: Ingrid Peterson, *Clare of Assisi: a biographical study;* Margaret Carney, *The first Franciscan woman;* Marco Bartoli, *Clare of Assisi* (American edition).

8. We read in the *Legend of Perugia:* "It is not surprising that fire and other

creatures at times showed their respect for him, since, as we who were with him have seen, he loved and respected them with such charity and affection, took so much joy in them, and was moved to such concern and pity over them, that if anyone did not treat them properly he was upset."

The absence in Francis of the ambivalence toward creation that characterizes the Christian tradition may be explained in part by his lack of formal education. Had he had one, he would probably have been schooled in Neoplatonic categories that looked askance at material creation as a path to God. See Roger D. Sorrell, *St. Francis of Assisi and nature, tradition and innovation in Western Christian attitudes towards the environment* (Oxford: Oxford University Press, 1988).

9. A number of theologians address themselves specifically to creation theologies. Examples include Claus Westermann, *Creation* (1974); Jürgen Moltmann, *The future of creation* (1977) and his 1984–85 Gifford Lectures, *God in creation;* Gibson Winter, *Liberating creation: foundations of religious social ethics* (1981); John Cobb, *Is it too late?* and *God and the world;"* Matthew Fox, *Original blessing* (1981) and *The coming of the cosmic Christ* (1988); William Butterworth, *Theology of creation;* Zachary Hayes, *What are they saying about creation?*; Dorothy Soelle, *To work and to love: a theology of creation* (1984); Sallie McFague, et. al. (eds.), *Liberating life: contemporary approaches to ecological theology* (1990); Thomas Berry, *Befriending the earth* (1991).

10 . See Marco Bartoli, *Clare of Assisi*, p 12.

11. Margaret Carney, *The first Franciscan woman*, pp 150–154.

12. Placid Hermann (trans), *XIIIth century chronicles; Jordan of Giano, Thomas of Eccleston, Salimbene degli Adami* (Chicago: Franciscan Herald Press, 1961), Section 55.

13. Although we will not examine descriptions of Clare's relationship to Jesus, it is obvious that a consuming relationship with the incarnate God is what fuels her life. Clare summarizes this attitude in her second letter to Agnes of Prague. Clare says of Jesus:

> O most noble Queen, gaze upon [Him] consider [Him]
> contemplate [Him]
> as you desire to imitate [Him].

The other important relationship to be considered is obviously that between Francis and Clare. One senses that their relationship was characterized by a spirit of love, mutual solidarity, comfort, respect and admiration.

14. We suffer from a perennial misunderstanding about the virtue of humility—one that emphasizes false self-abnegation, denial of gifts, refusal to become a self. This virtue has been especially problematic for women, whom the Church encourages to be humble and to sacrifice a self that too often has not had a chance to develop.

15. Elizabeth Petroff, "A medieval woman's Utopian vision: the Rule of Saint Clare of Assisi" in Libby Falk Jones and Sarah Webster Goodwin (eds.), *Feminism, Utopia, and narrative* (Knoxville: University of Tennessee Press, 1991).

16. W. Heisenberg, *The physicist's conception of nature* (London: Hutchinson, 1958), p 29.

17. Brian Swimme laments: "Scientists dropped out of religion because theologians and preachers had nothing interesting to say about the universe. Then, too, they stopped sitting in the pews because the preachers kept explaining to them that their passions and interests, their meaning, their central devotions in life are unimportant—or irrelevant and footnotes to the real truth." See "Science: a partner in creation" in Anne Lonergan and Caroline Richards (eds.), *Thomas Berry and the new cosmology* (Mystic CT: Twenty-third Publications, 1988), p 85.

18. Jürgen Moltmann proposes a model of co-operation and communication to replace the dysfunctional subject-object model. In this new model, nature is no longer the subjugated object of humans, but a cohesion of open-life systems with its own subjectivity. Two subjects with different subjectivities enter into a mutual relationship with one another. See *The future of creation* (Philadelphia: Fortress Press, 1979), pp 128–129.

19. "The scientific enterprise has produced a creation myth that offers humanity a deeper realization of our bondedness, our profound communion not only within our species, but throughout the living and non-living universe" (Brian Swimme, "Science: a partner in creation" p 86).

20. Sallie McFague, *Models of God: theology for an ecological, nuclear age* (Philadelphia: Fortress Press, 1987), p 70.

21. One must also note the very harsh ascetical practices in which Clare and many medieval women engaged at great cost to their bodies.

22. McFague, *ibid.*, p 74.

23. *Ibid.*, p.77

24. See John Bennett, "On the theological use of Whitehead's thought," *Journal of Religious Studies* 8 (Spring 1980), p 7.

St. Francis and Ecology

Thomas Murtagh, OFM*

Several years ago, on 29 November, 1979, John Paul signed a document proclaiming Francis of Assisi the patron saint of ecologists. Now, whatever Francis was, he was not an ecologist. Ecology is the study of the relation of plants and animals to their environment. Francis was not a student, let alone a student of science, even of the kind of science that was available for study in the thirteenth century. But it was by no means unreasonable for Pope John Paul to make him the patron saint of ecologists, for in that document he referred to Francis' "marvelous gift of fostering nature," and also to his Canticle of Creatures.

"Fostering nature"—a very apt description of what Francis did, but not all that helpful in distinguishing Francis from all the others who in one way or another have fostered or are fostering nature. Try to distinguish, just for yourself, the difference between ecologist, nature lover, environmentalist, animal lover, pantheist, animal liberationist —do you appreciate the difficulty? So, for the moment, let us leave this important question and concentrate on what it was about Francis that moved Pope John Paul to refer to his "marvelous gift of fostering nature." And let us look, not so much at the phrase itself, but at what we know from the sources about Francis' accomplishments in this area.

* This article originally appeared as: "St. Francis and Ecology," *The Cord* 39/4 (April 1989): 99-109. Reprinted with permission.

THE SOURCE OF FRANCIS' GIFT

How did Francis get this gift? The sources really tell us very little. Was he born with it? Although some authors hint at this as an explanation, there is nothing in the sources to support such an explanation. And if he was not born with this gift, he must have developed it during his life. And again there is very little that might indicate how this gift might have developed, although there are many and varied references to its presence.

Before his conversion Francis thoroughly enjoyed life; it was he who was the life of the party. But after his conversion he rejected life's pleasures, its good aspects, in his efforts to lead a penitential life. We are familiar with Francis' encounter with the leper, that incident that in later years he saw as the central moment of his conversion. In introducing this incident Celano writes:

> "Francis," God said to him in spirit, "what you have loved carnally and vainly you should now exchange for spiritual things, and taking the bitter for sweet, despise yourself, if you wish to acknowledge me." (2 Cel 9).

In his Testament Francis (related how when he embraced the leper, "That which seemed bitter to me was changed into sweetness of soul and body." But he did not say that he found the same sweetness in some of his other penitential practices like sprinkling ashes on his food, or fasting for most of the year, or spending sleepless nights in prayer. Some have even seen in Francis' complete rejection of the things of this world a trace of the Catharist or Albigensian heresy, which was widespread at the time, and which rejected everything connected with the body as evil. We do not need to posit a Catharist influence to explain Francis' conduct. In the traditional spirituality of his time there was acknowledgement of a twofold path to God, the negative way and the positive way—with emphases respectively on negation of the earthly and on the positive practice of virtue. There is no doubt that Francis took the negative rather than the positive way, that he started by rejecting earthly pleasures. So there must be at least a good argument that his appreciation of the worth of created things came only when he came close to God, and saw in creation a reflection of God's own goodness. St. Bonaventure, in his *Itinerarium, The Soul's Journey to God*, wrote of how the soul may move closer to God in various stages, starting with the traces, the footprints of God that can be found in created things, and only at the last stage requiring an acceptance of the crucifixion; but at no stage does he indicate that this is the path that Francis followed.

To me a logical (even if not developmental) source was his love of Our Lord, the love that grew stronger throughout his life of abnegation. We are all familiar with how Francis focused himself on Christ and made him the centre of his life, and strove in every way possible to be like him. If Francis thought he could find direction for his own life through anything Christ did or said, he made use of it.

Can you think of any words that have for you personally a special meaning because of how they are associated with your past experience, or with a particular person, or with your ambitions or your deepest thoughts? Such personal connotations can greatly enrich our reflections and our prayer, and can have a deep influence on what we do. Francis was well aware of how Scripture is applied to Our Lord in the liturgy, and through his reflection found a wealth of personal meaning in the scriptural phrases. Listen to this passage from the *Mirror of Perfection* (SP 118):

> Next to fire he had an especial love for water, because it symbolizes holy penitence and tribulation, and at Baptism the soul is cleansed from its stains and receives its first purification. So whenever he washed his hands he chose a place where the water would not be trodden underfoot as it fell to the ground. For the same reason, whenever he had to walk over rocks, he trod reverently and fearfully, out of love for Christ Who is called The Rock: so whenever he recited the psalm Thou wilt set me high up on a rock, he used to say with great reverence and devotion, Thou hast set me up at the foot of the rock.
>
> He told the friar who cut and chopped wood for the fire that he must never cut down the whole tree, but remove branches in such a way that part of the tree remained intact, out of love for Christ, Who willed to accomplish our salvation on the wood of the cross.
>
> In the same way he told the friar who cared for the gardens not to cultivate *all* the ground for vegetables, but to set aside a plot to grow flowers to bloom in their season, out of love for Him Who is called The Rose on the plain and the lily on the mountain slopes. Indeed, he told the brother-gardener that he should always make a pleasant flower-garden, and cultivate every variety of fragrant herb

and flowering plant, so that all who saw the herbs and flowers would be moved to praise God.

What a marvelous passage! How an environmentalist of today would love Francis' wishes, even though he might see no sense in, might thoroughly disagree with his reasons. Look at the individual things Francis referred to: Water—and clearly a reverence for water, not for some intrinsic property, not because of its usefulness to us and the need to keep it as unpolluted as possible, but because of its connection with the sacrament of Baptism. Then Rocks, or if you like, the Landscape—and again not for some intrinsic beauty it has, or for its usefulness—whatever the arguments between miners and environmentalists, or because it has a religious significance in itself (although here we are closest to Francis' reasoning), but because Christ is referred to as "the Rock." And then Trees—to use them as firewood but not to kill the tree in the process.

When I joined the Order there was one particular paragraph in our Constitutions which I presume was based on this wish of Francis:

> Trees, whether for fruit, ornament or the convenience of the Friars, may not be cut down without the consent of the Discreets and the permission of the Provincial, unless there be question of a dead tree soon to be replaced by a new planting, (1921 Const. #324)

Anti-woodchipping groups would again rejoice, although Francis is not arguing out of a desire to preserve a particular habitat and so keep safe the ecological network that had developed, but because Christ was nailed to wood from a tree. And the Garden! To leave a place for flowers, not the specially developed flowers that we can buy down at the nursery, but wild-flowers that would bloom in their own time. Some years ago I was in Italy, and I was amazed at the way the Italians used every bit of space for their gardens: There were plots alongside the railway lines and alongside the roads; what was growing in these plots differed, although there were usually several things in each plot. In one area grape vines would predominate, in another tomatoes, and there would be beans, and other plants I could not identify, but there was one thing they had very definitely in common: every square metre of ground was cultivated (I could tell, just from this, when we passed over the border into France!) And Francis was telling the friar gardener not to clear all the ground, but to leave a part where the wild-flowers could bloom! And the reason for this was the phrases about "Rose" and "Lily" taken from scripture and applied to Christ.

And finally in that passage we are given another reason why Francis wanted this: to encourage everyone to praise God.

As a postscript to this section, listen to Celano rhapsodizing about this aspect of Francis' character:

> A simple piety and pious simplicity! Toward little worms even he glowed with a very great love, for he had read this saying about the Saviour: I am a worm, not a man. Therefore he picked them up from the road and placed them in a safe place, lest they be crushed by the feet of the passerby. (I Cel 80)

THE BOND BETWEEN FRANCIS AND CREATURES

There can be no doubt about the scriptural and liturgical inspiration for these actions of Francis. But there was more than this to how Francis regarded and treated creatures. Francis found joy in creatures because he saw the goodness of God in them. And there was a definite bond between Francis and creatures that was mutual, two-sided. There are many accounts in the early biographies, but this passage from St. Bonaventure recounts several with relative brevity:

> Another time St. Francis was offered a live hare at Greccio. He put it on the ground and left it free to go where it pleased, but the moment he called it, it jumped into his arms. He held it affectionately and seemed to pity it like a mother. Then, warning it gently not to let itself be caught again, he allowed it to go free. But every time he put it on the ground to let it off, the hare immediately jumped into his arms, as if in some mysterious way it realized the love he had for it. Eventually Francis had the friars bring it off to a safer place in the woods.
>
> In the same way a rabbit which was caught on an island in Lake Trasimene was afraid of everyone else, but entrusted itself to Francis' embrace as if that were its home. When he was crossing Lake Piediluco on his way to Greccio, a fisherman offered him a water-bird. Francis took it gladly and then opened his arms to let it off but it would not go. The saint stood there praying with his eyes raised to heaven, and after a long time he came back to himself and once more encouraged the bird to fly away and praise God. When he had given it his blessing, the bird showed its joy by the

movements of its body and then it flew off. On the same lake he was offered a live fish which he addressed as brother, as usual, and put it back in the water beside the boat. The fish played about there in front of him, as if it were attracted by his affection, and would not go away until he gave it his permission with a blessing. (LM VIII, 8)

If there were just one of these stories, we could say, "Isn't it a charming story," and never for a moment believe it actually happened. But there are several, all speaking of a special way in which animals acted towards and responded to Francis. In the above passage Bonaventure has linked a series of stories about how animals wanted to stay in Francis' company; but there are also many other stories which illustrate how animals paid heed to what Francis told them. Edward Armstrong, in his book, *Saint Francis: Nature Mystic*, dismisses these stories as inventions, making remarks like:

> The element of truth in the story is that Francis was the sort of person to whom people would naturally bring a distressed animal. (p. 192)

Probably true, but not necessarily, because thirteenth-century Italians were not the animal lovers that many twentieth-century Anglo-Saxons are. And, even if true, not enough. For me Armstrong is carrying skepticism too far. We have heard of people who have a special bond with animals, who can inspire trust in animals who are normally afraid of humans. Francis was obviously such a person.

This bond that Francis had with animals was not universal. There were some creatures with whom Francis had no special affinity. About a year before his death, Francis was living in a small cell in a friary near the Poor Clares at San Damiano.

> His eyes caused him so much pain that he could neither lie down nor sleep, so to speak, which was very bad for his eyes and for his health. A few times he was on the point of resting and sleeping, but in the house and in the cell made of mats, that had been made ready for him, there were so many mice running around here and there, around him and even on him, that they prevented him from taking a rest; they even hindered him greatly in his prayer. They annoyed him not only at night but also during the day. When he ate they climbed up on his table, so much so that he and his companions were of the opinion that it was diabolical intervention. (LP 43)

A very clear description of what happens during a plague of mice! And Francis seemed powerless against this invasion.

And there were some insects that Francis had little time for. In *The Golden Sayings of Brother Giles* we find:

> He also used to say that ants were not very pleasing to the Blessed Francis, because of their exceeding solicitude in collecting their food. (Ch. VIII)
>
> And when Francis wanted to rebuke "a certain brother in a certain place who never went out for alms but always ate more than several together at table," he addressed him,
>
> Go your way, brother fly, for you want to eat the sweat of our brothers and to do nothing in God's work. You are like brother drone who wants to be first to eat the honey, though he does not do the work of the bees. (2 Cel 75)

Not the words of one who understands the workings of the environment, the necessity of drones for the future of bees, the environmental niche that flies occupy! Yet a very moral Francis, who expects insects also to observe moral behaviour.

It is worth noting that Francis was not a vegetarian; he did not eat much meat, because he fasted so often and going without meat was part of the regimen of fasting at that time, but on occasion he did eat meat. There was one occasion recorded by Jordan of Giano when Francis was in the East, and the times for fasting were extended by the vicars he left behind to look after the Order. When Francis learned of this, he was sitting at table "where meat had been placed before him for him to eat." He consulted Peter of Catanii, "My lord Peter, what shall we do?" Peter evaded the issue, "Ah, my lord Francis, whatever pleases you, for you have the authority." Finally Francis decided, "Let us then eat, according to the Gospel, what has been placed before us." (Giano 12) And there are his wishes regarding the celebration of Christmas one particular year:

> When the question arose about eating meat that day, since that Christmas day was a Friday, he replied, saying to Brother Morico: "You sin, Brother, calling the day on which the Child was born to us a day of fast. It is my wish," he said, "that even the walls should eat meat on such a day, and if they cannot, they should be smeared with meat on the outside." (2 Cel 199)

The Canticle of Creatures

There was another aspect of how Francis viewed creation. The liturgy is full of psalms and canticles of praise for God, including many that call on creation to praise God. The one that comes to mind most readily is the Canticle from the Book of Daniel, the *Canticle of the Three Young Men,*

> Bless the Lord, all works of the Lord, sing praise to him and highly exalt him for ever, (Can. 3:35)

going through the whole list of creation, calling on all creation to praise the Lord. Francis was familiar with this, and often prayed in this way. In his *Letter to All the Faithful* we find, "let every creature in heaven, on earth, in the sea and in the depths, give praise, honour, and blessing to Him." Yes, Francis saw all creatures praising God in a fitting way, all the creatures, that is, except man; as he remarked in one of the Admonitions: "And yet all the creatures under heaven, each according to its nature, serve, know, and obey their Creator better than you." (Adm. 5) And that is probably part of the reason why Francis wanted a part of his garden filled with flowers "so that all who saw the herbs and flowers would be moved to praise God." (SP 118)

But now we come to difficulty. When John Paul II proclaimed Francis the patron saint of ecologists, he referred to his Canticle of Creatures. We would certainly expect that Francis' Canticle would reflect all that we have spoken of so far, would hopefully go further because it was written only about a year and a half before his death, when he was aware that he did not have so long to live, and so might have brought some clearer insight to his view of creation. But there is no mention of sister lark, or brother lamb, or sister flower or brother tree. The Canticle is built around the four classical elements, earth, water, air and fire, with an introduction about the sun, moon and stars, and two bits tacked on at the end (we know the occasions when they were added) about peace and death.

We should not be surprised about the inclusion of Sister Water, we have seen the special reverence in which Francis held her. Nor should we be surprised about the inclusion of Brother Fire. There are several anecdotes about the special regard Francis had for Brother Fire; one will suffice.

One day when he was seated near the hearth, his linen drawers caught fire the whole length of his leg without his being aware of it. He felt the heat, but when one of his companions saw that his clothes were burning and hurried to extinguish them, he said to him: "No, my dearest brother, don't harm our Brother Fire." He did not let him put it out.

This is typical of the attitude Francis took to Brother Fire; the story goes on:

> The brother ran to find blessed Francis' brother guardian and led him to the place. They extinguished the fire but against Francis' will. He did not even want them to extinguish a candle, a lamp, or fire, as one does when it is no longer needed, so great was his tenderness and pity for that creature. (LP 49)

So the presence of Brother Fire is explained and Francis also had devotion to Brother Sun, because God "through him gives light to our eyes by day," (SF 119) and in Scripture the Lord is called The Sun of Justice.

But that does not explain the inclusion of Sister Moon and the stars, of Brother Wind and Mother Earth, nor does it explain the exclusion of all the animals, especially his favourites, brother lamb and sister lark.

There is another aspect of our difficulty. Writers on things Franciscan nearly always refer (to the extent that it is virtually a truism) to how closely St. Clare followed St. Francis, that Clare was the most perfect follower of Francis, that Clare was the best exponent of Francis' teaching. Yet on this particular area of the position of creatures, and on the special relationship that Francis had with them, Clare is virtually silent. Apart from a few simple references of the type that could be expected from anyone, there is only one statement of her outlook, and that is found in the proceedings of the Cause for her Canonization. One of the witnesses was Sister Angeluccia.

> The witness also said that whenever the blessed Mother sent the lay sisters outside the monastery, she admonished them that they should praise God for every beautiful green and flowering plant they saw; and that for every human being they saw; and for every creature, always and in all things God must be praised. (Witness 14: De Robeck, p. 223)

So we must look elsewhere to find an answer to our question.

When Francis wrote the main part of the Canticle (The other parts

came later), he had borne the marks of the stigmata for about six
months, and he had found from God an answer to his fears about the
future of the Order (that the Order was God's and not Francis'). Yet he
was severely afflicted with a disease that made him nearly blind and
ultrasensitive to any light, and other sickness made it clear that he did
not have long to live. It is from this position of pain and peace that the
Canticle makes sense; pain, because it can purify, clear away the dross
and the unessential, and make clear the basics; peace, because without
peace of heart how could anyone who was suffering at all compose such
limpid, lyrical lines. I do not claim to find in the Canticle what Francis
saw in it, only a realization that when I am in a comparable situation of
pain and peace I will have an understanding. Eloi Leclerc, at the end of
his book, *The Canticle of Creatures*, refers to his own experience during
the Second World War to explain his personal appreciation of the
Canticle. It is April 1945, and he and four other Franciscans are part of a
trainload of people being moved they know not where by the SS.

> Black night fills our souls. And yet, on the morning of April 26
> when one of us is in his last moments and the light has almost left
> his eyes, what rises from our hearts to our lips is not a cry of
> despair or rebellion, but a song, a song of praise: Francis of Assisi's
> Canticle of Brother Sun! Nor do we have to force ourselves to sing
> it. It rises spontaneously out of our darkness and nakedness, as
> though it were the only language fit for such a moment.
>
> At such a moment, astounding though it seems, we experience
> wonder before the world; we experience the sacred in the world.
> Such an experience is possible only in extreme deprivation of soul
> and body. Only in utter distress and need can we fully appreciate a
> mouthful of bread, a sip of water, a ray of sunlight, and now and
> then, like a visitor from another world, the warm greeting of a
> passerby. (Pp. 234-35)

This does not give *the* answer to our question. It tells us the direction
one person was looking when he found *an* answer.

FRANCIS AS AN ENVIRONMENTALIST

But we still have other questions to answer.

In the cloister of Santa Maria degli Angeli (the basilica that encloses
the original small church of the Portiuncula, and also where the major

religions of the world started their special day of prayer for peace), there is a statue of St. Francis, a rather special statue. Francis is standing there with his arms folded, looking upwards, presumably in prayer, and resting on his arms is a nest, and in the nest are two doves. The special thing about this statue is that the doves are live. Now I am virtually certain that Francis never supported a nest of doves like this. And I am certain that many who see that statue gushingly exclaim, "How cute!" or "How lovely!", and feel quite sentimental.

In the *Fioretti* we find what is probably the best known of all stories about Francis and animals: "How St. Francis Tamed the Very Fierce Wolf of Gubbio." (Fior 21) Since the story is so well known, just a brief outline. The town of Gubbio was being menaced by a fierce wolf. Francis was visiting the town, heard about the wolf, and resolved to do something about the situation. He halted the wolf's attack on him with the sign of the cross, gave him a sermon on the evil of his ways, and persuaded him to live at peace with the townspeople. In return they would feed him. And for the next two years, until the wolf died, the pact was kept by him and the townspeople. This never happened, although there may be some trace of historicity in a bandit nicknamed "Wolf." It is the kind of story about Francis that can lead animal lovers to exclaim, "isn't he wonderful!", and feel quite sentimental.

Neither of these things, the statue nor the story, is historical. Yet both capture well what was Francis' attitude towards creatures: On the surface a mere lover of animals; yet once one looks more deeply, one finds a respect, even a reverence for animals, and a presumption of basic equality. There is an expectation that animals also have moral duties. There is a personal charism that creates a bond with animals. There is the basic conviction that God is reflected in each creature; that is why there is the basic equality; that is why creatures are brother and sister. And there is the perceived need for every creature to praise the creator.

At the beginning of this talk I issued a challenge, to distinguish between ecologist, nature lover, environmentalist, animal lover, pantheist, animal liberationist. And there still remains one question, indeed our basic question. How does Francis fit into this gallery? I offer you a framework to help in working this out, a triangle with the three vertices of God, man, and creation, a triangle whose sides represent the relationship between each pair of vertices. For an atheist the picture is simplified—to a straight line. Without God, the only relationship is between man and nature. A pantheist sees equality (in some form or other) in the two lines connecting God to man and to creation. And so he also has a straight-line picture. For those whose picture is a triangle, different views will produce quite different relationship along that bottom line connecting man and creation.

Back in the seventeenth century Rene Descartes wrote about,

> practical [philosophy], by means of which, knowing the force and action of fire, water, air, the stars, the heavens, and all the other bodies that surround us, as distinctly as we know the various crafts of our artisans, we might also apply them in the same way to all the uses to which they are adapted, and thus render ourselves the lords and possessors of nature. (Leclerc, p. 11)

"Lords and possessors of nature," not an attitude that would appeal either to Francis or to environmentalists, and so an attitude that illustrates how much Francis was an environmentalist.

In some ways Francis was less than an environmentalist, because he did not have the knowledge and understanding of the interrelationship (at the natural level) between different plants and animals that distinguishes the environmentalist from the mere animal lover or nature lover. Yet Francis was also more than an environmentalist. How many environmentalists of today could we find that have Francis' charism of a special friendship with animals; and how many could honestly refer to animals as brother and sister. Yet it is mainly in what is added through the vertical dimension of the relationship with God that Francis' relationship with creation is more than what any environmentalist can find. And that, of course, is the aspect of Francis that made him a saint, and made him eligible to be appointed the patron saint of ecologists.

"The Canticle of Brother Sun" and the Value of Creation

Eric Doyle, OFM*

People from very varied backgrounds and of quite different levels of intelligence describe certain experiences as mystical or as filled with mystical enlightenment. From what mystics write these seem to fall into two categories.

First, there are experiences which are simply incommunicable. They may concern reality as a whole or some specific part of it. But there are no words to say what was experienced. This is the sense in which Wittgenstein uses the word mystical: "There are, indeed, things that cannot be put into words. They *make themselves manifest*. They are what is mystical."[1] The law of this incommunicability is absolute and indiscriminate. It binds without distinction all who have these experiences. And so with Wittgenstein we must conclude: "Whereof one cannot speak, thereof one must be silent."[2]

Secondly, there are mystical experiences which, though not incommunicable, need more than ordinary language to express them. We may have heard the spirit in the wind, or seen the beauty of a spider's web laced with dew, or been transfixed by the pied-wagtail's darting this way

* This article originally appeared as "'The Canticle of Brother Sun' and the Value of Creation," in *St. Francis and the Song of Brotherhood and Sisterhood*, ([New York: The Seabury Press, 1981] St. Bonaventure, NY: The Franciscan Institute, 1997), 41–59. Reprinted with permission.

and that. Most of us, however, have to be content with the silence imposed by our powerlessness to find the language to describe what we experienced.

Fortunately not everyone is doomed to that silence. There are some who can invent new words and create fresh symbols to disclose what was experienced. This is the way of the philosopher-mystics. There are others who can fashion poetry, the unfamiliar use of very familiar words. This is the way of the poet-mystics. Both philosopher and poet use words in such a way that these point beyond themselves. They thus communicate what cannot be put into ordinary language, and to a limited extent they unveil the world of mystery and the mystery of the world.

The Canticle of Brother Sun gives St. Francis a sure place among poet-mystics. It is a prime example of mystic poetry which reveals his experience of the fundamental unity and coherence of reality.

Francis did not understand himself as an isolated subject facing objects in the world. He saw himself as one love-center in a universal brotherhood and he expressed this in *The Canticle*. Indeed, as the key to Einstein's universe is contained in the devastatingly short statement that time is relative, so is the key to Francis' universe found in the tremendously simple belief, the grace of brotherhood in Christ, which is given to every creature. The vision of the universe which *The Canticle* presents is as fresh and relevant today as it was when Brother Pacificus first sang it.[3]

With these introductory remarks in mind let us now turn to the text of *The Canticle:*

The Canticle of Brother Sun[4]

Most high, all powerful, good Lord,
Yours are the praise, the glory and the honor and
    every blessing.
To you alone, Most High, they belong
    and no man is worthy to pronounce your name.
Be praised, my Lord, with all your creatures,
    especially Sir Brother Sun,
    who is day and by him you shed light upon us.
He is beautiful and radiant with great splendor,
    of you, Most High, he bears the likeness.
Be praised, my Lord,

through Sister Moon and the Stars,
in the heavens you formed them clear and
precious and beautiful.
Be praised, my Lord, through Brother Wind
and through Air and Cloud and fair and all Weather,
by which you nourish all that you have made.
Be praised, my Lord, through Sister Water,
who is very useful and humble and precious and pure.
Be praised, my Lord, through Brother Fire,
by whom you light up the night;
he is beautiful and merry
and vigorous and strong.
Be praised, my Lord,
through our Sister Mother Earth,
who sustains and guides us,
and produces diverse fruits with colored flowers and herbs.
Be praised, my Lord, by those who pardon for love
of you, and endure sickness and trials.
Blessed are they who shall endure them in peace,
for by you, Most High, they shall be crowned.
Be praised, my Lord, through our Sister Bodily Death,
from whom no man living can escape.
Woe to those who die in mortal sin.
Blessed are those whom she will find in your most holy will,
for the second death will do them no harm.
Praise and bless my Lord and give him thanks
and serve him with great humility.

In much the same way as Rublev's icon of the Trinity, but in words, *The Canticle* holds out invitation to participate in what it is communicating. While reading it, I have felt myself to be part of a total unity. It is an affirmation of being, and so it confirms one's sense of the value of one's own existence. It brings reality to a fine point at which it is revealed that all beings are held in unity through a vast and intricate network of love relationships. And because the potency to love all creation is in everyone of us, so too is the power to create. By love and creativity the self and the world blend into ever finer unity. In loving we create, and by creating we discover pathways to the future.

As a prayer of praise to God the Creator, *The Canticle* is a sublime expression of the authentic Christian attitude to creation, which is to accept and love creatures as they are. St. Francis did not romanticize nature into something other than itself, nor was he an undiscerning idealist in regard to it. For example, he disliked idleness intensely; he saw it as characteristic of the fly and the drone:

> There was a certain brother... who never went out for alms but always ate more than several together at table. When the saint observed that he was a friend of the belly, one who shared the fruits without sharing the labor, he once said to him: "Go your way, brother fly, for you want to eat the sweat of your brothers and to do nothing in God's work. You are like brother drone who wants to be first to eat the honey, though he does not do the work of the bees."[5]

According to Brother Giles, Francis was never too pleased with ants because of their solicitude for the morrow.[6] Francis referred to his body as brother ass. On one occasion, when plagued with lust, he took off his clothes and beat himself with his cord, saying: "See, brother ass, thus is it becoming for you to remain, thus is it becoming for you to bear the whip...."[7]

On another occasion, he cursed a sow that killed a new-born lamb. Hearing of the deed he exclaimed: "Alas, brother lamb, innocent animal, you represent what is useful to all mankind! Cursed be that evil beast that killed you; let no man eat of it, or any beast either."[8] He also predicted a bad end for a greedy robin, who even when he had his fill, drove his brothers away from the food. The robin perished by drowning.[9]

These episodes raise the uncomfortable question about innocent suffering and the pain caused unwittingly by predatory animals. It will be considered in a wider context in chapter ten. It seems, however, that St. Francis felt that the world would have been a better place if animals did not kill one another, and it is a feeling I share totally.

We should not fail to notice that Francis does not exclude the fly, the drone, or the ass from the brotherhood of creation. We can assume that he also included the sow and the ants in the universal brotherhood, even though he does not call them sister and brothers.

Nature for Francis was not just a reflection of human activity and reactions, because this would have been to destroy the unique value of other creatures. They are not mirrors of us, but like us, they reflect God. He began with equality: we are all created arid we are all brethren.

Francis believed the doctrine of creation with his whole heart. It told him that the entire universe—the self and the total environment to which the self belongs (microcosm and macrocosm)—is the product of the highest creative power, the creativity of Transcendent Love. By creation, God brings to being what did not exist, and then in love he lets it be itself. Consequently, his belief in creation did not have a constricting effect on Francis, nor did it inhibit him in any way. On the contrary, it liberated him, which is precisely what genuine belief ought to do.

Like the Creator, Francis loved creatures by letting them be, by encouraging them to grow in their uniqueness and by sharing with them their being themselves. Human beings, we proclaim, are made in God's image. God not only created all creatures, he made a covenant with them after the Flood: "And God said, 'This is the sign of the covenant I make between me and you and every living creature that is with you, for all future generations: I set my bow in the cloud, and it shall be a sign of the covenant between me and the earth'" (Gen. 9:12–13). God knows and loves the otter as the otter, the scarlet pimpernel as the scarlet pimpernel, grains of sand as grains of sand. As images of God, it is our privilege to do the same.

The mystical experience which gave birth to *The Canticle* was a creative encounter with reality. An encounter is creative when it brings about new being by an increase in being. It causes to be what did not exist prior to the encounter: the self becomes more truly the self; reality becomes more truly reality.

The Canticle, in fact, has all the marks of having come from the highest form of creative encounter, namely, contemplative union with God, which can be experienced at a number of levels. In the case of St. Francis, contemplative union was never exclusively his relationship with God, but in and through God with all other beings, whether humans, animals, plants, or the elements. Union of this kind has not even a shred of selfishness, and it has no ulterior motive. All lines of communication are open and the union between the self and the not-self is of such a kind that the inner and the outer are one. Yet there is no fusion, the individual is not lost in the great All; on the contrary, the union differentiates. Since we belong to creation organically, full union with its origin which is God, or full union with it through any part of it, makes an individual more truly a self. This is why his love of all creatures made Francis ever more unique, ever more original. His love heightened his sensitivity and endowed him with the precious gift of heart-sight.

This spiritual sense in Francis was linked so finely to his ocular vision that not only did he experience the obscure through direct union of love with God, which is ecstasy, but he also penetrated to the inner essence of every creature he encountered, and in that he experienced its unity, truth, goodness, and beauty.

Self-realization is linked unconditionally to participating in the existence of other selves and other centers in the universe. To say those beautiful and mysterious words, "I love you," is to give expression to the most genuine form of self-love possible. Love of the other is authentic love of self, for it is the union and harmony of the total self. To love myself truly and really, I must love the not-self with all my being. Although the words "I love you" have been said and heard in English millions upon millions of times, they have never been said twice; indeed they have never been said twice in any language in the history of speech. They are always new, always fresh, always being said for the first time. They are words which come from a creative encounter. In loving others lies our creativity in its most pristine form. To love is to be in relation with another, creating a bond between the self and a part of the world, and so ultimately between self and all creation. If one person can love one other person, one unique animal, one flower, one special place on this earth, there is no reason in principle why that love cannot stretch out to embrace every single creature to the furthest reaches of space.

Because everyone can love and be loved, everyone has within him the seeds of contemplation and the gift of creativity. It is, of course, true that things go terribly wrong for some people. Many are deprived and oppressed, and life can be so cruel that even the kindest person can be made callous and bitter. Hideous and hateful crimes can bring one at times very close to despair. But even so, I believe that a person can never lose the capacity to love, and no one can ever become totally unlovable. Nothing can dislodge the seeds of contemplation nor take away the gift of creativity through love. And the reason why is the mystery at the heart of everyone.

There is about human beings—to speak only of them—an element which cannot be reduced to anything the physical sciences have discovered about human life. As Theodosius Dobzhansky has convincingly presented it:

> Genes make the origin of culture possible, and they are basic to its maintenance and evolution. But the genes do not determine what

particular culture develops where, when, or how. An analogous situation is that of language and speech—genes make human language and speech possible, but they do not ordain what will be said.... There is no such thing as a gene for self-awareness, or for consciousness, or for ego, or for mind.[10]

Nor can this element of mystery be explained, as far as I can see, by any knowledge or information supplied by the psychological or sociological sciences.

When we begin to reflect on our existence in the world, we learn at once that we are called in freedom to account for the responsibility we feel for our existence. The primary significance of the question "What is humanity?" is the mystery of openness and transcendence it reveals. To be human is to be mystery in the world. Mystery does not mean vagueness, haziness or "easy-way-outness" from what appear to be insuperable problems or unanswerable questions about ourselves. Mystery is what we go on discovering about ourselves. Mystery is the "never-the-last-wordness" of our existence. It is this which makes false the saying "You never miss what you've never had." We are always waiting, searching, watching, listening.

Experience tells us that there is a factor in us beyond sense data which explains the extraordinary creations by some human beings, like poetry, philosophy, music and art, and the extraordinary creations by all human beings such as devotion, thinking, loving or praying.

One way of describing the mystery within us is to say that we are a unity of matter and spirit. In this unity is located the divine spark which is continually striving to burst into the flame of love without limits. But it needs our free cooperation. Even the slightest effort to do so bears fruit at once in a growth of awareness of other beings. This growth leads one to spend more time with other people, with animals, with nature as a whole. One begins really to listen to what people are saying, actually to listen to what the birds are singing; one learns what soft rain really feels like as it is allowed to fall gently on the face and caress it. All the while we are grasping more clearly the innate worth and unique being of individual creatures. We come to know too that we are individual creatures ourselves. Then we acknowledge in thankfulness and humility that we really are part of nature. And in acknowledging this, we recognize how contrary to God's will it is and destructive of justice and peace, that we should be at enmity with any part of it or with any creature in it.

Creativity gives birth to creativity. *The Canticle of Brother Sun* evokes a creative response, and in responding to it we are in process of creating ourselves. It addresses us in the depths of our being. We come to understand that there is a relationship between ourselves and the rest of creation, and this relationship is super-eminently fraternal.

Every experience of beauty, truth, love, unity, or goodness, is shot through with suffering and sadness. These proceed from the certain knowledge that the end always comes, that death is still among us. The beauty of the germander speedwell fades, and then one morning she is no longer there at all. Inexorably, the final note is reached in a Mozart Mass or a Bach Cantata. Each time I listen to Mozart's *Ave verum* and the *St. Matthew Passion* by Bach, I long to hold on to the notes of "Esto nobis" and to those of the line "In tears of grief dear Lord we leave thee." On several occasions I have tried to hold on to them by playing them over and over again. But silence is still reached at last. Of the paralyzing knowledge that those we love must die, it is not possible to speak. So in all loveliness and joy is found some suffering and sadness. These, however, can be bitter or they can be sweet. But they need not embitter us, for suffering and sadness can generate compassion. They can be sweet. Would life have been better and more bearable if we had never known the flower that has faded, never heard the Mozart Mass that has ended, never loved the friend who has died? If we think it would have been better, then perforce our suffering will be bitter.

The Canticle of Brother Sun is an emphatic "*no*" to these questions. Without the flower, Mozart, or those we love, there would have been no suffering, no sadness, on their account; but then there would have been no joy, no loveliness, either. In fact, there would hardly have been any life worth living at all. Francis is telling us in *The Canticle* that it is better to be than not to be. He is proclaiming the absolute value of being over non-being. And so true is this that even were we to experience it but once it would be enough, it would have meaning in itself for all eternity, to have spotted a fire-fly for a moment in the evening air; to have prayed in St. Piran's oratory in Cornwall; to have heard the haunting melody of Allegri's *Miserere*; to have caressed the water bubbling from the spring beside St. Martin's church at Canterbury; to have looked into another's eyes and found there total acceptance, devotion, understanding, and love. All belief in a life hereafter should therefore make us love life here so much the more, and not one fraction less. This belief should bring us to long for the transformation of this earth and the ultimate saving of all that makes it what it is, and without which it is not, and cannot be, the earth.

The remarkable circumstance about the composition of *The Canticle* is that Francis, being almost totally blind, was unable to see the beauty of the world of which he wrote such lovely words. This very circumstance may well be the most significant point about *The Canticle*. It is certainly the key to a profounder insight into its meaning than the text of itself provides. It is a recognized fact, of course, that people who go blind or who are struck blind, after having had good sight, generally develop in time a more acute sense of hearing and even a more delicate sense of touch. But this does not explain how Francis was able to compose *The Canticle*. He had not been blind long enough for his other senses to have developed in any appreciable manner.

All beautiful words and music come from the mystery of personhood, welling up from the inner depths. It is therefore not so remarkable that Francis, though blind, was able to write a song about the beauty and unity of creation. He was already one with himself and with the world, and the world was one in him. By the unity which he experienced, Francis found himself endowed with the sixth sense of heartsight, or what he himself once described as "the eyes of the spirit."[11] This is the way of seeing which the fox confided as a very simple secret to the Little Prince: "It is only with the heart that one can see rightly; what is essential is invisible to the eye."[12] The sun, the moon and the stars, the wind and the earth, the fire and the water were within him. And by the light of the inner sun, he saw the loveliness of everything.

There are depths upon depths in each of us far beneath the surface of immediate experience. All that takes place there has more lasting influence on the formation of the self than anything that goes on at the level of conscious awareness. The sad fact is that most people hardly ever advert to the existence of these depths.

Even when they do, their reaction, because of fears or misunderstanding, is often to repress the knowledge of their presence or to pretend, in the name of being "practical," that they are not really there at all.[13] Such reactions have a tragic element in them, because advertence to the presence of these depths within is a crucial stage in the process of integration of the inner and the outer, of the ego, the self and the cosmos. It is the beginning of the end of estrangement from the world.

Without this integration, there can be no inner or outer peace, and no cure of alienation in any of its forms. All of us, in one way or another, need to be integrated, and the world needs us to be integrated in order to increase the richness and diversity of its being.

Integration will not necessarily be the same for each person. And certainly it will not always mean having to attend fully to the unconscious, though it will always involve the unconscious in some way. For certain people it may require the total acceptance of themselves as lovable or the complete recognition that there is someone of irreplaceable value inside them. It may mean the shaking off of some unconscious and irrational dependence, or the removal of a symptomatic fear or anxiety, by discovering its causes. It may mean for some the clear recognition of possessing the one precious talent, the foundation and condition of all other talents: one's own unique being.

In the Parable of the Talents, the man who received the one went away and hid it. When he was called on to give an account of it, he replied: "Master, I knew you to be a hard man, reaping where you did not sow and gathering where you did not winnow; so I was afraid and I went and hid your talent in the ground" (Matt. 25:25). It has always seemed to me a legitimate enough interpretation to take this one talent for unique personal existence. We all receive the talent of our own being in all its originality and unrepeatability. And this should be the antidote in every case where a person considers self unlovable. To go away and hide this talent, or to deny one's own value, not only prevents one's being from developing (gaining interest, one might say, as in the parable), it also deprives the world of a precious addition to its treasures.

Besides these, however, integration will mean for many people attending fully to the unconscious as it breaks in upon their conscious lives. Far more are called on to achieve this than we may imagine. Integration is at times an arduous task, but no one should shrink from it. It may well begin in a mystical experience filled with the numinous,[14] and if this is repressed or denied through fear or ignorance, then the unconscious will wreak havoc on the conscious life. To return to the Parable of the Talents. In this case, the one talent may be interpreted as a mystical experience. If it is hidden through fear (repressed), then the Master (the unconscious) will surely demand full retribution.

The process of integration of the self is not achieved at the surface of life, but in the inmost depths of our being. It is important to stress that inner integration is a process. As it grows apace, it gradually brings the *persona* to understand the unity of the vast complexity of the cosmos. Manifestly, this process cannot happen automatically. It is conditioned, and the conditions are, firstly, *self-surrender,* total self-abandonment to the Holy when it reveals itself; and secondly, that form of *prayer* which is peaceful listening to hear the eternal "Yes" and joyful responding of "Amen" flowing from love and back into it, expressing total affirmation and complete acceptance of all creatures and every form of life.

Francis of Assisi fulfilled these conditions by his poverty and his life of prayer. There is not a millionaire on earth who loves his riches more than St. Francis loved poverty. His poverty, which he called Lady Poverty, was not a matter of economics. It was a liberation from all attitudes which barred the way to union of the ego with the self, with God, and with all creation. His dispossessing of himself was the sign of this union with all being. Dispossession of self leads to a new possession of oneself by communion with reality other than the self. At the outset of his new way of life, which we limply call his conversion, he stood before God and the world and stripped himself naked. He dispossessed himself of everything, not only of material possessions, but also of that pride which judges all things by the short yardstick of what is rational, which conceals deep-rooted fears, misunderstanding and ignorance in the face of the vastness and richness of reality, and which turns a person in upon self to be locked away in that cell of terrible darkness, which is interior blindness.

Thomas of Celano, speaking of Francis at prayer, tells us that he so centered himself on what he was asking God that he was "not so much praying as having become himself a prayer."[15] However we may interpret this extraordinary statement, it serves to emphasize that prayer in the first place is a way of being someone, and only then a saying of something.

The Gospel of Luke records that the disciples asked Jesus to teach them how to pray: "He was praying in a certain place, and when he had ceased, one of his disciples said to him, 'Lord, teach us to pray, as John taught his disciples'" (Lk.11:1ff.). I am convinced that it was the sight of Christ at prayer that brought them to ask him to teach them how to pray, and not just because John the Baptist had taught his disciples.

We should remember that they were Jews who asked Jesus this. To anyone familiar with the Old Testament it will be clear that the Jews certainly knew how to pray. The Book of Psalms is a school of prayer. Yet they asked Christ to teach them to pray. The reason was that when they saw him at prayer, they saw that he was his prayer. They saw him then as the Christ in a way they had not seen before. They saw him as the Son. And it was this that made them ask him to teach them to do and be the same. He taught them to say *Our Father.* Those two words express a network of relationships, brothers and sisters, sons and daughters. That means the *Our Father* is first about being someone and only then about saying something.

The way of being that is prayer is a way of being related to God, to other people, and to all creation; it is not only a relationship with God. This approach to prayer must be carefully distinguished from "saying prayers," which flows from prayer understood as being someone. The person who prays that is, enters with full awareness into a relationship with reality hears the "Yes" of divine affirmation pronounced over his own being. By this he is enabled to accept self ever more completely, not just passively, but actively, by responding "Amen," which is the personal affirmation of oneself made possible by God. Through complete acceptance of the self, genuine self-love is generated. The person who loves self authentically and truly also loves and accepts others: humanity, animals, plants, stones, rocks, that is, all creation, and says to it from the depths of his being the "Yes" of total affirmation. In return he hears from everything a reciprocal "Yes." Then together all pronounce in harmony the great "Amen" of cosmic affirmation to God. In his love of creation, as mentioned earlier, God accepts it totally and, at the same time, he lets it be in complete autonomy. The practice of prayer makes a person like God, precisely in the way in which he loves his creation. Consequently, prayer can never be reduced to the purely private sector; it cannot be separated from love of creation. If it is, then it ceases to be prayer and becomes at best introspection, and at worst selfishness by withdrawal from concern for creation. Where prayer is considered an escape from the world, it is no longer prayer.

I hope I will not be taken as proposing the simplistic solution to our problems, that if we pray, all will be well and the problems will go away. What I am stressing, with so many other writers today, is that the malaise of western civilization is spiritual and this needs to be met with spiritual means. One of these is prayer, in the sense in which I have been discussing it. The greatest challenge to organized religion in the western world now is whether it can guide individuals along the paths of their own inner depths, and show how the riches in these depths can be recognized, accepted, and put at the service of all creation; and, closely related to this, whether it can teach people to commune with God and nature. That religion has the means to do this cannot be doubted, I think; that it will see it as its chief task in the long run is probably predictable. But the long run is not satisfactory, because in the meantime, many people will become estranged from creation when this might have been avoided, and because organized religion will be responsible for failing in one of its primary duties.

There are techniques, both ancient and modern, of east and west, which teach their practitioners to cope with stress and eliminate it from their lives. While these techniques are admirable and have done an enormous amount of good, they cannot be equated with prayer. This attends to God as really and truly present to the world and, according to the Christian faith, to God as a community, as an integral unity-in-diversity, bearing the distinct names Father, Son and Spirit. It is not the task of religion simply to show us how to relax and rid ourselves of stress in a busy life, and remain content with that. Its duty is to lead us into God's presence at the point where we are, and to teach us how to commune with him. Through this we enter peacefully into deeper union with creation. The personal relationship between God and self, which attending to his presence engenders, leads ultimately to a disappearance of stress. Peace flows from prayer, and the alleviation of stress is a by-product of peace.

We should try to find fifteen minutes each day (the basic minimum) simply to be in the presence of God as Transcendent Love, not to ask for anything (that can be done at other times, for example, during the bidding prayers at Mass), but just to be there with God because he is God, dwelling in everlasting serenity and peace. It should be made as structural to the day as reading the morning paper, taking afternoon tea, or whatever else we have made indispensable elements in our lives.

There is nothing complicated or esoteric about it. One places oneself in the presence of God. This can be done quite simply by centering the attention of the heart on God, with some such words as: "Most holy God, I adore you"; or "Great God, I love you"; or by repeating the words "Holy God" or just the one word "God." Some people also like to trace the sign of the cross in the air, on the floor, or on the forehead. The words chosen should be repeated continually for the stated time. The posture taken is irrelevant. One can lie down, sit, kneel, stand or walk, go outside, stay in one's room or go to the chapel.

If the mind wanders, it should be brought back to God gently through what has now come into the mind. So, for instance, let us suppose one becomes aware that the mind is thinking about a friend or loved one, about a pet gerbil, or is planning how to answer a letter. This should be shared with God, and one should speak to him for a while about it. Then in continuity, with what is in the mind, one should pray: "And you, great God, love Helen more than I shall ever be able to, for you are the source of all love"; or "And you, great God, love the little gerbil, for all life comes from you"; or "And you, great God, are the origin of all words and by your Word all things were made." From these or similar words one then returns calmly to the words with which the prayer began.

In this approach, creatures are not considered as "distractions" in prayer, but pathways to closer union with God. Creation comes from God, it speaks of him and proclaims the glory of his goodness. How could it be a distraction when it bears in so many different ways his vestige, image and likeness? For this reason we should strive to correct every doctrine of prayer, be it Christian or other, which teaches its disciples that creation *is* a distraction from God, or that prayer should begin by emptying the mind of all that is not God. The weakness, and to some degree the error, of situating prayer in the mind is that when it wanders, prayer is thought to have ceased.

Prayer should begin with centering the will on God, loved for his own sake. The strength and correctness of locating it primarily in the will is that no matter how much the mind wanders or is "distracted," unless one withdraws the will from God by an act revoking the desire to pray, prayer does not cease either during "distractions" or even outside the time of prayer .

If more people would spend fifteen minutes each day in God's presence, peace and love would increase proportionately. Periods thus spent are precious oases in life when love flows from us through us, and back to us from God and creation. And the first-born daughter of love is peace among those who love. By contributing to the growth of love and peace on earth, we are realizing the dream of a world without war, in which there will be no weapons of destruction, not even hoarded secretly by the limp excuse of defense.

The ecological problem reflects the inner human problem of alienation as well as selfishness. Man is alienated from himself and this has alienated him from the rest of creation. Alienation from the self cannot be cured without inner integration and self-acceptance, and there can be no self-acceptance unless we accept that we are accepted by God. And we cannot come to a realization that we are accepted by God if we do not attend to him, surrender ourselves, and become contemplatives.

Prayer reveals to us that we belong to the world in all its staggering and wonderful complexity. The world is our home.

There is no vacuum between one person and the next, between a human being and the air, between a flower and a child. The self does not simply terminate at the surface of the skin, it continues out to the furthest reaches of space. *Homo sapiens* is an earthman; he is more, he is a universeman. That is what St. Francis was: *homo universalis*, man who had united in himself the whole of reality, so that there was no separation in him between the inner and the outer man. For him there was no longer an "in-here" and an "out-there," but simply a unity-in-being which banished all estrangement.

The contemplative loves creatures as they are. Water, for example, is loved for itself, not because it is full of sprites and ethereal things, but because it is a creature like himself. As a creature, water is our sister. And it is hardly normal to pour toxic acid into your sister! It is, moreover, completely abnormal and utterly immoral to assemble parts of creation (creatures like our-selves) and hurl them back at creation in the form of deadly bullets and lethal bombs. We have to stop misusing creation in any of its forms as means of destruction, because this makes it a house divided against itself.[16] What we fashion from the world must be put to the service of all creatures, in order to establish a more peaceful, caring, and sharing atmosphere around the globe.

It will be clear that in advocating the practice of daily prayer with a view to reaching the state of contemplation, I am not suggesting that prayer is a form of escapism into some idealistic world, nor a way of avoiding responsibilities. In fact prayer is a highly political form of activity, because it reveals the precise kind of relationship which exists between God and individual persons, and this has immediate repercussions on life in society. The awareness of acceptance by God, which prayer brings, is acceptance by the God we address as our Father. And whether we say *Our Father* individually or collectively, by these very words all "privatization" of religion is ruled out from the start. Moreover, in prayer God is recognized unambiguously as Sovereign Lord of life and death, as the Almighty, Most Just, and Most Merciful One. In him alone is absolute power and authority, and from him alone all other legitimate power and authority are derived as from their unique source. God's absolute power and authority judge (that is, vindicate or repudiate) every form of power and authority in the world.

Prayer reveals that we cannot shirk responsibility for injustice in the world. In the light it sheds on our existence as we engage in it, our trivialization of evil is shown up in all its shabbiness and absurdity. We come to see that what we call grave sins really lie in our "neutrality," our inactivity, our silence in the presence of injustice in the world. These rise up before us and condemn us. Prayer also brings to the surface of consciousness what we have repressed, especially our share in the collective guilt for exploitation and alienation in other parts of the world. Each one of us knows in his heart of hearts that no man is an island.

It does matter therefore that individuals make sacrifices on behalf of the underprivileged and work for justice even against terrible odds, odds in fact as terrible as national governments in one year spending on armaments two pounds for every star in our galaxy, or £200,000,000,000! Each one who shares what he has with others makes the world that much more a better place by contributing to growth in solidarity.

In prayer, one learns that intercessory petitions to God for the poor, the lonely, and the oppressed, are in fact commands from God to us to do something for them. By God's illuminating grace, we are made sensitive to the needs and sufferings of others, and our obligation to help them is made all the more serious by the fact that in intercessions we are speaking to God about them. Prayers of this kind are always calls to action. To pray for the deprived in the bidding prayers at Mass demands that we share our resources with a deprived person in the vicinity. Just to pray in these circumstances is simply not enough.

There is an intimate relationship between contemplation and action. We cannot in good conscience profess God as our Father if we ignore that there are brothers and sisters of his Son who get only enough to eat to keep them starving till tomorrow. As contemplation for St. Francis was closely linked with washing the suffering and disfigured bodies of the lepers around Assisi, so for us it is tied up with efforts to establish justice and peace at the local and international levels.

In its tiniest detail, creation spoke a word to St. Francis and this is evidently the reason why he said we should be obedient to all the beasts and to the wild animals. The word *obedience* is derived from the Latin *oboedire*, which means not only to obey, but also to listen and to hearken. He who listens attentively always hears a word addressed to him. And a word evokes a response, and a response carries with it a responsibility. As the fox told the Little Prince: "You become responsible, forever, for what you have tamed. You are responsible for your rose."[17]

Francis responded to the word spoken to him by creatures with a love and a reverence which distinguish him as one of the most mature and responsible human beings ever to have lived. Everything was endowed with a value and a dignity peculiarly its own which forbade him even to think of dominating anything, because that would have been to enslave it. And there is nothing more calculated to destroy the value, dignity, and uniqueness of a creature than enslaving it in any form.

Francis was a man of peace. His first greeting was always for peace. This was no empty platitude, but the result of an inner life at peace with itself, with God, and the world. As a poet, a mystic, and a man of peace, Francis seems to unite in himself the aspirations of all men for inner and outer peace and the teachings about peace of all the religions of the world. Of course, outer peace is impossible without inner peace. So it is that he added a verse to *The Canticle* on pardon and forgiveness.

It is not important for everybody to write poetry, but it is crucial for everybody to become a contemplative, and in that sense a mystic. There is no one in the whole world, known or unknown, great or small, who has not received the call from the inner depths to the mystery of unity, but there are many who ignore it. *The Canticle of Brother Sun* is the summary of the experience of one who heeded the call. That call is a precious gift held out to all without distinction of race, color, or creed. And if more people answered it the world would be enhanced not only with more lasting peace, but also, I fancy, with more poetry, art, and music.

It is easy enough to admire the sentiments of *The Canticle* and easier still to dismiss them winsomely as just a little too idyllic to be shared by us. Francis, it may be said, belonged to another world altogether, one gone by which we can never recapture. But it is not the world view of the middle ages that we want to retrieve, but Francis' belief in the universal brotherhood. We must be on our guard not to fall into the trap of neutralizing *The Canticle* by reducing it to a lovely piece of medieval romanticism. The vision it expresses is of lasting significance and universal relevance.

St. Francis was full of surprises. If it is a little startling to learn that he called poverty his lady, it comes almost as a shock to find death addressed as sister. Yet this is precisely what St. Francis does in *The Canticle:* "Be praised, my Lord, through our Sister Bodily Death." Such a sentiment must surely sound strange to the ears of twentieth-century people, whose attitude to death has grown so callous and indifferent. But then an attitude to death is a reflection of an attitude to life. We cheapened life and this led inevitably to a cheapening of death.

Francis valued all life so much that he knew as by instinct that it does not slip away into nothingness at death. He loved all God's creatures without exception, and love has eternity written into it.[18] What person in love is indifferent that his love might finally reach an end? Why do we want our love to last forever? Indeed, how did we learn to say "always" and "forever"?

Not only did Francis call death his sister in this poem, he actually welcomed death into his life as his sister when he learnt from the doctor that he was dying. This would have been impossible without his love of poverty. Poverty and death belonged together in his life. Death was infinitely more than a passivity to be endured. It was the final act of surrender, the last sacrament of total poverty. He had given his life completely to Christ, so that it could not be taken away from him. Hence he did not fear that death could rob him of anything. Moreover, through integration of the inner and outer man, death's ambiguity was removed for Francis, and its power over him destroyed. It became his companion on the passage to another life. Thus, paradoxically, by loving life in all its forms, he learned to love death as his sister. And so man's implacable and most deadly enemy was made at last his friend.

Notes

1.   Ludwig Wittgenstein, *Tractatus Logico-Philosophicus*, trans. D.F. Pears and B.F. McGuinness, introduction by Bertrand Russell, FRS (London: Routledge & Kegan Paul, 1976) 6.522 (p. 73).

2. This is the translation by A. Kenny, *Wittgenstein* (Penguin Books, 1976) 4.
3. Francis was evidently too weak to sing it himself. He had been able to sing earlier. Celano tells us that he sang before his conversion (1 Cel 2) and in his description of him mentions that he had a sweet voice (1 Cel 83). See *Omnibus*, 230, 298. We also know that he composed music. See *The Writings of Leo, Rufino and Angelo*, 171: "During those days and in the same place, after he had composed the Praises of the Lord for his creatures, St. Francis similarly composed some holy words with a tune *(quedam sancta verba cum cantu)* for the greater consolation of the poor Ladies of the house of San Damiano, especially as he knew that they were very grieved at his illness."
4. This is my translation of *The Canticle*. In an earlier version I used throughout the second person singular. On reflection I concluded that this gave it just too much of an archaic flavor: see Eric Doyle, OFM, "Ecology and The Canticle of Brother Sun" in *New Blackfriars* 55 (1974) 392–402, esp. 395–96.
    Here I wish to draw attention to the remarkable and beautiful study of *The Canticle* by Eloi Leclerc, OFM, *The Canticle of Creatures: Symbols of Union. An Analysis of St. Francis of Assisi*, trans. Matthew J. O'Connell (Chicago: Franciscan Herald Press, 1977). The book was published originally in French: *Le Cantique des Créatures ou les Symboles de l'Union* (Librafie Arthème Fayard, 1970.) Père Leclerc set out to find "in the primary cosmic meaning another meaning that is of the interior order" (viii). He found the key "to a reading of Francis' *Canticle* in terms of the interiority it reflects" in the following text by Paul Ricoeur, *The Symbolism of Evil*, trans. Emerson Buchanan, (New York: Harper & Row, 1967) 12–13: "To manifest the 'sacred' on the 'cosmos' and to manifest it in the 'psyche' are the same thing. ...Cosmos and Psyche are the two poles of the same 'expressivity'; I express myself in expressing the world; I explore my own sacrality in deciphering that of the world." *The Canticle* is interpreted as "the symbolic expression of an experience that unfolds in the night of the soul" (xii). The book, however, does not play down the cosmic, realistic aspect of the text. Père Leclerc does not interpret *The Canticle* as an allegory. As he recognizes himself, and in fact demonstrates in the course of the book, the interior and exterior cannot be separated in any satisfactory interpretation of St. Francis' mysticism. His mysticism consists precisely in a most balanced synthesis of the interior and exterior worlds of human experience. However, Père Leclerc's study is concerned with *The Canticle* primarily as a symbolic expression. I am concerned with it chiefly as a cosmic hymn and what it has to teach us in respect of the ecological crisis. This cosmic character of *The Canticle* cannot of course be separated from its symbolic dimension. The unity of the interior and exterior elements of *The Canticle* are treated in this chapter. Not everyone is in agreement with Père Leclerc's interpretation: see Gagnan Dominique, OFM Cap., "L 'âme de François d'Assise sous le prisme de la psychanalyse d'après Eloi Leclerc" in *Collectanea Franciscana* 47 (1977), 317–47.

5. 2 Cel 75 in *Omnibus*, 426.

6. *Golden Words. The Sayings of Brother Giles of Assisi*, with a biography by Nello Vian, translated from the Italian by Ivo O'Sullivan, OFM (Chicago: Franciscan Herald Press, 1966) 70, n. 177.

7. 2 Cel 116 in *Omnibus*, 459.

8. 2 Cel 111 in *Omnibus*, 454.

9. 2 Cel 47 in *Omnibus*, 404–05.

10. Theodosius Dobzhansky, *The Biology of Ultimate Concern* (Collins: Fontana, 1971) 72.

11. *The Admonitions*, I, "The Blessed Sacrament" in *Omnibus*, 79.

12. *The Little Prince*, 68.

13. Jung, *Psychology and Religion*, 183–4.

14. Ibid., 184.

15. 2 Cel 95 in *Omnibus*, 441.

16. The "common good" concerns all creation; see M. Longwood, "The Common Good: An Ethical Framework for Evaluating Environmental Issues" in *Theological Studies* 34 (1973), 479–80: "Our conception of the common good must obviously include the whole biotic community, since the quality and health of human life is integrally tied to the quality and health of the lives of all other members of the biosphere. There is, after all, only one ecology, not a human ecology on the one hand and a subhuman ecology on the other."

17. *The Little Prince*, 70.

18. B.C. Butler, *Why Christ* (London, 1968) 32: "In love the desirousness that found a lowly expression in appetite for food appears transfigured and in some sense inverted. The lover, in the narrower sense of love between persons, gives himself to the beloved; gives not merely his bodily self or physical life, not merely his time and trouble, his thought and admiration, but his own self in its inwardness; hence he would wish to live forever, always as the beloved's."

St. Francis of Assisi's Canticle of Creatures as an Exercise of the Moral Imagination[1]

Thomas A. Nairn, OFM[*]

David Tracy explains that "every classic contains its own plurality and encourages a pluralism of readings."[2] This aspect of the classic aptly refers to Francis of Assisi's short vernacular song, *The Canticle of Creatures*. After nearly eight centuries, commentators continue to attribute a variety of meanings to the song. This short study will investigate three contemporary interpretations of the *Canticle*, those by Eric Doyle,[3] Eloi Leclerc,[4] and Roger Sorrell[5] to ascertain how contemporary authors view the song. It will then suggest that another possible interpretation, one which demystifies nature, may be more adequate to the medieval world view and to the circumstances of the song's composition. Since this demystification also entails an assertion of true human freedom, one may properly describe the *Canticle* as an exercise in *moral* imagination.

I need to express one caution, however, as I begin this project. I am viewing the poem from the point of view of a moralist, not that of a historian. Although I believe that the interpretation I offer corresponds with what Francis says about the origin of the *Canticle*, as well as with what a person of his culture and world view might understand, this

* This article originally appeared as: "St. Francis of Assisi's *Canticle of the Creatures* as an Exercise of the Moral Imagination," in Kathleen Hughes, ed., *Finding Voice to Give God Praise*, (Collegeville, MN: The Liturgical Press, 1998), 202–13. Reprinted with permission.

interpretation is as much an *exercise* of moral imagination as it is a description of that moral imagination I claim was exercised by Francis. Nevertheless, I do believe that an overlooked interpretation of the *Canticle*, one which at least complements those mentioned above, is a call to moral conversion.

THE *CANTICLE* AND THE EARLY BIOGRAPHIES

Although the *Canticle* is mentioned by Thomas of Celano and possibly by Bonaventure,[6] detailed descriptions of Francis' composition of the song are found primarily in the *Legend of Perugia* and the *Mirror of Perfection*.[7] According to these latter sources, St. Francis composed the *Canticle* in three parts at three distinct times during the last two years of his life. The first, dealing with nature (or, as I will suggest, with the cosmic elements), was composed while Francis resided at San Damiano during the winter of 1224–25; the second part, dealing with reconciliation, written to heal a feud between the archbishop and the *podestià* (mayor) of Assisi; and the final part, calling upon "Sister Death," written shortly before Francis died.[8]

If one accepts the account of the *Legend of Perugia*, the event which occasioned the composition of the original section of the *Canticle* was a dream or vision that St. Francis experienced in which God assured him of salvation. The following day he explained this dream to the brothers:

> God has given me such a grace and blessing that he has condescended in his mercy to assure me, his poor and unworthy servant, still living on this earth, that I would share his kingdom. Therefore, for his glory, for my consolation, and the edification of my neighbor, I wish to compose a new "Praises of the Lord," for his creatures. These creatures minister to our needs every day; without them we could not live; and through them the human race greatly offends the Creator. Every day we fail to appreciate so great a blessing by not praising as we should the Creator and dispenser of all these gifts.[9]

He went on to tell his brothers the manner in which they were to sing the new *Canticle*:

> His heart was then full of so much sweetness and consolation that

he wanted Brother Pacificus, who in the world had been the king of poets and the most courtly master of song, to go through the world with a few pious and spiritual friars to preach and sing the praises of God. The best preacher would first deliver the sermon; then all would sing the "Praises of the Lord," as true jongleurs of God. At the end of the song, the preacher would say to the people: "We are the jongleurs of God, and the only reward we want is to see you live a truly penitent life."[10]

Thus by Francis' own admission (according to the *Legend of Perugia*), the purpose of the composition was simply to thank God for the creatures, who minister to human needs and through whom humanity offends God through lack of proper appreciation, and to lead people to penitence.

"A PLURALISM OF READINGS"

Given the fact that the *Legend of Perugia* portrays Francis as giving such a straightforward explanation regarding his purpose in composing the *Canticle*, it may seem pointless to search for another meaning. Yet, if Tracy's understanding of a classic's plurality of meanings is appropriate, each generation must be involved in the task of interpretation.[11] Thus, in spite of a basic agreement among themselves, the three commentators in question have each developed somewhat different interpretations of the meaning of the *Canticle*, ranging from a response to ecological problems (Sorrell) to an expression of the deepest archetypes of the human unconscious (Leclerc).

The authors all acknowledge a dependence of the *Canticle* upon the Liturgy of the Hours as it would have been recited during the time of Francis. They recognize the parallels between the *Canticle* and two liturgical texts which were frequently repeated during the hour of Lauds: Psalm 148, recited every morning, and the *Canticle of the Three Young Men* (Dan 3:56–88), recited every Sunday and feast day.[12]

According to these commentators, Francis' special contribution is in his use of the titles of "brother" and "sister" by which he addresses the creatures. Sorrell explains that by means of these titles Francis "en fraternizes all creation in God—accepting the creatures into his spiritual family as brothers and sisters.... The tenderness and feeling in this action should not be doubted, since Francis, in an emotional and final way, had given up his first family and reached out in turn to his friends, followers, and fellow creatures as his second family."[13] For Doyle, the terms disclose the "structure of reality," a brotherhood and sisterhood that "transcends all barriers and becomes a primarily spiritual relationship, founded upon recognition of a common origin in the sovereignly free, all-loving, creative will of God."[14] Leclerc speaks of these titles as "rooted in, and inseparable from, a profound affective and esthetic experience.... [expressing] a genuine love and a 'sense of union with the being and life of Nature' (to use Scheler's words)."[15]

When trying to ascertain Francis' specific purpose for composing the *Canticle*, however, each comes to a different conclusion. Doyle suggests: "It was not only the attractiveness and loveliness of creation that moved St. Francis... it was also the selfishness of human beings.... [The *Canticle*] is a protest against the misuse of creatures."[16] For Sorrell, the message of the *Canticle* is similarly "appreciative and ecological":

> It is appreciative in that people are instructed to value creation on at least three levels: the symbolic (the sun as signifying God), the aesthetic (Brother Fire as beautiful), and the utilitarian (the sun gives light, the earth feeds people). It is ecological in that it explicitly rejects a view of creation that would objectify it and take it for granted as being worthless and irrelevant unless it proves serviceable to humanity.[17]

Leclerc concentrates on the mystical, contemplative aspect of the song:

> The *Canticle of Brother Sun* is both praise of the cosmos and a hymn to the inner depths. When read according to its full meaning it proves to be the expression of the spiritual experience. What this brotherly praise of creatures, to the honor of the Most High, ultimately reveals to us is an approach to God that involves the saint simultaneously in a humble, fervent communion with all creatures and in the soul's opening of itself in its own innermost depths.[18]

Thus these commentators share what I believe are somewhat modern presuppositions, on the one hand an aesthetic vision of nature and on the other, at least for Doyle and Sorrell, the understanding that material creation is being threatened by humanity.

THE MEDIEVAL WORLD-VIEW

The expositor of medieval popular culture, Aron Gurevich, has suggested that "whenever we come across something in medieval texts that seems to point to an aesthetic relationship with nature, we have to ponder very carefully the specific complex of ideas and feeling underlying the case in point."[19] To the extent that this is true with the interpretations in question, one may ask whether they correspond either to the world view of Francis or to the circumstances in which Francis apparently composed the *Canticle*. If the creatures described in the song are actually threatened material creation, then the song is indeed ecological and appreciative. But what if the creatures mentioned in the *Canticle* meant something else to Francis and his contemporaries?

The Cosmic Elements

A striking feature of *The Canticle of Creatures* is, in fact, the sorts of creatures that Francis chooses to call "brother" and " sister." Those familiar with the early biographies know of Francis' fondness for calling both animate and inanimate creatures by these titles.[20] Yet the *Canticle* limits itself only to the cosmic elements of sun, moon, stars, earth, air, fire, and water. This limitation seems deliberate, especially given that the apparent liturgical models of the song, Psalm 148, and *The Canticle of the Three Young Men*, continue the praise of God in animate creation. Sorrell seems to miss this point, explaining that the song refers to "physical creation" in a way that "reveals a deep appreciation of the natural environment."[21] Leclerc (and to a lesser extent, Doyle) is better here, acknowledging that the song indeed names the cosmic elements. However, following Erhard-Wolfram Platzeck, he indicates that medieval cosmology cannot explain the *Canticle*.[22] Although I agree with Leclerc that the song is not simply reducible to a hymn praising the medieval cosmos, I believe that the medieval understanding of a foundational place of the cosmic elements in the then known universe is an essential backdrop for Francis' enterprise.

How would the educated or uneducated contemporary of St. Francis view the cosmic elements described in the *Canticle?* Characteristic of the agrarian culture of the time, people used water, earth, and fire as remedies to heal illness.[23] For the educated, Aristotle's astronomy[24] and his natural philosophy[25] already enjoyed a popularity in the twelfth century.

The sublunar universe was seen as composed of various mixings of the four elements, each of which in turn was reducible to various combinations of two pairs of contrary qualities (hot/cold and moist/dry). Air resulted from the union of the qualities hot and dry; fire, hot and moist; earth, cold and dry; and water, cold and moist. As philosophers used the qualities to explain motion and change, they also believed that the elements themselves were composed of "opposing powers which maintain an inherently unstable equilibrium."[26] It was this fundamental instability in the elements themselves that allowed a general transmutation from one substance to another and became the basis for the science of alchemy.[27] Brother Elias, Francis' successor as Minister General of the Order, was said to have pursued alchemy "with enthusiasm," ensuring that other friar alchemists were attached to his residence in Assisi.[28]

The Cosmic Elements and the Human Person

Gurevich explains that our contemporary perspective of disjunction between subject and object did not exist in the Middle Ages. He speaks of "a world-view which makes no clear distinction between the human body and the world it inhabits.... [A person's] properties as an individual and as a member of a group, on the one hand, and the properties of the earth he tilled within the confines of that group, on the other, were not sharply delineated, but remained intertwined in the social mind."[29] The boundary between the self and the world was a fluid one. In viewing the world, the medieval person was also viewing the self.

Thus, in the early Middle Ages, not only philosophers and theologians but also troubadours and poets saw the person not merely as a part of the larger world but rather as a "microcosm" reflecting the larger "macrocosm" and revealing a parallelism between the person and the world. The four elements whose combinations were responsible for the world humanity inhabits were the same four elements that constitute the human person. Gurevich shows this parallelism in a variety of ways:

> Repeatedly, medieval thinkers strove to embody the idea of the microcosm and macrocosm in graphic illustrative form. In the allegorical drawings illustrating the works of Abbess Hildegard of Bingen, the macrocosm is represented in the shape of the symbol of eternity—a circle, which Nature holds in her hands, while she in her turn is crowned by divine Wisdom. Within the circle is placed

the human form—the microcosm. He bears within himself heaven and earth, says Hildegard.... In one of the miniatures decorating the words of the Alsatian Abbess Herrad of Landsberg, man-microcosm *[sic]* is surrounded by the planets and the four cosmic elements—fire, water, earth and air.[30]

If the cosmic elements were the foundation both of the world and of the person, it would seem that an appropriate reading of the *Canticle* would not be that of ecological awareness or of a response to human alienation from nature. Such readings would seem to demand a separation of the person from nature that was simply not part of the medieval mind. Yet if this is not the case, what then is the misuse of creation to which Francis attempts to respond by composing the *Canticle?* Perhaps the elements should not be seen as exploited *by* humanity but rather as influences *upon* humanity.

For the typical person in the Middle Ages, the elements of sun, moon, and stars would not have been seen as creatures inferior to humanity but rather as powers which affected human fortune:

That... power emanated from the heavens and affected the earth was made virtually self-evident to Ptolemy and almost everyone else by the behavior of the Sun and the Moon. By analogy with, and extrapolation from, these two most prominent celestial luminaries, the other planets and stars were also assumed to cause a never-ending succession of terrestrial effects. Because celestial bodies possessed different powers and had different positions, their effects also varied. Depending on a complex set of relationships, planets and stars could cause either beneficial or harmful effects.[31]

Similarly, earth, air, fire, and water affected the very identity of the person. Gurevich notes:

The elements of the human body were identical, it was held, with the elements forming the universe. Man's *[sic]* flesh was of the earth, his blood of water, his breath of air and his warmth of fire. Each part of the human body corresponded to a part of the universe: the head to the skies, the breast to the air; the stomach to the sea; the feet to the earth.[32]

Combination of the contrary pairings of the qualities of hot/cold and moist/dry were the foundation of human temperament, and thus the four elements were related to the four humors: Earth related to the melancholic temperament, air to the sanguine, fire to the choleric, and water to the phlegmatic.[33] Imbalance among the four created illness and disease, both physical and mental. The constant goal of medicine in the Middle Ages was the same as that of natural philosophy, to restore balance among the elements.[34]

Another Possible Interpretation:
An Exercise of Moral Imagination

It is Leclerc who describes the *Canticle* as a creation of the religious imagination. He suggests that it is the imagination that "makes us 'see' the physical reality in a certain way by imposing on it an existence created by the imagination itself."[35] Referring to the *Canticle*, he claims that the song "contains a selection of material images whose 'imaginary' character, though not thrust upon us, is definitely asserted."[36] Thus Leclerc maintains that it is through the imagination that Francis adds value to creation: "Matter to which a value has been given is matter that as it were expands under the action of unconscious interior values."[37]

Having investigated how people of the Middle Ages understood the cosmic elements, one must ask whether this interpretation of adding value (or of defending threatened creation) coheres both with the medieval world view and with the circumstances of the composition of the song. If we return to the *Legend of Perugia*, we see that the *Canticle* was born of a particular religious experience of Francis, his profound realization that he would share in the reign of God. This experience became the occasion for a composition "for the glory of God, for my consolation, and for the edification of my neighbor." By means of the song, he also wanted to acknowledge that through creatures humanity has offended God because of lack of proper appreciation. Finally, he asked that the friars sing the *Canticle* as a means to move their audiences "to true penitence." In thanksgiving for his own salvation and to lead to *human* penitence, Francis speaks of the creaturehood of the cosmic elements.

Noting these circumstances, one needs to discover what factor this exercise of the imagination created that led Francis' contemporaries to "see" differently and thus be moved to penitence. Analyzing the brief strophes that name the elements, one sees in each a movement toward

God and a movement toward humanity. Brother Sun, for example, bears the likeness of God, yet he brings day to the human race. Sister Water is both useful to humans and precious, a term Francis normally reserves for the Eucharist.[38] Brother Air and all the weather's moods are means by which God cherishes all creation. Sister Earth is our mother through whom God feeds humanity. Thus Francis characterizes the cosmic elements in relation to God and in service to humanity. But these images of the *Canticle* are vastly different from the portrayal of the cosmic elements in the previous section. This choice of images, when seen against the background described above, is significant. Could Francis be making the claim that, when confronted with the cosmic elements, humanity must remember that they are *merely* creatures of God? If this is a plausible interpretation, then the use of the terms "brother" and "sister" in referring to the elements performs not only a relational function but a relativizing function as well. The terms may not "add value," imaginatively bringing nature up to the level of humanity, but rather bring the cosmic elements, understood as elements which influence humanity, down to human level.

By means of the concrete images of the song, Francis stressed that his contemporaries should see the value of the elements as inseparable from humanity on one hand and from God on the other. Gurevich explains that this was a persistent theme in the Middle Ages: "In so far as nature did not contribute to knowledge of God, it was devoid of value; if it hindered [humanity] from drawing near to God, then it was seen as evil, a manifestation of satanic powers."[39] When read in this context, the *Canticle* is a proclamation regarding the proper place of the cosmic elements. The focus of the song remains the praise of God. In fact, the lack of appreciation which Francis decries is not the lack of appreciation for creation but rather for creation's God. The elements are misused when they do not move humanity to such praise of God.

If the proper role of the elements points humanity to God, then God and not the elements is the true influencer of humanity. If this explanation is at all adequate, however, the *Canticle* says more about humanity than it does about the elements. Creation, which includes even the cosmic elements, serves God in serving humanity. But as humanity accepts its place as the microcosm of this universe it must also appreciate its own vocation in serving God. It is in this calling that humanity finds true freedom. It is noteworthy that Thomas of Celano relates: "He called all creatures *brother,* and in a most extraordinary manner, a manner never experienced by others, he discerned the hidden nature with his sensitive heart, as one who had already escaped into the freedom of the glory of the sons of God."[40] Can the moral vision of the *Canticle* be a call to such freedom achieved in conversion? Such an interpretation may also show more adequately than the others described above the coherence of this original section of Francis' song with those sections he added later, addressing reconciliation and the welcoming of Sister Death. The entire *Canticle* becomes a proclamation of praise to God in humanity finding its true freedom in serving God.

CONCLUSION

The notions of vision and moral imagination are becoming more and more a part of the vocabulary and methodology of Christian ethics. When applied to the *Canticle,* they enable one to see the song in a manner different from other contemporary interpretations. *The Canticle of Creatures,* by demystifying the cosmic elements and by examining the basis of human freedom, becomes a call to moral conversion.

APPENDIX

The Canticle of the Creatures [41]

Most high, all-powerful, all good Lord!
    All praise is yours, all glory, all honor
    And all blessing.
To you alone, Most High, do they belong.
    No mortal lips are worthy
    To pronounce your name.
All praise be yours, my Lord, through all that you have made,
    And first my lord Brother Sun,
    Who brings the day; and light you give to us through him.
How beautiful is he, how radiant in all his splendor!
    Of you, Most High, he bears the likeness.
All praise be yours, my Lord, through Sister Moon and Stars;
    In the heavens you have made them, bright
    And precious and fair.

All praise be yours, my Lord, through Brothers Wind and Air,
      And fair and stormy, all the weather's moods,
      By which you cherish all that you have made.
All praise be yours, my Lord, through Sister Water,
      So useful, lowly, precious, and pure.
All praise be yours, my Lord, through Brother Fire,
      Through whom you brighten up the night.
      How beautiful is he, how gay! Full of power and strength.
All praise be yours, my Lord, through Sister Earth, our mother,
      Who feeds us in her sovereignty and produces
      Various fruits with colored flowers and herbs.
All praise be yours, my Lord, through those who grant pardon
      For love of you; through those who endure
      Sickness and trial.
Happy those who endure in peace,
      By you, Most High, they will be crowned.
All praise be yours, my Lord, through Sister Death,
      From whose embrace no mortal can escape.
Woe to those who die in mortal sin!
      Happy those she finds doing your will!
      The second death can do no harm to them.
Praise and bless my Lord, and give him thanks,
      And serve him with great humility.

Notes

1.   I know Gilbert Ostdiek less as a liturgist than as a teacher, colleague, and brother in community—one whose imaginative and playful creativity has often challenged me to imagine in new ways. I therefore dedicate this essay dealing with St. Francis and the moral imagination to him in thankfulness for this gift of the imagination that he has shared with me.

2. David Tracy, *The Analogical Imagination: Christian Theology and the Culture of Pluralism* (New York: Crossroad Publishing Company, 1981) 113.

3. Eric Doyle, *St. Francis and the Song of Brotherhood* (New York: Seabury Press, 1981).

4. Eloi Leclerc, *The Canticle of Creatures: Symbols of Union* (Chicago: Franciscan Herald Press, 1977).

5. Roger D. Sorrell, *St. Francis of Assisi and Nature: Tradition and Innovation in Western Christian Attitudes Toward the Environment* (New York: Oxford University Press, 1988).

6. See 1 *Celano* 80 and 109; 2 *Celano* 213 and 217; and a possible allusion to the *Canticle* in St. Bonaventure's *Major Life of St. Francis* 9, 1. Quotations from the early Franciscan sources are from Marion Habig, *St. Francis of Assisi, Writings and Early Biographies: English Omnibus of the Sources for the Life of St. Francis* (Chicago: Franciscan Herald Press, 1972).

7. *Legend of Perugia* 43–4, 50, and 100; *Mirror of Perfection* 100–1 and 118–23. Since contemporary authors suggest that the *Mirror* is dependent upon the *Legend of Perugia*, I will use the *Legend* as my basic source. See Sorrell, *St. Francis and Nature*, 120.

8. Sorrell, *St. Francis and Nature*, 98.

9. *Legend of Perugia*, 43.

10. Ibid.

11. Tracy, *Analogical Imagination*, 115–24.

12. Sorrell, *St. Francis and Nature*, 99; see also Leclerc, *Canticle of Creatures*, 4. Raphael Brown also acknowledges a "possible indirect liturgical source in an eleventh-century Advent hymn." See "Appendix VIII" of Omer Englebert, *Saint Francis of Assisi: A Biography* (Chicago: Franciscan Herald Press, 1965) 441.

13. Sorrell, *St. Francis and Nature*, 127.

14. Doyle, *St. Francis*, 63.

15. Leclerc, *Canticle of Creatures*, 11–12.

16. Doyle, *St. Francis*, 67.

17. Sorrell, *St. Francis and Nature*, 123.

18. Leclerc, *Canticle of Creatures*, xiii.

19. Aron J. Gurevich, *Categories of Medieval Culture* (London: Routledge and Kegan Paul, 1985) 65.

20. See, for example, St. Bonaventure's *Legenda Major* 8, 6–11.

21. Sorrell, *St. Francis and Nature*, 125.

22. According to Leclerc, the ordering and the values given to the elements are contrary to that followed by medieval cosmology. See Leclerc, *Canticle of Creatures*, 21. See also Erhard-Wolfram Platzeck, *Das Sonnenlied Des Heiligen Franziskus von Assisi: Zusammenfassende Philologisch-Interpretative Untersuchung mit Aeltestem Liedtext und Erneuter Deutscher Ubersetzung* (Werl: Dietrich Coelde Verlag, 1984) 29.

23. Aron J. Gurevich, *Medieval Popular Culture: Problems of Belief and Perception* (Cambridge: Cambridge University Press, 1988) 83.

24. Prudence Allen, "Hildegard of Bingen's Philosophy of Sex Identity," *Thought* 64, no.254 (September 1989) 233.

25. Gurevich, *Categories*, 56–7.

26. Gad Freudenthal, *Aristotle's Theory of Material Substance: Heat and Pneuma, Form and Soul* (Oxford: Clarendon Press, 1995) 2.

27. See Titus Burckhardt, *Alchemy: Science of the Cosmos, Science of the Soul* (Baltimore: Penguin Books, 1967).

28. Wilfred Theisen, "The Attraction of Alchemy for Monks and Friars in the 13th–14th Centuries," *The American Benedictine Review* 46, no.3 (September 1995) 242–3.

29. Gurevich, *Categories*, 45.

30. Ibid., 59.

31. Edward Grant, *Planets, Stars and Orbs: The Medieval Cosmos*, 1200–1687 (Cambridge: Cambridge University Press, 1994) 572.

32. Gurevich, *Categories*, 57.

33. Scott Russell Sanders, "Ancient Quartet," *Parabola* 20, no.1 (February 1995) 8.

34. See, for example, Urban T. Holmes, *Medieval Man: His Understanding of Himself, His Society, and the World* (Chapel Hill: North Carolina Studies in the Romance Languages and Literatures, 1980) 34–6.

35. Leclerc, *Canticle of Creatures*, 7.

36. Ibid., 5–6.

37. Ibid., 7.

38. Ibid., 8.

39. Gurevich, *Categories*, 64.

40. Thomas of Celano, "The First Life of St. Francis," 81. Celano alludes to Rom 8:21.

41. Habig, *Omnibus*, 130–1.

Discussion Questions

1. Murtagh states: "Above all, as Francis' turning to God unfolded, he was gripped by the fact of the incarnation, and nature became holy to him." What difference does the fact of the Incarnation make in how you deal with environmental issues?

2. Describe Francis' understanding of "poverty." How does his understanding connect with your own understanding of poverty? In what ways can Francis' understanding impact how we regard the earth, people, and our environment?

3. Share your reflections concerning what Doyle means when he says that St. Francis had "heart sight" when composing the *Canticle of the Creatures*.

4. Do you agree with Dreyer's assessment that Clare of Assisi's deferential attitude in relationships with others is relevant to the environmental crisis? Share why you agree or disagree.

5. What have you learned about the spirituality of St. Francis and St. Clare? What do you find appealing in their spiritualities? To which of these spiritualities do you most naturally relate? Why?

6. William Short defines "sin" in Franciscan terms as: "the will to possess." Is this understanding helpful in thinking about the environmental crisis? Explain.

For Further Reading

ST. CLARE OF ASSISI

Bodo, Murray. *Clare, A Light in the Garden*. Cincinnati, OH : St. Anthony Press, 1979.

Carney, Margaret. *The First Franciscan Women: Clare of Assisi and Her Form of Life*. Quincy, IL: Franciscan Press, 1993.

Miller, Ramona and Ingrid Peterson. *Praying With Clare of Assisi. Companions for the Journey*. Winona, MN: St. Mary's Press, 1994.

Peterson, Ingrid J. *Clare of Assisi: A Biographical Study*. Quincy, IL: Franciscan Press, 1993.

ST. FRANCIS OF ASSISI

Armstrong, Regis J. *St. Francis of Assisi: Writings For A Gospel Life*. A Spiritual Legacy Book. New York: Crossroad, 1994.

Bodo, Murray. *Francis, the Journey and the Dream*. Cincinnati, OH: St. Anthony Press, 1972.

Bodo, Murray. *The Threefold Way of Saint Francis*. New York: Paulist Press, 2000.

Boff, Leonardo. *Cry of the Earth, Cry of the Poor. Ecology and Justice Series*. Maryknoll: Orbis Books, 1997.

Dennis, Marie, et. al. *St. Francis and the Foolishness of God*. Maryknoll: Orbis Books, 1993.

Doyle, Eric. *St. Francis and the Song of Brotherhood and Sisterhood*. [Reprint of St. Francis and the Song of Brotherhood, New York: Seabury Press, 1981] St. Bonaventure, NY: The Franciscan Institute, 1997.

Sorrell, Roger D. *St. Francis of Assisi and Nature: Tradition and Innovation in Western Christian Attitudes Toward the Environment*. New York: Oxford University Press, 1988.

ENGLISH TRANSLATIONS OF PRIMARY SOURCES

Armstrong, Regis J., trans. and ed., *Clare of Assisi: Early Documents*. Revised Edition. St. Bonaventure, NY: Franciscan Institute Publications, 1993.

Armstrong, Regis J., J.A. Wayne Hellmann, William J. Short trans. and eds.,

Francis of Assisi: Early Documents, Volume I - The Saint. New York: New City Press, 1999.

Armstrong, Regis J., J.A. Wayne Hellmann, William J. Short trans. and eds., *Francis of Assisi: Early Documents*, Volume II - The Founder. New York: New City Press, 2000.

Armstrong, Regis J., J.A. Wayne Hellmann, William J. Short trans. and eds., *Francis of Assisi: Early Documents*, Volume III - The Prophet. New York: New City Press, 2001.

PART THREE

Saint Bonaventure of Bagnoregio: Cosmic Christ

Born in 1217 at Bagnoregio, a small town in between Viterbo and Ovieto in the Papal States, St. Bonaventure was baptized Giovanni (John) di Fidanza (after his father who was a physician). Between the ages of seven and fourteen he was dedicated to St. Francis[1] by his mother, Maria di Retellio.[2] Bonaventure attended classes at the Faculty of Arts at the University of Paris in 1236–42.[3] In 1243 he began his theological studies as a novice of the Franciscan Order in Paris.[4] He was licensed as a bachelor of Scripture and also made his profession of Perpetual Vows in 1248. Alexander of Hales was his "father and master."[5] In late 1250 or early 1251 he began to read the *Sentences* (Peter Lombard) as a *baccalarius Sententiarius* and simultaneously, he received training in preaching— between 1252–53. He finished reading the *Sentences* in Advent of 1252. In late November of 1253 he became a master of Theology and he began to teach exclusively at the Franciscan School. He was finally incorporated into the College of Regent Masters in 1254.[6] As Doctor of Theology he was Regent Master of the Franciscan School with official recognition by the university from 1254 until 1257. Still acting as Regent Master, he was elected Minister General of the Franciscan Order February 2, 1257. During his seventeen years as Minister General, he continued to teach at Paris as well as oversee the Order's business, making numerous trips to Spain, Germany, and Italy. He was appointed Cardinal Bishop of Albano by Pope Gregory X, and he played a major role in the reforms of the Council of Lyons. Bonaventure died at the Council of Lyons in 1274.

Without St. Francis of Assisi, there would be no Bonaventure as we know him, today. The philosophical and theological synthesis of

Bonaventure included, but went beyond, the mystical experience and spiritual reflection of the Poverello. The influence of Francis is seen primarily in the Christocentricity of Bonaventure's theology, viewed as an explication of the Poverello's Christ-piety and in his interpretation of Francis' religious experience.[7] For example, following Francis who frequently named God "Supreme Good," but utilizing the Pseudo-Dionysian notion that goodness is self-diffusive, Bonaventure calls God "*fontalis plenitudo*" (Font of All Goodness). Though the poetic and aesthetic mark of Francis, the nature mystic, is far from absent in the work of Bonaventure, the Seraphic Doctor gave the spirituality of the Little Poor Man of Assisi a philosophical and theological framework. The insights of Bonaventure recorded in the thirteenth century still serve to deepen our understanding of the relationship of God, the cosmos, and human identity in relation to God and the cosmos, today.

In this section, then, we uncover Bonaventure's grounding of a Franciscan creation theology and ecotheology. The excerpt from Hayes' "Bonaventure: Mystery of the Triune God," unfolds the main strands of Bonaventure's theology and philosophy.[8] While the modern reader may find Bonaventure's philosophical notions a strange medium for a conversation about the created world and the Creator, many theological insights can be gained by following Bonaventure's discussion. The alert reader can begin to identify some significant elements of this system for a Franciscan ecotheology. The second selection in this section by Hayes, "The Cosmos: A Symbol of the Divine," uncovers the key elements of Bonaventure's vision of the Creator and the created world.[9] In Bonaventure's work we find grounds, not only for the sacredness of creation in general, but for the value of each element in particular. Taken together, the two Hayes articles set forth a vision of the created world and the need to place that vision in conversation with the science of our day in order that the story of creation be told and understood in its various forms and dimensions. Just as Bonaventure engaged theology and philosophy with the science of his day, we must engage in an interdisciplinary conversation in our day. To leave the story of creation to either science or theology would be to neglect the fuller truth provided by consideration of both dimensions.

In order to understand Bonaventure one must be aware of the many dimensions of his thought and the two kinds of language he employs.[10] He uses both the language of the imagination and the language of metaphysics. It is important to note that Bonaventure sees the imagination and metaphysics as interconnected and he understands that they impact one another. As Hayes shows, at the core of Bonaventure's theology is the Doctrine of the Trinity.[11] Bonaventure understands the Trinity as divine exemplarity; that is—the immense fecundity of the Goodness of God expressed in the emanation of the Three Persons and flowing outward into the created cosmos.

At the level of the imagination, the world outside ourselves impacts our consciousness through our senses—touch, taste, smell, sound, and sight—and we make judgments about what we experience. Bonaventure held that because God created all things, we can know something about God by experiencing the created world.[12] However, our intellect is also involved in knowing. As we reflect on the information given us by our senses, we raise the metaphysical questions of interpretation and meaning. We move to the ontological level of finding the nature of the One reflected in the encounters brought by the senses. Here we see Bonaventure's use of the Platonic philosophical tradition to show that the nature of the created order is conditioned by the nature of the Creator, and all created reality is grounded in God.

Bonaventure explains the existence of the created world as the result of the tremendous fruitfulness of the goodness of God. As Hayes explains, Bonaventure addresses divine exemplarity by building on Pseudo-Dionysus' neo-Platonic principle that goodness is necessarily self-diffusive, and on the Victorine understanding of ecstatic love.[13] Exemplarity for Bonaventure expressed the fundamental claim that all created reality is grounded in God, and therefore manifests something of the mysteries of God in the created world. The nature of the created order is conditioned by the nature of the creator. The triune God expresses a productive love within the godhead that is the emanation of the Three Persons. The divine life of the God-head flows outward and is reflected in the created cosmos. The created world is therefore, *theophanic*—it images God in varying degrees. The theophanic nature of creation is at the heart of a Franciscan ecotheology.

All created things image God in some way.[14] As Hoebing illustrates: "All living things are vestiges of God whereas man who represents God closely and distinctly is an image of God. The man conformed to God by grace is a similitude because such a person represents God most closely."[15] Divine exemplarity finds culmination in the figure of Christ, the Incarnation of the Divine Word—the Art of the Father—in which the divine exemplarity is most concentrated. Creation is brought to transformative fullness in union with God in the conjunction of the divine archetype and the microcosm of creation.[16]

> So, when the divine exemplarity is focused so sharply in the self-expressive Word; when that Word enters into the most profound relationship to creation in the humanity of Jesus, this conjunction of the divine archetype and what Bonaventure calls the macrocosm (because something of all creation is in human nature) when that comes together, this is the synthesis of all that makes up the created cosmos. It is at that conjunction when the divine aim for all creation is brought to fruition.[17]

That is why God created—so that through love, the creation can be brought into the kind of transforming fullness in union with the divine.[18] And that happens first and to the fullest extent in Jesus. Given this vision, we could say that the world of creation has its own truth and beauty.[19] However, there is much more to this story. "Beyond this, each creature in itself and all creation is in its truest reality an expressive sign of the glory, truth, and beauty of God. Only when it is seen in these terms is it seen in its most profound significance."[20] Here is the basis upon which we can hold that each element of creation has intrinsic value, in itself.

Bonaventure's metaphysics grounds a whole series of metaphors revelatory of the cosmos and which express his understanding of creation. The Seraphic Doctor employed metaphorical language to show the relationship between God and the cosmos. For his presentation, Hayes selects seven of Bonaventure's metaphors—circle, water, song, book, window, micro/macrocosm, and the cross—to further illustrate the Seraphic Doctor's vision of the created world and how it reveals God.[21] Bonaventure's vision of the world of creation given at the level of metaphor and symbol is summarized by Hayes in this way:

> ...for Bonaventure, the relationship between creation and God can be expressed in two words—manifestation and participation. All things in the cosmos exist so as to manifest something of the mystery of God. And all things exist by virtue of some degree of participation in the mystery of being that flows from the absolute mystery of the creative love of God. An appropriate reading of the

book of the cosmos, therefore, gives us some sense of the divine goodness and fecundity; of the divine wisdom and beauty; of the divine intelligence and freedom; and of the relational character of the divine mystery of the trinity in which all of creation is grounded. It gives us some sense of the pain and tragedy of existence in a fallen condition.[22]

Though after the fall (Gen. 3), the human view of God's self-revelation in creation was obscured, it was not lost. Biblical and historical revelation supplements and clarifies what we see in nature and enables us to read the cosmic revelation with greater accuracy. The story of the love of God expressed in creation is elaborated in the Scriptures and modeled most perfectly in the person, life and ministry of Jesus. In the end, there is little excuse for those who do not heed the call to return to the Fountain Source of all Goodness, as Bonaventure exhorts:

Open your eyes, alert your spiritual ears, unseal your lips, and apply your heart so that in all creatures you may see, hear, praise, love, serve, glorify and honor God, lest the whole world rise up against you. For the "universe shall wage war against the foolish." On the contrary, it will be a matter of glory for the wise who can say with the prophet: "For you have given me, O Lord, a delight in your deeds, and I will rejoice in the work of your hands. How great are your works, O Lord! You have made all things in wisdom. The earth is filled with your creatures."[23]

Now it is one thing to speak about creation this way in a medieval setting where Christian theology and belief formed and contextualized the daily life for the vast majority. How does this fit with the contentions of some in our day who claim that religion and theology have nothing to say to each other? In the latter portion of his paper Hayes addresses Timothy Ferris and others of a similar opinion who maintain that cosmology can tell us nothing about God.[24] Hayes carefully argues that the real focus of concern is what questions we expect religion and science, respectively, to answer. Science and religion each rightfully address a different set of questions. The danger comes when either science or religion makes exclusive claims to have the entire truth and that one or the other is able to interpret all levels of meaning. Just as Bonaventure utilized and conversed with knowledge the science of his day made available as a way to begin to grasp the wonders of creation, so too, we need to be conversant with the information made accessible to us through sophisticated methodologies such as quantum physics, astrophysics, or ecology, and use that data as the subject of our theological reflection.

In his essay, Hoebing points to several ways the conversation between science and theology has already been significant. Scientists, such as J. Baird Callicott, hold that if we are to change the way we treat the natural world (and indeed, in our ecologically-threatened world we must), then we need to find ways to recognize the intrinsic value of the created world, not only its instrumental value.[25] Certainly for Christians of today, Bonaventure's vision of the Creator and the world of creation offers reason to assign intrinsic value to all in the created world. In this classic essay Hoebing shows how this assignment can be made, grounding one's reasoning in Bonaventure's philosophy and theology. As Bonaventure so eloquently stated:

> ...the entire world is a shadow, a road, a vestige, and it is also a book written without. (Ex.2:8; Ap.5:1) For in every creature there is a shining forth of the divine exemplar, but mixed with the darkness. Hence creatures are a kind of darkness mixed with light. Also they are a road leading to the exemplar. Just as you see a ray of light entering through a window is colored in different ways according to the colors of the various parts, so the divine ray shines forth in each and every creature in different ways and in different properties; it is said in Wisdom: *In her ways she shows herself.* (Wis.6:17) Also creatures are a vestige of the wisdom of God. Hence creatures are a kind of representation and statue of the wisdom of God. And in view of all of this, they are a kind of book written without.[26]

In our ecologically threatened world, may we be wise enough to follow Bonaventure's vision.

Notes

1. J. Guy Bourgerol, *Introduction to the Works of Bonaventure* (Patterson, NJ: St. Anthony Guild Press, 1964.), 3. Legend holds that he was healed of some illness by St. Francis of Assisi. However, that is not probable because the age to which Bonaventure assigns his dedication appears to be *pueritia*, a date after the death of Francis (October 3, 1226).

2. Ewert Cousins, *Bonaventure*, The Classics of Western Spirituality, ed. Richard J. Payne, (New York: Paulist Press, 1978), 4.

3. The dating of the life chronology of Bonaventure depends on the date established for his election as Minister General of the Franciscan Order. I follow John Quinn's study. See John F. Quinn, "Chronology of St. Bonaventure (1217–1274)," *Franciscan Studies* 32 (1972):173.

4. Bourgerol, *Introduction to the Works of Bonaventure*, 5–10.

5. Ibid., 4.

6. John F. Quinn, "Chronology of Bonaventure's Sermons," *Archivum Franciscanium Historicum* 67 (1974): 151–52.

7. Zachary Hayes, "Bonaventure: Mystery of the Triune God," in Kenan B. Osborne, ed., *The History of Franciscan Theology*, (St. Bonaventure, NY: Franciscan Institute, 1994), 45. See also Regis J. Armstrong, "Francis of Assisi and the Prisms of Theologizing," *Greyfriars Review* 10/2 (1996):196–98.

8. Ibid.

9. Zachary Hayes, "The Cosmos: A Symbol of the Divine," unpublished paper prepared for the USCC, Washington, DC, June 1997.

10. Ibid., 3.

11. Hayes, "Bonaventure: Mystery," 53–60.

12. In Chapter 2 of *The Journey of the Soul into God*, Bonaventure shows how the senses bring us in contact with God.

13. Hayes, "Bonaventure: Mystery," 56.

14. See Bonaventure, *Breviloquium* 2.12 [5:230], cited in Zachary Hayes, *Bonaventure: Mystical Writings*, Spiritual Legacy Series, (New York: Crossroad Publishing Company, 1999), 90. Note that all citations Hayes gives in this work are his translations from *Doctoris Seriphici S. Bonaventurae opera omnia*. 10 volumes. Quaracchari: Collegium S. Bonaventurae, 1882–1902. The first two numerals indicate the section of the text, the bracketed numerals indicate the volume and the page in that volume.

15. Phil Hoebing, "St. Bonaventure and Ecology," *The Cord* 40/11 (December,

1990): 342. Note that Hoebing's use of "man" is intended to include both female and male human beings.

16. Bonaventure, *Collations on the Six Days of Creation*, 1.13 [5:332], cited in Hayes, "Bonaventure: Mystery," 74.

17. Zachary Hayes, a lecture "Of God's FULLNESS We Have All Received: The Teaching of St. Bonaventure on Creation," June 12, 1997, at The National Franciscan Forum – *Franciscans Doing Theology*, Franciscan Center, Colorado Springs, CO. The videocassette of the lecture is included in Mary C. Gurley, "An Independent Study Program to Accompany *The History of Franciscan Theology*," Kenan Osborne, ed., (St. Bonaventure, NY: The Franciscan Institute, 1999).

18. See Hayes, "Bonaventure: Mystery," 63–64.

19. Bonaventure, *The Collations on the Six Days of Creation* 3.8 [5:344], cited in Hayes, *Bonaventure: Mystical*, 73.

20. Zachary Hayes, "The Cosmos," 6.

21. Ibid., 6–14.

22. Ibid., 13. See also Hayes, "Bonaventure: Mystery," 65.

23. Bonaventure, *The Journey of the Soul into God*, 1.15 [5:299], cited in Hayes, *Bonaventure: Mystical*, 77.

24. See Hayes, "The Cosmos," 14–24.

25. Hoebing, "Bonaventure and Ecology," 343–44.

26. Bonaventure, *Hexaemeron*. XII, 14, quoted in Ewert Cousins, *Christ of the 21st Century*, (Rockport, MA: Element, Inc., 1992), 152.

An Excerpt from
"Bonaventure: Mystery of the Triune God"

Zachary Hayes, OFM[*]

III. Sources of Bonaventure's Thought

The relation of Bonaventure's thought to the broader stream of tradition has been debated at length. There has been a tendency to think of Bonaventure as a faithful follower of Augustine and often as an opponent of Aristotle. It would go beyond the intent of this exposition to recount the history of the debate in this context, but a few remarks are in place.

While it is true that Bonaventure owed a great debt to the work of Augustine, it has long been known that this so-called great Augustinian departed from the African master profoundly in what has to count as a central area of his doctrinal teaching: the doctrine of the trinity. On the other hand, the Seraphic Doctor was deeply influenced by Augustine's insights into the problems of human knowledge and was unwilling to let them get lost in the controversies evoked by the growing influence of Aristotle.

Concerning the problem of Aristotle, one cannot read the, scholastic treatises of Bonaventure without being greatly impressed by the

[*] This article originally appeared as: "Bonaventure: Mystery of the Triune God." in Kenan B. Osborne, ed., *The History of Franciscan Theology*, (St. Bonaventure, NY: The Franciscan Institute, 1994), 43–93. Reprinted with permission.

extent of his knowledge and the depth of his understanding of the Stagirite. Bougerol, for example, claims that there are 1,015 citations from Aristotle in the writings of Bonaventure.[1] These citations include not only the *Organon*, but the *Physics*, the *Metaphysics*, the *Ethics*, and the *De anima*. On Bonaventure's own word, he preferred the view of Plato to those of Aristotle on topics such as exemplarity. He was clearly impressed with what Aristotle had to say about empirical knowledge. But he was unwilling to grant that there was really nothing whatever in the mind that was not first in the senses. For this did not seem to account for the interior world of human consciousness which, as any Augustinian realized, was itself a potential object of knowledge which seemed to be at least relatively independent of sensation in many ways.

To be convinced that Aristotle is wrong on a specific point or to think that an Aristotelian position might be good but not fully adequate is not to be against Aristotle in principle. It simply indicates an ability to read even an outstanding author with a critical sense. According to J. Ratzinger's argument, what commonly counts as anti-Aristotelianism is a polemic not against Aristotle as such but against a specific mediaeval philosophical movement which argued for the self-sufficiency of philosophy.[2] This was the issue raised by the so-called radical Aristotelians or Averroists. Bonaventure's vision was opposed to this radical view because, in his eyes, it seemed to assume a fundamentally flawed understanding of the human situation and of the goal of human life.

To speak of sources can raise another sort of problem. The presence of citations from "authors" in a medieval text is commonly taken to mean that the citation has the same meaning in the original author and in the writer making the citation. If this were the case, many medieval texts would be appropriately interpreted as mere mosaics of past viewpoints. In fact, however, this seems not to be the case. It has long been an axiom in medieval studies that, while the citation of authority was a very important aspect of an argument, for most medieval authors authority had a "wax nose." Wax softens in the heat of the hand and can be re-shaped into a great variety of forms. So authority can be easily twisted and turned to serve new purposes. It would probably be more to the point to envision a particular author not only borrowing from others, but appropriating the wealth of a tradition in a new, creative, personal synthesis.

Whatever one might say about this as a general principle, it seems quite appropriate in the case of Bonaventure. While every line of such a work as the *Itinerarium* might be traced to the inspiration of another figure in the history of Greek philosophy or of Christian thought, the text as a whole bears the distinctive characteristics of a uniquely creative mind. This means it is quite possible that what a particular citation was intended to mean by its original author is not necessarily identical with what it means as it appears in Bonaventure.

The discussion of the sources of Bonaventure's theology should distinguish between the religious-theological sources and the philosophical sources. Concerning the religious and theological sources, it is true to say that without a St. Francis of Assisi there would have been no St. Bonaventure as we know him. Bonaventure was deeply impressed by the spiritual reality that Francis lived. Even though he never met Francis face-to-face, the Seraphic Doctor lived from his earliest years under the influence of the followers of Francis. He was involved personally in the controversies about the mendicant movement both as a scholar at the University and later as General of the Order. For years he wrestled with the mystery of Francis and with the enigma of the Order that claimed Francis as its founder.

The influence of Francis can be seen at two inter-related levels. First, Bonaventure offers a sensitive, theological interpretation of the meaning of Francis' religious experience. That is, Francis himself becomes the object of theological reflection and interpretation. Second, the spiritual experience of Francis provides some of the foundational insights for Bonaventure's theological system. The consistent Christocentrism of the Seraphic Doctor's theology can be seen as nothing other than an elaborate theological explication of the Christ-piety of the Poor Man of Assisi. And the tendency of Bonaventure to emphasize the nature of God as fruitful, creative love can be seen to have roots in Francis' experience of God as "most high," and "supreme good" *(Praises To Be Said at All the Hours,* St. Francis of Assisi).

Among the religious sources of Bonaventure's theology the scriptures hold a prominent place. There is a sense in which, for Bonaventure, theology is but an appropriate way of reading the scriptures. Certainly, in his mind, theology should never arrive at positions that contradict the Scriptures. Citations from the Bible are frequent in his academic writings. But even more so, in his sermons we are confronted with what might be called "chains" of biblical texts joined by the preacher with simple Latin phrases. The Bible both in itself and in the tradition of Patristic commentaries on the text available in the *Glossa* and the collections of *Sentences* are indispensable sources of Bonaventure's theology.

From the theological tradition, the most obvious sources from the broader tradition are Augustine, Pseudo-Dionysius, Anselm, the Victorines, and Joachim of Fiore. In a narrower sense, Bonaventure was concerned with the tradition as communicated by the early friar scholars at the University of Paris. This involved in a particular way Alexander of Hales and John of la Rochelle. In the prologue to the second book of his *Sentence Commentary*, Bonaventure states that he had adhered to the "common opinions" of his masters in the first book, and intended to continue on the same path in the books that follow.[3] Bonaventure felt deeply indebted to his intellectual masters. But, with a genuinely original and creative mind, he shaped that tradition in new ways. And in his efforts to save the Order from possible self-destruction, he created new possibilities by wrestling with problems with which the earlier masters did not have to contend.

With respect to philosophy, in general Bonaventure developed outstanding skill in analyzing and communicating theological insights through philosophical principles and categories. The philosophical sources used by Bonaventure show a decided preference for the Platonic and neo-Platonic tradition on numerous issues, together with an extensive reading and a skillful use of Aristotle. A certain Platonizing tendency may be accounted for by the nature of the monastic, Augustinian, theological tradition which preceded the work of the high Middle Ages. Some specific sources of Platonizing materials in Bonaventure's writings are the *Liber de causis* and the works of Pseudo-Dionysius.

IV. POINT OF DEPARTURE

a. *Philosophy and theology*

Although he was well read in Aristotelian philosophy, Bonaventure rejected the view that any philosophy, including that of Aristotle, could be self-sufficient. Bonaventure's view on this was guided by basic decisions about the nature of Christian faith and its relation to human reason. He was convinced that, while philosophy at some level is concerned with ultimate reality in a way that is universally accessible to human reason, the experience of Christ and the Christian faith provides decisive clues as to the nature of ultimate reality that may, and in fact do, differ from those of the best known philosophies.

In Bonaventure's view, one of the primary functions of philosophy is to unify reality in the human mind. This unifying dynamism of philosophy is carried out principally in the discipline of metaphysics. It is clear in several of his major works that Bonaventure read the Platonic tradition to mean that the crucial metaphysical question was the question of exemplarity. On this point, Platonism was preferable to Aristotelianism in Bonaventure's eyes. It is precisely here that Bonaventure's faith plays a significant role since, for him, the question of exemplarity coincides with the Christological question. In the light of the Christ-mystery and its metaphysical implications, all purely philosophical metaphysics must stand open to correction and to possible completion in the light of the metaphysical implications of Christ.

From this starting point Bonaventure can view philosophy in a positive way and yet not expect it to fulfill a task which, in principle, is impossible for it. And since the Christ-mystery did not appear with full explicitness in human history until a particular time and place, it is not surprising to find that no philosopher prior to the coming of Christ was able to provide an adequate account of the nature of reality. Bonaventure, therefore, sees philosophy as an integral part of the spiritual-intellectual journey of humanity. But, by itself, philosophy is incapable of providing an adequate road-map for the journey.

Thus, it would not be fair to describe Bonaventure as either anti-Aristotelian or as anti-philosophical. He clearly knew and respected the great lights of antiquity, including Plato and Aristotle. Important as their contribution to the intellectual tradition may have been, Bonaventure simply did not find the work of any philosopher adequate to provide the way of wisdom of which humanity stands in need.

A close reading of his works indicates that Bonaventure was capable of performing well at the philosophical level. Recognizing that the insights of faith provide at least some external guidelines for what might count as significant philosophical reflection, Bonaventure operated philosophically on at least two levels. First, he developed intellectual positions on issues commonly recognized as philosophical in nature. And second, he developed theological positions through philosophical categories and principles.[4] Thus, his early writings, especially his

Sentence Commentary, and his *Disputed Questions* reveal a highly philosophical style of theology. But, like philosophy, this form of discursive
theology was seen to be but a step on the way to a mystical experience
of God.

The same Christological convictions which stood behind Bonaventure's approach to philosophy provided the underpinnings for a program of Christological inclusiveness whereby all the arts and sciences,
including philosophy and theology, could be incorporated into a unified
vision of the journey of creation to God. At the summit of this journey,
the soul is called in the spirit of Pseudo-Dionysius to move beyond all
epistemological categories of rational thought into the silence of a loving, mystical union with God.[5]

b.   A starting point in theology

Bonaventure is well-known as a Christocentric theologian. One
might expect, therefore, that his theological system begins with the
mystery of Christ. Since, with the exception of the *Collations on the
Hexaemeron*, none of Bonaventure's theological works are structured in
this way, we might well ask where one begins most appropriately in
treating the theology of the Seraphic Doctor?

There are two texts in his own writings that provide important
clues for locating the starting-point for entering into Bonaventure's theological world. The first text appears in his *Disputed Questions on the
Trinity*, and hence from his years in the academic arena of Paris. The second text appears in the *Collations on the Hexaemeron*, and hence comes
from his final work which was left unfinished in 1273, the year before his
death.

In the first text, Bonaventure speaks of the foundation of the entire
edifice of Christian faith.[6] This foundation, he argues, is the mystery of
the trinity. At first reading, this seems to be inconsistent with the long-
standing conviction that Bonaventure's theology is thoroughly and consistently Christocentric. The tension is obvious when this text is placed
next to the second text. In the second instance, Bonaventure is reflecting
on the possibility of overcoming the confusion which he feels is so pervasive in his own historical era. In that context, he asks explicitly:
Where are we to begin our reflections if we hope to arrive at true wisdom? His answer is unequivocal: We are to begin at the center of reali-

ty; and the center is Christ.[7] Only if we begin there can we hope to overcome the rampant debilitating confusion of the times and come to some genuine insight into the nature of reality and of human destiny. Here the mystery of the incarnation is emphatically foundational.

Which is really the foundation? Is it possible that both are foundational in some sense? Or is Bonaventure simply carried away by a kind of religious rhetoric when approaching two mysteries that certainly are basic to any Christian theological understanding? It is possible to see this in the following way. If Christianity is approached in terms of its eternal grounding, then the mystery of the trinity is foundational. But, if Christianity is approached in terms of the historical process whereby the Christian faith-vision emerged in human consciousness, then the mystery of the incarnation is foundational. That is, both are foundational. All depends on the perspective from which we approach them. And Bonaventure's statements, at first seemingly inconsistent from the perspective of logic, can readily be seen as intelligible and coherent within the broader context of his Christocentric vision.

When these two texts are read in relation to each other, it becomes clear that Bonaventure's Christocentrism is not in competition with theocentrism. Christ does not replace God in the structure of Christian faith and spirituality. On the contrary, Christ is the crucial historical point of departure for the Christian experience of God. And the experience of Christ has led Christians to expand the received monotheistic understanding to a trinitarian monotheism. The mystery of the triune God, therefore, is the eternal mystery of God in which the historical mystery of Jesus is grounded and into which that historical experience opens the eye of faith. The infinite mystery of God is not replaced by the finite reality of a human being. But the finite history of Jesus is perceived as the historical mediation of a divine presence in and through a finite symbol.

Bonaventure's own words confirm this dialectical relationship. In speaking of the trinity and the incarnation, he writes: "As in the eternal God there is a trinity of persons together with a unity of essence, so in God made man there is a trinity of natures together with a unity of person. These are the two roots of faith. Anyone who is ignorant of them will have no faith. They include the body, the soul, and the divinity. The holy Christ has a holy body; the holy Christ has a holy soul; and the holy Christ has the holy divinity."[8]

Where, then, does one take hold of the Christian symbol-system in the investigation of Bonaventure's theology? It seems that two ways are possible. Does one take the text of *the Hexaemeron* quite literally for what it says and begin with the mystery of Christ? This is a possibility. And it is an approach that could be of considerable interest in our own age with its discussions concerning Christocentrism. On the other hand, Bonaventure's own writings are not structured in this way. Recognizing the historical basis for the Christian tradition and being aware of the historical unfolding of that tradition, it seems advisable to follow the pattern of Bonaventure's own theological architecture. In laying out his theological structure, he consistently begins with the view "from above." It is not surprising to find this in the *Sentence Commentary*, since the author of such a commentary follows a topical plan laid down by Peter Lombard, the author of the *Book of the Sentences*. But the situation is different in case of the *Breviloquium*. This work is the closest Bonaventure came to producing a *Summa*. In writing it, he was not bound by the expectations of the academic discipline. In a sense, he was free to structure this work as he saw fit. It is significant, therefore, that after a brief and poetic prologue concerning the scriptures, Bonaventure turns immediately to the eternal foundation of his entire theological structure: the mystery of the Triune God.

This is the route we shall follow in our presentation. We will attempt to see the inner logic of the building blocks of Bonaventure's system and their inner relationship to each other. It is in the analysis of the building blocks that we will discover some of the distinctive qualities of the Seraphic Doctor's theology and some of the reasons for the shape it takes. For even though we begin with the mystery of the trinity, the system from start to finish is unabashedly Christocentric.

SYSTEMATIC VISION

In two striking texts Bonaventure has offered important clues as to the structure of his systematic theology. In the *Collations on the Hexaemeron* he writes: "This is the whole of our metaphysics: It is about emanation, exemplarity, and consummation, that is, to be illumined by spiritual rays and to be led back to the supreme Being."[9] And again: "For any person who is unable to consider how things originate, how they are led back to their end, and how God shines forth in them, is incapable of achieving true understanding."[10]

The neo-Platonic sound of this is unmistakable. Emanationism is a common form of neo-Platonic explanation of the move from the One to the many. The metaphysics of exemplarity has deep roots in the older Platonic tradition with its vision of Ideal reality. The tendency of neo-Platonic systems to draw the multiplicity of reality back into an undifferentiated unity gives rise to the symbol of a circle. It is this circle that the reader hears in Bonaventure's statements. "Our metaphysics" is about how things go forth from God and how things are led back to God, and about the archetypal model after which all created reality is shaped.

It is certainly the case that this circular symbol represents the outline of Bonaventure's entire theology and spirituality from the time of the *Itinerarium* to the time of the *Hexaemeron*. Bonaventure's theology from the time he left the university is above all the exposition of the ascent of the world back to God. "The theologian considers how the world, which was made by God, will be brought back to God."[11] And this is, above all, the work of reconciliation. The body of his theology, then, is framed by the two terms: *emanatio* and *reductio*. But the ancient neo-Platonic meaning of the circular symbol implied here has been profoundly altered in the encounter with the Christian faith. The neo-Platonic sense that created reality emerges from a primal cataclysm is transcended by a positive theological assessment of the goodness of finite reality. The neo-Platonic sense that in the end the empirical world would fade away is replaced by the Christian sense that the created cosmos is being led back to God. In a direct sense this reduction involves the human soul, but in an indirect sense it involves the human body and the whole of the material universe. Finally, the Platonic world of ideal reality is replaced with a trinitarian and Christological analysis of the eternal Word of God.

How does this vision of theology relate to Bonaventure's earlier works such as the *Sentence Commentary* and the *Breviloquium?* Since the earlier works are directly related to the university career of the Seraphic Doctor, and the later works were composed during his time as Minister General, one might be tempted to say that the early works represent what he thought in strictly theological terms while the later works are more spiritual and pastoral in nature. This, however, would be misleading. While the external, literary form of the late work differs greatly from that of the early writings, there are points of contact in the content of his theology that indicate a level of continuity together with discontinuity in the basic theological vision of Bonaventure. The development of these discontinuities represented in specific forms of emphasis and in the adoption of particular literary forms may be explained by the need to address the problems of the Order and the developments taking place in the university community which concerned Bonaventure persistently during his last years. The late writings, far from being only loosely theological, actually solidify and radicalize theological positions that had been with Bonaventure from his early years. It is legitimate, then, to take the later formulations as a statement of his mature theological vision and to interpret the earlier work from that perspective.

The following presentation will follow the Bonaventurean interpretation of the circular symbol. It will begin with the primal source of all going-forth in the mystery of the triune God and follow the movements of creation as it goes forth into history and is led back to God through the history of the human spirit as it moves to eschatological fulfillment. In the beginning is God. And in the end is God and the fruits of history.

1. *The Triune God: Source of All Emanation*

a. Human knowledge of God as supreme good

Some initial suggestions concerning Bonaventure's understanding of God appear in the questions he treats concerning the relation between God's being and truth. This matter is discussed in two places: First in the *Sentence Commentary*[12] and then in the *Disputed Questions on the Trinity*.[13] In the first instance, Bonaventure asks whether the being of God is true in such a way that it cannot be thought of as not existing. In the second case, he asks whether the existence of God is indubitable. In both cases, as K. Fischer has pointed out, the question is not about the divinity in itself. It is, rather, a question about human knowledge and doubt.[14] The basic question, for Bonaventure, is never about the existence or non-existence of God, but only about the impossibility of reasonably thinking of God as non-existing. The divine being is such, in Bonaventure's view, that there can be no rational doubt about God's existence. The fact that there are people who seem to be ignorant of God or who have doubts about the existence of God says nothing about God but suggests only that such people are limited by blindness and ignorance, and are not making proper use of their rational faculties. For example, one may have a faulty concept of God. In such a case, the denial of

God's existence is really nothing but the rejection of an erroneous idea of what God is. Or, one may draw inferences from insufficient data. Then, the rejection of God is simply a matter of bad logic. Or, one may fail to carry the process of reflection through consistently to the end in what Bonaventure understands to be the process of *reductio*. In such a case, one has simply stopped thinking too soon.

This conviction about the indubitability of God's existence has deep roots in the Augustinian, Anselmian tradition which was mediated to Bonaventure by Alexander of Hales and the other early masters of the Franciscans at Paris. There was a sense, for this tradition, in which the existence of God was a truth that was *per se notum*. The ontological argument involved was deeply indebted to the Anselmian formulation which defined God as "something than which nothing greater can be conceived." In such a formulation, the existence predicated of the subject is fully identical with the subject, hence the impossibility of logically affirming the non–existence of the subject.

The other major line of argument is strongly anthropological in nature. It runs roughly as follows: The perennial human thirst for truth, goodness, and happiness cries out for the existence of a truth and good-ness that does not fail in the end. Since all created truth and goodness is fragile, transitory, and insufficient, human experience in its deeper levels calls out for the existence of a supreme Truth and Goodness. The exis-tence of God, therefore, is a truth which, in some sense, is natural to human beings. It is called a *cognitio inserta* or "innate knowledge" and must be distinguished from any form of explicit knowledge. The *Summa Halensis* had spoken of an "habitual knowledge" of God which was naturally impressed in the human soul. Bonaventure seems to see an implicit knowledge of God as supreme Being to reside in the experience of being in our knowledge of finite realities. Speaking of the mystery of absolute Being, Bonaventure writes: "Remarkable, then, is the blindness of the intellect which does not consider that which it sees before all other things, and without which it can know nothing."[15] There is a sense in which God as the supreme Being is involved in every human act of knowledge which comes to judgments about the being of finite crea-tures. The process of human reflection, then, might be seen as a way of making this implicit knowledge explicit in human consciousness.

This line of thought is concerned primarily with the relation between being and truth. What sort of being is involved in the mystery of God that leads to such claims about the nature of human knowledge? For Bonaventure, as for Alexander of Hales, this is above all a question of the divine being cast in strongly Anselmian terms. Hence, the logical impossibility of thinking it to be non–existent follows. More specifically, it is a question of defining the nature of that being as the supreme good. This is a matter of investing the mystery of Being with a distinctively Christian face. The further implications of this understanding of God are developed in the doctrine of the trinity.

b. Trinitarian logic

It has long been recognized that Bonaventure's approach to the mystery of the trinity differs significantly from the Augustinian model which had dominated the theology of the Christian West for centuries. Before looking into specific aspects of the Bonaventurean model, two general observations can be made.

The first thing that strikes the reader of Bonaventure's works is that the Seraphic Doctor never develops an independent treatment of "the one God." The whole of the customary treatment of divine attributes and the divine intellect and win is discussed within the context of the doctrine of the trinity both in the *Sentence Commentary*[16] and in the *Breviloquium.*[17] The systematic treatment of the doctrine of the trinity constitutes the whole of Bonaventure's doctrine about God. Since the understanding of the divine attributes is worked out within the context of trinitarian reflection, the definition of these attributes is colored from the start by the trinitarian context. In this sense, the trinitarian vision of Bonaventure becomes the source for an ongoing corrective to the metaphysical tradition from which many of these attributes were derived. In an even more basic sense, the mystery of the trinity assumes genuinely metaphysical status in his thought since it involves a penetrating insight into the mystery of Being which does not negate the metaphysical doctrine of being as known to the philosophers of antiquity, but constantly holds it open to correction.[18]

Even a cursory reading of Bonaventurean material reveals yet another difference in his approach to the trinity. The discussion of the trinity, for Bonaventure, is not simply a prelude to theology which plays no significant, constructive role in the rest of theology. It is obvious that every major theological theme is structured by Bonaventure with reference to the mystery of the trinity. The trinity is, in the fullest sense of the word, a structural principle of the Seraphic Doctor's entire theological vision.

More specifically, a style of trinitarian thought that differed from the psychological model of Augustine had been sketched by two early Franciscans, Alexander of Hales and Odo Rigaldus. Following their inspiration, Bonaventure built an alternate trinitarian model by developing seminal ideas found in the writings of Pseudo-Dionysius and Richard of St. Victor. From Pseudo-Dionysius he drew the neo-Platonic principle of the necessary self–diffusion of the good. But the almost impersonal tone of the Dionysian definition of the good was modified by the Victorine mysticism of ecstatic love. From these two sources Bonaventure built his own vision of the trinity in the form of a metaphysics of love.

c. The internal emanations

While Augustine had struggled to conceive of the trinitarian persons as fully equal in every way, Bonaventure gave a peculiar emphasis to the mystery of the Father as the ultimate source of all, both within and without the Godhead. In the neo-Platonic tradition Bonaventure discovered the axiom: "The more a thing is prior, the more fecund it is and the more it is the principle of others."[19] Applied to God, this could be taken to mean that God is the source of all other beings to the degree that the divine reality is first. Since God is first in an absolute sense, the mystery of the divine being is the supremely fruitful source of all created reality. Bonaventure calls this attribute of God *primitas* or "firstness." It is related to fecundity (*fecunditas*). Together, these two concepts describe God as the fountain-head of all that is. As the primal good that exists only in the form of love, God is the creative principle of all created reality (*plenitudo fontalis*).

But, then within the Godhead Bonaventure traces a level of *primitas* back into the depths of the trinity itself where it is the Father who enjoys a "firstness" with respect to the other trinitarian persons. Since, among the persons of the trinity, it is the Father alone who is "not from another," it is in the Father that the most primal level of divine fullness, power, and fecundity lies. In the most basic sense, the Father represents the Godhead as the fontal source from which all else emanates, both the immanent emanations of the trinity itself, and through them the external emanation of creation.[20]

The difference between the Augustinian and the Bonaventurean model appears clearly with the discussion of the procession of the second person. Taking its inspiration from the dialectical structure of human consciousness, the Augustinian model thinks of the first procession as one that occurs *per modum intellectus*. The basic analogy is drawn from the manner in which the human mind generates an "inner word," the word of human consciousness and self-knowledge. This Augustine had called an inner word that exists within us before all vocal words.[21] In the Augustinian tradition, this provided the basic metaphor for expressing the generation of the second person of the trinity if one views God precisely as intellectual being.

In contrast with this, Richard of St. Victor took his point of departure from the statement of St. John: "God is love" (1 Jn 4:8). If God is both love and supremely perfect, the question of the trinity becomes: What is the most perfect form of love? Love, as Richard argues, must be proportionate to its object. Hence, if God's love is infinite, there must be an infinite object proportionate to that love. This cannot be creation, for creation—no matter how great—is and remains finite. Therefore, a solitary divine person would be impossible; for such a divinity would be incapable of fully sharing the divine goodness. Therefore, the perfection of God's love requires some form of plurality within God, some sort of a divine beloved, infinite as the Lover is infinite. Hence, there must be at least two persons in God. But the argument does not end here; for love reaches its perfection not simply when two persons love each other, but when their wills are united in the love of a third. Hence, if God is truly the most perfect form of love, there must be three persons in the one divine nature.

In a way that reflects this Victorine argument as well as the Dionysian vision of the good as "naturally" self-diffusive, Bonaventure describes the first trinitarian procession as an *emanatio per modum naturae, concomitante voluntate*. The second, reflecting the Victorine tradition, is called an *emanatio per modum voluntatis* or *per modum liberalitatis concomitante natura*. The primary principle of the first emanation is the divine nature precisely as the good; the primary principle of the second is the will as free and generous.

In analyzing the trinitarian dynamic as one of love, Bonaventure follows Richard of St. Victor in arguing that the three persons represent three modalities of love. The first is a love that is totally communicative and gratuitous *(amor gratuitus)*. At the other extreme is a form of love that is totally receptive and responsive *(amor debitus)*. And between these is a modality of love that is both communicative and responsive *(amor ab utroque permixtus)*. A similar structure appears when Bonaventure views the persons in terms of origin. There is one person who is origin only. There is one who is originated only. And between them is one who is both originated and originating.

In this almost geometrical pattern, the idea of a *center* begins to emerge. There is one person who lives at the center of the trinity. In this central person lives the fundamental structural law of all that is other than the Father. That person is found in the modality of a love which is both receptive and responsive. If, therefore, the Father is first in the most primal sense, the Son, reflecting the productivity of the Father and the receptiveness of the Spirit, is that person who anticipates all that is other than the Father. This includes the mystery of the inner-trinitarian Spirit and the reality of the created cosmos. This insight will become ever more crucial in Bonaventure's theology. This description of the trinitarian emanations amounts to a metaphysical analysis of the modalities of love. In the course of this analysis the second person is given an emphatically central position. As the Son is intermediate between the Father and the Spirit, so he is intermediate between God and the created world.

The Dionysian tradition has left its traces in the understanding of the emanation of the Son from the Father as the necessary emanation of the divine nature that expresses the fullness of the divine goodness and all that can come to be in the world from out of that goodness. The Victorine tradition has left its traces in the understanding of the emanation of the Spirit as an outpouring of the pure liberality of divine love. Thus, the analysis of the two emanations, in Bonaventure's theology, reflects a dialectical relation between nature and will, between necessity and freedom internal to the mystery of God. It has been argued that the first emanation expresses the radical identity of being and power while the second emanation expresses the radical identity of being, power and will.[22]

Bonaventure's argument might be summarized as follows: God is indeed the supreme good and is therefore, by nature, self-communicative. Thus, the truth of the neo-Platonic philosophical tradition is respected. But the supreme good subsists as a mystery of personal love, the nature of which involves free self-communication. This insight of the Christian religious tradition stands dialectically related to the philosophical tradition. God acts necessarily by virtue of what God is. But God is the Good in the form of personal love. Therefore, the mystery of self-diffusiveness must be articulated in terms of a dialectical relationship between nature and will in God; that is, in the dialectic between self-diffusiveness that is both necessary and free.

By situating necessity and freedom within the Godhead in this dialectical manner, Bonaventure, was able to articulate the immanent mystery of God as self-diffusive love that is entirely adequate to the divine nature within itself, and therefore to envision God as completely free with respect to anything other than the divinity. This is reflected in his insistence on the freedom of God with respect to the entire created order as well as to the order of salvation and grace.

d. The divine missions

Bonaventure's theology as a whole is, to a great extent, a theology of the divine missions. Since the very concept of mission is grounded in the theology of trinitarian emanations, the basic architecture of his theology is trinitarian. To speak of mission means that an eternal emanation has a temporal effect whereby it comes to be known expressly in history. In the strict sense of the word, only the Son and the Spirit can be sent, since only they come forth by way of emanation. Methodologically, it is only from the experience of the historical missions of the Son and the Spirit that Christians come to know the Father in a specifically Christian sense as the ultimate source of all emanation and hence of mission. The entire doctrine of the incarnation is nothing but a discussion of the mission of the Son. The mission of the Spirit is discussed in the doctrine of the church and the doctrine of grace.

The goal of the missions is not only to make the divine persons known to humanity. It is above all aimed at effecting the indwelling of the triune God as a personal presence in the human person and the corresponding transformation of the human person into an ever more perfect similitude of the trinity present to it. Visible mission is directed to the invisible mission of the personal presence of God in the soul of the human person. This is developed extensively in the doctrine of grace.

e. The logic of appropriation

The tradition of trinitarian theology had developed a form of predication called "appropriation." Bonaventure's understanding of appropriation is fully in harmony with his view of trinitarian reality. Appropriation is a form of predication through which something common to all three persons is predicated of one in particular. The primary purpose of such predication, for Bonaventure, is to highlight something of the personal character of a particular divine person. Appropriation depends, therefore, on some insight into the relation between the property of the person and the essential attribute involved. Thus, power, wisdom, and goodness are all essential attributes of the divinity as such. But power has a particular affinity with the property of Father as sourceless Source. And wisdom relates particularly to the Son as the Word of divine truth. And goodness relates to the mystery of the Spirit as that emanation of divine goodness which is by way of liberality. Thus, while these are essential attributes of God, they reflect the order of origin of the persons.

From this basis, Bonaventure was able to build a theological vision which is a clear example of what contemporary theology calls economic trinitarianism. He unfolds this vision under the conviction that God's will is free and unnecessitated relative to the created order, yet God acts in an orderly way. God is, indeed, gratuitous love. But God is also intelligent. From the notion of gratuitous love comes the conviction of the radical contingence of everything outside God. From the notion of intelligence comes the conviction of some sort of order. Both of these convictions are united in Bonaventure's concept of *convenientia*. In the light of this concept, every form of necessity is excluded both as to the structure of the world and as to its history. Nonetheless, Bonaventure's conviction concerning the orderliness of God's works leads him to a position of economic trinitarianism which seeks to delineate as carefully as possible the inner relation between the outer form of historical reality and the deepest content of that history which is the true self-communication to the world of the divine mystery as it is in itself: Father, Son, and Spirit. For, even though God has no internal need of the world, and is not motivated by anything outside the divinity itself, God yet creates a world whose structure and history is an appropriate expression of the mystery of the creative power of the Godhead. Since all of created reality bears some sort of imprint from its trinitarian source, a primary task of theology is to read the book of creation in such a way as to make the trinitarian mystery explicit.

2. Emanation

In the first book of his *Sentence Commentary* Bonaventure expressed a vision of creation that remained with him until the end of his life. Drawing on and expanding the scriptural image *(Eccles* 1:7) of a river which flows from a spring, spreads throughout the land to purify and fructify it, and eventually flows back to its point of origin, Bonaventure presents the outline of his entire theological vision.[23] In sum, the contours of the Christian faith are cast within the neo-Platonic circle of emanation, exemplarity, and return as this philosophical metaphor is reshaped by the Christian vision of faith. Viewed in terms of this symbolic structure, the doctrine of creation is the articulation of the mystery of absolute origin in God and of the beginning of a journey through history to a God-intended destiny. The doctrine of grace, salvation, and eschatological fulfillment constitutes the articulation of the successful completion of the journey. "Illumination is referred back to God in whom it took its origin. And there the circle is completed."[24] Salvation, therefore, is the actualization of the divine aim in creating. Embraced, as it were, by the two arms of the circle is the mystery of exemplarity, for all of created reality bears the marks of its divine origin and destiny within itself in a variety of ways.

a. The external emanation

The doctrine of creation, for Bonaventure, presupposes the doctrine of the immanent emanations that constitute the mystery of the trinity. This, in turn, is the explication of the mystery of God as the supreme Good which is fecund and productive both within the Godhead, producing the trinity, and without the Godhead, producing the cosmos as a reflection of the triune God. The causality of the creative principle is threefold, for it must act from itself (efficient cause), in accordance with itself (exemplary cause), and because of itself (final cause).[25] This triple causality is related to God's power, wisdom, and goodness, which, in turn, are appropriated to the persons of the trinity. By power, God creates; by wisdom, God rules; and by reason of goodness, God brings creation to completion.[26]

More specific themes of Bonaventure's theology of creation are set out in the following: "The whole of the universe has been produced in being; in time; from nothing; by one, supreme principle alone, whose power, though immense, has disposed all things with a 'certain measure, number, and weight.'"[27]

In clear and pointed language, this text sets out the basis from which Bonaventure will discuss alternate philosophical and theological positions concerning the origin of the created universe. The text is, first, an affirmation of creation in its most metaphysical sense as the act of the divine artist alone who confers existence after simple and unqualified non-existence. In the most basic sense of the word, therefore, creation is not the formation of beings from already existing materials. As the act in which finite existence is grounded, the creative act is in an unqualified sense the only source of finite being.

b. Creation a divine prerogative

Like most of the major thinkers of his age, Bonaventure understood the act of creation in the strict sense to be proper to the power of God alone. But in a development that seems peculiar to his own theology, he argued that the power of God is revealed specifically in the fact that God creates two extreme forms of finite being—material beings and spiritual being—and particularly in the fact that God creates between these two extremes a finite being in whom the extremes are reconciled in a harmonious way. That central creature in whom the extremes are united is humanity.[28] Not only does this indicate something of Bonaventure's vision of God's creative power, it suggests clearly the broad structure of his hierarchical view of the created order, including the central position of humanity within it. "Since humanity shares with all creatures, and since all things are created for humanity," it follows from several distinct perspectives that humanity can be said to hold a central place in the hierarchy of created beings.[29] This question will be treated further in the next section concerning exemplarity.

c. The divine aim

Bonaventure's elaboration of the trinitarian doctrine suggests why it is that he could maintain two convictions that ran counter to the thesis of an eternal and necessary world espoused by Avicenna and other Islamic scholars under the influence of Aristotle. First, a God who is tri-une as Bonaventure conceives God to be does not need the world in order to be God. It was his vision of the infinite, immanent fertility of divine love that allowed Bonaventure to break out of the logic of a nec-essary world. If the dialectic of necessity and freedom could be placed within the flow of life immanent to the divinity in emanations that are both necessary and free, then God can be thought of as infinitely self-communicative internally. Such a God could be entirely free with respect to anything outside the divinity. Given that, the second convic-tion follows. If there is a world, it does not exist necessarily but only by virtue of the free creative power of divine love. The world is radically contingent both in terms of its existence and in terms of its specific form. The act of creation can only be a free act of divine goodness and love. Is it possible to specify what this means in any further detail? Simply put, if God does not need the world in order to be God, why does God call the world into being?

Negatively, Bonaventure makes several points with unambiguous clarity. Nothing outside God serves as a motive for the divine act of cre-ation. Neither does God create out of any internal need, as if God were to gain something for the divinity itself. Positively, the Seraphic Doctor includes two dialectically related elements in his answer. These are expressed in the, words: *manifestare* and *participare*.[30] In the act of creat-ing, God calls forth a world that would manifest the divine glory. And God creates beings who are capable of participating in that glory. The first is Bonaventure's description of what is commonly referred to as "objective glory." The second is his description of what is commonly spo-ken of as "subjective glory."

When these two statements of the "divine aim" are separated and the first one is taken in isolation, the idea of a God who creates for the sake of "objective glory" invariably awakens the feeling that such a God must be terribly selfish or self-centered. Two things must be kept in mind. First, we are dealing with metaphorical language. And second, the two statements, in Bonaventure's view, are internally related to each other. Concerning the first, metaphors should never be pushed too far or taken in too literal a sense. Concerning the second, neither of these statements ought to be taken in isolation from the other.

If we imagine God as an artist and think of the way in which a great work of art says something about the artist simply by the fact of its existence as a beautiful object, we might gain a better insight into what is meant by objective glory. If the world is truly an objective expression of the goodness, truth, and beauty that resides in the mystery of God, then it cannot exist without—by the mere fact of its existence—saying something about the one who produced it. In this sense, it cannot exist without giving "objective" glory to God.

But this needs to be related immediately to the second "aim." For all good medieval theologians were convinced that a book that did not have a reader hardly made sense as a book. Similarly, a world that manifested the glory of God but did not include some creature capable of perceiving and reveling in that glory would make little sense. A world that "manifested" without the possibility of "participating" would, indeed, be a sort of selfish whim on the part of God. But a world that "manifested" in such a way that "participation" was possible could be seen as an expression of the gratuitous love of God who creates so that creatures might eventually come to participate in the mystery of the divine life itself. Thus, for Bonaventure, the most basic reason for the existence of created reality is simply the goodness of God who calls forth creatures capable of participating in the divine life, and places them in a world which is capable of awakening in them an awareness of and an active desire for such participation.

d. Creation and time

As the absolute source of finite being, the act of creation is also the beginning of time; for temporality is that mode of existence proper to finite beings. The possibility of an eternal world was part of the philosophical vision which Christian intellectuals in the thirteenth century were engaged within the development of their theological systems. It is commonly thought that Aristotle held that the world is eternal. Whether this is the case or not is unclear to Bonaventure. If Aristotle held that the world did not begin of its own natural power, he was correct, says Bonaventure. But if the Philosopher held that the world had no beginning of any kind whatsoever, he was definitely wrong.[31] Bonaventure was convinced that the very notion of an eternal production *ex nihilo* involved a logical contradiction.[32] There is, indeed, eternal production; but it is not a production *ex nihilo*. Rather, it is a process that is totally immanent to the eternal, triune God. The source of this production is the Father, and the term of this production is found in the persons of the Son and the Spirit, both of whom are co-eternal with the Father. This is a production, therefore, that involves no beginning. To be produced *ex nihilo*, on the other hand, means at least to undergo the metaphysical change of moving from non-being to being. That which is produced *ex nihilo*, therefore, begins to exist. It cannot be eternal. If faith provides clues into the nature of reality, then the logical implication of the concept of creation makes an eternal creation *ex nihilo* logically impossible.

While Bonaventure offers a number of philosophical arguments to support his view, it is very likely that his most basic concern is theological. Ratzinger has argued that Bonaventure's argument involved a theological understanding of history that differed from that of Aristotle who saw time and history as the realm of chance. The concept of time, therefore, was defined in terms that are more theological than philosophical.[33] Time is listed by Bonaventure among the first four things to be created. Time is not only the neutral measure of duration, as the Aristotelian view suggests. It is above all, for Bonaventure, the measure of going-forth.[34] To be a creature means to be situated somewhere on the circular line of emanation from and return to God. And events that take place in time are not just random occurrences but are ordered to a particular end which God has established for creation. From the beginning, creation unfolds as history, and time is the measure of where one stands in the historical movement toward God.

e. An ordered cosmos

Finally, though the power of God is infinite and beyond measure or human calculation, the product of that creative power, vast as it may be and rich in varieties of beings, is stamped with a certain intelligent order.[35] There is, first, an ordering among creatures with respect to each other. Over and above this, all things are ordered to their proper end.[36] More specifically, in Bonaventure's view, the created order reflects the order of the persons within the creative Trinity of which the entire universe is a reflection. That trinitarian relation is seen particularly in the threefold causality whereby the world is related to its Creator: efficient, exemplary, and final causality.

Bonaventure's understanding of the order of the created universe emphasizes the centrality of humanity. This seems almost inevitable when creation is viewed in terms of its origin in an intelligent God and in terms of its finality in the spiritual union between that intelligent God and intelligent creatures. If, in some sense, this offers clues as to why there is anything at all other than God, it is understandable that some form of hierarchical ranking would be found in relation to this vision of origin and destiny. In Bonaventure's terms, the material universe is simply incapable in itself of experiencing this destiny; for it is, by its very nature, incapable of any personal relation with God. It is, however, involved in this destiny, but only in and through the destiny of the spiritual creation. The divine wisdom, therefore, disposes all things in the universe in reference to this finality.

In a very compact statement, Bonaventure expresses his understanding of humanity's place in the ordered structure of the universe. In describing how corporal beings are formed through the influence of the heavenly bodies, he moves through the levels of minerals to plant life and on to sentient life. At the high point of this cosmic process, he focuses on what he sees as its most perfect result, the formation of human bodies. About this he writes:

> The heavenly bodies influence human bodies which are disposed for the most noble form, namely, the rational soul. The desire of the entire sentient, corporal nature is ordained to this form (the rational soul) and finds its end in this form. So it is that through this form, which is an existing, living, sentient, and intelligent form, the human body may be led back as if in the manner of an intelligible circle to its point of origin in which it is brought to perfection and beatified.[37]

From this, Bonaventure concludes:

> It is true without any doubt that we are the end of all existing things, and all bodily things exist to serve humanity by enkindling in human beings the fire of love and praise for the one who has made all things, and by whose providence all things are governed. So, this sensible machine of bodily beings has been formed as a sort of home for humanity by the supreme architect until such time as humanity should arrive at that 'house not made by human hands... in heaven.'[38]

What sounds at first like an unrelenting, anthropocentric charter for the human exploitation of the material universe is immediately defused by the specification of the manner in which the universe ought to serve humanity. The material world stands most properly at the service of humanity when it enables human beings to realize the end of God's creative activity by awakening in them the conscious appreciation, love, and praise for the Giver of the gift of created existence. It is thus that humanity gives a conscious, loving voice to what otherwise would remain a mute creation. In this sense, the destiny of the material cosmos is intertwined with that of humanity.

As that being in which the extremes of created spirit and materiality are united, humanity is related not only to the material universe but to the world of the angels as well. As created spirits whose spiritual faculties have God as their object, the angels can be said to be equal to humanity.[39] As pure, created spirits that have no orientation to union with matter, the angels can be seen as more perfect than humanity.[40] But in as far as humanity unites in itself both the world of spirit and that of materiality, humanity alone is a "microcosm" in the proper sense of the word. Viewed from this final perspective, humanity is said to be superior to the angels.[41] The destiny of the angelic world is related to human destiny in a number of ways. First, Bonaventure shares the common doctrine which sees the angels to be deputed by God as helpers for humanity on the journey through history. Second, Bonaventure sees the ranks of saved humanity as filling up the places in the angelic hierarchies vacated by the fallen angels.[42]

The world of angelic reality is structured by Bonaventure along the lines suggested in the work of Pseudo-Dionysius. He envisions three groups of angels, each including three choirs. The structure of the angelic hierarchies is based on the way in which each group and each choir reflects a property of God. This understanding of hierarchy involves no superimposed levels with no relation to one another, but rather a process of mediation through which the higher levels of the hierarchy function as channels of divine influence to the lower levels of the hierarchy, It is through the chain of being that makes up these hierarchies that the influence of God streams forth to reach into all areas of the spiritual life and to bring about more perfect God-likeness in all God's spiritual creatures.[43]

f. Universal hylomorphism

All finite beings are subject to change. Therefore, any theology or philosophy of creation must provide some insight into the dynamic of change. In his attempt to do this, Bonaventure emphasized that created, finite beings include not only bodily beings, but created, spiritual beings as well. How can one explain the changeable character of all finite beings, spiritual as well as corporal?

Under the influence of Alexander of Hales, Bonaventure argued in favor of a theory of universal hylomorphism. Everything that is subject to change is, to that extent, in a state of potentiality. This is true of angels and of the human soul just as it is true of corporal being. But if matter is the name for the principle of potentiality as such and not simply the name for the principle of potentiality in corporal beings, then matter in itself is neither spiritual nor corporal. It can be informed by either spiritual or corporal forms. In speaking of that sort of matter involved in spiritual creatures, Bonaventure uses the term "spiritual matter."[44] All changeable beings, therefore, including the angels and the human soul, involve some form of hylomorphic composition.[45] This theory is not only a metaphysical issue for Bonaventure. It serves a specifically religious-theological purpose as well, since it provides a way of clarifying the difference between the mystery of God as Pure Act and the essential mutability of every created being.

g. Light metaphysics and plurality of form

In developing his understanding of the structure of created beings further, Bonaventure departed from the more common understanding of Aristotelian hylomorphism in another significant way. Instead of accepting the doctrine of the unity of form, Bonaventure drew from R. Grosseteste and the Oxford Franciscans a form of light-metaphysics. According to this view, creatures are, indeed, composed of matter and form, but not necessarily of a single form. According to Bonaventure, the first form of all corporal beings is the form of light. Light in this instance is designated by the Latin word *lux* and is distinguished from *lumen* (radiation) and *color* (the empirical form in which light is perceived). In Bonaventure's view, light is the most general form of all bodies, and is indeed the most noble of all forms. There is, in fact, a hierarchy among creatures determined by the degree to which each is informed by light.

Hence, in the world of the physical cosmos, the highest and most noble level of the material universe is the empyrean sphere. As its very name implies, this is the fiery sphere; it is the realm of pure light.[46]

Opaque as earthly beings seem to be, it remains the case nonetheless that each being contains something of the form of light. "All bodies naturally participate in the light."[47] Bonaventure envisions an influence of light at all levels of the material universe, regulating even the formation of the earthly minerals. In a sense, light prepares matter to receive other forms. It is through the influence of light that all complex bodies are generated out of the four basic elements, for "the power of light harmonizes the contrary qualities of the elements in composite beings."[48]

This theory of light implies a rejection of the Aristotelian theory of the unity of form which would be favored by Aquinas. In fact, Bonaventure argued in favor of a plurality of forms in a position similar to that of Avicenna, Avicebron, and Albert the Great. If light is understood to be the first and most general form, then, besides light, each individual being has a special form. It follows that each being has at least these two forms.[49] The theory of the plurality of forms in Bonaventure involves a distinct understanding of the function of form. The function of form is not merely to give rise to one specific being. But, precisely in forming specific being, it prepares or disposes matter for new possibilities. There is, indeed, such a thing as a final form. But this is arrived at only at the end of a process involving a multiplicity of forms along the way. For example, Bonaventure did not accept the position that such a noble form as the human soul could be united directly with prime matter without the work of intervening forms. This position he maintained until his final lectures where he referred to the opposite view as unreasonable or insane.[50]

h. Seminal reasons

This suggests that Bonaventure thought of matter not as inert but as having an inner dynamism toward change, and eventually toward union with spiritual reality. This dynamic orientation he spoke of as an "appetite."[51] In a broader sense, he saw the level of material being as a seedbed laden with possible forms of beings that will unfold in time. Here he adopted Augustine's theory of seminal reasons to express the active dynamism of matter. The Augustinian theory is explained by means of the Aristotelian principle that forms are educed from the potency of matter. Rather than posit an immediate, direct action of God for the creation of each new form in the course of the development of created beings, Bonaventure posited the presence of forms as virtual realities in the matter from which individual beings are constituted. Thus, material reality is not inert and passive but is full of active powers virtually present from the beginning and educed into an actual diversity of beings in the course of history through the agency of specific creatures. All forms with the exception of the human soul are co-created with matter and have resided in matter virtually since the creation of the world. The eduction of a new form does not mean the creation of a new essence, but merely the appearance of a new disposition.[52]

3. Exemplarity

If, at one level, Bonaventure sums up his metaphysical vision in three words—emanation, exemplarity, return—at another level he argues that there is a sense in which the most basic metaphysical question is simply that of the exemplar, or the original model in whose likeness all things have been shaped. Here the great Platonic tradition is given a specifically Christian content; for, as is clear from Bonaventure's trinitarian theology, the exemplar in a preeminent sense is the Word who lives at the very center of God and who, as incarnate, is the center of all created reality. Here is the key to Bonaventure's conviction that the greatest metaphysical question cannot be answered—and perhaps not even asked—in ignorance of the incarnation. We are here at the core of a vision which involves a truly cosmic Christology. The reality of Christ pertains to the very structure of reality: as Word, to the reality of God; as incarnate Word, to the reality of the universe created by God.

Bonaventure's understanding of exemplarity operates at two interrelated levels: first, there is a trinitarian exemplarity; and second, there is the specifically Christological exemplarity. The basis for both types of exemplarity is rooted in the doctrine of the divine Ideas.

a. Divine Ideas

Bonaventure's treatment of the necessity of the divine Ideas is deeply indebted to the tradition of Augustine which, in turn, is heir to the Platonic vision of antiquity. In its philosophical form, exemplarity postulated a realm of archetypal reality which transcended material beings and which was reflected in a shadowy way by the sensible things of the empirical world. For the Christian doctrine of exemplarity, this Platonic world of archetypal realities was placed inside God and became identified with the eternal, creative Ideas in the mind of God. God was understood to be an intelligent creator who produced things through Ideas much as a human artisan produces an artifact that reflects an idea in the artisan's mind.[53] The question of the divine Ideas, then, is the question of the original model in the mind of the divine Artist which is reflected in the objects of creation in various ways.

In Bonaventure's theology, the divine Ideas are closely related to the emanation of the divine Word within the trinity. In reality there is only one divine Idea. It is simply identical with the full act of God's self-knowledge. In this act of self-knowledge God knows all that the divinity *is* within itself and all that it can do *ad extra*. Since this divine self-knowledge is simply God's being at the high point of its self-awareness, it can be called a likeness of God that is fully equal to God. In this sense, there *is* only one Idea, and its content is infinite. But in so far as the divinity, knowing itself, knows all that *it* can produce in the created realm, both those things that will in fact be produced and those which are mere possibilities that will never exist, it is possible to speak of a multiplicity of Ideas expressing this relation of the mind of God to the world of creation. As the representation of God and the model of all that God can and will in fact produce, the divine Idea is called the Word of God. As such, the Idea *is* simply the truth of all things, both the truth of God and the truth of the created world grounded in the divine truth.[54]

On first hearing, this may sound quite similar to the Augustinian psychological model of the trinity. Yet there is a considerable difference of emphasis. The model of Augustine has a stronger contemplative tone and suggests the divine mind resting in itself. The model of Bonaventure, with its Dionysian and Victorine background, suggests that the self-consciousness of God is that of a being who is by nature self-communicative love. The divinity is aware of itself, then, precisely as fruitful, expansive love. It follows, therefore, that in that first, necessary emanation of love that is the generation of the Word (Idea), the inner tendency of love to be self-communicative is expressed both in the primal Idea, and in its tendency to freely expand outside the realm of the divine life into the world of created reality. Thus, it is not surprising that Bonaventure describes the Ideas in terms of an almost active tendency to be projected outward.[58] As love, God's being is expressive being. The divine being is being that presses outward from within to its otherness. The first otherness is the immanent Word who can be called the otherness of the Father. The second otherness is the created universe. The universe is, therefore, the external language-system in which the content of the immanent Word is expressed outside of God. It is, in Bonaventure's metaphorical language, a book written outside. The content of the external book is the internal book of God's immanent Word.[56] The divine Ideas, then, are endowed with the expressive power of the divine nature. This helps to clarify the frequency with which Bonaventure speaks of the Word as the eternal Art and to use the very active metaphors of artistic creation for the creative dimension of God.[57]

b. Universal analogy

The doctrine of exemplary Ideas leads inevitably to a doctrine of universal analogy. Each individual object in the created world and the whole of the world taken together in unity reflect something of the creative Artist who, in the very act of creation, has given external expression to the internal world of the divine Ideas. The same is true of the history of the world. Even though creation can never give adequate expression to God's act of self-expression, there is a sense in which the cosmos, even in its limited condition, is an external objectification of the divine consciousness.

c. Levels of trinitarian exemplarity

It is possible to speak of exemplarity in the philosophical sense in a way that makes no reference to the trinity or to Christology. Bonaventure's view of exemplarity, however, is thoroughly shaped by his Christian convictions. Hence, his doctrine of exemplarity is developed very explicitly in both trinitarian and Christological terms. As we have already seen, the creative source of the world is the mystery of the creative love that is the trinity. We have seen this relation between God and world first reflected in the threefold causal relation of efficient, exemplary, and final causality. But Bonaventure's reflection on the structure of created realities searches out trinitarian reflections at ever deeper levels. The text cited at the beginning of this discussion of creation indicates a vague triadic structure: all things are created with a certain "measure, number, and weight." This implies a very distant echo of the trinitarian source of creation. From here, Bonaventure leads the reader eventually to a remarkable vision of the outcome of the spiritual journey: "Therefore it follows that eternal life consists in this alone, that the rational spirit, which emanates from the most blessed trinity and is a likeness of the trinity, should return after the manner of a certain intelligible circle—through memory, intelligence, and will—to the most blessed trinity by God-conforming glory."[58] Here the trinitarian intimations to be found in the material world come to the fullest expression in the world of the human spirit and its grace-filled journey into God. And the text offers hints as to how Bonaventure employs the Augustinian trinitarian analysis. Augustine had suggested two ternary structures in his analysis of human consciousness: *mens, notitia, amor,* and *memoria, intelligentia, voluntas.* It is in these triadic structures of the world of the human spirit that creation comes closest to God through its awareness of and response to God's personal, gracious presence mediated through creation. While Augustine applied these triadic patterns primarily to the construction of the psychological model of the trinity, Bonaventure used them most commonly in their more basic anthropological sense.

Between the two extremes of trinitarian exemplarity indicated above, Bonaventure describes the whole of the cosmos as a hierarchy of beings, each reflecting the trinity in some way, but not all reflecting it in the same way. The principle on which the hierarchy is built is the degree of similarity between the creature and the Creator, between the copy and the model after which the copy is shaped. Bonaventure writes: "the created world is like a book in which its Maker, the trinity, shines forth, is represented, and can be read at three levels of expression: namely, as a vestige, as an image, and as a similitude. The reality of the vestige is found in all creatures; that of the image is found only in intellectual beings or rational spirits; and that of the similitude is found only in those creatures which have become conformed to God."[59]

These distinctions are to be understood in the following way. Every creature, because of its inherent unity, truth, and goodness, reflects God in terms of a threefold causality: efficient, exemplary, and final. This is not yet a reflection of the Trinity in the Christian sense. But it is a reflection of the three-fold causal activity of the one God. Such a reflection, therefore, is a shadowy anticipation of what will become explicitly trinitarian in the Christian context; for Christianity understands this one God to be triune. In Bonaventure's terms, such a reflection may be called a *vestige* (footprint).

Beyond this level, there are some creatures that reflect God not only as their cause but as their object as well. This includes the world of created spiritual beings whose spiritual powers are directed to God as the truth to be known, the goodness to be embraced in love, and the eternal beauty to be reveled in with joy. This level of representation is found in the angels as pure, created spirits and in humanity particularly by reason of the faculties of memory, intellect, and will. These faculties have God not only as their cause but also as the object which moves and regulates them.[60] Such a creature is called an *imago* (image). This level of creation is understood to represent God more closely and distinctly than a mere vestige.

Up to this point, Bonaventure is dealing with the structure of the created order precisely as creation. The universe as the result of God's creative artistry is structured in a way that reflects the divine mind in ever greater depth and intensity as one ascends the hierarchical structure from opaque matter to embodied spirit. The universe thus conceived has a profoundly sacramental character, for even at its most material level it has the power to lead the spirit of humanity to God.

There is yet a further level in Bonaventure's vision of exemplarity which moves from the level of created nature to the level of grace. It is at this level that Bonaventure speaks of the *similitudo* (similitude).[61] This level of God-conformed existence is found in every sanctified creature and hence in the good angels and in human beings who receive and respond to God's gift of grace. This will be treated in more detail below. For now suffice it to say that the life of grace is understood to involve a deepening and transforming of the image found in human nature into an ever deeper, more personal conformity to the eternal Exemplar.

Not only is the metaphysical structure of created reality a reflection of the trinity, but history also reflects the same mystery. Bonaventure here incorporates the triadic historical structure of the theological tradition and distinguishes three ages of history: the age of the law of nature; the age of the law of the scriptures; and the age of the law of grace.[62] In accordance with the logic of appropriation, in a broad sense each of these may be related to the trinity as a whole. But in a specific sense each historical age corresponds to one of the divine persons. Under this broad triadic structure, he situates the Augustinian schema of six stages of salvation history, culminating in the seventh age of the Sabbath rest. As we will see below, this structure will be transformed in his later works through the influence of Joachim of Fiore and through

Bonaventure's own attempts to come to a more adequate understanding of St. Francis and the meaning of the Franciscan Order in the sweep of history.

d. Christological exemplarity

The issue of exemplarity, which is first of all a philosophical matter, quickly becomes a theological issue and is inseparable from Bonaventure's doctrine of the trinity. God is the exemplar, and God exists always and only as a trinity. But the road does not end there. There is a sense in which the trinitarian exemplarity is compacted into that person who stands at the center of the trinity: the Word, or the Son. The primal relation in which all other relation is grounded is the mutual relation between Father and Son. If the Father is identical with totally self-communicative love, and the Spirit is a love that is totally receptive, between these two modes of love stands a form of love that is both receptive and responsive. And that is the Son. Thus, the mystery of the Son reflects both the reality of the Father and that of the Spirit. As the Father's self-expression, the Word is the openness of the Father to the other in all its forms. As the primal self-expression of the Father, the Son is the primal *ratio exprimendi*; and "every creature cries out the eternal generation."[63]

To speak of the second person as Son is to speak of him solely in terms of his relation to the Father. To speak of the same person as Word is to speak of him in terms of all the other forms of divine self-expression which are co-spoken in the primal speech of the Father.[64] In summary, the Son of the Father's love is the eternal Word and the Image of the Father in such a way that he is simultaneously the ground of all other relations. In as far as the entire mystery of the trinity is compacted into the Word, he is the exemplar of creation which, while spoken in the Word, bears the stamp of the entire trinity which finds its expression in the Word.

As Bonaventure argues in several places, the possibility of God's creative activity rests in the triune nature of the divinity. This is but another way of saying that if the divine mystery were not supremely communicative in itself, it could not communicate being to the finite. But the weight of this supremely communicative being is focused in the emanation of the Son-Word who is the openness of God to all that is other. Only a self-communicative God can be a creator in Bonaventure's view, and the weight of that self-communication falls upon the Word as the necessary and exemplary condition for all created being. Thus, when this Word becomes incarnate in the history of Jesus, the principle of all otherness appears in that history. The center of God is now at the center of created reality.

4. Return

a. General statement

The world moves out from the inner-divine movement of creative love into its own existence. As the world pours out from God, it is shaped in the likeness of the divine exemplar. And the movement out from God is internally oriented to the return of creation to its divine source. What was originally the neo-Platonic circle of emanation and return has now become the overarching framework of the Christian theology of creation *(exitus)* and salvation *(reditus)*. The circle is a symbolic expression of the conviction that creation is the movement of finite being from nothing into historical existence and ultimately to that fullness of personal life in union with God that Christians understand to be salvation. Creation and salvation, though distinguishable conceptually, are inseparably related. In its fullest sense, salvation is the actualization of the deepest potential that lies at the heart of created reality by reason of the creative love of God.

This circular, neo-Platonic metaphor is set in the general framework of economic trinitarianism described earlier. This relation between creation and salvation is grounded in the unity of the Word that stands as the ontological condition for all of God's action *ad extra*. The visible creation is the objective expression of the Word that lies at the center of the divinity. There is a unity that binds the eternal mystery of the Word with all created existence and all human knowledge, for all of these are in some way related to the reality of the Word. It is the same Word, in varying forms and degrees of intensity, that sounds forth from God from the beginning of creation through the history of humanity to the incarnation of the Word in the history to Jesus. It is the same Word that lies at the heart of the church as a community of faith endeavoring to shape itself and its life around the mystery of Jesus, the Word incarnate. The theology of the return of creation to God is, in essence, the theology of history. If we move this line of thought but a step further, it appears that eschatology is the attempt to articulate that point at which the curve of creation and history bends back on its point of origin. It is the doctrine of the ultimate fulfillment of the created order.

If one envisions the doctrine of creation as the story of the journey of created reality from God into history and back to God, the same metaphor serves to express the contours of the spiritual journey whereby, in the human microcosm, the destiny of the macrocosm is worked out. If the visible creation is the objectification of the spiritual Ideas of God, humanity in its spiritual powers is, as it were, the subjectivity of the created world. Humanity is that point at which creation has become capable of reading the mind of God in the book of the universe. If the objective world is the diffusion into multiplicity of what is fundamentally one in God, the drawing of the multiplicity of creation back into a unity in the human soul so that the world comes back into harmony with God is the goal of the spiritual and of the cosmic journey. The world comes back to God in and through the human journey. God has invested humanity with an exalted destiny.

But between creation and the return is the historical fall of humanity. Thus, the world in which we exist is not only a created and finite world. It is a fallen world as well. We find all our relations with ourselves, with others, and with the physical cosmos to be opaque and distorted. Hence, we find ourselves in our historical condition to be inadequate to the noble task God has given us.

The return of creation to God, then, is in essence a journey through history, and the fulfillment of the universe is inseparably related with that of humanity. How, then, are we equipped for the journey? The answer to that question lies in Bonaventure's understanding of human nature. And if we find ourselves to be inadequate to our task, how are we to meet our inadequacy and overcome it? For Christian faith, this is the issue of the salvific meaning of Christ. How, then, does Christ relate to this human and cosmic context?

b. Anthropology

Central to Bonaventure's understanding of humanity is the conviction that the human person is created as an image of God. This fact is reflected in the unity of the soul and its trinity of powers: memory, intellect, and will.[65] Memory is understood here in a larger sense than we normally give to the word. We commonly think of memory as the power to retain a consciousness of the past. For Bonaventure, the term certainly includes that. But in his usage, it embraces also our awareness of the present and some fore-knowledge of the future.[66] Beyond this and in a deeply Augustinian sense, memory is seen to be that place in the soul in which it holds some of the most basic principles of intellectual thought and the axioms of the sciences. These are not to be thought of as objects of conscious, objective awareness, but as *a priori* principles that the human mind uses in shaping its conscious knowledge.

Viewed as the power that embraces past, present, and future, therefore, memory bears a certain analogy with God's eternity. And viewed in terms of the principles of cognition which it contains, memory is one the most primal levels of preconscious contact with the divine Ideas.[67]

The power of the intellect is related to the cognitive functions of the soul. Its task is to understand the terms, propositions, and inferences by which human knowers structure their knowledge and give it verbal expression, and even develop it further by means of logical reasoning.[68] The intellect, therefore, is related to judgments about the reality of things. Such judgments are about the being of things. When the process of judgment is carried out fully, the intellect arrives at a concept of being in the most basic sense; that is, it comes to the concept of absolute being. A similar conclusion comes from the analysis of syllogistic reasoning. The conclusion, for Bonaventure, indicates that the intellect is in contact with a divine principle which illumines the human intellect and enables it to know with a certitude which the intellect itself cannot account for.

The function of the will or the elective faculty is found in deliberation, judgment, and desire.[69] These three activities are involved in the process of coming to proper judgments about the good. Such judgments are made in the light of laws that transcend the soul itself. And the desire of the human heart directs it toward that which is the highest good. Hence, the analysis of the elective faculty, like that of the intellect, indicates a close relation between the human soul and the reality of God as supreme truth and goodness.

By reason of these three faculties, therefore, human beings may be said to be created in the image of God and may be seen as *capax Dei*. Particularly by virtue of our intellect and will we are equipped to discover truth and embrace goodness. We find ourselves situated in a world of material beings. Our task is to discover the truth and goodness of reality first in and through the visible universe; then in and through the interior world of human consciousness and in the transformation of the soul and its powers through grace; and ultimately in the purely spiritual world of God. By so doing, we align our human reality with the truth and goodness that is God. While that alignment is first of all a matter of the soul, the body is involved in it indirectly. Ultimately the entire material cosmos is involved. And that alignment of creation with God is the goal of the spiritual journey. This journey, as it is described in the *Itinerarium*, reaches a high point in the most impressive meditations on the mystery of the trinity and of Christ, ending in what Bonaventure sees as a truly experiential knowledge of God in mystical union. At this point, Bonaventure reaches to the Dionysian tradition to speak of a knowledge of the divine in darkness.[70] The entire cosmos has become a ladder through which the human spirit can climb up the hierarchy of created reality to the supreme Good, the mystery of the trinity that is mediated to us through the mystery of Christ, there to rest in loving, contemplative union with God.

While the *Itinerarium* presents the return to God as the journey of the individual soul, the *Collations on the Hexaemeron* situates the dynamic of this individual journey in the broader context of world history. Reflecting the influence of Joachim of Fiore's theology of history, Bonaventure is arguing here about a goal not only for the individual but also for a larger community which he calls the *ecclesia contemplativa*. It is in this contemplative, mystical moment that the world, through humanity, is brought back to God.

c. The mystery of Christ and the return

It hardly needs to be argued that the spiritual journey of St. Francis of Assisi was centered around the figure of Jesus Christ. Inspired by the Christ-centered spirituality of their founder, the early Franciscan theologians gave distinctive traits to the theological image of Christ. Among those working in the middle of the thirteenth century, none carried out this theological task with greater consistency or power than Bonaventure. With this the analysis of the return of creation moves beyond what might seem to be a purely philosophical analysis or a metaphysical meditation on being. It now takes on specific characteristics drawn from the history of Christ. Moving from the level of a Christ-centered spirituality, Bonaventure develops a conscious statement of the principles implied in such a spirituality and unfolds its systematic implications in a stunning theological vision that is both personal and cosmic, both symbolic and metaphysical, both deeply spiritual and remarkably speculative in character.

1. Christ the center

Much of Bonaventure's Christological insight is synthesized in his concept of Christ as the center. The seeds of this vision are present already in his early *Commentary on John*, particularly in the explanation of the prologue of that Gospel. There the Seraphic Doctor offers a thoroughly Logos-centered theology of revelation.[71] In the broadest sense, God's revelation is found in the whole of the created universe. In a more specific sense, it is found in human nature. But in its most adequate form, it is found in the person of Jesus Christ.

Undergirding Bonaventure's vision is the conviction that all of God is communication *ad extra* takes place through the mystery of the divine Logos which is the immanent self-expression of God. All external expression of God is a form of symbolic communication of the immanent self-expression of God. Therefore, while there is a growth in the process of historical revelation, there is a principle of continuity that relates all forms of revelation to one another positively. Cosmic revelation is not nullified by the biblical revelation, nor by the revelation brought by Christ. Rather, in Bonaventure's view, the original, cosmic revelation has been rendered dark and opaque through the reality of sin. The book of cosmic revelation has become illegible, like an unknown language. One of the principal functions of the historical revelation of biblical history is to enable humanity to read the primal revelation of creation in an appropriate way. The book of nature is not nullified but is made legible again by historical revelation.[72]

This understanding of the revelatory character of creation and of history is held together by the affirmation of the identity of the divine Word as *increatum*, *incarnatum*, and *inspiratum*.[73] As *increatum*, the eternal Word lies at the very center of the mystery of the triune God. As *incarnatum*, the same Word lies at the center of creation, both in a metaphysical sense and in an historical sense. As *inspiratum*, the same Word resides at the center of the spiritual life by the power of the divine Spirit through whom the Word becomes the *verbum inspiratum* in the human heart. It is, however, through the history of Jesus of Nazareth as the incarnate Word that the mystery of the Eternal Word comes to most explicit consciousness. In Bonaventure's own formula, Jesus is both the temporal and the eternal exemplar.[74] His historical life is the exegesis in time of the eternal mystery in which all created reality is grounded. As the historical manifestation of the eternal exemplar of all reality other than the Father, Christ offers more than a mere moral example. He embodies the very principle of all moral existence in the historical style of his life.

It is, therefore, from the history of Jesus that Christians learn to read the genuine meaning of the book of creation, both in nature and in human reality. And as they come to shape their lives after the historical life of Jesus, they enter ever more deeply into personal union with the Word that lies at the center both of created and of uncreated reality.

From this it becomes clear why Bonaventure, in his own way, would share the common Franciscan concern for the humanity of Jesus. For that humanity, in Bonaventure's view, is the key that unlocks to us the meaning of all reality: created and uncreated. This is not simply a concern for a human nature in the abstract. Rather, it is a concern for the actual shape which the life of Jesus took in history. Following the inspiration of Francis, Bonaventure emphasizes the significance of the poverty of Jesus and particularly the mystery of the cross. This is an issue not only of piety and spirituality but of systematic theology as well. For in a very particular way the mystery of the cross suggests insights into the mystery of divine love as well as insights into the dynamism of the spiritual way to God.

This highly Christocentric vision is unfolded by Bonaventure at two distinct but interrelated levels. The first level is that of the spirituality of the *imitatio Christi*. Here Bonaventure provides an account of the spirituality of Francis. He then searches for the scriptural underpinnings of that spirituality. It is here that the paradigmatic significance of the life of Jesus becomes obvious. The moral teaching and example of Jesus have normative significance in the spiritual search for an authentic human existence. Spirituality is, above all, the journey of the human soul "into God." And that journey is made by conforming one's personal life to the mystery of the eternal Word enfleshed in the history of Jesus. (See section g below for further details on spirituality.)

As a university scholar, Bonaventure discussed the standard questions that the theological analysis of the hypostatic union must attempt to clarify. From one perspective, this represents his attempt to provide a grounding for the spirituality of *imitatio* and its attendant Christ-image. In what sense can the living of such a spirituality draw one into a healing and integrating relation to reality? From another perspective, this project involves questions about the meaning of such terms as nature, person, hypostasis, and various forms of union. How shall one conceive the mystery of Christ in its essential structure without doing violence to God or to creation? At this level, Bonaventure demonstrates his exceptional ability to employ all the tools of philosophical analysis in the service of theology.

2. *Speculative Christology*

It is significant for Bonaventure that the Christian faith proclaims not simply that God became flesh, but that the Word, specifically, became flesh. There is something particularly fitting about this faith-claim, for there is a special relation between the divine Word within the trinity and the human reality which he assumed as his own in history. The character of this relation is elaborated by Bonaventure from a variety of perspectives. We have mentioned above that in the order of creation, humanity appears as an image of God. In the context of trinitarian theology, the second person is known not only as the Word, or the Son, but also as the Image. Thus, in the mystery of the incarnation, the created image is filled with the eternal, exemplary Image. In this way humanity reaches its fullest participation in the divine archetype and thus the deepest fulfillment of its potential.[75] From yet another perspective, in as far as the second person is the center of the trinity and the center of the divine exemplarity, when precisely that person enters into a personal union with humanity, he enters into his rightful place as the center of all created reality. It is for this reason that Jesus can be seen as the universal center of meaning.[76]

Not only is it fitting that the incarnation should involve the Word specifically, but it is also fitting that the union should be with a human nature and not with some other creature.[77] Since humanity, including within itself both material and spiritual reality, is the most express imitation of God within the entire realm of creation, and since human nature, by virtue of its spiritual dimension, is ordered immediately to God, it is most appropriate that the actual hypostatic union should take place with a human nature.[78]

Even the historical circumstances in which the mystery of the incarnation is located can be said to be appropriate. For the simplicity and poverty of the life of Jesus, and especially the tragic outcome of his ministry on the hill of Calvary, can be seen as a statement about the nature of divine love. In the context of the poverty controversy, Bonaventure develops this issue extensively into a theology of divine condescension and compassion. Seen from this perspective, the divine compassion becomes the archetype for the form of love to which human beings are called.[79]

Much of Bonaventure's academic discussion is a search for the conditions under which such a thing as a hypostatic union between God and creation could be conceived as genuinely possible. That is, if one accepts the faith-claim of Christianity as the starting point, one is led to ask what this must imply in our understanding of God. And what must it imply in our understanding of the structure of the created world? From the side of God, the possibility of an incarnation is grounded in the prior possibility of God being a creator. This, as we have already seen, is grounded further in the mystery of God as a triune mystery of self-communicative love. Against this background, Bonaventure argues that there is nothing contradictory to or derogatory to God's perfection in the concept of a hypostatic union. Therefore such a union is to be thought of as at least possible without doing violence to God.[80]

From the human side, Bonaventure's understanding of human nature consistently argues that, by virtue of its spiritual dimension, humanity has an inner ordering to immediacy with God. Without arguing that humanity has a right to such immediacy, Bonaventure argues that we are capable of such a relation. This capability is the most noble potency of the universe. While we cannot bring this potency to act by our human powers alone, it can be brought to act by virtue of a divine initiative. When this happens, the created order finds its highest form of fulfillment. This is what Bonaventure understands the hypostatic union to involve. Christ is the purest actualization of a potential that lies at the heart of the created order.

It is Bonaventure's conclusion, therefore, that both from the side of God and from the side of human nature, such a thing as an incarnation is not only possible; indeed, it is the most appropriate way of crowning the actual created order which God has in fact called into being. But the Seraphic Doctor consistently refuses to describe the incarnation as necessary, for that would be to place limits on God which no creature has a right to do.

To ask about the possibility of an incarnation in the broader context of Bonaventure's theological world-view is not to ask about a divine absentee landlord visiting a world otherwise devoid of God. On the contrary, as the Bonaventurean theology of creation emphasizes, the world of creation is already a place of divine presence. The theological understanding of human nature, furthermore, and the trinitarian doctrine of divine missions and divine indwelling, elicits the image of a world in which God is present not only as an efficient, sustaining, and perfecting cause, but as an indwelling, spiritual presence. This theology of creation evokes the sense of a world which, in its material reality, mediates an awareness of the divine to the created spirit which dwells within it, and which, in its spiritual reality, is open to and yearning for a divine presence which can be given only by the free action of God. In this sense, when God comes into the world, God comes into his own (*Jn* 1:11). This coming is not a change of physical place. It is, rather, a matter of spiritual presence to that which, by virtue of the act of creation, was formed as a potential recipient of the divine. In such a world, an incarnation *is* not an unwelcome intrusion of a foreign God. It is, in fact, but the fullest realization of the most noble potential in the created order.[81]

When pushed for a definition of this union, Bonaventure suggests that there is no adequate definition available. He writes that the hypostatic union consists in this, that one of the divine persons who, from eternity, has been a hypostasis of the divine nature "becomes the hypostasis of a human nature" in time.[82] That is, the divine person of the Word exercises a hypostatizing function relative to the human reality of Jesus in such a way that the Word is the regulative principle operating in the human life of Jesus.[83] What distinguishes this action of God from all other creative activity is that God is not only the efficient cause of the creature. In this instance, one of the divine persons becomes the personal ground for the very existence of the created effect. He draws the creature to himself. He assumes the created nature as his own.[84]

In searching for an analogy that might serve to clarify this relation between the human and the divine natures in one hypostasis, Bonaventure chooses that of a tree that is grafted onto the root of another tree. Each tree maintains its identity, but both draw their life from one root. The trees are united in such a way that neither undergoes substantial change, nor are they blended into a third nature different from either of the trees. Neither can be said to be essentially dependent on the other, but the original tree can be said to predominate in the sense that the grafted tree lives from the root of the original tree. With this analogy, Bonaventure wishes to affirm that there can be no relation of mutual dependence between God and creation; and since the divine nature is superior to the human, the union between God and creation can take place only if God actively draws the human nature into such a union. Since a union of natures would seem to involve some change in the terms of the union, only a union in person would be possible without doing violence to the divine and human natures. Finally, as Bonaventure sees it, the human nature is, as it were, grounded in the divine root.[85]

Since, in Scholastic thought, there is an intrinsic relation between being and knowing, it is inevitable that when the Christ–mystery is approached in terms of its essential structure, theology will be moved, at some point, to reflect on the impact this most intimate relation with God would have on the human intellect and will of Jesus. In this sense, the question of Jesus' human knowledge and freedom becomes an important matter for speculative theology.

In his *Sentence Commentary* and in his *Breviloquium* Bonaventure treated both the question of Jesus' human knowledge and the question of his freedom. The question of his knowledge found its third and most elaborate treatment in a set of seven *Disputed Questions on the Knowledge of Christ*. Bonaventure's treatment of these issues suggests a tension between the theological tradition which tended to deal with Christ in terms of the divine wisdom alone and the more recent tendency, especially among Franciscans, to give greater emphasis to the human reality of Jesus.

Because of the hypostatic union, it was impossible for most Scholastic theologians to assume that the human mind of Jesus actually started as a *tabula rasa*. But was there no development of knowledge in him of any sort? In his *Sentence Commentary*, Bonaventure used the distinction between habitual knowledge and actual knowledge as a way of addressing this question. By virtue of the hypostatic union, Jesus would have known both habitually and actually all that pertains to the essence of beatitude. But those things which do not pertain to the essence of beatitude would have been known only habitually, while an actual knowledge of them would have unfolded successively in relation to Jesus' empirical experience.[86]

The *Disputed Questions* make no reference to this distinction. Instead, Bonaventure employs a distinction between apprehension and comprehension. In these terms, one might attribute to Christ a comprehensive knowledge of finite reality; of everything, past, present, and future. But when we shift to the relation between the created, finite mind of Jesus and the infinite mystery of God, it is impossible that his created intelligence could comprehend God. Here Bonaventure appeals to the mystical tradition of Pseudo-Dionysius to suggest a form of ecstatic knowledge in which the finite mind of Christ is constantly drawn beyond itself in the direction of the infinite mystery which it never comprehends. This ecstatic knowledge is, in fact, the most important aspect of the relation of the created intellect to the infinite mystery of God.[87]

The discussion in the *Breviloquium* shows a certain parallel with the views of Alexander of Hales. Here Bonaventure attributes to Christ all the forms of knowledge that the theological tradition had associated with the perfection of created, intelligent beings at all stages of history, including the state of original innocence. Here Bonaventure distinguishes between an "infused habit" and an "innate habit."[88] Here as in the other two treatments, Bonaventure is clear that one must affirm a created habit of knowledge in the intellect of Jesus, and that the created intellect of Jesus, like every other created intellect, cannot comprehend the infinite mystery of God. While there is something different about the psychology of Jesus because of the hypostatic union, this difference should not be understood in such a way as to equate Jesus' human knowledge with divine omniscience.

As the affirmation of a human intellect is a part of the broader affirmation of the integral humanity of Christ, so is the affirmation of a human will and freedom. At the level of the human will, Bonaventure distinguishes between the sensual will and the rational will. This is basic to his treatment of Christ's acceptance of suffering and death as an act of perfect obedience to God. The sensual will, by reason of its very nature, does not desire suffering. In normal circumstances, this would be quite acceptable. But, in dealing with the suffering involved in the passion and death of Jesus where such suffering appears to be the consequence of following God's will, this becomes a problem. How is Jesus to be seen as perfectly obedient in these circumstances? It is at the level of the rational will that Jesus accepts what his sensitive nature rejects. It is at this level that his human will is subject to and in harmony with the will of God. Thus, the distinction between a sensual and a rational will makes it possible for Bonaventure to see in Christ a perfect act of subjection to the divine will that does not exclude some form of tension in the human experience of Jesus.[89] Concerning the rational will of Christ, specifically, Bonaventure argues that this will was so deeply conditioned by the grace of the hypostatic union that it was confirmed in the good. It would have been impossible for Christ to choose anything contrary to the will of God.[90]

3. Christ and the theory of illumination

Related to the treatment of Christ's knowledge in the *Disputed Questions* is a most unusual element of Bonaventure's Christology. Unlike most of his contemporaries, the Seraphic Doctor sees a specific epistemological significance in the Christ-mystery. In the *Disputed Questions* this appears in the fourth question which is, in essence, a detailed discussion of the epistemology of illumination.[91] The same matter is presented in another form in the sermon *Christ, the One Teacher of All*[92] and in *Sermon I* on the twenty-second Sunday after Pentecost.[93] The theory of illumination, which is commonly treated as a philosophical matter, is here given a specifically Christological interpretation.

Basically, the theory of illumination is an attempt to locate the metaphysical conditions for the fact of human certitude. In a world of ambiguity where neither the objects of our knowledge nor the human subjects knowing provide adequate grounds for certitude, it is undeniable, in Bonaventure's view, that human beings do have certitude about certain objects. Among those objects are some of the most basic principles of rational thought without which rational discourse would not be possible. The knowledge of such things is not derived from empirical experience. In fact, it seems to be operating already at the level of empirical knowledge as the human knower comes to make judgments about the objects of empirical experience. Even more is this the case at the level of explicitly logical, rational modes of discourse.

If such certitude is a fact of experience, and if it can be explained neither by the changing objects of experience nor by the fallible human subject, the question of the source of such certitude is inevitable. The answer to the question, for Bonaventure, involves some kind of divine cooperation or some form of contact with the divine ground of reality and therefore with the divine ground of truth. In Bonaventurean terms, this leads back to the divine ideas or the eternal reasons in the mind of God. In God, of course, the ideas are not multiple but one. Only in reference to creatures are they said to be multiple. In the theory of illumination, the divine ideas function as a regulatory and motivating influence that illumines the human mind so that it is enabled to judge in accordance with the eternal truth. The ideas are not the direct object of human knowledge, but are "contuited" obliquely, as it were, in the experience of finite beings.

The understanding of the ideas, in turn, leads to the mystery of the Word in whom the Ideas are expressed within God. What is said of the ideas must now be said of the Word, namely, that the Word exercises a regulatory and motivating influence in human knowledge. But that is the Word that has become incarnate in the mystery of Christ. Here again we meet the relation between trinity and Christology so basic to Bonaventure's system. He writes: "Even though the whole of the trinity is the light of understanding, nevertheless, it is the Word who is by nature the principle of expression."[94] Or even more pointedly, he writes: "The principle of being is identical with the principle of knowing."[95] But all of creation is brought into being in and through the Word. Therefore, the Word is involved in all knowledge. For human knowledge is that process whereby the macrocosm is brought into the microcosm of human consciousness and unified in the human mind as it was first of all unified in the mind of God. And all of reality is unified in the mind of God in the form of the eternal Word.

This provides the systematic basis for Bonaventure's conviction that, from one side, all of created reality is, at root, an expression of the content of the eternal Word, and that from the other side, all human knowledge somehow pertains to that Word and no certitude is possible without the operation of the Word in the context of human knowledge. From this systematic vision, it is an easy step to the Bonaventurean notion of Christ as the inner teacher of the soul.

4. Soteriology

The soteriology of Bonaventure may be described as multidimensional. Regardless of any specific interpretations of the textual tradition, it is fair to say that for Bonaventure, the meaning of Christ should never be limited to the overcoming of sin. There is a prior and more basic sense in which the fact of the incarnation in itself stands as the highest act of God's creative work and as the completion of the cosmic order. Following Bonaventure's logic, one cannot say that, given the fact of creation, an incarnation would be necessary. But one can argue that given the actual order of creation, the incarnation is, in fact, the completion of this created universe. One can argue further that, since the created order has been enmeshed in a history of sin, the actual form that the incarnation takes will be thoroughly shaped by that fact.

Notes

1. J. G. Bougerol, *Introduction to the Works of Bonaventure*, p. 39.
2. J. Ratzinger, *The Theology of History in St. Bonaventure*, p. 119ff.
3. *II Sent.* (II, 1).
4. J. Quinn, *The Historical Constitution of St. Bonaventure's Philosophy*, p. 841ff.
5. *Itin.* (V, 295–313).
6. *Qq. d. de trin.* q. 1, a. 2 (V, 51ff).
7. *Hex.* 1, 1 (V, 329); 1, 10 (V, 330).
8. *Hex.* 8, 9 (V, 370).
9. *Hex.* 2, 17 (V, 332).
10. *Hex.* 3, 2 (V, 343).
11. *Hex.* 1, 37 (V, 335).
12. 1 *Sent.* d. 8, p. 1, a. 1, q. 2 (I, 53).
13. *Qq. d. de trin.* q.1, a.1 (V, 45).
14. K. Fischer, *De Deo trino et uno*, p. 90.
15. *Itin.* 5, 3–4 (V, 308.)
16. 1 *Sent.* d. 2–d. 48 (I, 50ff).
17. *Brevil.1* (V, 210–218).
18. *Itin.* 5 & 6 (V, 308–312).
19. *Liber de causis*, prop. 1 & 17.
20. *Qq. d. de trin.* q. 8 (V, 112–115).
21. *De trin.* 15, 22.
22. Fischer, *De Deo Trino et uno*, p. 299.
23. 1 *Sent.* prooem. (I, 1–6).
24. *De reduc.* 7 (V, 322).

25. *Brevil.* 2, 1 (V, 219).
26. *Hex.* 16, 9 (V, 404).
27. *Brevil.* 2, 1 (V, 219).
28. II *Sent.* d. 1, p. 2, a. 1, q. 2 (II, 41–43).
29. II *Sent.* d. 1, p. 1, div. text. (II, 13–14).
30. II *Sent.* d. 1, p. 2, art. 2, q. 1. (II, 44).
31. II *Sent.* d. 1, p. 1, a. 1, q. 2, resp. (II, 23).
32. II *Sent.* d. 1, p. 1, a. 1, q. 2, fund. 6 & resp. (II, 23) and *Hex.* 4, 13 (V, 351).
33. Ratzinger, *The Theology of History*, p. 138ff.
34. II *Sent.* d. 2, p. 1, a. 2, q. 3, resp. (II, 68).
35. II *Sent.* d. 13, dub. 3 (II, 332).
36. I *Sent.* d. 43, a. u., q. 3, resp. (I, 772) and IV *Sent* d. 46, a. 1, q. 3, fund. 2 (IV, 960).
37. *Brevil.* 2, 4 (V, 221).
38. *Brevil.* 2, 4 (V, 222).
39. *Brevil.* 2, 6 (V, 224).
40. II *Sent.* d. 16, a. 2, q. 1 (II, 401).
41. II *Sent.* d. 16, a. 2, q. 1, resp. (II, 401).
42. II *Sent.* d. 9, a. u., q. 5 (II, 250).
43. *Hex.* 21, 2 (V, 314).
44. II *Sent.* d. 17, a. 1, q. 2, resp. (II, 414–415).
45. II *Sent.* d. 3, p. 1, a. 1, q. 1 (I, 89ff) and d.17, a.l, q.2 (II, 421ff).
46. *Brevil.* 2,3 (V, 221).
47. II *Sent.* d. 13, a. 2, q. 2 (II, 321).
48. *Itin.* 2, 2 (V, 300); also *Brevil.* 2, 4 (V, 221).
49. II *Sent.* d. 13, div. text. {II, 310).
50. *Hex.* 4, 10 (V, 351).
51. *De reduc.* 20 (V, 324).
52. II *Sent.* d. 7, p. 2, a. 2, q. 1 (II, 197).
53. II *Sent.* d. 1, p. 1, a. 1, q. 1, ad 3 (II, 17).
54. I *Sent.* d. 35, a. u., q. 2 (I,605), *Qq. d. de sci. Christi*, q. 3, resp. (V, 13–14); *Hex.* 1, 13 (V, 331); *Hex.* 3, 4. (V, 343).
55. I *Sent.* d. 35, a. u., q. I (I, 601).
56. *Brevil.* 1, 8 (V, 216).
57. *Hex.* 1, 13 (V , 332).
58. *Qq d. de trin.* q. 8, ad 7 (V, 115).
59. *Brevil.* 2, 12 (V, 230).
60. *Itin.* 3, 2 (V, 303).
61. II *Sent.* d. 26, a. u., q. 4, ad 2 (II, 639).
62. *Brevil.* prol., 2 (V, 203).
63. I *Sent.* d. 27, p. II, a. u., q. 3, resp. (1,487) and *Hex.* 11, 13 (V, 382).
64. *Comm. in Joan.*, 1, 6, q. 1 (VI, 247).
65. *Itin.* 3 (V, 303ff.).
66. *Qq. d. de myst. trin.* q. 5, resp. (V, 90).

67. *Itin.* 3, 2 (V, 303).
68. *Itin.* 3 (V, 304).
69. *Itin.* 3 (V, 304).
70. *Itin.* (V, 295–313).
71. *Comm in Joan.* 1, 6, q. I (VI, 247); also I *Sent.* d. 27, p. 2, a. un., q. 1 (I, 481ff).
72. *Hex.* 2, 20 (V, 339–340); 13, 12–13 (V, 389–390).
73. *Itin.* 4, 3 (V, 306); *Brevil.* 4, 1 (V, 241); and *Hex.* 3, 2–32 (V, 343–348).
74. *Apol. paup.* 2, 12–13 (VIII, 242–243).
75. *Itin.* 6, 7 (V, 312) and *Brevil.* 4, 1 (V, 241).
76. *Hex.* 1, 10–39 (V, 330–335).
77. III *Sent.* d. 1, a. 1, q. 1, ad 4 (III,11).
78. III *Sent.* d. 2, a. 1, q. 1, resp. (III,38).
79. *Apol. paup.* 7, 7–8 (VIII, 274–275) and 1, 10 (VIII, 238–239).
80. II *Sent.* d. 1, a. 1, q. 1, corp. (III, 9ff.).
81. *In nat. Dom.* II (IX, 110).
82. III *Sent.* d. 1, a. 1, q. 2, resp. (III, 12–13).
83. III *Sent.* d. 10, a. 1, q. 3, resp. (III, 230–232).
84. III *Sent.* d. 5, a. 1, q. 2, resp. (III, 125).
85. III *Sent.* d. 6, a. 2, q. 1, resp. (III, 158).
86. III *Sent.* d. 14, a. 1–3 (III, 295–324).
87. *Qq. d. de sci. Christi* q. 7 (V, 40).
88. *Brevil.* 4, 6 (V, 246–247).
89. III *Sent.* d. 17, a. 1, q. 3, ad 1 (III, 369).
90. III *Sent.* d. 12, a. 2, q. 1, resp. (III, 265–267).
91. V, 17–27.
92. V, 567–574.
93. IX, 441–444.
94. *Hex.* 11, 13 (V, 382).
95. *Hex.* 1, 13 (V, 331).

The Cosmos,
a Symbol of the Divine

Zachary Hayes, OFM[*]

When I heard the learn'd astronomer,
When the proofs, the figures, were ranged in columns before me,
When I was shown the charts and diagrams, to add, divide,
    and measure them,
When I sitting heard the astronomer where he lectured with much
    applause in the lecture-room,
How soon unaccountable I became tired and sick,
Till rising and gliding out I wander'd off by myself,
In the mystical moist night-air, and from time to time,
Look'd up in perfect silence at the stars.[1]

I begin with this poem of Walt Whitman for a very specific reason. My intent is not to put down the significance of scientific knowledge about the cosmos. On the contrary, I believe that such knowledge is of great importance for humanity. But I do want to suggest with Whitman that scientific knowledge about the cosmos is not the whole picture for us. Even the best positive knowledge and explanation of things does not necessarily tell the whole story. "In the mystical moist night-air, and from time to time," after I had taken into account everything the scientists of astronomy had to say, I "Look'd up in perfect silence at the stars." What

* This paper was originally prepared for the USCC, meeting in Washington, June 1997. Used with permission from the author.

Whitman is pointing out we might call the importance of the contemplative moment in the human experience of the cosmos. And with that, the concern of this meeting enters the picture. Knowing is not all there is; explanation does not account for everything. Reality is multi-dimensional, and the human reaction to reality is similarly multi-dimensional. Before we engage in scientific knowledge, we relate to the cosmos in other ways. One of these ways is through the human imagination.

In reflecting on this, I wish to lead us through two stages. For the first stage we shall reach back to a period of time when the role of the human imagination was of basic importance in the human perception of the universe. The time I am concerned with is the thirteenth century. The author I will appeal to is the Franciscan, St. Bonaventure di Fidanza. And I will present his view not by giving a detailed account of his metaphysics of creation, interesting though it is in its own way. Rather I shall give only a general description of this metaphysics and then I shall draw out a number of the principal images and metaphors used by Bonaventure which appeal largely to the imagination. It is through these that Bonaventure describes the universe and its relation to the divine— remarkably concrete images which are related to his metaphysics and help to interpret its meaning.

Recognizing the immense changes in the human perception of the physical cosmos that have entered into the Western understanding of reality since the days of Bonaventure, I will attempt in the second stage to look at the kinds of insights suggested by the wealth of Bonaventurean metaphors and to ask whether anything similar to his reading of the cosmos is possible for us today in the face of the radical changes in our understanding of the physics of created reality.

IMAGINATIONS, METAPHORS, COSMIC REVELATION IN THE THOUGHT OF BONAVENTURE

One of the interesting aspects of Bonaventure's theological style is the fact that it is so multi-dimensional. It is clear that Bonaventure was keenly aware of the metaphysical dimension of philosophy and theology, of its relation to the intellect, and of its tendency to more abstract language. His great academic writings make it clear that he understood this well and could operate at this level with great skill. It is equally clear that he operated just as easily at the level of the imagination and was fully at home in the highly symbolic and metaphorical language involved at that level.

Imagination, as he understood it, has to do with the kind of sense-generated images that are created when the sensible world outside the human subject impinges on that subject through the five bodily senses. Thus, there are aural images, visual images, and images corresponding to all the other senses through which the outside world impinges on the interior world of human consciousness and knowledge. Such images are generated with the first kind of contact that the human person has with the world in which it is situated. There are, at this level, sense-images and sense-judgments concerning the objects the person encounters. For example, we readily say that this is a beautiful sound, a pleasant color, an ugly shape, etc. All this involves what, for Bonaventure, is a primal level of the human encounter with the world of sensible realities. There are, of course, other levels. For example, the process of sensation moves to the process of intellectual awareness, or abstraction, and of judgment. These take place not at the level of the senses but at the level of the human intellect. It is at this level, that of intellectual knowledge, that metaphysical questions and language enter into the picture.

This sort of distinction may help us understand how it is that Bonaventure's treatment of creation reveals at one level a series of remarkable metaphors and images, and at another level a profound understanding of the metaphysical implications of the Christian doctrine of creation. The second level simply indicates at the level of reflective thought the basis in reality for what is experienced at the first level prior to reflective thought. Thus, for the reflective theologian, what we are about to describe in metaphors and images is simply the experiential description of what is called in more theoretical, metaphysical language the divine exemplarity. The term *exemplarity* is rooted historically in the Platonic philosophical tradition. When it is used by a Christian theologian such as Bonaventure, it expresses the conviction that all of created reality is grounded in the divine archetypal reality and manifests the mystery of the divine in the created realm to some limited degree. We might give a summary statement of Bonaventure's understanding of exemplarity in the following way.

His view begins with the sense of the immense fecundity of the goodness of God. This is expressed first internally within the godhead in the mystery of the trinity. God is not simply a static, monadic being.

Rather the mystery of the trinity suggests that the divine reality is a mystery of productive love. This love is first of all productive within the godhead expressing itself in the fullest sense in the emanation of the persons of the trinity. But this internal divine fecundity flows outward in the free, loving act whereby God calls into being a created cosmos. This cosmos, in Bonaventure's understanding, is through and through *theophanic:* God-revealing. All of created reality manifests, in a variety of ways and levels, the richness of the divine life from which it flows.[2]

In the language of exemplarity, all created things are at least vestiges or footprints of the divine. Beyond this, intelligent beings are images of the divine, reflecting the mystery of God even more deeply than the non-intelligent cosmos. And intelligent beings are in essence a potential to yet a deeper realization of God-likeness which is realized in the transformation brought about by grace. This level is called a likeness of the divine. Now, since the divine is always the mystery of the trinity even though it is not always known precisely as such, it follows that at every level, there is some reflection not simply of God as being, but of God as the mystery of triune love. At the most basic level, all of creation reflects God who is its origin, its exemplar, and its final end. This triadic relation is not yet clearly known in terms of three divine persons, but it may be seen as a first intimation of what will eventually become known as a tri-personal mystery of divine love.

The high point of this vision is the figure of Christ who is the incarnation of the divine Word. The Word is seen by Bonaventure to be the *Ars Patris* in which the divine exemplarity is most concentrated. Since the exemplarity of God is focused most sharply in the self-expressive Word, when that Word enters into the most profound relation to a human nature in Jesus, this represents the conjunction of the divine archetype with the created microcosm which is, in turn, the synthesis of all elements that make up the created cosmos. It is in this point of conjunction that the divine aim for creation is brought to fruition. And that which has happened in Christ—that most profound union with God through which the humanity of Jesus is radically transformed—is the anticipation of what God wishes for all of the cosmos.

This is a vision in which we can say that the world of creation has its own truth and beauty. But this is not the entire story. Beyond this, each creature and the whole of creation is in its truest reality an expressive sign of the glory, truth, and beauty of God. Only when it is seen in these terms is it seen in its most profound significance. Only when creation is seen in terms of the self-diffusive love that is its source and its final end is it seen for what it truly is. Thus, any positive knowledge about the world such as we find in the sciences may be important information about how the world works physically. It must, however, be held open to the religious vision in which humans may discover—beyond the factual information of the sciences—a framework of value and of ultimate meaning which is not accessible to the sciences as such but is crucial for the successful living out of human life.

With this as the setting, we shall look at several examples which give expression to this vision at another level: the level of metaphor and symbol.

1) Circle/River The image of the circle appears in a variety of ways in Bonaventure. At one level, it is a symbol of the divine trinity itself. Bonaventure borrows from the Neo-Platonic tradition to describe God as an intelligible circle, whose center is everywhere and whose circumference is nowhere.[3] At another level, the circle may be seen as a symbol of the origin of all things in the creative fecundity of God and the return of creation to the same mystery of divine love as their final end. The symbol of the circle can be rendered in another way if the circle is thought of as a river. For as we read in *Ecclesiastes* 1:7, the river returns to its point of origin. This reading of the Scriptural text is drawn from the Latin translation in use in the university context of the thirteenth century. It envisions the river flowing from the immensity of the sea and eventually returning to the fullness of its point of origin. The divine trinity, then, can be seen as the fountain-fullness from which the river of reality flows, both within the mystery of God in the form of the triune life of love, and outside the divinity in the form of creation.[4] The river, then, is a particular way of envisioning the Neo-Platonic circle of expansive goodness.

2) Water A river is but one of the forms in which we encounter water. And water itself is a powerful metaphor. The trinitarian God of productive, creative love, as we have seen above, can be compared to a living fountain of water. Flowing from that fountain as something known, loved, and willed into being by the creative love of God is the immense river of creation. The world of nature in its vastness is the expression of a loving, intelligent creator. As a reflection of the richness of the creative source, the cosmos can hardly be one-dimensional. On the contrary, like water, it has many dimensions and diverse qualities. If, for example, we think of water in the form of the oceans, it suggests the overwhelming fullness of creation as it flows from the depths of God. Like an ocean, the cosmos is deep and contains many levels of meaning. If we think of water in the form of a river, we can see how it reflects the movement and fluidity of the cosmos.

Thus, for Bonaventure the metaphors of the circle, the river, and water elicit a sense of the immense diversity, fertility, and fluidity of creation. No one form of created being is an adequate expression of the immensely fertile source that resides in the divine, creative love. Therefore the diversity of beings which in fact exist in creation are a more appropriate form of divine self-expression. But, as the river eventually closes back on its point of origin, so creation is a dynamic reality, directed in its inner core to a fulfillment and a completion with God which is the mysterious fruit of its history .

3) Song The universe may be compared with a beautifully composed song. In this case, Bonaventure reaches back to one of the metaphors of Augustine.[5] Several elements stand out in his use of this metaphor. First, it is clear to Bonaventure that one does not appreciate a song if one hears only a part of it. It is necessary to grasp the whole of the melody if one is to appreciate it fully. And second, a melody is not simply a series of notes in juxtaposition. A well-crafted melody relates individual notes to other notes in terms of pitch and rhythm in such a way that the true significance of the individual note can be discerned only through the network of relations which constitute the melody. And third, Bonaventure shares with many of his contemporaries a fascination with the constructive significance of number or mathematics both with respect to the created order as a whole and with respect to music specifically. There is, in the depths of the human spirit, a desire for a certain numerical proportion which must be present in the structure of the melody if it is to work effectively.

If we then think of the cosmos in terms of this metaphor, it suggests the need for a sense of wholeness, a sense of the dynamic inter-relatedness of all the elements that make up the melody of the cosmos, and the hope that there is, in the context of the wild diversity of creatures, some principle of unity and order.

4) Book "The first principle created this perceptible world as a form of self-revelation so that through the world, as through a mirror or a footprint, humanity might be led to the love and praise of God, the Artist. Accordingly, there are two books, one written within, namely the eternal Art and Wisdom of God; and the other written without, namely, the perceptible world."[6]

When speaking of the relation of the cosmos to God, Bonaventure speaks of a book "written and without." The content of the book is first written in the consciousness of God in the form of the divine Word. That Word contains all that the divine is in itself, and all that God can call into being outside God. When that Word is expressed externally, what comes into being is the created cosmos, the form in which the Word of God's consciousness becomes visible and audible as the book "written without." Bonaventure describes this much as we can see the relation between our own interior consciousness, and the words, both vocal and written, in which our interior world becomes present in something outside our mind.[7] Clearly this is a way of expressing what today we think of as cosmic revelation.

Using the same metaphor of the book, Bonaventure speaks elsewhere of three books: the book of creation, the book of Scripture, and the book of Life.[8] Here the metaphor serves as a means of drawing out the relation between the cosmic revelation and the historical revelation. The book of creation which is the primordial revelation has become illegible for humankind because of human blindness caused by sin. Bonaventure writes that it has become like an unknown language, "like Greek or Hebrew."[9] Therefore, the book of Scripture is given to us not to annul the cosmic revelation but to help us in reading the book of the cosmos. And the Book of Life, the high point of revelation, is the mystery of Christ. In him we find the most express statement of the meaning of the two other books. By reading these books in harmony, we can discern the multi-leveled manifestation of God in created reality and in history.

We should not make the mistake of thinking that the book of the Bible offers special information about the physical workings of the cosmos. This is not really its concern. What it offers is a spiritual vision and a framework of values within which to situate the kind of information which we might derive from empirical experience. Thus, when Bonaventure speaks of the physical cosmos, he draws not on specific biblical sources but on what counted as general information about the cosmos available at his time. His vision of the physical cosmos is that of

Aristotle or Ptolemy and not one that could be found with any explicitness in the Bible.

In his final work, the *Collations on the Six Days of Creation*, Bonaventure describes the multiple forms of wisdom contained in the works of creation. He uses the same metaphor of the book to relate creation to Christology and to the mystery of the trinity, the two foundational mysteries of the Christian faith.[10] Having described the entire created order as a rich representation of the divine wisdom, Bonaventure concludes that:

> It (the cosmos) is a book written without. And so when the soul sees these things, it seems to it that it should move through them from shadow to light, from the way to the end, from the vestige to the truth, from the book to that true knowledge which resides in God. To read this book is the privilege of the highest contemplatives, not of natural philosophers; for the latter know creatures only in terms of their physical essence, and do not consider them also as signs.[11]

5) Window At the time Bonaventure was giving his last major series of collations at Paris in 1273, the cathedral of Notre Dame had only recently been completed. It stood in splendor not far from where his lectures were taking place. And just a short distance from the cathedral was the remarkable building known as Sainte-Chapelle which had been built during Bonaventure's student years at Paris. One can hardly visit these two masterpieces of Gothic art on a sunny day without being overwhelmed by the orgy of light and color displayed in both of them. And when one thinks about the medieval fascination with the physics, metaphysics, and mysticism of light, it is easy to come to the conclusion that Bonaventure may well have had these two buildings with their elaborate displays of stained glass in mind when he wrote:

> In every creature there is a shining forth of the divine exemplar, but mixed with darkness: hence there is a sort of darkness mixed with the light. Also, there is in every creature a pathway leading to the exemplar. As you notice that a ray of light coming in through a window is colored according to the shades of the different panes, so that divine ray shines differently in each creature and in the various properties of the creatures.[12]

Light is a metaphor for the divine reality. The colored window with its myriad shapes and colors is a metaphor for the created cosmos. Thus, as the colored patterns on the floor of the cathedral are generated by the physical light pouring through the glass, so the remarkable patterns of created things are generated by the divine creativity which shines through differently in each individual thing and in each property of each thing. The cosmos is, as it were, a window opening to the divine. And the rich variety of creatures and their specific qualities is a reflection of the depth and richness of the mystery of the divine.

6) Microcosm/macrocosm Again, sharing a common medieval conviction, Bonaventure uses the image of the microcosm and the macrocosm to express the relation of humanity to the cosmos. It will be recalled that according to the physics of the medieval period, all of the material creation is made up of the elements of earth, water, fire, and air. And beyond the material order , there is an order of created spiritual reality. These are the elements that make up the macrocosm. When we turn to humanity, we discover that in a representative way, something of all these elements are present in the human being. Our bodily nature is made up of the same elements which make up all other material beings. And when the body is seen to be united with a created spiritual principle, it is clear what Bonaventure can mean when he says that something of every creature is in human nature. In some sense, then all creation is present in the microcosm that constitutes the human being. And when Christ, in his created human nature is transfigured in the mystery of the resurrection, Bonaventure can see here the beginning of the transfiguration of the cosmos.[13]

In a very basic sense the view of the theologian expressed in these metaphors is a theological explication of what Bonaventure said elsewhere concerning St. Francis' perception of creation:

> In beautiful things he saw Beauty itself and through his vestiges imprinted on creation he followed his Beloved everywhere, making from all things a ladder by which he could climb up and embrace Him who is utterly desirable. With a feeling of unprecedented devotion he savored in each and every creature—as in so many rivulets – that Goodness which is their fountain-source. And he perceived a heavenly harmony in the consonance of powers and activities God has given them, and like the prophet David sweetly exhorted them to praise the Lord.[14]

7) Cross The reality of the cross provides a remarkable symbol by which Bonaventure relates the whole of cosmic reality and its history to the revelation of the Scriptures. Scripture, he writes, deals with the entire universe, "the high and the low, the first and the last, and all things in between. It is, in a sense, an intelligible cross in which the entire structure of the universe is described and made to be seen in the light of the mind."[15] In order to understand this cross, we must know God as the first principle of all reality. With respect to the world, we must know how things were created, how they fell, and how they were redeemed through the cross of Christ, how they will be reformed by grace and healed through the sacraments, and how they are finally to find either eternal glory or eternal pain.

In summary, for Bonaventure, the relation between creation and God may be expressed in two simple words: manifestation and participation.[16] All things in the cosmos exist so as to manifest something of the mystery of God. And all things exist by virtue of some degree of participation in the mystery of being that flows from the absolute mystery of the creative love of God. An appropriate reading of the book of the cosmos, therefore, gives us some sense of the divine goodness and fecundity; of the divine wisdom and beauty; of the divine intelligence and freedom; and of the relational character of the divine mystery of the trinity in which all of creation is grounded. It gives us as well some sense of the pain and tragedy of existence in a fallen condition.

Taking this all into account, we can say with Paul, "We see now through a glass, darkly" (1 Cor. 13: 12). Because of human sinfulness, the book of the cosmos has become obscured for us. It is, as it were, a language which humanity has a difficult time reading. Therefore, God has provided a key for deciphering the meaning of the cosmic revelation, namely the Scriptures and above all, Christ. This historical revelation does not replace the cosmic revelation, but enables us to read it more effectively.

II. CONTEMPORARY COSMOLOGY AS REVELATORY

Now, the question for us is whether the cosmos as we see it today can be read as a revelation of the mysterious richness of divine being. Can we look at our kind of world and say in the words of Bonaventure: "Whoever does not see is blind... Whoever does not hear is deaf... Whoever does not praise God in all these effects is mute... the entire universe will rise up against such a person."[17] Or in the words of Thoreau, "The morning wind forever blows, the poem of creation is uninterrupted; but few are the ears that hear it."[18]

There are those who maintain that scientific insights into the *what* and the *how* of the cosmos tell us nothing about God. For example, in his most recent book, Timothy Ferris asks what cosmology can tell us about God. "Sadly, but in all earnestness, I must report that the answer as I see it is: Nothing. Cosmology presents us neither the face of God, nor the handwriting of God, nor such thoughts as may occupy the mind of God."[19] His discussion of the issue then seems to focus on attempts to prove the existence of God, or to show from the insights of the sciences that God must have created the universe; and he warns—rightly—against the tendency to fuse the disciplines of science and theology.

Whatever one may think about the argument from design, the cosmological argument, and the ontological proof, (and there are forms of all these arguments which are interesting and tempt even a number of scientists), it is my view that proving the existence of God in such ways is not the real issue. Of greater importance is to show to what extent a religious faith may be seen not as childish immaturity but as a responsible vision of the meaning of reality and of human life, and then to search out the possible coherence between the insights of science and those of theology.

It may well be that science, precisely as science and by virtue of scientific methodology, knows nothing about God. This is not a problem as long as we do not claim that science alone defines the range of meaningful discourse. There are clearly other dimensions involved in the human relation to the cosmos. It is my conviction that the entire range of human experiences and questions ought to be brought to bear on our attempts to understand who we are and what sort of world we live in. Science provides important and helpful insights into the physical origins and workings of the cosmos. And it raises important questions that must be addressed by the theologian. The arts, philosophy, and religion open us to other levels of concern about values and meaning, and hence to other levels of questioning.

Religion does not need to appeal either to the sciences or to philosophy to provide its starting point. This might have been the understanding of an older form of apologetic. But what is of interest to a reflective religious believer at the present time is the question as to whether we may see a certain sort of coherence between the concerns of religion and the insights of science. This is a question not of fusing science and religion but of conversation between two important dimensions of human experience. Is it possible to ask whether a person who believes in the Christian God can look out at the physical cosmos with the lens of contemporary science instead of with the lens of an archaic medieval physics? And if the believer does this, what does such a person see in the cosmos? How can the cosmos, viewed in the light of the best empirical knowledge available to us through the sciences, be said to manifest the mystery of God to those who believe in God, and who believe that the physical universe which is described by the sciences is the universe which God is creating? What follows is an attempt to draw out some possible ways of approaching the issue.

Clearly we do not find the kind of geocentric, stable, hierarchically structured cosmos which pre-modern people such as Bonaventure would find. Neither do we find the mechanistic and utterly predictable cosmos of Newtonian thought. But we do find a cosmos which evokes a profound sense of its seemingly impenetrable mystery. Apparently boundless in space and time, or at least beyond our power to imagine, it is a dynamic, unfolding, organically interrelated cosmos, marked by some degree of unpredictability together with forms of order which are at times unexpected and yet remarkable in their beauty. (I have in mind the phenomenon of chaos theory and of fractals.)

The conviction of pre-modern Christianity, as we have seen in the case of Bonaventure, was that if one learns to read the book of the cosmos correctly, one will discover something of God's wisdom, beauty, power, and love. To see the cosmos as a theophany means to see the various forms and rhythms of nature as at least distant reflections of divine qualities. Is that possible for us today? If we think of the cosmos as book, then we might ask what are the words in that book; how are they to be pronounced; how are they spelled? And what is the grammar of the book? And if we think of the words as part of a song, we might ask what does the song sound like when you hear the whole? Like any book, the book of creation has different levels of meaning.

1) Science sees the cosmos in its incalculable immensity both in space and in time. The vision is overwhelming. There are those today who feel it is quite reasonable to suggest that the cosmos, for all its immensity and complexity, just "happens to be." There are many who

are convinced that the cosmos is contingent in this sense, and that there is no rational reason for asking anything beyond the fact that it happens to be. But the very nature of the cosmos as science describes it gives rise to the question that appears at the end of S. Hawking's *Brief History of Time*. There he describes how after we have given a complete description of *what* the cosmos is and *how* it works, we are still left with the question as to *why* it is, and *why* we human beings exist in it. Should we ever succeed in answering this question, says Hawking, "we would know the mind of God."[20] My immediate reaction to this statement is to suggest that the kind of *why* that emerges when we have given a full and adequate account of the physics of the cosmos is no longer a scientific question. Nor is it a question that can be dealt with by means of scientific methodology.

It seems, however, that this is one of the primal questions of humanity, and it refuses to go away. In fact, unless it is consciously and deliberately stifled, it seems to emerge with even greater power today than in the past. Can one look at the cosmos in modern terms and not ask with a profound sense of awe: Why? What is it all for? It may well be that such a question, in the final analysis, is not a scientific question and cannot be discussed in scientific terms. Yet the question refuses to go away. This was the sort of question that in the past expressed the sense of awe before the mystery of existence. And it seems to do so today, as long as we do not arbitrarily limit the range of meaningful discourse to the sort of questions that can be dealt with by the positive sciences. It was the sort of wonderment in the face of what seemed to be so radically contingent that led people to see the contingent cosmos grounded in some form of mysterious necessity; to see the relative as grounded in some mysterious Absolute.

It seems to me that today, precisely because of the world-view communicated to us by the sciences, we have even more reason to ask such a question, regardless of how we may attempt to answer it. Pursuing the scientific venture consistently to the end (if we ever succeed in doing that), we arrive at that persistent limit-question: Why is there anything at all when it does not have to be? Then one understands the long-standing tradition that maintained that it was a sense of awe that gave rise to philosophical reflection. It is the same sense of awe that is reflected in theological reflection on the primal source of the cosmos and of the purpose of it all.

2) Viewed from another perspective, this cosmos reveals a baffling number of diverse forms of created things. This has been the focus of E. O. Wilson's extensive work over many years on the diversity of life. We might think also of S. J. Gould's recent book.[21] At one level this book is an argument about the apparently haphazard character of the process commonly called evolution. At another level, the book is an argument about the variety of life forms "within the full house of our planet's history of organic diversity." Without going into Gould's argument against the idea that evolution is a movement toward more excellent forms of life that finds its summit in humankind, what is interesting for our purposes here is the other side of the argument; namely, that there is one discernible trend in evolution, and that is the emergence of an ever greater variety of organisms. Hence, the title: *Full House*. Thus, from a scientific perspective, the emergence of such prolific diversity is a fact that cries out for some interpretation. While Gould has his own rather cynical interpretation, faith and theology can see the same diversity as an expression of the divine fecundity of being poured out in such richness that it would not be appropriately expressed in a single form or even in a few forms of created being. While the limited nature of the physics of the cosmos as it would have appeared to Bonaventure could evoke a sense of the richness of the divinity, it seems to me that the contemporary vision of physics can do so even more emphatically. Who can look at and study the teeming life forms of this planet and not ask: What has God done? What sort of God has done this? Certainly not a God who calculates according to the principles of modern economy. Perhaps the metaphor of ocean might be more appropriate to evoke the sense of the fullness of divine being reflected in the cosmos. And what might this suggest concerning a proper respect for even the smallest creatures and their place in the cycles of life?

3) Scientists today are inclined to see a universe of things intimately intertwined at all levels. Think, for example, of the search for the "ultimate particle." By and large, it had been assumed that the subatomic particles—over a hundred of them have been identified—are isolated and independent particles. Yet in the "quark" research which led to the discovery of the sixth and final (?) quark at Fermilab in 1995, it was discovered that quarks can be discerned only in groups. And if quarks are really the end of the line in the search for the ultimate building blocks, this may mean that the so-called building blocks are not isolated

monadic blocks, but are relational complexes. This points to the possibility that the cosmos is really "systems within systems" all the way down and all the way out. If this is the case, then it seems that created reality is through and through relational.

With that in mind, we can recall that the core insight of the traditional trinitarian concept of God; namely, that the divine reality is intrinsically relational in character. It may well be, then, that Christian believers today can see the cosmos, as did Bonaventure in his own time and place, as grounded in and as reflecting the relational character of the trinity. Similarly, if the trinity is thought of, as it is in the tradition, as a unity of many, it may be thought of as reflected in the cosmic system of systems; a union of many and not simply a universe of individual things only extrinsically related to each other .

4) Science operates on the assumption that the cosmos is intelligible, while chaos-theory raises the awareness of the limits to predictability and intelligibility. Faith and theology can see this as pointing to its own conviction that since created reality is grounded in a God who is both intelligent and free, creation might then be intelligible but not necessarily in a totally mathematical form. One expects some form of intelligibility because of the divine intelligence. But one would not be surprised if things are not totally predictable, because of the divine freedom. A Christian, then, would expect the created order to have the quality of what we might call "intelligible contingence." This means that its final unifying formula may not take the form of a purely mathematical equation, and that the purely mechanical model of Newtonian physics will not be the final word. In fact, chaos theory seems to indicate that this is the case. Methodologically, it may be that we are searching for factual correspondences between elements of creation rather than for strictly logical necessities.

5) Contemporary science sees humanity to be deeply imbedded in the cosmic material process out of which life emerges, and eventually conscious life with intelligence and freedom. Humanity in a pre-modern world, as we have indicated above, was seen to be a microcosm of the macrocosm. In pre-modern times, one would not think of evolutionary connections, nor of stardust in us, but one did think of humanity as containing in itself in a representative way all that makes up the cosmos. That is, the human being contains within its own development from conception onward the mineral, the vegetative, the animal, and finally

the rational dimensions of the cosmos. Thus, through the body, humanity is integrated in the material world; and through the soul, humanity is integrated in the world of created spirits. (In medieval terms, this means the world of the angels.) Humanity is the point of integration of these two dimensions. By reason of its intelligence and freedom, humanity differs from the non-living, the vegetative, and the purely sensible world. By reason of its bodily dimension, it differs from any purely spiritual, created being. This might be seen as a medieval way of trying to account for the intimate integration of humanity in the cosmos together with a sense of humanity's distinctiveness. We are not otherworldly creatures. We are profoundly of the world. Yet we have a distinctive place and role because of the spirit that animates us. We are embodied spirit. While *modern* science is still puzzled by the spirit-functions of the human being, it is convinced, though for different reasons, that humanity, while embedded in the chemical cosmic process, possesses a distinctiveness which the Christian theologian thinks raises important moral, ethical questions.

6) We have spoken of Bonaventure's suggestion of a cosmic cross. Is it possible in any way for us to relate to such a symbol? The first thing that strikes me in this regard is the remarkable ambiguity of nature. The world of nature is not just a realm of unmitigated beauty. It is profoundly marked as well by the struggle for life. All around us, and even in ourselves and in our relation to each other, we find that life comes from life. There is a pervasive movement to more and fuller life which moves through pain, struggle, and death. If we think of Christ as the embodiment of the cosmic-word, we might ask: Does the figure of the man on a cross suggest the deeper significance of what we find in the cosmos—or at least on our planet—at every level? Holmes Rolston III has described nature as prolific and as problematic.[22] Pain and struggle are built into the structure of the cosmos as it moves toward life in a variety of forms. We seem to be confronted with perpetual perishing, as Whitehead once wrote. New life comes from what looks like destruction. Are lower forms of life simply destroyed, or are they transformed as they are taken up into higher life? Rolston describes the inner structure of this process of nature as a "suffering through to something higher." Can one see this as an anticipation at the cosmic level of what is most clearly affirmed in the experience of Jesus and the cross? Rolston speaks of a "cruciform" creation. Given this sort of cosmos, we might

want to think of God not only as a Benevolent Architect, but also as a Suffering Savior.

CONCLUSION

In all this, nature can still be seen as a revelation of God. It is through nature that God brings us into being and sustains us. To know nature more deeply is to sense its mystery, its depth, and its value. It is to know nature as an image of the sacred; a sacrament of the divine. The cosmos truly speaks to us of God. But what it says is difficult to discern. Yet, in all this, we see "through a glass, darkly" (1 Cor. 13:12). The ambiguity of the cosmic revelation is relieved for us, at least to some extent, by the revelation of the Scriptures and the revelation of Christ.

When we look at the cosmos from a Christological perspective, we can say that God loves and cherishes the world and all in it. God desires that the cosmic order be brought to a fulfilling completion which is anticipated in the personal destiny of Jesus as the risen Christ. Thus, we are in a position to be serious about the sacred character of the world of nature without turning it into God. And when we look from a cosmic perspective, we can say that, in the final analysis, the cosmos is not cold and indifferent, but finally beneficent and life-giving. In Christian terms, we can say that the creative power that generates and sustains cosmic reality including humanity and draws out its ever new forms of being is a power that is loving, personal, forgiving, and fulfilling. In Christ we discover that the true nature of creative power is enacted as "humble love." We find that for human beings, the appropriate way of interrelating with each other and with the world around them is through the ethics of self-giving love, even though the world operates on the basis of other principles in other dimensions. And in Christ we find the hopeful vision for a successful outcome for the entire cosmic process, even though the future seems quite dark and unpredictable when we view it simply in terms of the empirical sciences.

I close with the following words of Langdon Gilkey:

> If in nature the divine power, life, and order (law) are disclosed through dim traces, and if the divine redemptive love is revealed only in ambiguous hints in and through the tragedy of suffering and death, it is in the life of Israel, in the life and death of Jesus, in the promises to the people of God, and in the pilgrimage of that

people, that all of this is disclosed in much greater certainty, clarity, and power. Moreover, when once God is known in this historical disclosure to the community, then these traces in nature themselves relinquish much of their dimness and become genuine signs of the power and the order of the will of the God of faith.[23]

Notes

1. Whitman, Walt, *The Complete Poems*, ed. Francis Murphy (Penguin Books, N. Y., 1975), p. 298.

2. *Itinerarium* 2, 11 (V, 302). References to the works of Bonaventure are to the Quaracchi edition. In the parentheses, the Roman numeral refers to the volume number, and the Arabic numeral refers to the page number.

3. *Itinerarium* 5, 8 (V, 310).

4. I *Commentary on the Sentences*, Prooemium (I, 1ff).

5. *Breviloquium*, Prologue, #2 (V, 204).

6. *Breviloquium* II, 11 (V, 229); *Itinerarium* 6,7 (V, 312).

7. *Sermo II in Nat. Domini* (IX, 106–110).

8. *Quaestiones disputatae de mysterio Trinitatis*, q. 1, a.2 (V, 55).

9. *Collationes in Hexaemeron* 2, 20 (V, 339–340).

10. Ibid.

11. Op. cit., 12, 15 (V, 386).

12. Op. cit. 12, 14 (V, 386).

13. *Dom.II in Quad., Sermo I* (IX, 218); and J. G. Bougerol, *Sermo 16*, p. 250 in: *Sancti Bonaventurae Sermones Dominicales, Bibliotheca Franciscana Scholastica Medii Aevi*, 27 (Grottaferrata, Rome, 1977).

14. *Legenda Major 9*, 1 in: *Bonaventure*, ed. and tr. E. Cousins (Paulist Press, N.Y., 1978) p. 263.

15. *Breviloquium*, Prologue, #6 (V, 208).

16. II *Commentary on the Sentences*, d.1, p.2, q.1 (II, 44).

17. *Itinerarium*, 1, 15 (V, 299).

18. Henry David Thoreau, *Walden* (Time Inc., N.Y., 1962) p. 83.

19. *The Whole Shebang: A State of the Universe(s) Report* (Simon & Schuster: N. Y., 1997) p. 303–304.

20. *A Brief History of Time: From the Big Bang to Black Holes* (Bantam Books: N. Y., 1988) p. 174–175.

21. *Full House: The Spread of Excellence from Plato to Darwin* (Harmony Books: N.Y., 1996).

22. "Does Nature Need to be Redeemed?" in: *Zygon* 29 (1994) 2, p. 205ff.

23. "The God of Nature," in: *Chaos and Complexity: Scientific Perspectives on Divine Action*, ed. R. Russell, N. Murphy, A. Peacocke (Vatican City/ Berkeley, 1995) p. 212–213.

St. Bonaventure and Ecology

Phil Hoebing, OFM*

In this paper I wish to explore the thought of the thirteenth century theologian and philosopher, St. Bonaventure, in the belief that Bonaventure's thought can contribute some concepts and attitudes to the present ecological discussion. In the twentieth century many voices, scientific, philosophical, theological, conservationist, and preservationist, have expressed a deep concern about our ecological crisis. These people have observed the damage that man has done to his world and have offered explanations as to how man has gotten into this crisis and also recommendations as to how to ease or solve the crisis. Many who have studied the twentieth century predicament with the environmental problems are convinced that man must change his attitude toward the world around him before any major change will occur in man's treatment of our land, air and water with its many forms of life.

For the formulation of the current questions I will first give a brief sketch of the positions of Aldo Leopold and Lynn White. White who has a great admiration for St. Francis, does, I believe, misrepresent Bonaventure's relationship with St. Francis.

Aldo Leopold, whose book A *Sand County Almanac* was posthumously published in 1949, was among the first ecologists to call attention

---

* This article originally appeared as "St. Bonaventure and Ecology," *The Cord* 40/11 (December 1990): 336–45. Reprinted with permission.

to the need for a land ethic. Leopold, a conservationist, a scientist, a writer, and a university professor, was deeply concerned with the state of the world in which we are living. In his many articles and lectures Leopold summarized his views in a number of pithy statements, such as, "many incorrectly believe that a stump is a sign of progress." Leopold was among the first in the U.S. to challenge the American way of conservation, recreation and sportsmanship. When he saw how timbers were being destroyed, whole species of wild life eliminated, and rivers and lakes polluted, he called for a change of attitude. Leopold proposed a land ethic which called for love and respect for the world, the plants and the animals.

> It is inconceivable to me that an ethical relation to land can exist without love, respect and admiration for land, and a high regard for its value. By value, I of course mean something far broader than mere economic value; I mean value in the philosophical sense.[1]

In this book *In Defense of the Land Ethic*, J. Baird Callicott discussed in detail the views of Aldo Leopold whom he refers to as a seminal environmental philosopher. In his book of essays Callicott tries to spell out the underlying assumptions and principles on which Leopold based his ethics of the environment. He takes exceptions to the views of contemporary philosophers, such as John Passmore, Robin Attfield and H. J. McCloskey, who for one reason or another do not put much credence in Leopold's views. In support of the land it can be argued that one of Leopold's most important contributions to an ethics of the environment is his concern for the biotic community. Leopold's interpretation of the position of man in the world is that man is a member and not a conqueror of the land. The implications of this view are manifold because all of nature is interconnected and interdependent. Callicott summarizes the principles of the land ethic in the following manner.

> According to the land ethic, therefore: Thou shalt not extirpate or render species extinct; thou shalt exercise great caution in introducing exotic and domestic species into local ecosystems, in exacting energy from the soil and releasing it into the biota, and damaging or polluting water courses; and thou shalt be specially solicitous of predatory birds and mammals. Here in brief are the express moral precepts of the land ethic. They are expressly informed—not to say derived—from the energy of the environment.[2]

In discussing some of the causes of our environmental problems, Lynn White, in a presentation to the AAAS meeting in 1966, suggested that the Judeo-Christian tradition must share some of the blame for our present ecological crisis. His argument was partly based on the first chapter of Genesis.

> And God blessed them and God said to them, "Be fruitful and mul-tiply, and fill the earth and subdue it; and have dominion over the birds of the air and over every living thing that moves upon the earth." (Gen. 1.28)

White suggested that Adam and Eve took this command very seri-ously as did their followers so that today man dominates nature and uses it as he pleases. As White concluded his presentation he noted that at least one person did not follow the traditional view of man's dominance and that man was St. Francis of Assisi. Francis, a radical in his time, did not follow the common view that man was to dominate nature but rather saw all creatures as having a certain equality. Because of Francis' appreciation of nature, White concluded his presentation with these words:

> Possibly we should ponder the greatest radical in Christian history since Christ: St. Francis of Assisi. The prime miracle of St. Francis is the fact that he did not end at the stake, as many of his left-wing followers did. He was so clearly heretical that a General of the Franciscan Order, St. Bonaventure, a great and perceptive Christian, tried to suppress the early accounts of Franciscanism.[3]

Some authors might view White's view as expressing only the tradi-tion of Genesis and that if one looks further into the Bible one will also find that man is asked to be the gardener and caretaker of the Garden. (Gen. 2, 15) The story of man's position in Eden is found in the J-tradi-tion which pictures man in a different light than does the P-tradition. The J-tradition is compatible with many of the modern concepts of the ethics and the environment such as those of Leopold and Callicott. The Franciscan view of nature as exemplified by Francis and Bonaventure is also compatible with the view that man is a steward and caretaker of nature.

I suggest that Francis' vision and life were central to Bonaventure's philosophical-theological synthesis. To develop this claim, I suggest, at the risk of oversimplifying, three main views on the relationship of man to nature that can be discerned in the Western World. The first position is the dominance view which believes that all of nature is a commodity to be used, manipulated and enjoyed by man. The stewardship view believes that man does not have absolute control of nature but must use it wisely and respectfully in accord with God's plan. The third position, known as the "participation in nature" view, is found in Eastern thought and in some Western thinkers. This view believes that all of nature is interconnected and that man himself is also a part of nature. Since Darwin's "Origin of Species" many twentieth century writers, for a number of reasons, have espoused this position. St. Francis is classified with those who accept the interconnectedness of nature and the participation view.

One often sees the statue of St. Francis in a birdbath or in a flower garden. These would seem to be appropriate places for his statue provided one understands why St. Francis loved the birds and preached to them and why he admired the beauty of the flowers. One must avoid two extremes when considering Francis and his love of nature. First of all, Francis is clearly not a pantheist, even though he sees the presence of the Creator in everything. Celano writes about Francis and his attitude to all creatures:

> The realization that everything comes from the same source filled
> Francis with greater affection than ever and he called even the
> most insignificant creatures his brothers and sisters, because he
> knew that they had the same origin as himself.[4]

The second extreme position to avoid would be to make Francis a sentimentalist and a naturalist. Francis realized that things were good because they came from God and can lead man back to God.

> In every work of the artist, he praised the Artist. Whatever he
> found in the things made he referred to the Maker. He rejoiced in
> all the works of the hands of the Lord and saw behind things pleas-
> ant to behold their life-giving reasons and cause. In beautiful
> things he saw Beauty itself; all things were to him good... through
> his footprints impressed upon things he followed the Beloved
> everywhere; he made for himself a ladder by which to come even to
> his throne.[5]

The footprints of the Creator in creation and the ladder by which man can ascend to union with God are concepts developed by Bonaventure in his "Journey of the Mind to God" and in many of his other writings. Like all the professors in the thirteenth century he could not help but be involved in the controversy over Aristotle and his thought. Although Bonaventure saw much good in the works of Aristotle, his own metaphysics took a different direction, being influenced by the Greek Fathers, the Pseudo-Dionysius, St. Augustine and the Victorines. In developing his synthesis of man's relationship to God, Bonaventure employed the Trinitarian theology of the Greek Fathers as the keystone for his view. His views on emanation, exemplarism and the return of creation to God are intimately connected to his concept of the Trinity as essentially dynamic. Bonaventure developed his subjectivity along the lines of Augustine whom he admired very much and referred to him as "The greatest of the Latin Fathers." In his works he quoted St. Augustine more than three thousand times. Bonaventure was a student and friend of Alexander of Hales who introduced him to the Victorines, the Pseudo-Dionysius and through him, to the Greek Fathers. Bonaventure's view of God as essentially dynamic has a different perspective than that of Thomas Aquinas, his contemporary. Moreover, the Neoplatonism of the Pseudo-Dionysius differed from the Neoplatonism of Augustine. The dynamic God with his exemplarism and illumination has a more intimate role to play in the creation and development of the universe than a God who is interpreted to be more transcendent than immanent. In his synthesis Bonaventure attempts to synthesize the apparently opposite interpretations of God's role with the universe.

The Pseudo-Dionysius had a great influence on the thirteenth century thinkers and especially on St. Bonaventure. Bougerol in his book writes:

> The Areopagite's teaching is hard to summarize. We may say, however, that his influence on Bonaventure was threefold: he gave Bonaventure a viewpoint, a method, and a few fundamental themes. Bonaventure himself says: "The first (dogma) is exposed chiefly by Augustine, the second (morals) by Gregory, and the third (the end of both), or mystical anagogy by Dionysius."[6]

Bonaventure held the view that to have a "true metaphysics" one has to be concerned with emanation, exemplarity, and consummation. The metaphysics, thus, had to consider creation, the ideas of God in creation, and the return of creation to God. Bonaventure states this in his *Collationes in Hexaemeron:*

Through the first Truth, all come back as the Son expresses it: "I have come forth from the Father and have come into the world. Again I leave the world and go to the Father." (*Jn.* 16, 28) Likewise let anyone say: "Lord, I came out of You, the Supreme Being: I will return to You and through You, the Supreme Being."

Such is the metaphysical Center that leads us back, and this is the sum total of our metaphysics: concerned with emanation, exemplarity, and consummation, that is, the illumination through spiritual radiations and return to the supreme Being.[7]

Ewert Cousins insists that the metaphysics of Bonaventure must be grounded in his theology of the Trinity and that the act of creation takes place because of the dynamism in the Trinity.

the root of Bonaventure's doctrine lies in his conception of the Father as dynamic, fecund source of the Trinitarian processions. In examining the Father, Bonaventure employs two principles: the principle of fecund primordiality and the principle of the self-diffusion of the good. Both of these principles he applies to the divinity in relation to creation and to the Father in the Trinity.[8]

Because Bonaventure believed that the Trinity is dynamic he was able to join two conceptions of God that appeared to be irreconcilable in Western thought, namely, the self-sufficiency of God and the self-communication of God. Bonaventure unites both in his theological synthesis. He did so by appreciating St. Francis' vision that the whole of creation is an expression of God's love. Love becomes the means of reconciling the concepts as Cousins states:

For Bonaventure God's self-sufficiency and self-communication are so intimately united that his principle can be stated as follows: Because He is self-sufficient, he is absolutely self-communicating.[9]

Being a Christian thinker, Bonaventure could not accept either an eternal universe or a necessary universe. Without going into the arguments as to why he opposed both Aristotle who postulated an eternal universe and the Arab philosophers who accepted a necessarily created universe, Bonaventure argued that the world was created in time, that the world was created from nothing, and that it was created freely by God. In the *Breviloquium* Bonaventure writes:

Having summarily considered the trinity of God, it is proper to speak next of creation. Briefly, the following must be held. The entire fabric of the universe was brought into existence in time and out of nothingness, by one first Principle, simple and supreme, whose power, though immeasurable, disposed all things by measure and number and weight.[10]

The second important theme of Bonaventure's metaphysics is concerned with exemplarism. Bonaventure believed that Aristotle had made a fundamental error in separating the Ideas from God. In his unique way, Bonaventure places the Ideas in the second Person of the Trinity and makes them the exemplar ideas of all the individuals in creation. Surely, this relates to the idea of emanation because creatures reflect the perfections of God and God can be found in all of His creatures. Francis knew this intuitively but Bonaventure structures a theological explanation with his exemplarism. He often states in his writings that God can be found in two books; the book of Sacred Scripture and the book of nature. Regarding the question; "Whether God is Knowable through Creatures" he writes:

> I reply; it must be said as the cause shines forth in the effect, and as the wisdom of the artificer is manifested in his work, so God, who is the artificer and cause of the creature, is known through it.[11]

And again:

> From this we may gather that the universe is like a book reflecting, representing, and describing its Maker, the trinity, at three levels of expression: as trace, as image and as likeness. The aspect of trace is found in every creature; the aspect of image in the intellectual creatures or rational spirits; the aspect of likeness, only in those who are God-conformed. Through these successive levels, comparable to the rungs of a ladder, the human mind is designed to ascend gradually to the supreme principle who is God.[12]

That God is the exemplary cause of all creatures is at the very center of Bonaventure's metaphysics. Bonaventure reasoned in this way: if God created the world He would act, not in a blind manner, but rather in an intelligent way. Bonaventure was convinced that Plato erred when he put the Ideas in a world apart from God because it is necessary that these Ideas exist in the divine intellect. It would be more correct to say that these ideas or patterns are in God and that he acts according to them. Being a Christian and a believer in the Trinity he develops his interpretation of the ideas along these lines. God is supremely intelligible to Himself and comprehends Himself in a single act, but in performing this act, he equals himself. This similitude, as a Christian knows, is the Divine Word, which is equal to God and expresses all His being, all His power and all His knowledge. *(Hex.* III, 4, v. p. 343) It is in the understanding of the Uncreated Word that everything is known and understood. In his interpretation of the exemplar ideas in the Word, Bonaventure differs from some of the other medievalists by stressing the activity of the divine Intellect in the production of the Ideas. Besides being representations of the essence of God, which are imitable by creatures, they are also active. Bonaventure compares them to the ideas of an artist who plans to produce a work of art. God knows the creatures through His Ideas which are not universal but individual and specific. Thus, Bonaventure in explaining the relation of creature to creator used his doctrine of analogy.

One of the characteristic features of Bonaventure's exemplarism is his doctrine that every creature is an analogy of God. Since all things are made according to their pattern in the divine ideas, they bear the seal of their descent. There are many degrees of analogy between the creature and God, namely, shadow, vestige, and image. A rock, for example, represents God in a distant and indistinct way, a vestige represents God in a distant but distinct way. All living things are vestiges of God whereas man who represents God closely and distinctly is an image of God. The man who is conformed to God by grace is a similitude because such a person represents God most closely.

All creatures must bear the "seal of the divine" because they are made according to the patterns in the divine Word. Bonaventure, like his teacher, Alexander of Hales, emphasizes the positive aspect of analogy in seeing creatures as reflections of the creator. In treating analogy in this way there is no longer an infinite distance between God and the creature.

Bonaventure saw analogy as the structural law of creation. Since all things are made according to their pattern in the divine ideas, all things bear the seal of their divine descent. All things are analogies of God. Man, however, being the image of God in this world of analogies, has the central position because he is able to appreciate the various levels or analogies and refer them back to their Maker.

Consummation or the return of creatures is the third part of Bonaventure's metaphysics. In the return of creatures to God, man plays a central role in the synthesis of Bonaventure. Man is a composite of the spiritual and the corporal and is the natural mediator between creation and God and the rest of creation becomes a mirror which reflects the perfection of God. The visible world is a book through which, God, the artist, proclaims His infinite perfection. Bonaventure admits that man can view nature simply as objects to be appreciated in themselves or he can see them in their symbolism which gives them real meaning. Until man sees creatures in their relationship to their Creator he does not really understand his position in the world or the value of nature.

After briefly considering a few of Bonaventure's basic ideas one sees that he is in agreement with St. Francis in his love for nature. With his exemplarism, his analogy of creatures with God and man's central position in the return of things to God, Bonaventure has given a philosophical-theological rationale for Francis' exuberant and enthusiastic love of nature.

St. Bonaventure, because of his metaphysics of exemplarity and analogy, can make a contribution to the twentieth century discussion of ecological ethics. Many writers argue that man must see the intrinsic value in nature to change man's use of nature. If nature has only instrumental value then it can be used in any way by man but if it has intrinsic value then it must be respected for that value. Bonaventure, with his metaphysics, has given nature an intrinsic value.

Today some authors like to speak of the intrinsic value of nature rather than discuss the rights of animals. Callicott, for example, in responding to Peter Singer and Tom Regan, discusses the intrinsic value of species and the need to preserve those species. Although the men who lived in the thirteenth century had different problems and attitudes than the people living in the twentieth century they did realize the intrinsic value of nature. They had different reasons for their views than some twentieth century ecologists as the Franciscans saw things as valuable because they came from the goodness of God. Contemporary writers see things as intrinsically valuable because all of nature is interconnected. Since every species is valuable because all things in nature are interdependent, man is harming himself by his destruction of species. The thirteenth century thinkers did not realize the danger of eliminating species because they did not have such a problem. It would be hypothesizing to say what Bonaventure and Francis would say about our current ecological crisis. There are so many situations in Francis' life where he showed respect and concern for the world and its creatures that it is easy to put words in his mouth. For example, when St. Francis delivered his famous sermon to the birds he was expressing a special concern and respect for the flock of birds that listened attentively to his words.

One may speculate as to St. Bonaventure's comments on problems that were unknown in the thirteenth century. Since that time science and technology, although they have solved many of man's problems, have not been without questions regarding their values and development. Some ethical questions that are discussed frequently in our daily newspapers are the following: Do animals have rights? Is it ethically permissible to use animals for medical experiments that will benefit only humans? Does the non-human and non-animal world have any moral rights or moral status? Is it ethical to have animal farms whose only purpose is commercial? Do members of endangered species have more rights than members of a species that is not endangered? What is the status of such predators as the mountain lion and the timber wolf? Does our present generation have an obligation to future generations? Do future generations have a right to a beautiful and unpolluted world?

These questions are difficult to answer but there is another problem which seems unique to the last years in the twentieth century. This is the problem of species extinction. Conservationists tell us that from 1600 to 1900 species became extinct at the rate of about one every four years. From 1900 to 1950 the rate of extinction was about one a year. If man continues to exploit in the future as he has during the last forty years, conservationists think the extinction of species would be more than a hundred a day. This is seen as one of the biggest problems in our ecological crisis. If all of nature is interconnected how many species can nature lose before it is harmed beyond repair?

These questions may seem very distant both in time and in concept from a thirteenth century Franciscan teacher at the University of Paris. As one reads Aldo Leopold's "Thinking Like a Wolf," which is an essay on the need for the wolf, one appreciates his message on attitudes. During his early years as a conservationist, Leopold was adamant in his view that the wolf had to be destroyed because it was ruining the deer population. He took part in wolf hunts and wrote articles advocating the extermination of the wolf. Later in life his view is the exact opposite because he came to realize that by eliminating the wolves the deer became overpopulated and seriously damaged the forests when their food became scarce. He learned that it was more difficult to repair the damage done to the forests by the hungry deer than it was to replace the deer destroyed by the wolf. He learned that all of nature is interconnected and that to destroy parts of nature is to weaken and harm all of nature.

In struggling to find answers to the many problems in our ecological crisis many writers, like Leopold, believe that we must learn to see the intrinsic value of nature. They believe strongly that the non-human world does not exist solely for the manipulation of man. Bonaventure certainly gave an intrinsic value to all of nature in that it reflects the perfections of God, but he also viewed nature in an instrumental way. He would advocate a reasonable use and appreciation of God's world in which man lives. In his *Retracing the Arts to Theology* Bonaventure, for example, considers hunting as an external art that also leads one to God. It would seem that Bonaventure, with his metaphysics, would be able to offer valuable concepts to a twentieth century discussion on ecology from both a philosophical and a theological aspect.

In his thoughtful New Year's address Pope John Paul II called on all people to respond to our ecological crisis which he called a "moral problem." He specifically addressed himself to those people without any particular religious conviction, to those people who believe in God but are not Christian, to the entire body of Christians and to the Catholics. In our discussion of Bonaventure and his philosophical-theological principles it is fitting to conclude with Pope John Paul's conclusion to "Peace with All Creation":

> In 1979, I proclaimed St. Francis of Assisi as the heavenly patron of those who promote ecology (cf. Apostolic Letter "Inter Sanctos": AAS 71 (1979), 1509l). He offers Christians an integrity of creation. As a friend of the poor who was loved by God's creation—animals, plants, natural forces, even Brother Sun and Sister Moon—to give honor and praise to the Lord. The poor man of Assisi gives us striking witness that when we are at peace with God we are better able to devote ourselves to building up that peace with all creation which is inseparable from peace among all peoples.

It is my hope that the inspiration of St. Francis will help us to keep ever alive a sense of "fraternity" with all those good and beautiful things which almighty God has created. And may he remind us of our serious obligation to respect and watch over them with care, in light of that greater and higher fraternity that exists within the human family.[13]

Notes

1. Aldo Leopold, *A Sand County Almanac.* (Oxford University Press, 1987), p. 223.
2. J. Baird Callicott, *In Defense of the Land Ethic.* Essays in Environmental Philosophy, (State University of New York Press, 1989) p. 91.
3. Lynn White, "The Historical Roots of Our Environmental Past." *Science,* March 10, 1967, Vol. 155, Number 3767: 1203–1207 p. 1206.
4. Celano, *Lives of St. Francis, his Writings and Early Biographies.* English Omnibus, ed. Marion Habig, O.F.M. (Franciscan Herald Press, 1972) p. 692.
5. Celano, p. 494.
6. José de Vinck, *Introduction to the Works of Bonaventure* (trans. from the French of J. Guy Bougerol, O.F.M.) St. Anthony Guild Press, 1963) p. 40.
7. José de Vinck (trans.) *The Works of Bonaventure.* Vol. V. *Collationes on the Six Days* (St. Anthony Guild Press, 1963).
8. Ewert Cousins, *Bonaventure and the Coincidence of Opposites.* (Franciscan Herald Press, 1978) p. 101.
9. Cousins, p. 102.
10. José de Vinck trans. *The Works of Bonaventure,* Vol. II. *The Breviloquium* (St. Anthony Guild Press. 1963) p. 69.
11. Richard McKeon, ed and trans., *Selections from Medieval Philosophers, St. Bonaventura* (Charles Scrihner's Sons, 1930) p. 131.
12. *Bonaventure* (trans. José de Vinck) Vol. II, p. 104.
13. Pope John Paul II. "Peace With All Creation." *Bulletin Institute for Theological Encounter with Science and Technology* (Winter, 1990, Vol. 21, No.1.), p. 10.

Discussion Questions

1. Consider Bonaventure's understanding of who God is: "Because He is self-sufficient, He is absolutely self-communicating." How does this relate to your own understanding of God? Discuss your conception of some implications for your life in relationship with the environment that flow from viewing creation as a form of God's self-communication.

2. How did Bonaventure view the human person? Discuss your own anthropology.

3. Reflect on Bonaventure's "Doctrine of Universal Analogy" (See Hayes, "Bonaventure: Mystery of the Triune God"). Respond to the concept of being a co-creator with God. Can you give any examples of being a co-creator with God, from your own experience?

4. Bonaventure's metaphysics was an attempt to present a cohesive, coherent, and consistent account of reality as a whole. Bonaventure held that for a Christian, such an account must include: (1) *emanation* [creation], (2) *exemplarity* [the ideas of God in creation], and (3) *consummation* [the return of creation to God]. Discuss how Bonaventure's metaphysics helps us gain respect for the ecosystem in our time.

5. For further consideration: Research St. Bonaventure's composition, "The Tree of Life" and discuss its importance for our understanding of ecotheology. [See Ewert Cousins, trans. and ed., *Bonaventure: The Soul's Journey into God; The Tree of Life; The Life of St. Francis*, Classics in Western Spirituality, New York: Paulist Press, 1978, 1–48 and 119–175]

For Further Reading

Bettoni, Efrem. trans. Angelus Gambatese. *Saint Bonaventure*. Notre Dame, IN: University of Notre Dame Press, 1964.

Bougerol, Jacques Guy. trans. José de Vinck. *Introduction to the Works of Bonaventure*. Paterson, NJ: St. Anthony Guild Press, 1964.

Cousins, Ewert H. *Bonaventure and the Coincidence of Opposites*. Chicago: Franciscan Herald Press, 1978.

Cusato, Michael F. and F. Edward Coughlin, eds. *That Others May Know and Love: Essays in Honor of Zachary Hayes, OFM, Franciscan, Educator, Scholar*. St. Bonaventure, N.Y.: Franciscan Institute, 1997.

Doyle, Eric. trans., ed., and intro. *Bonaventure, Saint, Cardinal, Ca. 1217–1274. The Disciple and The Master: St. Bonaventure's Sermons on St. Francis of Assisi*. Chicago: Franciscan Herald Press, 1983.

Foley, Pascal F. ed. *Proceedings of the Seventh Centenary Celebration of the Death of Saint Bonaventure*. St. Bonaventure University, St. Bonaventure, N.Y., July 12–15, 1974. St. Bonaventure, NY: Franciscan Institute, 1975.

Gerken, Alexander. "Identity and Freedom: Bonaventure's Position and Method." trans. Miles Parson. *Greyfriars Review* 4/3 (1974): 91–15.

Hayes, Zachary. *Bonaventure: Mystical Writings*. Spiritual Legacy Series. New York: Crossroad Publishing Company, 1999.

Hayes, Zachary. "Christ Word of God and Exemplar of Humanity: The Roots of Franciscan Christocentrism and Its Implications for Today." *The Cord* 46/1 (1996): 3–17.

Hayes, Zachary. *The Gift of Being: A Theology of Creation*. New Theology Studies 10. Collegeville, MN: The Liturgical Press, 2001.

Hayes, Zachary. *The Hidden Center: Spirituality and Speculative Christology in St. Bonaventure*. New York: Paulist Press, 1981.

Hayes, Zachary. *A Window to the Divine: Creation Theology*. Quincy, IL: Franciscan Press, 1997.

Pompei, M. Alfonso. "The Role of Christ in Human Knowledge According to St. Bonaventure." trans. Edward Hagman. *Greyfriars Review* 6/2 (1989): 211–35.

Quinn, Mary Bernetta. *To God Alone the Glory; a Life of St. Bonaventure*. Westminster, MD: Newman Press, 1962.

Ratzinger, Joseph. trans. Zachary Hayes. *The Theology of History in St. Bonaventure*. Chicago: Franciscan Herald Press, 1971.

Spargo, Emma Jane Marie. *The Category of the Aesthetic in the Philosophy of Saint Bonaventure*. St. Bonaventure, NY: Franciscan Institute, 1953.

ENGLISH TRANSLATIONS OF PRIMARY SOURCES

Works of Bonaventure. 6 volumes. St. Bonaventure, NY: Franciscan Institute, 1956–. (Each volume has a helpful introduction to the texts.)

The Works of Bonaventure. 5 volumes. [Paterson, NJ: St. Anthony Guild Press, 1960–66] Reprinted by Franciscan Press, Quincy, IL.

What Manner of Man? Sermons on Christ by St. Bonaventure. Trans. Zachary Hayes. [Chicago: Franciscan Herald Press, 1974] Reprinted by Franciscan Press, Quincy, IL.

PART FOUR

Blessed John Duns Scotus: Cosmic Mutuality

John Duns Scotus was born in 1265 at Duns, Berkwickshire, Scotland. Named after St. John the Evangelist, he was raised in a devout Christian family, frequenting the Abbey of Melrose for catechism classes. In 1280 he completed the novitiate of the Franciscan Friars Minor at Dumfries, Scotland. Following his ordination to the priesthood in 1291 by the Bishop of Lincoln, England, he studied philosophy at Cambridge and then at Oxford. He lectured on the *Sentences* of Peter Lombard at Oxford until 1302, then traveling to Paris for further study. In June of 1303 he was banished from France because he objected to an appeal by King Philip IV to oppose Pope Boniface VIII. He was likely at Oxford until April of 1304. The banishment did not hold, however, and he returned Paris and was named Regent Master in Theology in 1305. He lectured in Paris until his relocation to Cologne, Germany, in 1307 to take charge of the Franciscan House of Studies. Because of the precise and subtle philosophical distinctions that define his work, he became known as the "Subtle Doctor." On November 8, 1308, John Duns Scotus died in Cologne at the young age of 42.

The Franciscan scholar John Duns Scotus is important for ecotheology for several reasons. First, like Francis and Bonaventure before him, he recognized God as the creator of all and therefore saw creation as a source of God's self-revelation. Yet, Scotus came to that understanding in his own unique way, and his reflections provide distinct insights that can assist us as we wrestle with our current ecological crisis.

As Osborne explains,[1] Scotus was a realist and he understood that all in the created world somehow had its source in God. Scotus had a worldview that envisioned good and evil, virtue and sin, the angelic and the demonic as all under the governance of God. However, God was not known only through empirical observation, but also through divine revelation. Thus, the reality of the humanity of Jesus as revealed in scripture is also included in the reality with which Scotus deals. The vast diversity of creation leads Scotus to a wonderful conclusion, namely that the God revealed in such a creation, the First Principle, is absolutely necessary, yet utterly free, and the created world is equally utterly contingent.

Such an utterly free God did not *have* to do anything. Thus, the entire created world is pure grace and gift. For the modern reader it is quite a stretch to understand the depth and profundity of this insight. As Osborne points out, Scotus holds that God has primacy in three ways: of efficiency, finality, and eminence.[2] God is *necessary*, simply because there is *nothing* that could bring about God or "make God happen." However, what was most important for Scotus, and for us is that God is more than the "uncaused cause" of created things, God is *love*.[3] Because God is absolutely free, God is absolutely loving and this love is absolutely eminent. For our purposes, this insight speaks loudly to the kind of attitude we need to have in relation to the created world. If the entire creation—ourselves included—is God's free gift of love, how dare we abuse it? If in absolute divine freedom God generously provides such vast diversity and abundance in creation, how dare we withhold what is needed for the flourishing of our human sisters and brothers *and* entire ecosystems? At present, many of the world's economic systems operate on the presupposition of scarcity with an eye only toward satisfying the greed of a few human elites who profit from the mining or harvesting of particular elements of the earth's wealth.

But Scotus' insight draws us into an understanding of God that is deeper still. The Subtle Doctor stresses that the reason God created was not just to display God's abilities, but rather to demonstrate God's own glory and God's own love. Before the beginning of time, Scotus contends, God freely intended the Incarnation. Simply stated, according to Scotus, the reason for the Incarnation, in the first place, was God's free and eternal decision to have (outside himself) someone who could love him perfectly. Through the humanity of Jesus, God expressed the absolutely free divine desire to communicate divine love in a contingent and finite world. This free expression eventually played a redemptive role for humanity as well.

In Scotus' view, the Incarnation was not necessitated by human choice to sin, for that would effectively subject God to the permission of sin. Rather, the Incarnation represents the manifestation of God's eternal glory and God's intent to raise human nature to the highest point of glory by uniting it with divine nature. Understood in this way, the Incarnation is a paradigm for human beings as partners with God in the ongoing co-creation and co-redemption of the world. Christ embodies the divine message that human actions are pleasing to God, human persons are pleasing to God and humans are loved by God. The fact that, according to Scotus, God's freedom and liberality inspired the Incarnation provides a positive enhancement (divinization) of human nature. God, in Scotus' view, is a creative artist who selected the human nature as the "material" most fitting to receive the highest glory of subsisting in the person of the Word.[4]

One strong implication for ecology suggested by this understanding of the Incarnation is that humans have a particularly Christ-like role to play in the cosmos. That role is to love God in God's self and in the entire cosmos which is God's self-expression. Because the entire cosmos in some way resembles Christ, the "first born of all creation," (Col 1: 15–20) we must cherish creation as we reverence Christ. This is the finest example of orthodox panentheism.[5]

Just as God freely and lovingly chose the distinct self-expression of the Incarnation, so too, God intends the unique particularity of everything in the created world. Scotus explains this reality utilizing the philosophical category, the principle of *haecceitas* (individuation or "thisness").[6] As Osborne points out, "Scotus makes the claim that individuation must be based in the very substance of a thing or a person, not in some accidental aspect of a thing or person."[7] *Haecceitas* makes a singular thing what it is and differentiates it from all other things (of common nature) to which it may be compared (because of its commonality).[8] The implications for ecology are vast.

Haecceitas potentially affects human relating in general because it affects how we understand contingent reality as thoroughly laced with the absolutely free and loving intent of the divine. Humans are created by God with freedom to choose good/evil, right/wrong, yet are unconditionally loved by God. Humans are not loved by God simply as a species, but each is loved in her/his person—their individual essence. Just as human value is enhanced by such intimate regard, so too the value of all elements of the cosmos is revered. Not only is each element of the cosmos different in its accidental characteristics, but each is distinct in its very essence. If this is the case, then for Christians, issues of biodiversity must be considered in this light. Not only are entire species of great worth, each particular being is valued in particular for its own sake.

As Séamus Mulholland claims, Scotus' doctrine of *haecceitas*, the Primacy and Predestination of Christ, as well as his other teachings bear implications for Christian spirituality. At the heart of each of these understandings is Love, which is God. Mulholland states: "They (the teachings) are the conclusions of a man of prayer and deep spiritual serenity, for in Scotus, the ultimate aim of all theology is union with God and this is also the ultimate aim of spirituality."[9] Scotus does not treat the usual medieval question, "...if man had not sinned, would Christ still have come?". Instead, Scotus asks: "whether Christ was predestined to become the Son of God."[10] By asking the question this way, the emphasis is shifted from the activities of humans to the love of God. In absolute freedom "God's will is that he be loved outside himself by someone who can love perfectly. He foresees the intensity of the union between Christ and himself who loves him as he loves himself. Christ therefore, one concludes from this, is the center of all creation, all of which has its beginning, source, and end in the love God has for himself in Christ most perfectly."[11] This activity unfolds a story of love, intimacy, union, redemption, acceptance, gratitude, goodness and creation. Creation, Christ and the human family are formed in love and drawn toward the end of ultimate union with God.

But it is to a very specific and individual intimacy that we are drawn. Scotus' *haecceitas* "concerns itself ...with the absolute unique individual distinction of originality that is the result of God's free loving creative activity and effects every animate and inanimate thing."[12] It is in this utter uniqueness that God loves each and every thing for its own sake in and of itself. There is no insignificant being! A spirituality based on "thisness" calls forth a profound regard for life, hope, and respect for the uniqueness of God's creation and the ever-present love of God.

It is this spiritual celebration of God's freely expressed love in creation and the Primacy of Christ that William Short finds in the poetry of Gerard Manley Hopkins. As the first born of all creation, Christ is the model after which all the created world is fashioned. The materiality of Jesus and the materiality of all of creation alike, is the result of the absolutely free loving expression of God. As Short points out, each distinct created thing or person enacts themselves. In the process of enacting themselves each thing or person is simultaneously enacting or manifesting Christ.[13]

Scotus' understanding of nature stands in contrast to other scholastics, such as Thomas Aquinas, whose theory of the analogy of being held that "true being exists only in God and all other being is derivative, pointing toward true being, but only weakly and indirectly."[14] Scotus' theory of the univocity of being holds that each created being in its own singular manner expresses the total image of the Creator. So when we observe the natural world or other persons, we see "things are/do themselves. That doing/being themselves is their doing/being Christ."[15]

Short uses Hopkins to illustrate Scotus' notion of *haecceitas*. In contrast to Thomas Aquinas' view that things have two components—matter and form, Scotus claims there is a third component—"being *this* grape: *haec*, 'This'."[16] "Here is the corollary of the incarnation—God became *this* Jewish carpenter: this unique, unrepeatable, specific creature is the incarnate Creator. From this belief one can conclude that things are God-like in their specificity. Things deserve the respect of our attention, for whatever *is* is because of Christ."[17]

In the final article in this section, Mary Elizabeth Ingham draws on John Duns Scotus' ethical thought. The human person is created by God and given a free will. Though we might be forced to *act* against our will, each of us is solely responsible for choosing or willing something. According to Scotus, our human heart has two affections: the first is directed at self-preservation; the second, is directed outward toward others. It is the second affection, the affection for justice, that Ingham suggests is what undergirds our ecological concerns today. Our affection for justice moves us to do what is fitting and treat nature with appropriate dignity. Sadly, in freedom, we humans often choose selfishly.

If we do follow our affection for justice, Ingham states, "The result is a dynamic of mutual love and expanding inclusivity."[18] Such a stance would also enable us to live into the right relationships characteristic of the Reign of God. This, according to Ingham, would require each of us to develop: *A self-reflexive stance* toward our own lives, *a critical awareness of injustice* around us, and the *courage to act as quickly as possible* on behalf of justice.[19]

As we have already suggested, Ingham proposes, Scotus is relevant for our day on several counts. His moral vision is rooted in an optimistic view of the human capacity to be morally active in the world. Our will for self-preservation and our affection for justice can work together to respond rationally to the command to love God, neighbor and self. Scotus is also optimistic about creation. The created world has all powerful, free, generous Love as its source. Thus, all reality is good and beautiful. The moral life involves all that is our environment and our efforts to strengthen and enhance our mutual relations. Scotus' view is both organic and dynamic. All reality progresses through the present toward a future that potentially includes greater integration and awareness. Ingham concludes: "If relationship and mutuality are appropriate human goods, then they are moral goals. Accordingly, all persons have a right to share equally in the resources of the earth."[20]

We can sum up the significance of John Duns Scotus' philosophy and theology for ecotheology and ethics as follows: God created the world in absolute freedom. But, more, God is Love. Out of a desire to be loved perfectly God chose the human form as the material in which to express the Masterpiece of creation, Jesus Christ. Each thing and person of creation is an expression of God in its own right. The created world and all that is in it is good and thus, there is great hope for humans and all of creation. In our ecologically threatened world, humans need to follow their affection for justice and inclination to live in mutual relation with all of creation.

Notes

1. Kanan B. Osborne, "Incarnation, Individuality, and Diversity," *The Cord* 45/3 (1995): 21.
2. Ibid., 22.
3. Ibid.
4. John Duns Scotus, Ordinatio III.7.q.3, trans. Allan B. Wolter "John Duns Scotus On the Primacy and Personality of Christ," in *Franciscan Christology: Selected Texts, Translations and Essays*, Franciscan Sources No.1, ed. Damian McElrath, (St. Bonaventure, NY: Franciscan Institute Publications, 1980), at 151: "Now the sequence in which the creative artist evolves his plan is the very opposite of the way he puts it into execution. One can say, however, that in the order of execution, God's union with a human nature is really prior to his granting it the greatest grace and glory. We could presume, then, that it was in the reverse order that he intended them, so that God

would first intend that some nature, not the highest, should receive the highest glory, as he bestowed natural perfection. Then secondly, as it were, he willed that this nature should subsist in the Person of the Word, so that the angel might not be subject to a [mere] man."

5. Panentheism is the belief that all things are imbued with God's being in the sense that all things are *in* God. God is more than all that is and is a consciousness and the highest unity possible.

6. John Duns Scotus, *John Duns Scotus: God and Creatures*, trans. Felix Alluntis and Allan B. Wolter, "Glossary," at 511: "*haecceitas*, (from the Latin *haec*, this): The term means literally, 'thisness.' It designates the unique formal principle of individuation that makes the nature, which all individuals of the same species have in common, to be just this or that individual and no other. Scotus regards it as a distinct positive formality over and above the common nature of the individual (natura communis)."

7. Osborne, "Incarnation, Individuality, and Diversity," 25.

8. Eric Doyle, "Duns Scotus and Ecumenism," in *De Doctrina I. Duns Scoti*, vol. III, Acta Congressus Scotistici Internationalis Oxonii et Edimburgi, 11–17 September 1966 celebrati, Camille Bérubé, ed., (Roma: Cura Commissionis Scotisticae, 1968), at 460: "The uniqueness, the unrepeatable something of all things, is what gives them their intrinsic and eternal value. There is about everything, every person, an originality that gives new insight into reality, another aspect that has never been seen before. Each person enters into a new enriching relationship of knowledge and love with every new person met, with every new thing encountered."

9. Séamus Mulholland, "Christ the *Haecceitas* of God: The Spirituality of John Duns Scotus' Doctrine of *Haecceitas* and the Primacy of Christ," *The Cord* 40/6 (June 1990):167.

10. Ibid., 168.

11. Ibid., 169.

12. Ibid., 170.

13. William Short, "Pied Beauty: Gerard Manley Hopkins and the Scotistic View of Nature," *The Cord* 45/3 (1995): 30–31.

14. Ibid., 31.

15. Ibid., 32.

16. Ibid., 34.

17. Ibid.

18. Mary Elizabeth Ingham, "A Certain Affection For Justice," *The Cord* 45/3 (1995): 15.

19. Ibid.

20. Ibid., 17.

The Franciscan Doctor*

Philotheus Boehner, OFM**

To intellectual honesty and obedient faith, John Duns Scotus adds the Franciscan spirit. Understanding cannot be the last goal, high though its value is in the hierarchy of values. The highest value is Charity. Scotus shows that the opponents of the primacy of love claim the authority of Aristotle, who thinks that the acts of the intellect and not the acts of love dispose to Wisdom. But Scotus has in his favor a much better arid higher authority...

What use is speculation, to enjoy deep insights into the highest truths, if it does not lead to the highest act of the human personality, loving surrender to God as revealed in Christ...? Hence, Scotus does not consider theology a speculative science. Its highest purpose is not to inform about truth and to know God only in a scientific way; theology is a practical science, and its purpose is to instruct us about and lead us to the highest "praxis," to Charity, that is the Love of God...

It follows that man [sic] has to know, above all, that he is a creature,

---

* From: Philotheus Boehner, OFM: "The Intellectual Personality of Duns Scotus." *The History of the Franciscan School*, Part 3, *Duns Scotus.* Unpublished lecture notes (St. Bonaventure University, St. Bonaventure, NY, 1945) 123–24.

** This article originally appeared as: "The Franciscan Doctor," *The Cord* 45/3 (May–June 1995): 37–8. Reprinted with permission.

and that, as a creature, he comes from nothing and tends toward nothingness. Even in reasoning, he tends toward nothingness...

From this, humility in reasoning and the necessity for prayer follow naturally. Human effort is certainly necessary. Otherwise we would wrong God, the Creator of our powers. In this ...Scotus dignifies human nature; ...but human nature... has its limits and consequently man has to turn to the Father of Lights in prayer. Scotus, the knight of truth, is also a great fighter and a man of great prayer. If we open his *Treatise on God as First Principle*, we see an impressive picture. The knight of truth first lays down his weapons and, kneeling down and folding his hands, he prays; ...and then he puts on his armor, takes his weapons and fights the struggle of truth in painstaking logic. Time and again he does the same, praying for help from God, until he reaches his highest point in the last chapter where his fight and struggle for insight transform themselves into a long prayer of great beauty, strength and ardor. Here metaphysical speculation and religious fervor are harmoniously united. His charity, humility and spirit of prayer, therefore, authorize us to call Duns Scotus a *Doctor Franciscanus.*

If we may be allowed to compare St. Bonaventure and Duns Scotus, at first sight two quite different types of mind, we shall find that in spite of all their differences, they are both true Franciscans. St. Bonaventure, the *Doctor Seraphicus*, is an intellectual personality who does not reason without emotion, ...circulating around the object of his intellect in a restless love until the fulfillment of this love is reached in the highest mysticism. Duns Scotus, the *Doctor Subtilis*, is an intellectual personality who, with strictly objective reasoning and a rigid asceticism of the intellect, gives his *placet* to a statement *only* if his logic is satisfied. At the same time, however, Scotus is a humble scholar, a prayerful theologian, whose ultimate goal is the love of God. Both Scholastics may have different ways, but both have the same goal. The one calls it *unctio*, the other *charitas*. Therefore, their ways cannot be in opposition. On the contrary, their different ways are integrating parts of a real Franciscan philosophy and theology. It would be a loss to Franciscan science if it should lack the Seraphic Doctor's *pie et alta sentiendum est de Deo* [devout and profound feeling toward God]. But, Franciscan science would be in perpetual danger of falling into an uncontrolled mysticism if the Subtle Doctor's intellectual asceticism were wanting.

Incarnation, Individuality and Diversity: How Does Christ Reveal the Unique Value of Each Person and Thing?

Kenan B. Osborne, OFM[*]

Kenan B. Osborne, OFM [*]

INTRODUCTORY OBSERVATIONS

In Robert Sokolowski's recent book, *Eucharistic Presence: A Study in the Theology of Disclosure*, the author, a priest of the archdiocese of Hartford teaching philosophy at The Catholic University of America, describes necessary and contingent being in this way:

> To turn everything in the world into the contingent... would be to equate the contingency that marks the world as a whole with the contingency that is found as part of the world. The consequence of such a confusion, of course, would be another confusion regarding necessity; the necessity by which God exists would be equated with the necessity that is part of the world, and the divine choice to create would be assimilated to events that take place within the contingent domain of the world. God's choice would then appear as a "merely contingent" event and would take on the quality of being arbitrary. Cajetan criticizes Scotus for making this mistake.[1]

Thomas de Vio Cajetan was a Dominican who lived in the sixteenth century at the time of the Council of Trent. Cajetan at that time had written: "How uncultivated and upstart is Scotus' way of speaking...

* This article originally appeared as: "Incarnation, Individuality, Diversity," *The Cord* 45/3 (May–June 1995): 19–26. Reprinted with permission.

when he calls the divine will 'the first contingent cause.' It is nefarious to speak of contingency in the divine will."[2] This is the only reference to John Duns Scotus in Sokolowski's book—and he is quoting Cajetan!

How easy it appears to be, even today, to dismiss the thought of Scotus and to do this by simply citing another author, in this case, Cajetan. This particular instance is remarkable, since Sokolowski states clearly in his introduction—the very first sentence in fact—that he wants "to discuss a type of theological thinking that draws on the philosophical resources provided by phenomenology."[3] Oddly enough, one of the masters of phenomenology, Martin Heidegger, wrote his doctoral thesis on John Duns Scotus, a philosopher whom Sokolowski cites but once. Moreover, one wonders whether Sokolowski has truly understood the insights of Scotus on the issues of necessity and contingency. What he has presented above is really a superficial picture of the thought of Scotus on the theme of contingent and necessary being.

I did not write a doctoral thesis on John Duns Scotus, but in my youthful days when I was a senior in college, I did write a final paper for my philosophy professor, Geoffrey Bridges, OFM. My paper was different from the ones to which he was accustomed. The theme was *haecceitas* or "thisness" as found in Scotus. The style, however, was a whimsical platonic dialogue between myself and John Duns Scotus, which took place in a small boat called the Shenandoah adrift in Whelan's lake, where we college students often went for picnics. In the dialogue, I kept asking Scotus: "What does it mean to be an individual? What does it mean to be a person?" Scotus' thought responds to such questions with valuable insights. Even though his work bears all the hallmarks of medievalism, and we, on the other hand, are living in the so-called post-christian age and on the very threshold of the third millennium, nevertheless we can learn from Scotus today.

In order to place these questions in a clear way and to offer some answers to them, I would like to take a walk with you through some Scotistic positions in order to comprehend some of the essential background and reasoning of "thisness" which Scotus himself perceived.

Scotus: A Christian Realist

First of all, Scotus was a believing realist, both ontologically and epistemologically. This means that his Christian faith penetrated his human real life. For Scotus there was indeed a God and there was indeed a created world. The world actually existed, and it existed in its details long before any of us began thinking about it and naming the things in it. Scotus in this regard was neither a nominalist, nor a solipsist, nor an idealist. Although the realist position which he espoused cannot logically be proven and must serve only as a presupposition, Scotus accepted the reality of the world about him, both epistemologically and ontologically. However, he was a *Christian* realist, and as such he accepted in faith the existence of God, the incarnation, the church, and all the other major tenets of the Roman Catholic faith. His was a medieval faith, untouched by the many pluralistic, secularistic, even atheistic questions of contemporary life. It is against this background of Christian realism that he asked the question: what is "thisness"?[4]

HIS METHODOLOGY

In order to understand the mystery of God, at least to some degree, Scotus places on the table of observation all of creation, that is, every finite, created being. Nothing is to be left out. The environment is certainly there, with its physical nature and its vegetative and animal life. Human life is also there, with every person from Adam and Eve to those living at the close of the thirteenth century and even those who were yet to come. The angels, too, are placed on this observation table. Scotus adds one other keenly important creature to this table of observation: namely, the humanity of Jesus, the most important, the most perfect, the most wonderful of all God's creatures.

However, not only are the good aspects of finite being spread out on this table of observation, but also the misshapen aspects, the sinful aspects are also there, including satan and the legions of demons. It is a table on which there is good, indeed the most wonderfully good, and on which there is bad, indeed the most dreadfully evil. Through this mass of creatures, both good and evil, Scotus looks for a God who is not only the God of the good, but also the God of the weak, the God of the sinful. What kind of a God can this be?

I find this methodology very helpful for us today, since in many ways our scientific and secularistic world asks us to consider a God of the totality. We cannot have religion only in one small part of our life and science in another part of our life. We cannot be schizophrenic, either religiously or scientifically. This is of advantage in today's religiously plural world, for were Scotus alive today he would place on the table of observation Buddhism, Hinduism, Islam and all other religious groups. He would place on the table all the atoms and sub-atomic particles as well as the processes of thermo-nuclear dynamics and electromagnetics. When all created and finite beings known to us would finally be placed on the table, Scotus would then ask: given all of this data, what kind of a credible God accounts for this multiple form of finitude? It is within this observational methodology that Scotus seeks the meaning of "thisness."

GOD: THE FIRST PRINCIPLE

Given this massive array of the Christian "real" world, Scotus then asks: what God is mirrored here? This Scotus attempts to answer in his book: *A Treatise on God as First Principle.*[5] While this work might seem very abstract and challenging, nevertheless, it is an important basis for understanding Scotus. In an introductory essay to this treatise, Allan Wolter reminds us that the First Principle [God] can be understood in three ways: as cause of all that is (efficiency), as ultimate end or purpose for which all exists (finality), or as first in the order of relative perfection (eminence).[6] Further on Wolter writes: "If the whole of creation depends upon God's free decision, then any factual or existential statement about the world will be radically contingent."[7]

Scotus looks at our world and realizes that God is absolutely free— nothing created is necessary; God did not *have to* create anything; all is gift and grace. God, the first principle, is both absolutely necessary and at the same time absolutely free. Most medieval theologians stressed that God as first principle was a necessary being. Scotus, on the other hand, in a fairly unique way, stressed the absolute freedom of this necessary God.

What one hears in the writings of Scotus is an emphasis on the free willing of God, on a free contingent willing of a necessary God, but a willing of contingent beings nonetheless. In *A Treatise on God as First Principle*, Scotus presents God as the efficient cause of all created beings, but he also stresses throughout chapter three of this treatise that God as First Principle is absolutely necessary and absolutely free; that there is a triple primacy—of efficiency, finality and eminence. Since such a God as First Principle has no efficient cause of God's own being, God is necessary.[8] This is the *aseitas* [the uncaused cause] of so many medieval writers. However, in Scotus' view, finality and eminence are of higher value than efficiency. It is not the "how" but the "why" which is important. *Aseitas* simply says that there is no beginning, no other cause. This term speaks of the "how" or better, the lack of any "how." God, however, is much more than one who has no beginning, no cause. God is *love* and this is the "why" or the finality and eminence. Nor is God simply love; God is absolutely free love; and this absolutely free love is absolutely eminent. Meaning, not origin, has primacy of place. For Scotus, "thisness" of created beings can only be understood in the light of this absolutely eminent and free God, who in love wills each and every contingent being.

CREATION

Freedom is reflected in God's freely creating contingent beings. Efficient causality is indeed present, i.e., "how" contingent beings arise. But *final* causality, i.e., "why" they are created, is for Scotus of greater significance. God does not create just because God can create. God creates for a purpose, namely, God's own glory and God's own love. Let us return to the table and look over all those items of this creative God. We see our environment, we see our first parents and all other persons, we see ourselves, we see our sins, we see the sins of all men and women and we see that special created, finite, contingent being which we call the humanity of Jesus.

It is in the *Reportatio* that Scotus clearly "de-links" the incarnation from the fall of Adam and Eve, but already in the *Ordinatio* he had begun this process.[9] In a well-known passage he writes:

> Therefore I argue as follows: in the first place God loves himself. Secondly, he loves himself in others and this is most pure and holy love. Thirdly God wills to be loved by another who can love him perfectly and here I am referring to the love of someone outside God. Therefore, fourthly, God foresees the union between the Word and the creature Christ who owes him supreme love, even had there never been the Fall.... In the fifth place, he sees Christ as Mediator coming to suffer and redeem his people because of sin.[10]

Here Scotus is speaking primarily about God, the First Principle, creating the world we know. This is a passage which is primarily theological and only secondarily christological; it says something about God first and only then something about Christ. This theocentric interpretation is based on the structure of the passage: i.e., Scotus says that God first…, then God second…, then God third…, etc. In this view, Jesus, in his humanity, indeed sacramentalizes the finality of God's whole world, a world in which human freedom and human mis-freedom (sin) exist. The whole world is sacramentalized, not just the "nice" part of it. The incarnation, then, begins, one might say, with the very first act of God *ad extra*—the first creative moment of our world. The incarnation is a process moving through the history of our created world, and with each subsequent step the meaning of the world, the finality of the world, the "why" of the world emerges to some degree in a clearer way. We are finding out more about the incarnation than ever before. It is an ascending experience. Like climbing a mountain, the higher one goes, the wider and broader one's perspective.

In the Jesus-event, a major revelation of the meaning of creation, the "why" of creation, takes place. This is what the world and its history are all about. But this Jesus-event includes not only his life and death, his preaching and healing, but also his resurrection, his ascension, his sending of the Spirit and his eschatological place at the right hand of God. This is where Jesus was always meant to go. The Church itself is part of this process, since the resurrection of Jesus and our own resurrection are intrinsically one. More strongly put, the Christ at God's right hand cannot be understood except in and with the mystical body of Christ here on earth.

This is what it's all about. This is what it's always been about. Where Jesus went we are meant to go and have always been meant to go. This is the *Christus totus*, the whole Christ, of which the *Catechism of the Catholic Church* speaks when it asks "Who celebrates the sacraments?" and answers "The *Christus totus.*" The full meaning of incarnation is not that Jesus has a human and a divine nature, but that Jesus has a human nature and we, all of us, all human beings, are related to it. One might say that the incarnation as a process is still continuing and will continue until the eschaton, until the "why" of God's free action to create reaches its own fullness. All that is, all that has ever been, is related to incarnation. Only with this understanding can we realize the height and depth, the length and breadth of "why" there is something finite and not nothing at all except God.

Scotus certainly did not believe that a "greater-than-Jesus" would ever appear. The Jesus in his statement above is the risen Jesus, the eschaton Jesus, not simply the Jesus who walked this earth and died. In Scotus' thought, it is Jesus who gives the greatest glory to God. Scotus did, however, believe that *none of this was necessary.* Even the humanity of Jesus, even the incarnation itself was not "necessary." The humanity of Jesus, just as my own humanity, is contingent. Only God is necessary and only God is absolutely free. From the point of view of the *absolute power of God,* God could have done quite otherwise. From the point of view of the *actualized power of God,* God freely and contingently acted in a specific way. Why, one might ask, did God choose this specific way of creating something? For Scotus, the only reason is God's love and God's desire to express this divine love in a contingent and finite world. Only within this framework can one begin to understand what Scotus wants to say about "thisness."

HAECCEITAS OR "THISNESS"

We have almost finished our walk, brisk and quick as it has been. Let us pause now, thinking over the details which Scotus has pointed out, for it is against the background of all these details that Scotus addresses the issue of "thisness." In his early Oxford lecture on individuation, Scotus begins by noting that a stone is singular long before we perceive it. It has its own unity of singularity before we call it a stone.

There is indeed an *epistemological* "thisness," which means that we often perceive individual things first of all through accidental individual characteristics. We see that someone is tall, short, thin or fat. Only in and with time do we begin to appreciate the "individual person" beneath these observable appearances. This is epistemological "thisness," but Scotus and others had much more in mind than merely epistemological individuation. Scotus wanted to talk about *essential* "thisness," essential individuation, ontological *haecceitas.*

At the beginning of his discussion on this matter, he rejected several views which other theologians of his time had proposed: 1) that all one needed were the four Aristotelian causes, material, formal, efficient and final, to account for individuation; 2) that individuation is based on quantity; 3) that individuation is based on negation; 4) that individuation is based on matter. Scotus makes the claim that individuation must be based in the very substance of a thing or person, not in some accidental aspect of a thing or person. There is a form connected to the very substance of a being through which individuation takes place. I cannot simply put on or take off my individuality. It belongs to my very essence. Elizabeth Ingham summarizes this: "It [*haecceitas*] grounds the substantial being internally and points to individuality at the core of each thing, not as a function of the material component, but as the internal instantiation of the substantial being."[11]

Wolter, at the end of his preface on the text and translation of Scotus' early *Oxford Lecture on Individuation* writes:

> In the *Ordinatio* revision of this seventh question, Scotus makes an important claim, that where rational beings are concerned it is the person rather than the nature that God primarily desired to create. His remark is in answer to an objection that individuals do not pertain to the order of the universe, for order is based on priority and posteriority, and individuals are all on a par with one another. Not only do individuals pertain to the order of God's universe, Scotus replies, but in communicating his good as something befitting his beauty in each species, he delights in producing a multiplicity of individuals. And in those beings which are the highest and most important, it is the individual that is primarily intended by God. Viewed from this aspect, Scotus' doctrine of thisness applied to the human person would seem to invest each with a unique value as one singularly wanted and loved by God, quite apart from any trait that person shares with others or any contribution he or she might make to society. One could even say "thisness" is our personal gift from God.[12]

God, then, does not want primarily to create "human nature," an abstraction, but this particular human person.

Haecceitas, Ingham writes, refers to that positive dimension of every concrete and contingent being which identifies it and makes it worthy of attention.[13] Scotus elaborates an understanding of reality imbued with freedom, contingency and attention to the particular.[14] Even more, this singularity is especially important for the human person as a *moral person*. In this regard, Scotus alters his general approach which favors final causality and focuses the individual on his or her own efficiently causing will. The individual actually causes events to happen. Scotus leads us to ask: What does it mean to be myself? Of what am I a cause? What will I, in my particular life, cause to happen through my own free choices?

We have free will, and it is particularly in this free will that we evidence the image of God. We cannot claim that we are part of a process which is cosmic and beyond our control. Rather, we are responsible individual persons with individual wills, and we do cause good and also cause evil. Free will is not the choice to sin or not to sin, but simply choice. It is our perception of the harmony of goodness and our choice of this harmony of goodness which is at the basis of our moral action. Here again we see the importance of the individual over the general, the concrete over the abstract, the person over the nature.

Notes

1.   Robert Sokolowski, *Eucharistic Presence: A Study in the Theology of Disclosure* (Washington, DC: The Catholic University of America Press, 1993) 48.
2.   Cajetan, *Commentary on St. Thomas Aquinas*, Summa theologiae, I, 19, 3, Leonine Edition (Rome: Sacra Congregatio de Propaganda Fidei, 1888).
3.   Sokolowski, 5.
4.   Cf. Allan B. Wolter, "The Realism of Scotus," *The Philosophical Theology of John Duns Scotus*, ed. Marilyn McCord Adams (Ithaca, NY: Cornell University Press, 1990) 42–53.
5.   John Duns Scotus, *A Treatise on God as First Principle*, trans. and ed. Allan B. Wolter, OFM (Chicago: Franciscan Herald Press, 1966).
6.   Scotus, xiii.
7.   Scotus, xvii.
8.   Scotus, 42–72.
9.   Cf. Mary Elizabeth Ingham, CSJ, "John Duns Scotus: An Integrated Vision," *The History of Franciscan Theology*, edited by K. B. Osborne (St. Bonaventure, NY: The Franciscan Institute, 1994) 220.
10. Scotus, *Reportata Parisiensia* III, d. 7, q.4, n. 5.
11. Ingham, 210.
12. Allan B. Wolter, *Duns Scotus' Early Oxford Lecture on Individuation* (Santa Barbara, California: Old Mission Santa Barbara, 1992), xxvii.
13. Ingham, 190.
14. Ingham, 198.

Christ: The *Haecceitas* of God
The Spirituality of
John Duns Scotus' Doctrine
of *Haecceitas* and Primacy of Christ

Séamus Mullholland, OFM[*]

It may at first glance seem odd that I have chosen to reflect upon the spirituality of Scotus when he is known as a theologian and philosopher, but on closer inspection it is not odd at all. Scotus' theological and philosophical investigations and conclusions burn with a love for God, Christ, creation, and humanity. He is a thinker, not just of profound intellectual insight, but of profound spiritual insight also. It is love which is the central motivating force, and principle tenet of his life and work. It is love which is the essence of Franciscan spirituality whether it be found in the writings and life of Francis, Clare, Bonaventure and a host of other Franciscan writers, thinkers, mystics and saints and it is love of God which predominates.

Yet, Scotus' spirituality has not been given the attention it deserves for too often, even among Franciscans, his insights are seen as theological or philosophical "hair-splitting," He is presented as some kind of Scholastic Iago: subtle, scheming, devious, a thinker who can take apart a word, phrase or sentence and manipulate it to serve his own purposes. He is more feared in the avoiding than understood in the confronting. Scotus: the Harbinger of Nominalism; the initiator of everything that is decadent in philosophy and theology: Scotus, the linguistic gymnast

[*]   This article originally appeared as; "Christ: The *Haecceitas* of God," *The Cord* 40/6 (June 1990): 165–72. Reprinted with permission.

who somersaults, cartwheels and vaults with finely tuned nuances and veiled half-implied eccentricities and subtleties of language and thought. But there is more to him than that for I believe he is not only one of the great theological and philosophical teachers in the Franciscan tradition, but also one of the great spiritual teachers.

The most frequently used epithet of Scotus is "Subtle Doctor" which does not have the same celestial attractiveness about it as Thomas', "Angelic Doctor," or Bonaventure's, "Seraphic Doctor," and too often this epithet is used in a pejorative and derisive sense. But as Hamlet said, "...to my mind it is a custom more honored in the breach than in the keeping." (Hamlet; 1, 111). So, I use the epithet, "Subtle" in the breach and not the keeping; for though he was intellectually subtle, he was subtle in love also. It is a subtlety which is rooted in love, a gifted vision of God, the unique individuality of Creation, and the place and role of Christ in God's redemptive plan, and the absolute freedom of God, particularly in Christ's predestination and the Immaculate Conception.

In all the reading, study and thinking about Scotus that I have done and continue to do, a question persistently raises itself in my mind: how could Scotus have arrived at the spiritual depths of his doctrines (let alone the theological philosophical depths), if he had not already experienced them as realities in his own life? I find it impossible to believe that Scotus did nothing but abstractly think and reason like some Scholastic Mr. Spock. Indeed those who use his epithet pejoratively may think of him as Caesar did of the even subtler Cassius: "...Mark him ...he thinks too much... such men are dangerous..." (Julius Caesar, I, 11). Where ignorance is bliss, when approaching Scotus it is folly to pretend to be wise by avoiding him; the result is fear and lack of understanding and yet Scotus is a fertile bed of spiritual richness.

As a Franciscan myself and a Scotist, l am struck by the fact that Scotus' own Franciscanism is very often almost overlooked, or at best, an afterthought or irrelevancy in his life. It is an uninteresting biographical fact yet it is crucial to any spiritual understanding of him. His work burns with a Franciscan vision which has much to teach us today. The doctrine of the Primacy and Predestination of Christ; *haecceitas*; primacy of the Will; and his defense of the Immaculate Conception, as well as his ethics, are intimately part of the Franciscan tradition, its vision of the world and its humanism.

He entered the Order at a very young age and one may assume that this was because his desire to join the Friars was very strong. Perhaps he had heard the Friars preach in his native Scotland, or had seen them; whatever the case, one may also assume that he had some love for Francis when he joined. One may further agree that Bonaventure may be closer in "spirit" and in time to Francis, but I have always viewed this as setting limits on interpreting Francis' life and vision. New interpretations of his life and work and vision are essential if the needs of any age are to be met so that the vibrant, charismatic ever-newness of the Spirit of Francis and Franciscanism can be a prophetic witness in every climate and not be lost to complacency, cynicism and compromise. I believe Scotus does this in his own age, for what we receive from Bonaventure in poetry in his own writings, we receive in realism and conceptualization in Scotus. One might call him the "metaphysical wing" of Francis.

Yet it is the "Subtle" doctor who breaks with a whole tradition and asserts the Will over intellect; who limits what philosophy can conclude or reach; who teaches the Predestination of Christ. It is the "Subtle" doctor, who when Augustine, Thomas and even Bonaventure, cannot hold to the Immaculate Conception, solves their problem (and that of the Church) by moving it away from human necessity to divine freedom of will (for which alone he should be canonized). One might ask and wonder why Bonaventure could not hold to the Immaculate Conception—a question which has not been asked or even investigated. However, what holds these theological and philosophical teachings together in unity is not intellectual or linguistic subtlety itself, but I believe his experience of them in his own life. Even in Scotus' ethics it is Love which dominates.[1] They are conclusions of a man of prayer and deep spiritual serenity, for in Scotus the ultimate aim of all theology is union with God and this is also the ultimate aim of Spirituality.[2]

His teachings attest to the spirituality of his own life which is within the understanding of mysticism in the Scholastic tradition.[3] He was not an emotionless thinker, nor was he removed and transcendentally mystical or spiritual; he was, rather, a man bewildered in love at the intensity of God's love revealed in creation, Scripture, theology and most perfectly, in Christ—and is this not what Francis is doing in the Canticle of the Creatures which is poem, prayer, mystical union, theology, and praise all in one? Scotus is undeniably a son of Francis and it is the doctrine of the Primacy and Predestination of Christ which is the most eloquent witness to the depth of his Franciscanism, his prayer and mysticism.

THE SPIRITUALITY OF SCOTUS' DOCTRINE OF CHRIST

In turning to consider the spirituality of Scotus' doctrine I am constantly struck by the beauty of the phrase "*Summum opus Dei*"[4] which the late Eric Doyle, OFM, translated as "God's Masterpiece." Here Scotus manifests the poet in himself as well as mystic: and not only here, for one need only read the opening and closing prayer of *De Primo principio* to see not just his poetry but also his prayerfulness.[5] And I venture to suggest that the doctrine of "haecceitas" is of significance here, for what Scotus says about the unique distinction of everything as being "this" and not "that" can equally, be applied to God's Masterpiece for I believe in this context that Christ is the "haecceitas" of God.[6]

The question of Christ's Predestination was not new when Scotus came to consider it, but as Scotus thought differently from others before him so too he approaches this question differently.[7] It had been considered from the hypothetical standpoint in the question, "if man had not sinned would Christ still have come?" The question is not only hypothetical but is also negative in its implications for spirituality where it is man's actions which occasion God to act. Though the question is hypothetical it implicitly limits the absolute freedom of God to be God as God.

Scotus does not ask this question and indeed would never have asked such a question because he moves away from considering the question in hypothesis and so in a negative manner, to a consideration of divine freedom, will and love and so arrives at a positive soteriology, anthropology and spirituality. Scotus says that we do not know what God may or may not have done if man had not sinned;[8] when he treats of the question he does so based purely upon what he concludes of Christ's absolute predestination to be Son of God before all time. He therefore takes what is essentially a theological question and moves it into a spiritual dimension by starting not with man's sinfulness and need for redemption, but the absolute freedom of God's love. Scotus' question is "whether Christ was predestined to be the Son of God." Scotus' answer based on the love that God is, is yes. Christ's predestination is absolute and unconditional and sin has nothing to do with it. He cannot and will not believe that God's Masterpiece would never have taken place because there was no sin to bring it about.

Here, spirituality is at the service of theology first and foremost and again the basis of Scotus' doctrine is love. He cannot accept that if Adam had not sinned the greatest love would never have been given to

God because the love of men which is less than perfection had not been refused—and the love of men cannot have nor ever possess the same intensity as Christ's love. It is impossible, Scotus holds, to accept that God would have accepted the lesser over the greater; thus, Christ was always absolutely and unconditionally predestined to be the Son of God; it is the perfection of Christ's love which constitutes the Primacy he has and his predestination and no other reason.

Spirituality takes precedence over theology here for although the doctrine has profound theological significance, it has a profounder spiritual significance particularly for understanding the Universal Kingship of Christ over creation. Scotus' doctrine hinges on God's love for himself and his will to be loved by others in himself.

Scotus says that God is first and foremost and formally love. He loves himself and wills himself to be loved in others and that those who love him come to perfect union with him (the end to which theology and spirituality look forward). Love is reason itself for its own loving and in God there is one act of loving. He loves himself most perfectly; in loving himself in others the love is ordered and holy and it diffuses itself. God's will is that he be loved outside himself by someone who can love perfectly. He foresees the intensity of union between Christ and himself who loves him as he loves himself. Christ therefore, one concludes from this, is the center of all creation all of which has its beginning, source, and in the love God has for himself in Christ most perfectly.[9]

The "motive" for the incarnation then is God's freely willed, freely given, freely creating love. Scotus' teaching from a spiritual point of view is about the goodness of God, how God sees man in love in Christ; it is about love and redemption, intimacy and union, acceptance and gratitude, the goodness of creation—and not sin and death, estrangement and loss, rejection and self-pity, and creational dualism.

This is Francis of Assisi's Canticle and spirit from a different, though undoubtedly Franciscan, viewpoint. Scotus has the same vision of the created order as Francis; he is closer to Francis than many would consider, for he knows that without this love there is nothing and if there is nothing there is chaos. The core spiritual message of the Doctrine of the Primacy of Christ in Scotus is that of experiential love; God's love is its own reason (the Immaculate Conception is a point in case), its own cause and so is the cause of everything else. As Francis saw with the poet's eye, Scotus sees with the reflective eye: creation, Christ, and the human family are constituted in love and it is through this love that we are brought deeper and deeper into the mystery of God in union, the end to which we all look forward.

THE SPIRITUALITY OF *HAECCEITAS*

I do not wish to discuss the metaphysics of "haecceitas" in great detail in what is essentially an article on spirituality; however, some treatment is necessary if the spiritual dimension is to be explored.

In Scotus the mind apprehends both being and objective truth but he goes on to say that objectivity of human knowledge involves certain positions for which philosophy does not allow.

Agreeing with Thomas, Scotus says that human knowledge depends upon experience but he rejects the necessity of a "divine illumination" of the intellect. Scotus, however, did not agree with Thomas' idea that the human mind does not know individual things directly or immediately.[10] He believed that the mind does have an intellectual, albeit somewhat confused, intuition of the individual thing itself. His reasoning is sound: how could the mind abstract the universal from the particular or individual without any previous intellectual intuition of the individual. If the mind abstracts at all it abstracts from what it knows.

Scotus demonstrates this in his Socrates example: Socrates is a man and Plato is a man but there is in both a human nature which is itself "indifferent" to being the nature of Socrates and Plato. In other words we can distinguish in Socrates his "Socratesness" from his human nature which is not identical with it. What then is the distinction? It is not a distinction between separable things (not even the divine power could separate them). Nor is it merely a mental-intellectual distinction. It is a "formal objective distinction." Again, reason and sensation are distinct objectively but they are not separable in the way body and soul are separable—the power of both could not be separated without the destruction of the soul. So it is a distinction in formalities rather than in separable things.

This is the core of "haecceitas" and there is a deep spirituality in it because this realism of Scotus attests to the fact that there exists in each individual thing a nature distinct from its "haecceitas" (though he does not attribute the same nature to all members of the same species).

Haecceitas concerns itself from a spiritual point of view with the absolute unique individual distinction of originality that is the result of God's free loving creative activity and effects every animate and inanimate thing. As each person is individual and distinct in their "thisness," even from their own human nature, so too is every bird, flower, tree etc. The doctrine of Christ's Primacy attests to his own uniqueness for he is the only Son of God. He is utterly and absolutely unique in himself; his haecceitas is his Christness—original and individual: he is a sense the "haecceitas" of God present to the world.

Haecceitas then is not simply about metaphysical delineations of form, genus, species, substance, essences and so on but it is also about humility in accepting the glory of God in the most insignificant of created things. Gerard Manley Hopkins spiritualized it as "inscape" in his poetry, particularly in "Pied Beauty." Francis does the same in the Canticle by naming each thing as individual Brother or Sister and in the great prayer of thanksgiving before the Eucharist.

There is as much Christological depth in this doctrine as in that of the Primacy and it has a very positive anthropological and psychological dimension to it. Underpinning all these teachings is the unity in love which exists between God and his creatures each one of which is unique, not just among the species but of and within itself and to itself in God's creative activity. Thus even the metaphysical dimension of Scotus' thought is rooted in love.

Francis always began with the love of God and his own experience of it. Scotus too belongs in this category: he begins with the love of God in his Predestination and Primacy doctrines; Primacy of the Will; haecceitas; his ethics, psychology and anthropology. He has the same depth of feeling and desire that Francis has, though he expresses and contextualizes it differently. It led Francis to call Christ, "Brother"; to thank God for him who knew our human experience. It led him ultimately to La Verna to experience the pain and suffering of this love.

Love of God, love of Christ, love of creation, love of man in all his array of gifts and talents, Scotus experiences it as much as Francis, Clare, Alexander of Hales or Bonaventure. He not only loves God but is in love with God's love. He is beyond doubt a great spiritual master in the Franciscan tradition, a mystic and, I believe, a saint.

His teachings are deeply significant for our own times: filled with faith and hope; love and longing; a respect for life: a respect for the uniqueness of God's creation and the ever-present love of God. What a pity he died so young. I regret what might have been, but as Gilson says, "such regrets are useless." His works radiate not only intellectual power, but spiritual power also filled with love, intimacy, prayer, mysticism and the unity which he saw his whole life and work bringing him towards.

As a Scotist, as a Franciscan, as a Celt, as a disciple I pray daily, that the church may recognize not just his intellectual genius, theological orthodoxy, or philosophical subtleties, but also the sanctity of his life; for Scotus was a man who knew by experience the love of the God he wrote, thought, speculated and reflected about. Like Francis he was a simple man of prayer and love.

Notes

1.   See the excellent translation and study by A. B. Wolter, *Duns Scotus on the Will and Morality*, CUP, 1986, esp. last 3 chapters.
2.   *Opus Oxoniense*, Prol., q.3, a. 4, n.12.
3.   See P. Tillich's remarks about Scotus' mysticism in *A History of Christian Thought*, SCM, London, 1968, p. 126.
4.   Scotus' full teaching on the Predestination of Christ is to be found in *Ordinatio* III, d.7. (Vives edition, XIV, 348–9, 354–5) and *Reporta Parisiensis*, III, d.7, q.4 (Vives edition, XXIII, 301–4).
5.   An excellent translation can be found in A. B. Wolter's *John Duns Scotus: A Treatise on God as First Principle*, Franciscan Herald Press: Chicago, 1966, 1.1, 1.2 p.3, 4.94, p. 150.
6.   I am aware that Scotus teaches that God's essence alone has no need of any individuating principle since it is individuation in itself *(de se haec)*. I use the term in a spiritual sense and not creedal.
7.   See ref. note 4. In these two cases Scotus always begins with asking about Christ's Predestination: Ord. 111 *Utrum Christus praedestinatus fuerit esse Filius Dei?* Rep. Par.: *Utrum Christus sit praedestinatus esse Filius Dei?*
8.   As note 7 has suggested, there is nothing in his works treating of the question in the way it had been framed before him. He does mention the hypothesis of Adam not sinning but in Scotus this too must be understood in terms of what he says concerning Christ's predestination.
9.   *Rep. Par.*, III, d. 7 q. 4 no.5 op. cit., 303.
10   See the variety of its use in *Op. Ox.* I, d. 2, q. 4 a. 5, n. 41–45 *Op. Ox.*, I, d. 8, q. 4, a. 3, n. 17 and cf I, d. 2, q. 7, nn. 43–44.

Pied Beauty:
Gerard Manley Hopkins
and the Scotistic View of Nature

William Short, OFM*

INTRODUCTION

On the third of August, 1872, a group of Jesuit scholastics arrived on the Isle of Man for vacation. One of them noted in his journal: "At this time I had first begun to get hold of the copy of Scotus on the Sentences in the Baddely library and was flush with a new stroke of enthusiasm. It may come to nothing or it may be a mercy from God." His journal entry for that day continues, "But just then when I took in any inscape of the sky or sea I thought of Scotus."[1]

In this presentation, I would like to examine the Christology of Scotus as it touches the question of Nature. And to do this I will use the writings of that Jesuit journaling during his holiday on the Isle of Man. His name is Gerard Manley Hopkins. We may find it easier to read Scotus through Hopkins (and I think this is a valid way) than to attempt reading the original, which even scholars often find difficult both for its ideas and its expression of them. The British Jesuit Hopkins was reading the British Franciscan Scotus, with whom he shared the experience of the intellectual life of Oxford. Hopkins speaks our lan-

* This article originally appeared as: "Pied Beauty: Gerard Manley Hopkins and a Scotistic View of Nature," The Cord 45/3 (May–June 1995): 27–36. Reprinted with permission.

guage and lived close to our time. He died in 1889 at the age of 45. I will leave it to you to determine if this way of approaching Scotus is congenial. I hope it will be.

In his poem; "Duns Scotus's Oxford," we hear Hopkins rejoice in the privilege of simply being in the same place where Scotus once lived and worked. After describing the city, he reflects on Scotus:

> Yet ah! this air I gather and I release
> He lived on; these weeds and waters, these walls are what
> He haunted who of all men most sways my spirits to peace.
>
> Of realty the rarest-veinèd unraveller; a not
> Rivalled insight, be rival Italy or Greece;
> Who fired France for Mary without spot (#21).

The Problem of Nature

A convert to Rome from the Church of England, Hopkins entered the Jesuit novitiate shortly after completing a brilliant undergraduate career at Oxford. His training was in late nineteenth-century Catholic theology, the Scholasticism of the manuals and within the strongly anti-worldly spirituality of his time. Hopkins felt himself morally or spiritually misformed because of his fascination and delight with specific individual things, especially the things of nature, a fascination observed by others. A Jesuit brother who had lived at Stonyhurst while Hopkins was a student there, remembers him in this way:

> One of Hopkins' special delights was the path from the Seminary to the College. After a shower, he would run and crouch down to gaze at the crushed quartz glittering as the sun came out again. "Ay, a strange yoong man, crouching down that gate to stare at some wet sand. A fair natural 'e seemed to us, that Mr. 'opkins."[2]

This fascination, this sensual delight in the things of nature, became a problem for Hopkins, something he felt he must suppress or discipline through asceticism in order to conform himself to the search for "heavenly things," "the things that are above." It was a mercy of God that during his theology days he came across the works of Scotus in the library of the Jesuit theologate at St. Beuno's in Wales. J. Hillis Miller, in his lovely study of Hopkins and Christology, says: "Ultimately, with the help of Scotus and other theologians, Hopkins broadens his theory of the Incarnation until he comes to see all things as created in Christ."[3]

This was a revelation. It was also the solution to that severe problem of conscience that had plagued Hopkins since his conversion. On reading Scotus he found a theologically positive view of the specific and individual. He discovered Christ in matter. This discovery he expressed in both prose and poetry in his journals. One of those journal entries speaks of this new-found delight in nature: "As we drove home the stars came out thick: I leant back to look at them and my heart opening more than usual praised our Lord to and in whom all that beauty comes home."[4]

This same delight is expressed in the following stanza from Hopkins' early masterpiece, "The Wreck of the Deutschland," written in memory of a group of Franciscan sisters:

> I kiss my hand
> To the stars, lovely-asunder
> Starlight, wafting him out of it; and
> Glow, glory in thunder;
> Kiss my hand to the dappled-with-damson west;
> Since, tho' he is under the world's splendour and wonder,
> His mystery must be instressed, stressed;
> For I greet him the days I meet him, and bless when I understand (#5).

Hopkins' writings may be seen as an example of Scotus' understanding of the Incarnation. The poet attends to the specific—even the minutest details—like the tiny, crushed quartz crystals of the sand in the path at Stonyhurst. From a Franciscan perspective, the reason this makes sense is that the tiny grains of sand are eucharistic, with a small "e" if you like, but truly eucharistic, the extension of the Incarnation in matter.

Listen to a selection from Hopkins' journals where he records his observations of clouds in the sky:

> ...below the sun it was like clear oil but just as full of colour, shaken over with slanted flashing "travellers," all in flight, stepping one behind the other, their edges tossed with bright ravelling, as if white napkins were thrown up in the sun but not quite at the same moment so that they were all in a scale down the air falling one after the other to the ground.[5]

CHRIST AS EXEMPLARY CAUSE

Here is the key to Nature as an American amateur Scotist sees it. The humanity of Jesus—even more emphatically the *body* of Jesus—is the point of God's creating everything. In Scholastic terms, the humanity of Jesus is the *exemplary cause* of creation. This is the model on which God models everything else: those white napkins of sunlight, stars, snails, raindrops, oxygen, magnesium, protons, grapes, every shade of the color purple, coffee beans, volcanoes: each of them and the relation each has with every other thing. They do something. What they do is, in odd language, themselves: they do themselves. Consider two other poems of Hopkins, "God's Grandeur" and "Pied Beauty." In each we see a world filled with God's presence and an intense attention to particularity and diversity. In these poems, all things are doing themselves; they are "themselving":

> The world is charged with the grandeur of God.
> It will flame out, like shining from shook foil;
> It gathers to a greatness, like the ooze of oil
> Crushed ....
> ...nature is never spent;
> There lives the dearest freshness deep down things;
> And though the last lights off the black West went
> Oh, morning, at the brown brink eastward, springs
> Because the Holy Ghost over the bent
> World broods with warm breast and with ah! Bright wings
> (God's Grandeur, #8).

> Glory be to God for dappled things—
> For skies of couple-colour as a brinded cow;
> For rose-moles in all stipple upon trout that swim;
> Fresh-firecoal chestnut-falls; finches' wings;
> Landscape plotted and pieced-fold, fallow, and plough;
> And all trades, their gear and tackle and trim.

> All things counter, original, spare, strange;
> Whatever is fickle, freckled (who knows how?)
> With swift, slow; sweet, sour; adazzle, dim;
> He fathers-forth whose beauty is past change:
> Praise him (Pied Beauty, #14).

The grape grapes, the star stars, coffee coffees, a volcano volcanoes.

Each doing this is being itself, doing what it is. Hopkins calls this "do-being" (a Frank Sinatra kind of theological term).

UNIVOCITY OF BEING

This do-being is doing-Christ. That is what all things were formed to do. This can be difficult to understand—perhaps it is also difficult to experience. It may be best to say what this is *not* before trying to say what it is. And then we can talk a bit more about the "why" of this.

What is *not* the relation between a grain of sand and Christ? The sand-grain is not just a *symbol* of Christ, though it can be that if we work at it. But that requires the grain to *stand for something about* Christ. Let us say we decide that the grain of sand, because it is small, makes us think of the humility of Christ. This is a very familiar use of religious language. What have we done? We have abstracted, identified an adjective about the sand-grain, "small," with an adjective about Christ, "humble." We have taken a quality of a thing and associated it with a quality of a person. But the sand-grain isn't all that important, a small acorn or a small tomato could do the job just as well. They are dispensable, interchangeable. They are *used* to achieve some other purpose, to teach a lesson, usually a moral lesson.

And whether we use the sand, the acorn or the tomato, the *thing* can produce only a reference to some quality or aspect of Christ: humility or some other description *about* Christ. This kind of association is perfectly fine to do, of course, but it can get tiresome. It is theologically grounded in the more common Thomistic view of nature based on the theory of analogy of being. According to this theory, true being exists only in God, and all other being is derivative, pointing toward true being, but only weakly and indirectly.

What fires Hopkins—though he only comes to articulate it through reading Scotus—is that the sand-grain, by being/doing itself, directly and immediately *does* God, who is incarnate, Christ. And it does that quite well without my having to sit and cogitate about "small" or "humble." Here is Hopkins painting this perception in a sonnet:

> As kingfishers catch fire, dragonflies draw flame;...
> Deals out that being indoors each one dwells;
> Selves—goes itself; *myself* it speaks and spells,
> Crying *What I do is me: for that I came.*

I say more: the just man justices;
Keeps grace: that keeps all his goings graces;
Acts in God's eye what in God's eye he is—
Christ—for Christ plays in ten thousand places,
Lovely in limbs, and lovely in eyes not his
To the Father through the features of men's faces (#34).

What is "Christ-y" is the sand doing sand: it is noun-verbing and not adjectiving. And the sand-grain sanding is doing *all* of Christ, not just this or that aspect of him, smallness or humility or whatever.

This expresses the profound notion of Scotus known as the "univocity of being." This subject has been explored by several scholars.[6] We might say that this perception, common to both Scotus and Hopkins, allows for a direct connection between our awareness of a thing and our awareness of Christ. J. Hillis Miller explains this more precisely:

> The idea of the univocity of being leads to a different view of nature (from that of Thomism), and therefore to a different kind of poetry. In this view natural things, instead of having a derived being, participate directly in the being of the creator. They are in the same way that he is. Each created thing, in its own special way, is the total image of its creator. It expresses not some aspect of God, but his beauty as a whole. Such a view of nature leads to a poetry in which things are not specific symbols, but all mean one thing and the same: the beauty of Christ, in whom they are created.[7]

In his journals Hopkins makes the following entry that renders this idea rather well: "I do not think I have ever seen anything more beautiful than the bluebell I have been looking at. I know the beauty of our 'Lord by it.'"[8] And he expresses it, as well, in his poem, "The Windhover, To Christ our Lord":

> I caught this morning morning's minion, kingdom of daylight's
>   dauphin, dapple-dawn-drawn Falcon, in his riding
> Of the rolling level underneath him steady air, and striding
> High there, how he rung upon the rein of a wimpling wing
> In his ecstasy! Then off, off forth on swing,
> As a skate's heel sweeps smooth on a bow-bend: the hurl
>   and gliding
> Rebuffed the big wind. My heart in hiding
> Stirred for a bird,—the achieve of, the mastery of the thing!...

No wonder of it: shéer plód makes plough down sillion
Shine, and blue-bleak embers, ah my dear,
Fall, gall themselves, and gash gold-vermilion (#13).

It seems to me that such a perception requires a different kind of discipline of the observer/participant of Nature (me or Hopkins or you.) The job is not to get lots of ideas about stuff that can then be lined up with ideas about Christ. The job is to observe closely, attentively, carefully that things are/do themselves. That doing/being is their doing/being Christ. Again, in Hopkins' own words:

...the just man justices;
Kéeps gráce: that keeps all his goings graces;
Acts in God's eye what in God's eye he is—
Christ (#34).

HAECCEITAS

It is each particular thing which does this being-Christ. This grape be/does Christ in dark purple on the left-hand side as I face it and in more crimson mixed with mauve on the right side where it has a fine dusting of gray-brown near the stem where the mold is. Put simply, it is/does only its own grape, not the one next to it or above it in the bunch. We notice its uniqueness when we look at it carefully.

Elisabeth W. Schneider gives an example of this minute observation from Hopkins' journal:[9]

Oaks: the organisation of this tree is difficult. Speaking generally no doubt the determining planes are concentric, a system of brief contiguous and continuous tangents, whereas those of the cedar would roughly be called horizontals and those of the beech radiating but modified by droop and by a screw-set towards jutting points. But beyond this since the normal growth of the boughs is radiating and the leaves grow some way in there is of course a system of spoke-wise clubs of green—sleeve-pieces. And since the end shoots curl and carry young and scanty leaf-stars these clubs are tapered, and I have seen also the pieces in profile with chiselled outlines, the blocks thus made detached and lessening towards the end. However the star knot is the chief thing: it is whorled, worked round a little, and this is what keeps up the illusion of the tree: the leaves are rounded inwards and figure out ball-knots. Oaks differ much, and much turns on the broadness of the leaf, the narrower giving the crisped and starry and Catherine-wheel forms, the broader the flat-pieced mailed or shard-covered ones in which it is possible to see composition in dips etc on wider bases than the single knot or cluster. But I shall study them further.

Schneider tells us that he did exactly that, and in a journal entry eight days later declared, I have now found the law of the oak leaves."[10]

Here we touch the Scotistic notion of *haecceitas*, being *this* thing and not *that* next thing that looks a lot like it. In the more common Thomistic view, things have two fundamental components, matter and form. The form of a grape, for example, is "grapeness" and the matter includes the physical attributes of sweetness, roundness, sugar and skin. Scotus adds a third component: being *this* grape: *haec*, "this."

Here is the corollary of the incarnation-God became *this* Jewish carpenter: this unique, unrepeatable, specific creature is the incarnate Creator. From this belief one can conclude that things are God-like in their specificity. Things deserve the respect of our attention, for whatever is is because of Christ.

SOME OBSERVATIONS AND QUESTIONS

Instead of any further description of Scotus' Christology of Nature seen through the lens of Hopkins' poetry, I wish at this point to make some suggestions about what this Christology might look like in practice.

1. Close, even minute, observation and attention to *things* is revelatory, is a truly contemplative act. A deep gazing *into* things can allow glimpses of Christ. The close analogy is that of traditional Eucharistic devotion-gazing on the consecrated bread of the Eucharist, pondering the invitation, "Ecce Agnus Dei." Behold (that is *look* and *see)* Christ: wheat flour baked, juice of grapes crushed. Here in ordinary Near Eastern food see the Creator of the universe.

In a similar way, gaze on this leaf, this stone, this molecule, this hand, this shadowy light streaming through this window—and behold! (Hopkins would say *inscape!*) *Ecce: look* and *see*: creature and Creator marvelously 'oned,' co-present, with no less of identity for the creature or the Creator.

* *A brief excursus. There may come to mind the intuition expressed by*

another Jesuit, Pierre Teilhard de Chardin, in his work entitled Hymn of the Universe. *Teilhard developed his scientific-mystical intuition without any conscious reference to Scotus. And he, like Hopkins, was much misunderstood, eventually silenced by his superiors, for his views. Yet there was for Teilhard also a direct and happy meeting with the work of Scotus. While in Hong Kong after a period of research in China's interior, he met the Sicilian Franciscan Father Allegra, a devoted Scotist.*

Allegra listened to Teilhard's description of his growing awareness of the "cosmic Christ." He then mentioned the strong affinity he noted with Scotus' Christology. Teilhard, as Allegra reports, exclaimed, "Voila! La theologie de l'avenir!" ["There it is! The theology of the future!"] His conversations with Allegra on Scotus began on that note and continued during Teilhard's stay in Hong Kong.

It is hard to avoid the observation that two of the most innovative Jesuit authors of the late nineteenth and early twentieth century had such strong affinity with the theological intuition of Scotus even before discovering his works. This suggests to me that there may be many in our own day, as in the past, who perceive the creation in a way very similar to that of Scotus, without ever having read Scotus. *End of excursus.

Whether we consider the work of Hopkins in literature, or that of Teilhard in paleontology, it seems clear that a careful examination of nature, poetically or scientifically, is theological and Christological. This confirms the strong assertion of Roger Bacon, one of Scotus' Franciscan predecessors at Oxford, that studying the natural sciences was important for a proper understanding of theology. In fact the Oxford Franciscans for centuries held the natural sciences in a place of special honor in their *studium*. We might ask ourselves: "What honor do we pay to scientific work as Franciscans today?"

We speak often enough of experience as the starting point of Franciscan theology. Do we include the experience of natural-scientific work in this view? Or is it only the experience included in the human sciences (psychology, sociology, anthropology)? These are certainly important and not to be neglected. But what honor do we render to biology, zoology, botany, environmental studies, geography, physics, chemistry? Are these perceived as important to our mission of evangelization, pointing to the presence of Christ among us?

2. What importance do we give to the creation around us? In the places we live and work what message, what Good News, about the cre-

ation do we communicate? Is each *thing* reverenced? Are *things* used eucharistically? Do we create things and places of beauty that call attention to the importance of things—or are our places a hodge-podge of things tossed without thought to fill up empty spaces?

3. Some sustained contact with nature needs to be a fundamental component of our Franciscan life. A trip to the ocean, a walk in the hills, working in the garden, working with wood or stone or metal or glass—manual labor—these are important not primarily for what they *produce*, but for their inherent Christ-contact. This could imply that many activities considered "hobbies" or "avocations" among our brothers and sisters should be given more careful attention and encouragement, whether photography, painting, poetry, or flower-pressing. These are not "trivial pursuits." As Hopkins wrote to a friend, "I think that the trivialness of life is, and personally to each one ought to be seen to be, done away with by the Incarnation."[11]

Work with people and the experience of loving community are essential, but not sufficient. Close, regular, even daily attention to the wider world of creatures is fundamental to our spiritual life as Franciscans. Without it, we begin to lose living contact with Christ in his most widely-extended body, the universe. Obviously, much more could be said. But the saying of it may be better yours than mine. Let me close with words from our Franciscan brother, the Jesuit, Hopkins:

> All things counter, original, spare, strange
> Praise Him!

Notes

1.   Jnl 161, quoted in Maurice B. McNamee, S.J., "Hopkins: Poet of Nature and of the Supernatural," *Immortal Diamond: Studies in Gerard Manley Hopkins,* ed. Norman Weyand, S.J. (NY: Sheed & Ward, 1949) 228. (The word "inscape" is a Hopkins' invention, meaning "more than what you see" or "that which makes a thing what it is"; "its particularity" [author's note].) Poetry selections from *Poems and Prose of Gerard Manley Hopkins,* ed. W. H. Gardner (NY: Penguin Books, 1985) with corresponding numbering.

2. Humphry House and Graham Storey, eds., *The Journals and Papers of Gerard Manley Hopkins* (London: Oxford University Press, 1959) 408, quoted in J. Hillis Miller, "The Univocal Chiming," *Hopkins: A Collection of Critical Essays,* ed. Geoffrey H. Hartman (Englewood Cliffs, NJ: Prentice-Hall, 1966) 89.

3. Miller 111.

4. House 254.

5. House 207.

6. See Allan B. Wolter, OFM, *The Transcendentals and Their Function in the Metaphysics of Duns Scotus* (Washington: The Catholic University of America Press, 1946) 31–57. See also Cyril L. Shircel, OFM, *The Univocity of the Concept of Being in the Philosophy of John Duns Scotus* (Washington: Catholic University Press, 1942) and Etienne Gilson, *Jean Duns Scot* (Paris: 1952).

7. Miller 113.

8. House 199.

9. Elizabeth W. Schneider, *The Dragon in the Gate: Studies in the Poetry of* G. M. *Hopkins* (Berkeley and Los Angeles: University of California Press, 1968).

10. House 144–46, 364n. Quoted in Schneider 116. In his study of "The Dialectic of Sense-Perception" in Hopkins, Geoffrey H. Hartman gives another example from Hopkins' journals about this kind of close observation. He notes, "Even when, as in a snowfall, it seems least possible to remark the individual forms of things, Hopkins still manages to do so":

    It tufted and toed the firs and yews and went to load them till they were taxed beyond their spring. The limes, elms, and Turkey-oaks it crisped beautifully as with young leaf. Looking at the elms from underneath you saw every wave in every twig... and to the hangers and flying sprays it restored, to the eye, the inscapes they had lost (123).

11. Quoted in Claude Colleer Abbott, ed., *The Letters of Gerard Manley Hopkins to Robert Bridges* (London: Oxford University Press, 1955) III, 19. In Miller 111.

A Certain Affection for Justice
The Here and Now of Praxis:
Human Freedom
and Acts of Justice

Mary Beth Ingham, CSJ*

I. INTRODUCTION

Duns Scotus' commitment to the importance of the Incarnation and to the primacy of Christ appears clearly when he talks about human freedom and acts of justice. Scotus has a "this world" attitude which shines through his texts. He admires the intricacy of reality and affirms the value of each individual. His thought inspired the Jesuit poet Gerard Manley Hopkins. For Scotus, the kingdom is truly here—even though we cannot see it yet—the future is now, in germ, awaiting our acknowledgment of its presence: our free response to the gifts of God around us. In this article I discuss Scotus' thought in terms of its moral significance for us today. By this I mean the aspects of his moral philosophy which contribute to a contemporary understanding of our place in the world and the ways in which we might act to bring about the Reign of God. This discussion involves an awareness of the present moment and what it calls forth in us, the realization of the importance of human freedom for our response, and the human attraction to justice in the form of right relationships.

* This article originally appeared as: "A Certain Affection for Justice," The Cord 45/3 (May–June 1995): 11 –18. Reprinted with permission.

II. THE PRESENT MOMENT: A HERE AND NOW OF PRAXIS

As we look around us we see a world spinning out of control. Even Bette Midler's popular song "From a Distance" places God pretty far away—as if even God doesn't want to get too close to what's really going on here. Descartes' *clock-maker* image is an attractive one for believers today. It is just too difficult to reconcile the infinite goodness of God with the present chaos. But as Christians, and especially within the Franciscan tradition, we must acknowledge both the tragedy of today and the intimate presence of God: a God who must spend a good deal of time weeping with those who suffer and who long for the Kingdom to be revealed in all its fullness.

Politically, our world is in fragments. Eastern Europe struggles after the breakdown of the communist society. Ethnic rivalries in former Yugoslavia horrify us with inhuman actions. The movement of peoples throughout Europe provokes the response of Right Wing Nationalism, and we are all reminded of Nazi Germany. But the horrors are not limited to Europe. In Africa we have witnessed events in Somalia, Rwanda, Ethiopia. Glimmers of hope shine forth in South Africa, but these glimmers are, unfortunately, the exceptions rather than the rule. The international community is unable (perhaps unwilling) to enter conflict-ridden situations and normal citizens say, as did the marvelous character in the film *Grand Canyon*, "this is not the way things are supposed to be."

Not the way things are meant to be. How do we know this? We know it deep in our hearts. We see the moral unraveling around us and we know that the society in which we live is deeply wounded. Children should not be in schools where they fear daily for their lives. How can any real education take place in an environment of fear? Citizens should not fear a system of justice "stacked against them." When the fundamental bond of trust disappears from a society, the ultimate disintegration of that society cannot be far behind.

The last ten years have changed the way we look at the world around us. The old, tried and true, cold war ideological balance is gone. We must admit, there was security in knowing who the enemy was: we were the *good guys*, they were the *bad guys*. There is no longer an "evil communist empire" against which we can raise our so-called standard of democracy. Capitalist societies must ask themselves the hard questions of justice, of equal opportunity, of oppression, of propaganda, of social sins that we so easily directed at communist nations and whose policies we so quickly condemned.

The spiritual *angst* of the late 20th century descends upon us all. We witness widespread disenchantment with the institution of religion and, at the same time, the growth of new age "natural religion." James Redfield's *The Celestine Prophecy*[1] has been a best seller for over a year. In this treatise-novel, people of good will seek spiritual liberation through a journey of self-help, meditation, aura-reading and personal enhancement. The beauty of nature and of creation affirmed in the first insights is ultimately transcended in a rapture-like experience of other-worldliness. The book documents a religious journey without need for a personal God, taking the best of all traditions and placing them side by side to climb out of the world, to get away (finally) from this "vale of tears," to reach that distant point where salvation is found, at one with Bette Midler's God—way out there, far away, where we can all find peace in spiritual oblivion.

Yes, the letter to the Romans rings true for us today. All creation yearns and longs for the revelation of the children of God. We groan with labor pains in which we intuit the nearness of death and destruction. The normal human reaction to pain? Run away, hide in drugs, in alcohol, in spiritual oblivion. Get away from here, get out of now—anywhere has to be better. After all, I have to take care of myself first; everyone else comes after me.

And the response of Scotus? This salvation you seek, this peace you long for, it's right here, it's right now. The faith-filled response of the spiritually mature means we "sit tight," hold our place and act as midwives in the birth of a "new heaven and new earth." The centrality of Christ for Scotus, for Franciscans, means that we have an incarnational commitment to remain right here "in the world," with muddy hands and dirty faces.

Scotus talks of *praxis* in light of the Incarnation, of persons transformed in Christ to be transformative agents, architects of the Kingdom, right here, right now. A deep spirituality, a oneness with Christ must support these persons. In their action for justice, they cannot be self-serving, but other serving. They must reach out of themselves in love toward a world bent on its own destruction, fascinated with death, with violence, with addictive behaviors. Our action for justice will bear no fruit unless we turn our gaze incessantly toward Jesus, both suffering and risen, and beg for the strength and the courage to be his emissaries among the living dead.

An image Scotus uses of the person perfected in Incarnational *praxis* is that of the musician. Just as the guitar player knows at each moment which string to pluck and which chord to play because of years of study and practice, so the transformed agent of change has trained carefully for moments of action. With agile fingers, such agents know what to do, they know how to be creative of beauty, they know what works and what doesn't.[2] They have tried for years to develop their talent. As any musician knows, training is not success. We often make the most progress through moments of failure.

III. RESPONSE OF PERSONS IN FREEDOM

More than any major medieval thinker, Scotus emphasizes the centrality of freedom for human action. Our own time is influenced by a strain of determinism which is often difficult to identify and even more difficult to overcome. My past has made me this way, my family has taught me how to relate to others, societal forces prevent me from acting as I might like. I am surrounded by Karma, by Fate, by factors which determine what I shall do.

Scotus acknowledges the presence of forces over which we have no control, but he affirms all the more strongly that freedom is the determining characteristic of rational beings.[3] Nothing is so much in my power as my own actions or reactions to events around me. Today we say, "Don't react, respond to life." Scotus might say, "Don't be forced, be self-determining in your choices." Acknowledge those aspects which determine, but find the corner of freedom and embrace it.

The self-determination of the human will means that no one can force me to will what they want me to. Of course, I can be forced to act, but not to assent. This basic human freedom is the seed for the much greater freedom to be creative of beauty, to affirm values, a freedom for goodness. Scotus calls this the affection for justice, and here he follows St. Anselm in his description of the motivation within the human heart.

The human heart has two affections: one directed toward itself, which we might identify with self-preservation, and one directed outward toward others. This second affection is characteristic of rational beings and is called the affection for justice. It is the orientation of rational beings toward right loving and right action. It is that critical piece in our makeup which asks the question: why am I doing this? Because this is a desire to give each what is due, Scotus and Anselm called it the affection for justice, since justice really involves treating all persons and objects as they deserve.[4] It is not limited to "social justice" or to dealings with persons. It is a stance outward toward reality. It undergirds the ecological concern today to treat nature in a manner fitting its dignity. The affection for justice is the human desire to *Do the Right Thing*, as Spike Lee's film depicts.

We have an affection for justice, but we don't always operate out of it. Too often our own desires come first. Our self-preservation instinct is getting all the attention when we care more about our personal property than about the cry of the poor, when the haves gang up on the have-nots and systematically exclude them from real dialogue, when conspicuous consumption takes the place of selfless sharing and when all decisions are made out of concern for the "bottom line." We can choose to act out of the affection for justice, but it must be our choice. The freedom which Scotus describes is a freedom for self-direction, for self-orientation toward goodness, toward an other-centered life based upon right relationships with nature, with persons, with God. But this freedom has been handicapped as a result of our sinful condition. Because of the sin of Adam and Eve, the human will carries an affection for possession which all too often governs the affection for justice. By grace the affection for justice directs the affection for possession: it is only with God's help that we overcome our natural self-centeredness.

The fullness of human perfection involves the right ordering of the two affections. When the affection for justice directs my life I see myself in my place and in my relationships with others. I look outside my own needs toward the needs of others. I work to help others just as others work to help me. The result is a dynamic of mutual love and expanding inclusivity.[5]

IV. Right Relationships and the Reign of God

What would it mean for us today to embrace freely, to own and act out of affection for justice?

First it would mean the development of a *self-reflexive stance* toward my own life. This means that I would consider prayerfully my own life journey, my own actions in light of the self-preservation or justice affections. This does not mean that I never think of myself, but only that I think of myself in an appropriate manner. I give myself the attention I deserve and turn my gaze more often toward others. I become aware of these two affections within me. I acknowledge that they are both natural and both healthy, but I work to keep them in their proper place. I ask as well for the grace to do this.

Second, I would work to develop a *critical awareness of injustices around me.* No situation is too small or unimportant to call for a response, an act which brings justice to birth in the daily setting. I might do this with others in an effort to enhance my own ability to recognize situations of injustice and work to improve them.

Third, I would try to develop the *courage to act as quickly as possible.* The here and now of justice means the right here and right now of justice. Our culture tells us to wait, to be careful, to avoid risks. I am not encouraging a foolhardy attitude, but St. Francis was given more often than not to foolish acts. Maybe our present moment needs the insanity of sanctity right here and right now. The person transformed in Christ knows immediately what to do, says Scotus, and acts quickly. We know that nothing energizes like action and nothing paralyzes like inertia. This swift judgment and action comes from years of training, of prayer, of carefully reading the signs of the times, of discernment with others.

The justice of right relationships involves a stance of mutuality which is suggested by Scotist thought. When we relate in justice to others, we raise them to equality with us or we lower ourselves to equality with them. This is the model of the Incarnation, of God-with-us. In Jesus we see the icon for our journey. He came to walk with us, to put himself at our level, to communicate the love of God to each of us, to create a relationship which ultimately brings us into union and communion with a God whose essence is right relationship, a Triune community.

V. THE SIGNIFICANCE OF SCOTUS TODAY

Like other medieval thinkers, Scotus rises above partial perspectives to offer an understanding of moral living which is closely related to a spirituality of goodness and love. He seeks to integrate partial viewpoints into an organic and dynamic description of human living. Moral living is not a mathematical problem nor a technological calculus, it is the human response to the particular events of a particular life. As a paradigm of integration, Scotus' moral vision offers several values that make it attractive today.

First, Scotus is optimistic about the human capacity to be morally active in the world. In the will's two affections we find a straightforward description of the desires within the human heart. Not only do we possess a desire for justice, but also a healthy desire for self-protection. Our will is constituted so as to respond rationally to the command of Jesus: love your neighbor as yourself. Both love of self and love of neighbor are required in moral living, and their proper relationship of mutuality must be the result of rational deliberation and choice.

The key to self-control lies within the constitution of the will. The moral dimension is natural and rational; it expresses what is best in the human person. Human choice in light of self and others moves naturally toward ordered and rational consistency if there is a moral community to support such growth. Natural affection for the good develops toward increasingly higher levels of moral awareness in a society where good is really rewarded and evil really punished.

Second, Scotus is optimistic about the goodness of creation. The Franciscan insight about the connectedness of all reality (divine, human, natural) informs his moral discussion. All reality is good and beautiful. This is why, for Scotus, moral loving does not so much involve finding those objects worthy of love (since all reality is good), but rather working out the intricate manner by which we can love reality as it deserves. My moral living involves my relationship to all beings which surround me and my efforts to strengthen and enhance that mutuality.

The value of relationship imbues the Scotist perspective. Since all reality is good, then my relationships with others ought to promote goodness. In addition, my relationship with God plays a key role in my moral living and my moral choices. My goal centers around the proper integration of all segments of my life into a beautiful, harmonious whole, both intentionally through charity and extensionally throughout my lifetime. The final goal is not a state of eternal rest, but rather an eternal dynamic life of mutuality, part of the cosmic journey of all things to God.

Scotus has a vision which is both dynamic and organic. All reality grows toward the future through the present. New levels of consciousness promote the integration of all aspects of human life into the "global village" or "spaceship earth." Moral living is part of this integration and moral choices promote the development and flourishing of life. The promotion of moral attitudes belongs not only to individuals but to families and to moral communities. For the human community, this means that society has a responsibility to promote values which sustain and promote human life. The need for moral communities is increasingly felt today as the fragmentation of the social fabric results in civic communities which are concerned to arm themselves at ever higher rates. The increase of violent crime gives tragic testimony to a civilization already in decline. For many there is no hope, no future, no reason to live.

If relationship and mutuality are appropriate human goods, then they are moral goals. Accordingly, all persons have a right to share equally in the resources of the earth. The consumption by the few at the expense of the many, the structures of sin which continue to oppress and dominate, the culture of death and destruction which sells contraceptives but no antibiotics to the poor of the Third World: none of these can be morally justified, nor should they be tolerated. The Christian moral vision, a vision of the sanctity of life and of each person, must continue to speak to such a world, to denounce systems of exploitation and dominance. We must speak to all—poor as well as rich, simple as well as learned, humble as well as powerful.

As friends of Jesus we do not belong to another world, we do not deal with people from a distance. Scotus' interest in a philosophical and theological discussion of God, of the Incarnation and of human freedom reflects the spirituality of Francis, a saint who saw the glory of God in the beauty of this world. Francis reached out to the dispossessed, he sought out the marginated and the powerless, he lowered himself to create mutuality with all and he worked for a more just distribution of the wealth of this earth. The time is now; the call is ours. As we move into the third millennium, let us embrace that same generosity which inspired Francis. Let us act freely to create right relationships of justice and mutuality in our world.

Notes

1. Warner Books 1993.
2. See my *The Harmony of Goodness: Mutuality and Moral Living According to John Duns Scotus* (Franciscan Press 1995).
3. See Allan B. Wolter, OFM, "Native Freedom of the Will as a Key to the Ethics of Scotus," *The Philosophical Theology of John Duns Scotus,* Marilyn M. Adams, ed. (Cornell University Press 1990), 148–62.
4. Wolter, 151–2.
5. See my "Scotus and the Moral Order," *The American Catholic Philosophical Quarterly* 67 (1993):127–50.

Discussion Questions

1. We know God, according to Scotus, through the univocity of being. How might this belief influence your understanding of creation?

2. a. Scotus held that God is both "absolutely necessary" and also, "absolutely free." Discuss the implications of this belief for how we understand the created world.

   b. Discuss how that understanding influenced Scotus' explanation concerning why the Incarnation took place.

   c. When taken together with Bonaventure's understanding of the Christic universe, what difference does all of this make in our approach to environmental issues?

3. How would Scotus answer the question: Why did God create? Does our belief about the origin and reason for the existence of the created world make a difference in our treatment of the environment?

4. Consider and discuss your response to Osborne's questions (26): What does it mean to be myself? Of what am I a cause? What will I, in my particular life, cause to happen because of my particular choices?

5. Recall Scotus' notion of *haeccietas* ("thisness"). Discuss your understanding of this principle and its relation to present day issues of biodiversity.

6. What difference does Scotus' understanding of God make in your approach to issues of the environmental crisis?

For Further Reading

Cross, Richard. *Duns Scotus.* New York: Oxford University Press, 1999.

Cross, Richard. *The Physics of Duns Scotus: The Scientific Context of a Theological Vision.* New York: Oxford University Press, 1998.

Ingham, Mary Elizabeth. *The Harmony of Goodness: Mutuality and Moral Living According to John Duns Scotus.* Quincy, IL: Franciscan Press, 1996.

Ingham, Mary Elizabeth. "John Duns Scotus: An Integrated Vision," in Kenan B. Osborne, ed. *The History of Franciscan Theology.* St. Bonaventure, NY: The Franciscan Institute, 1994.

Shannon, Thomas A. *The Ethical Theory of John Duns Scotus : A Dialogue with Medieval and Modern Thought.* Quincy, IL: Franciscan Press, 1995.

Shannon, Thomas A. and Mary Beth Ingham. "The Ethical Method of John Duns Scotus." *Spirit and Life* 3 (1993):1–99.

Wolter, Allan Bernard and Marilyn McCord Adams, eds. *The Philosophical Theology of John Duns Scotus.* Ithaca: Cornell University Press, 1990.

PRIMARY SOURCES IN ENGLISH TRANSLATION

John Duns Scotus. *John Duns Scotus' Political and Economic Philosophy.* Trans. Allan B. Wolter. Santa Barbara, CA: Old Mission, 1989.

John Duns Scotus. *John Duns Scotus: A Treatise on God As First Principle. Second Edition.* Trans. Allan B. Wolter. Chicago: Franciscan Herald Press, 1981.

John Duns Scotus. *John Duns Scotus: God and Creatures, The Quodlibetal Questions.* Paperback edition. Trans. Felix Alluntis and Allan B. Wolter. Washington, DC: Catholic University of America Press, 1981.

PART FIVE

Franciscan Praxis:
Peace, Justice
and the Integrity of Creation

An Internet search on the topic "ecology" yields well over a thousand "hits." It seems that everyone—lay person and expert alike—is somehow concerned about the environment and is trying to discover what needs to be done to preserve it or use the resources of nature properly. The authors and the editor of this book agree there is an environmental crisis, and each has addressed it from a Christian perspective, particularly through the resource of the Franciscan charism. But what do Christianity and the Franciscan way of life have to say to the *contemporary environmental movement?*

Michael J. and Kenneth R. Himes respond to that question, beginning with the wisdom of the late Richard McCormick who said that Christianity is "more a value raiser than a problem solver."[1] They suggest that Christianity's contribution to today's world is the value of companionship that comes down to us through the creation stories of the Hebrew Scriptures, the early Christian writers, and saints such as Augustine and Francis of Assisi. Today's need is for a definitive shift away from the U.S. notions of self interest and giving nature only instrumental value. It is imperative that humans realize their origins as the beings created in the *image of God*, who is revealed as a relational being. Additional clues about the importance of companionship between the non-human and humans comes in Gen 2:18, where the human is allowed to name the animals, not to gain power over them, but as a part of a process of seeking companionship.

It is in this very need of the human for something beyond the self that indicates yet another important truth about human existence, namely, the human is finite and contingent. In other words, poverty is the true condition of the human, yet the human is sustained through the love of God who is forever. One of the primary modalities God uses to sustain humans is their relationship with the created world. God's goodness and grace is known and revealed through creation, making it, in essence, sacramental. The Himes brothers remark: "Francis of Assisi's interweaving of poverty with the brotherhood and sisterhood of all creatures is profoundly Catholic because it is profoundly sacramental."[2] All of creation has value in itself and as a revelation of the Creator.

This insight about the sacramental character of creation gains force when considered along with Catholic social teaching. Pope Pius XII, for example, held that the right to private property is only secondary when measured against the common good. No element of creation can live fully by itself. Companionship with the non-human elements of creation implies that humans expand their moral imagination, engage in mutual relationship with the non-human, and give moral standing to them (for their own sake). Once rights to moral standing are recognized, those rights must be promoted and protected. Often, such promotion and protection requires political action, not from an ideological position, but from an inclusive position on social justice.

Indeed, Keith Warner has suggested that it is this kind of unified stance toward addressing the environmental issues of today that flows naturally from the values inherent in the Franciscan charism. He cites numerous examples that show three predominant themes are part and parcel of the Franciscan tradition. The three themes are concern about relationships, the life of penance, and an attitude of respectful deference toward the other. All human relating needs to be inclusive; it must consider how actions and decisions made within one relationship will impact all other possible relationships—between humans and God, between humans, and between humans and the non-human creatures. Francis' practice of penance was grounded in a value base deeply rooted in God's love demonstrated in the Incarnation. Francis responded to God's love in acts of humility, simplicity, service to the poor, hospitality and peacemaking.

So too, in the twenty-first century, where ecological, economic, social and political issues are intertwined and complex, Warner suggests that a wholistic method, modeled by Francis' integrated approach to God and the created world, is needed. Many people of good will are already

engaged in actions toward making the world more whole and holy—
protesting war, advocating for the poor and oppressed, or protesting
environmental destruction. Yet, there is evidence to show that stopping a
war does not necessarily shift a nation's economic priorities toward eliminating poverty. Nor does the priority of eliminating poverty require
development and industrial growth that respects the integrity of the
environment. And, destruction of the ecosystem frequently necessitates a
shift in human population and often becomes the occasion for war.
Warner insists that the works taken up on behalf of social justice, peacemaking, or advocacy for the environment must each consider the interrelationship of justice, peace and the integrity of creation.

Yet, James F. Edmiston shows that in order to champion someone or
something, one must know the subject quite intimately. He claims that
of the approximately 100 million species, most ordinary people know
only a few. Indeed those most people will name when asked—cats, dogs,
bears—"show our vertebrate bias. Colorful butterflies and moths receive
some attention, but only as they stimulate our emotions through the
visual spectrum."[3] Edmiston continues: "To personally know other creatures that are not like us can enable us to appreciate how our life inter-
acts with millions of other life forms."[4]

Francis of Assisi provides a clear example of one who knew numerous creatures for their own sake but also as revealers of God. From
Francis' experiences, a spiritual and intellectual tradition emerged and
his legacy is found in the work of Bonaventure, Scotus, and their successors. Edmiston shows how this spiritual and intellectual tradition has
enriched his own life and work as a nationally known entomologist, and
how he came to a "theology of biodiversity." Yard sweeps, soil extractions, and stream walks are three respectful and least intrusive ways he
recommends for people of all ages to begin to know the vast diversity of
the non-human world, and then, to begin to understand the world from
the perspective of the other creatures of creation. Edmiston concludes:
"Building relationships with other species can help rejoin information
with the soul... can promote connecting our spirituality with science...
will promote receptivity to national and international policies that can
reduce the reduction of biodiversity."[5]

One way the formal Franciscan communities and others inspired by
the charism of Francis and Clare of Assisi from around the globe have
begun to bring their familiarity with the non-human perspective to

bear on international policies is through work with the United Nations. In her article, Margaret Pirkl discusses the pioneering work of the Franciscans at the UN, particularly their involvement in the 1982 breakthrough document, "The World Charter of Nature." Pirkl illustrates how the seven major points that frame the document are highly compatible with the Franciscan vision and values.

Not only have the Franciscans at the UN been involved in developing a theoretical base for safeguarding the integrity of creation, they have promoted and participated in direct actions such as the planting of 20,844 trees in thirty-three countries, the celebration of the UN Environmental Sabboth, and the work on the Earth Charter.

While much good can be done within existing institutions such as the UN, at the beginning of the twenty-first century the influence of social and political structures that operate from a exclusive and non-participative power base still firmly dominate economic and government systems. Not infrequently, environmental concerns are simply ignored by those in positions of power, or compromises are made which lead to less than satisfactory solutions. The human conversion to an attitude that values the power of mutual relations has barely begun. And certainly, ethical reflection that can point the way to a future which joins the option for the poor with the integrity of creation is in its infant stages.

The various religious orders within the Church have begun to uncover their particular potential to contribute to the resolution of the many environmental issues of our day. The Benedictines and the Franciscans have perhaps been most active in this recovery of their spiritual, intellectual, and practical heritage. In the concluding article the distinct contributions of these two major traditions concerning the relationship between humans and the environment are discussed. While both charisms are firmly rooted in the Christian and Hebrew Scriptures and the doctrinal traditions of the Church, the Benedictines stress a relationship in which humans are stewards and owners of the land, while the Franciscans focus on the mutual relationship of humans with nonhumans and the role of humans as sojourners on the land. In the closing essay of this volume, I conclude: "Perhaps it is the case that the language of Benedict can more easily bridge the gap that exists between the Utilitarian and the Steward, but I claim that it is the Poor Man of Assisi who holds the paradigm for the kind of power needed for the future."[6]

Notes

1. Michael J. Himes and Kenneth R. Himes, "The Sacrament of Creation: Toward an Environmental Theology," *Commonweal* 117 (January 26, 1990): 43.
2. Ibid., 45.
3. James F. Edmiston, "'How to Love a Worm?' Biodiversity: Franciscan Spirituality and Praxis," in John E. Carroll and Keith Warner, eds., *Ecology and Religion: Scientists Speak*, (Quincy, IL: Franciscan Press, 1998), 291.
4. Ibid.
5. Ibid., 300.
6. Dawn M. Nothwehr, "Benedictine Responsibility and Franciscan Mutuality: Perspectives on the Relationship between Humans and the Environment," 16.

The Sacrament of Creation: Toward an Environmental Theology

Michael J. Himes & Kenneth R. Himes, OFM*

Something is in the air. Or is it in the water? A sense of ecological crisis looms over our planet. Interest in the environment is spreading. In Washington, Congress has been at odds with the White House over how to make the next clean air legislation tougher. And, lo and behold, officials in Los Angeles have gotten so serious about air quality they have proposed a plan for cutting down pollution that could make carpooling mandatory.

When the leaders of the seven industrialized nations met in Paris in the summer of 1989, their final communiqué gave evidence of just how "mainstream" environmentalism has become. That the president of the United States supports such ecological high-mindedness should come as no surprise. Recall the last presidential campaign when Messrs. Bush and Dukakis skirmished over who deserved to be called the environmental candidate.

For many, of course the environment has never not been an issue. Fetid garbage dumps, closed beaches, air you can see as well as breathe, the extinction of whole species—the causes for concern have long been with us. More recently interest has arisen in developing a religious response to the ecological crisis. Some have found the resources for such

* This article originally appeared as: "The Sacrament of Creation," *Commonweal* 117 (Jan. 26, 1990): 42–9. ©1991 Commonweal Foundation Reprinted with permission. For subscriptions, call toll-free: 1–800–495–6755.

a theology and spirituality in Eastern thought and practice. Others, like Joseph Sittler and Ian Barbour, seek out elements of the Christian tradition for the development of a "creation-centered" perspective.

At the same time a number of critics (Arnold Toynbee, Lynn White) have argued that the Christian tradition is suspect on the matter of the environment. They argue that Judaism and Christianity have fed an anthropocentrism which, intentionally or not, demeans the rest of creation as it exalts those who are a "little less than the angels" (Psalm 8:5). Certainly Hebraic monotheism declared that all others but Yahweh were "no-gods." Included among those denied divine status were the deities of Greek and Roman mythology who protected streams, mountains, and forests. It is possible to see in this demythologizing a loss of reverence for nature. Christianity's contribution to the problem—its celebration of the Incarnation—has promoted the centrality of humanity in the plan of creation and redemption and accorded secondary status to the rest of creation.

With a bit of poetic license and some ingenuity a few individuals (Thomas Berry, Matthew Fox) have sought to re-present the tradition and demonstrate a more sensible Christian attitude toward the created order. Some of this work has borne fruit, awakening among believers an interest in the environment and providing a degree of religious seriousness for addressing an issue that is more important and complex than the faddishness and trivialization which mass media politics inevitably encourages.

Despite these efforts, it is lamentable but true that the question still can fairly be asked, "What does Christianity have to say to the contemporary ecological movement?" That it has something to say is important to assert, but what it has to say is not primarily advice on public policy or clear moral judgments for settling disputes about economic growth versus ecological protection. In this regard, the Christian tradition is, in the words of Richard McCormick, "more a value raiser than a problem solver."

The values that Christianity points to in the cluster of issues raised by the environmental crisis is humankind's essential relatedness to nature, an understanding of the created order that is precisely what is at stake here. Too often the discussion over the ecosystem turns on arguments from self-interest, even if enlightened self-interest, a stance that we believe is fundamentally flawed.

Treating the environmental issue as primarily a calculation of long-term versus short-term interests maintains an attitude of instrumental rationality that is essentially part of the problem. The Jewish and Christian understanding of creation, at least in one of its strands is profoundly insightful and potentially transformative of modem ways of addressing the crisis of creation.

The needed transformation lies at the level of our deep convictions, our world view. The relational dimension of the Jewish-Christian heritage must replace the atomized individualism of our current outlook. The mentality of consumerism, the myth of progress, and our technological mind-set are all problematic in regard to the environment; they are also symptomatic. Each is the distortion of a human good, a distortion rising from the nonrelational anthropology of our age. If our environmental sensitivity is to change, the transformation must take place at the root of the problem. But that transformation is more convoluted than might first appear.

The human abuse of nonhuman nature has spurred a harsh reaction by defenders of the environment, who exhibit a brand of ecological activism, and environmental romanticism, that borders on the antihuman. Nature is idealized. The achievements of human civilization are disparaged. The environmental romantic, however, mirrors the fundamental outlook of the technocrats. Both see humanity at odds with nature. In one case this leads to calls for more effective ways of manipulating, subduing, and dominating nature. In the other, there is opposition to technology, economic growth, and development efforts. In both cases humanity is set in opposition to the rest of creation. Either alternative is unacceptable from a relational world view. To separate nature from human culture is environmental romanticism. To consider human culture apart from the nonhuman is to invite the impoverishment of the first and the devastation of the second.

The Jewish and Christian traditions put before us a world view in which humanity is not against nature but a part of it. Neither element is rightly viewed in isolation. The exploration of this relational anthropology is the basic contribution theologians can make to the environmental movement. We can examine the traditions to see which developments have been distortions, which trajectories misguided, which insights forgotten. The constructive task is to illustrate how the resources of the Jewish and Christian heritage can be used in promoting ecological wisdom.

LESSONS OF GENESIS

Like every myth of origin, the two Genesis stories of the beginning of all things (Genesis 1:1–2:4a and 2:4b–25) have been used to explain and justify the ways human beings relate to one another and to the nonhuman world. As narratives of how things came to be and depictions of how things were and presumably ought to be, these creation stories have been elaborated into cosmologies and theories of the soul and twisted into ideological support for male-dominance and industrial exploitation.

The first of the two stories has been the basis of both the overlordship and stewardship images for the role of humanity in the natural world. "Let us make the human being in our image and likeness... God blessed them, saying to them, 'Be fertile and increase; fill the whole earth and subdue it; have dominion over the fish of the sea and the birds of the air and all the living things that move on the earth.'" (Gen.1:26 and 28). Part of the human being's likeness to God is the exercise of dominion over the rest of creation. The twin images of being given dominion and being commanded to subdue the earth and all the creatures which fill it are closely connected with sovereignty. God's sovereignty is asserted often in the Hebrew Scriptures. Here the image and likeness of God, the human being, is entrusted with sovereignty. From the perspective of the first creation myth in Genesis, without such dominion and power over the rest of creation, the human being would not be "like God."

But there is a contrasting theme in this story. "And so God created the human being in God's image; in the divine image did God create the human being, male and female did he create them" (Gen.1:27). How is it that being created in the image of God results in the differentiation of male and female? Clearly the myth does not wish to attribute gender to God, much less dual bisexuality. The point is not that God is male or female or male and female, but that God is relational. The only God that the Hebrew tradition knows is the God who is about the business of creating; that is, the Hebrew Scriptures contain nothing about God *in se*, God considered apart from the creating God. Even in one of its creation myths, the Hebrew tradition envisions God as the God of the covenant, God in relationship. To be the image of this God, the human being must be relational. Humanity is sexed in order that human beings may be driven into relationship one with another.

This is a central theme of the second of Genesis' creation myths

(2:4b–25). The dominion motive is depicted in the first human being naming all the animals that God has made and led before him "to see what he would call them" (Gen. 2:19). All other creatures will be what the human being says they are—certainly an extraordinary statement of the power over creation given by God to humanity. But the context of this conferral is the human hunger for companionship. In the first of the creation myths, the first divine judgment on humanity is that it is "very good" (Gen. 1:31). That judgment is made on humanity differentiated into male and female, relational being. The first judgment of God regarding human beings in the second myth makes this even more explicit. Having fashioned the human being from the clods of the earth and breathed the divine breath into him, God announces that "it is not good for the human being to be alone" (Gen. 2:18). Again there is the insistence that human beings are meant to be in relationship to one another. Thus, in this second creation story, companionship is the explicit ground given for the creation of the two sexes. But it is important to note not only human beings are intended for relationship to one another. This is also the reason for the creation of "the various wild beasts and birds of the air" (Gen. 2:19). The natural world is not merely intended for subjugation by human beings but for companionship.

Dominion over the earth and all that it contains, the command "to fill the whole earth and subdue it"—certainly this conveys power. Such a claim to power by human beings over all nonhuman creation contains the possibility, all too often realized, of domination and exploitation of the earth. Clearly the claim to power must be balanced by the call to responsibility, the traditional appeal to stewardship. The relationship between humanity and the rest of creation has often been cast in the Jewish and Christian traditions as that of a caretaker, one charged by God with the maintenance of the earth. The nonhuman world has been given to human beings for our good, to be used responsibly for our self-development, to answer to our purposes and thus to fulfill God's purpose in creating it. To be sure, this stewardship image prohibited wanton wastefulness, the mere exploitation of nature by humankind. The world is presented as a garden given into our care to be tended and nurtured. But undeniably the role of stewardship carries the implication that non-human creation is to be used.

The theme of companionship, the relationship which exists not only between human persons but between humans and non-humans, has been largely submerged in the stewardship theme. We need to recover it.

Companionship implies mutuality. It excludes the reduction of either side of the relationship to a tool of the other's purposes. Martin Buber, so deeply rooted in the biblical tradition, explored the meaning of companionship under the rubric "I-Thou." The contrasting possibility is "I-It." The reduction of "thou" to "it" results from making the other into an extension of oneself. The other becomes *mine-my* husband, *my* wife, *my* parent, *my* friend, *my* student, *my* boss. "It" can be manipulated in order to fulfill the task which I set, for "it" belongs to me. "It" has no intrinsic value, only the instrumental value that I assign it. The other as "thou" cannot be possessed, can never become *my* "thou." When recognized and respected as "thou," the other is seen to be of inherent value, to be an end and not a means to an end.

As a human being can be reduced to an "it," so a nonhuman being can become "thou," in Buber's terms. "It" can be a possession but not a companion. "Thou" is always a companion. But in what sense, other than the mythology of the second creation story in Genesis, can one speak of the nonhuman world as companion to human beings? At a time of global ecological crisis, we certainly do not need a revival of the nineteenth-century Romantic poets' personification of Nature. Indeed, such personification is the very reverse of what Buber meant by treating the nonhuman world as "thou," for instead of allowing the other to be what the other is, personification insists that the other must be what I am if I am to enter into any relationship with it. Such personification is another, more subtle way of reducing the non-human other to "it."

AUGUSTINE AND FRANCIS

The Catholic tradition offers two important symbols that deserve to be explored as ways of reappropriating the biblical theme of companionship in creation: poverty and sacramentality.

In Book 9 of his *Confessions*, Augustine recounts an incident that took place shortly before the death of his mother, Monica, as they stayed at Ostia on their way home to North Africa after his baptism in Milan. Seated at a window overlooking the garden of their rented house, they speculated on the life of the saints in glory. As Augustine describes their experience, they entered into a rapturous ecstasy in which they had a foretaste of that life. Passing through all the spheres of the sun, moon, planets, and stars of their Ptolemaic universe, they came to the outermost limit of their own minds and transcended even that. All the heavenly spheres ceased their music, Augustine writes. Everything that exists by passing away, that is, all creatures, since the mark of creatureliness is temporality, fell silent after singing the song which they constantly sing: "We did not make ourselves, but were made by God who is forever" (Bk. 9:10, 25).

Eight centuries later, Francis of Assisi grasped the two central elements of this Augustinian song of all creation. As with so many charismatic men and women, the historic Francis has been lost in popular mythology. But two themes of the Franciscan legend seem rooted in Francis himself: poverty and the unity of all creatures. The singer of the Canticle of the Sun, who recognized the sun and moon, earth and air, fire and water, his own body, all animals and plants, and death itself as brothers and sisters, also entered into a mystical marriage with Lady Poverty. This Franciscan emphasis, which finds its legendary expression in Francis' preaching to the birds and the wolf of Gubbio, is grounded in one insight: all creatures are united in the depths of their being by the fact of being creatures.

The discovery of one's finiteness is the recognition of one's poverty. When one grasps the "iffiness" of one's existence, the shocking fact that the source and foundation of one's being is not in oneself, then one knows oneself as truly poor. To be poor in this fundamental sense is a definition, not a description. True poverty, the poverty of the spirit, is the realization that there is no intrinsic reason for one's being at all. In this fundamental poverty of creatureliness, there is equality. The human person has no more claim to intrinsic being than a plant or animal, a star or a stone. This is not in any way to deny the unique role which the human person plays in the divine economy. Indeed, in light of the Christian doctrine of the Incarnation, that role is one of extraordinary dignity. But the role given to humanity is as sovereignly the gift of God as is the role of every other creature. The human person is the point in creation to which the fullness of the self-gift of God can be given. But the human person has been *created* as such.

The doctrine of *creatio ex nihilo* is not a claim about *how* the universe came into being, but *why*. It is the Christian response to the question that Martin Heidegger held was the beginning of all metaphysics: why is there being rather than nothing? If the question seeks a reason within being itself, it is doomed to remain unanswered. The doctrine of *creatio ex nihilo* insists on the fundamental poverty of the universe: the universe has no intrinsic ground for existence. When all else has been said, when the heavenly spheres fall silent, Augustine knew, the great truth that must be proclaimed is that we—all of us individually and together—did not make ourselves. And so Francis saw that it was neither an act of human self-denigration nor an effusion of poetic personification to address the sun and the moon, the fire and the earth, and all animate and inanimate creatures as his brothers and sisters; it was the simple truth.

The only reason for anything to exist is the free *agape* of God. The universe exists because God loves it and wills to give God's self to it. Utterly dependent, creation is divinely gifted. Thus, to see creation as a whole or any creature in particular as what it is, namely, totally dependent on the gracious will of God, is to see revealed the grace which is its foundation in being. Since everything that is exists because of the free act of God—the overflowing *agape* that is the source of all being—then everything is a sacrament of the goodness and creative power of God.

The themes of creation and poverty intersect in the Catholic vision of sacramentality. A sacrament is not a stand-in for something else, a visible sign for some other invisible reality. The essence of a sacrament is the capacity to reveal grace, the agapic self-gift of God, by being what it is. By being thoroughly itself, a sacrament bodies forth the absolute self-donative love of God that undergirds both it and the entirety of creation. The Catholic community has recognized seven particular events as being revelatory of grace. But every creature, human and non-human, animate and inanimate, can be a sacrament. The more richly developed our sacramental vision, the more sacraments crowd in upon us. Francis of Assisi's interweaving of poverty with the brotherhood and sisterhood of all creatures is profoundly Catholic because it is profoundly sacramental.

This sacramental vision is by no means limited to the Roman Catholic church. When Jonathan Edwards described the marks of true conversion in his great *Treatise on Religious Affections*, he gave as the first mark of such affections that they "do arise from those influences and, operations on the heart which are *spiritual, supernatural,* and *divine.*" In explanation of this first mark of the converted, Edwards wrote that "in those gracious affections and exercises which are wrought in the minds of the saints, through the saving influences of the Spirit of God, there is a new inward perception or sensation of their minds, entirely different in its nature and kind, from anything that ever their minds were the subjects of before they were sanctified." The saints, to use Edwards' term, see reality differently from the unconverted. They do not see things that others do not see; rather, they see what everyone else sees but in a different way. They see everything in its relation to God: they see it as creature. Edwards' "new inward perception or sensation" is the ability to hear the song of all creation that Augustine and Monica heard, to see the community of all creatures as creatures that Francis saw. At the risk of "catholicizing" the great eighteenth-century Calvinist, one way of describing this "new inward perception" of the Edwardsean saint is the capacity for sacramental vision.

The cultivation of sacramental vision is the richest way of recovering the companionship motif of the Genesis stories that the Christian tradition has to offer in the current global ecological crisis. The discovery that every creature, including oneself, is a sacrament of the love of God that causes all things to be provides the deepest foundation for reverencing creation. The recognition of the other as a creature and, therefore, that which exists because it is loved by God cannot occur where the other is regarded as "it." By its nature a sacrament requires that it be appreciated for what it is and not as a tool to an end; in Buber's terms, a sacrament is always "thou." Since every creature can and should be a sacrament, so every creature can and should be "thou," a companion. But this sacramental vision demands unflinching recognition of the poverty of one's own being—for many too terrible to be true—and joyful acceptance of the absolute *agape* that supports one's own being—for many too good to be true. This requires the expansion of the imagination.

Paul Ricoeur has written that "we too often and too quickly think of a will that submits and not enough of an imagination that opens itself." Seeing the world sacramentally cannot simply be commanded. However necessary it may be for the survival of the planet in our time, sacramental vision cannot be made a moral imperative. It might better be understood as a Christian aesthetic that needs cultivation. The whole of Catholic praxis is training in sacramental vision. Liturgy and social action, marriage and parenthood, prayer and politics, music and dance and the visual arts, all educate us to appreciate the other as sacramental, worthy companions of our poverty and our engracedness. They teach us to see things as they are. In Gerard Manley Hopkins' words, "These things, these things were here, and but the beholder/Wanting." At present, "beholders" are desperately wanted.

ELEMENTS OF A NEW ETHIC

If the ecological crisis is to be addressed effectively, the ethic of individualism must be replaced with an ethic of companionship. Both creation myths in Genesis agree in their depiction of the human capacity for relationship as that which makes humanity "like God." The exaltation of the individual at the expense of the community, which in its crudest form becomes the "trickle-down" theory of social responsibility, stands in contradiction to this foundational insight of the Jewish and Christian traditions. Not surprisingly, this individualist ethic has debased the image of stewardship from participation in the creative activity of God into cost-benefit analysis. While it is important to attempt to reassert the stewardship motif in its pristine form, it is also necessary to strike at the heart of the problem, to confront impoverished and impoverishing individualism with the relational anthropology of the Jewish and Christian traditions. The crisis of the environment is directly linked to the problem of humanization. For unless nonhuman beings are treated as "thou," human beings will be treated as "it." This is why the appeal to self-interest cannot yield sufficient support in responding to the global environmental crisis. Such an appeal merely reinforces the basic problem. Far more adequate and far more faithful to the Christian tradition is the reappropriation of the companionship motif of the biblical creation stories.

The religious discussion of human responsibility toward creation must move beyond stewardship for the sake of both theology and the environment. Theologically, stewardship has been open to a deist interpretation whereby God is seen as having begun creation and then handed over care of it to humanity. When the image of stewardship dominates our imagination, God can be removed from the scene as human beings are given oversight of the earth and move to center stage in the drama of creation. Too easily the duty of caring for God's world becomes the task of shaping our world. Just as stewards are not anxious for the master's presence lurking over their shoulder, so humanity is content to keep God in a distant heaven.

Companionship evokes a different attitude toward creation. This difference in attitude will be reflected in an environmental ethic grounded on a relational anthropology. Such an ethic does not spring full-blown from the companionship theme. The movement from an over-arching frame of mind to an ethical method is more complex. What the companionship motif provides is an orientation that should guide us in devising an environmental ethic.

The first point of orientation that the companionship motif provides is the desirability of a transformed context within which to develop an environmental ethic. Governed by images of stewardship and ruled by precepts based on self-interest, our moral imaginations are unable to envision an environmental ethic that is adequate to the Jewish and Christian heritage. In contrast, images of companionship encourage the moral imagination to consider that more than the good of the individual self is at stake. Once the intrinsic good of creation is seen, then approaches to the environmental crisis that treat creation only as an instrumental good for humanity become inadequate.

Basic to any ethic is a determination of the moral standing of the "other" one encounters. The reduction of creation to "it" has promoted a loss of respect for nature and an attitude of instrumental rationality. Doing justice to the environment becomes difficult when the context of decision making is so one-sided. Rediscovering the "thou" dimension of all creation provides a corrective to the tendency to relate to nature only as "it" by moving beyond the technological vision of instrumental rationality to a reawakened sacramental vision of companionship. So fundamental a reorientation alters the context for assessing our responsibility toward the environment.

The context of mutuality created by an awareness of both the poverty and the sacramentality of all the created order should yield an ethic less prone to denigrate the intrinsic worth of non-human creation. The poverty of the entire created order forces us to acknowledge our ties with the rest of creation in its dependence upon the creator. At the same time the sacramentality of all creation prevents any debasement of our common creaturely state. Our poverty as creatures and our dignity as sacramental mediations of divine grace must be held in tension as twin aspects of our organic connection with all creation.

The second point of orientation for an environmental ethic is an expanded notion of the common good that includes non-human creation. The common good, in John XXIII's classic phrase in *Mater et magistra*, embraces "the sum total of those conditions of social living whereby people are enabled to achieve their own integral perfection more fully and easily." As a way of elaborating what those "conditions of social living" entail, John went on to list an extensive roster of human rights. Both Paul VI and John Paul II have continued to use the language of human rights when discussing the common good. Theologian David Hollenbach suggests that the use of human rights in recent Catholic social teaching is a way of specifying the essential *needs*, basic *freedoms*, and *relationships* with others that comprise the common good and serve human dignity. In this essay we have suggested a perspective that sees the created order as an "other" with whom we have a relationship and that this relationship is part of the common good. Protecting that relationship with *non-human creation* is properly one of the aims of *human* rights.

Various addresses of Pius XII are also important resources for social ethics. So, for example, while not denying the right to private property, Pius made it clear that property rights are not primary but secondary. Private property is always subordinate to the more fundamental right of all people to the goods of the earth. This reiteration of the priority to be given to the universal destiny of goods contains the germ of an important insight. Pius saw the relationship of humanity to the earth and the rest of its inhabitants as basic to the common good. There is no need to protect the environment by ascribing rights to nature or individual animal species. It is humanity's fundamental human right to share in the goods of the earth that is at stake in the ecological issue. Setting this human right in the context of companionship is necessary, however, to prevent the human right to the universal destiny of the goods of creation from being interpreted according to a narrow mind-set of instrumental rationality.

The third point of orientation for an environmental ethic concerns the means whereby an expanded notion of the common good can be safeguarded and promoted. Here too the tradition of Catholic social thought has something to offer. In *Pacem in terris*, John XXIII drew attention to the existence of the "universal common good." The unity of the human family was the basis for John's espousal of a common good that transcended national boundaries. In the same encyclical John noted that the "whole reason for the existence of civil authorities is the realization of the common good." The difficulty was that existing political institutions "no longer correspond to the objective requirements of the universal common good." Subsequent popes have continued John's move from a national to an international to a transnational plane when analyzing social questions.

Issues that touch upon the universal common good—and the environment is one of these—go beyond the competence of individual nation-states. It is necessary to develop vehicles that protect the well-being of the global environment. An international agreement like the Law of the Sea Treaty serves as an illustration of the kind of structure that the papacy advocates for the sake of the universal common good. In contrast, the tendency to define narrowly the self-interest of a nation— as the Reagan administration did in opposing the Law of the Sea Treaty or as Japan has done in resisting fishing and whaling treaties—remains a major obstacle to building effective vehicles for the universal common good.

The language of the common good challenges political arrangements not only at the level of transnational issues. Ours is a nation that has prized individual liberty and has a strong attraction to free market economics. But we cannot avoid asking what social mechanisms on a national level must be devised so that the varied activities of citizens are directed to the common good, understood as including the good of creation. Romantic calls for simpler lifestyles or ideological reliance on purely voluntary measures are simply insufficient. Debate on the specific nature of these necessary mechanisms requires political leadership notably lacking at all levels of government.

No proposed environmental ethic can avoid confronting the pressing question of the relationship between ecology and economic development. Are ecological concerns to be traded off for the creation of jobs in poor areas? Or vice-versa? Is industrialization to be discouraged in nations with undeveloped economies for the sake of preserving certain animal and plant species? The common good cannot be a mere abstraction which prescinds from specific social and historical conditions. Building a shared understanding on the matter of the common good and the place accorded to the environment among other goods is a crucial enterprise for true development.

In *Redemptor hominis* John Paul II opposes a false development that is "dilapidating at an accelerated pace material and energy resources, and compromising the geophysical environment...." This critique of forms of development that ignore the earth's ecosystem echoes an earlier position articulated by many third-world hierarchies. At the 1971 Synod the bishops stated that "such is the demand for resources and energy by the richer nations, whether capitalist or socialist, and such are the effects of dumping by them in the atmosphere and the sea that irreparable damage would be done to the essential elements of life on earth, such as air and water, if their high rates of consumption and pollution, which are constantly on the increase, were extended to the whole of mankind." Donal Dorr has suggested that the episcopal view helps explain the use of the strong language about exploitation that is found in many third-world pronouncements about the international economic system. For too long the presumption was that the task was to "raise" poor nations to the level of production and consumption found in richer countries. The 1971 Synod pointed out, however, that such a view, whatever other failings it has, ignores the abuse of the environment that has accompanied development based on the first-world model. This development has come at the price of exploitation of the earth.

An indirect form of exploitation is the overuse of the universal goods of the earth for the benefit of a few, penalizing people in nations where economic development was slow in occurring. The earth cannot sustain everyone at the level of consumption found in the first world. The first nations to undergo modern industrialization have used more than their share of the earth's resources. Nations seeking economic development must now compensate for the abuses of those who benefited from earlier exploitation of the earth. According to third-world leaders, the limits now proposed on development constitute an exploitation of poor nations. No consensus yet exists on how to reconcile ecological concerns and developmental needs, but some headway in resolving them is a *sine qua non* if the environmental movement is to make progress.

GETTING IT RIGHT

An attitudinal shift is foundational for dealing with the environmental crisis, and theology has a leading role to play in the endeavor. The main contribution of the Church in the ecological crisis should be to foster a correct attitude toward all of God's creation. The motif of companionship is an important initial stage for establishing the imperative of a new way of relating to the created order. Without that starting point, the problems of developing a politics and economics cognizant of the ecological common good will be multiplied.

There is the danger that the language of companionship could be understood as simply fostering romantic forms of opposition to technology. But a simplistic "back to nature" movement fomenting broad opposition to technology is a distortion of a proper theology of creation. Technology is an outgrowth of our own human nature as creative beings. Unless we do violence to ourselves, technology will continue. What is needed is the wisdom to direct the process of technological change, not to stop it. The primacy of ethics and politics over technology must be asserted. First, we must assess the human goods that technology must serve. Second, the political process is the arena in which many of the moral choices will be worked through and implemented. Effective political action must follow careful ethical reflection. To fail in either of these realms is to permit technology to slip beyond human direction. In order to guide change there must be a sense of the goods that are to be sought and an appreciation of the ranking of goods that may conflict. Only then can we know what goods technology must serve, what policy choices are to be made, at what price, and what institutional arrangements are required for implementation. From the outset, however, the scale of goods will be skewed unless humanity's relations with nature include an awareness of the "thou-ness" of creation.

Although, we believe, the retrieval of the companionship theme and a deepened commitment to the common good tradition are required criteria for the development of an environmental ethic, other criteria are also essential. The Jewish and Christian understanding of creation should not be wedded to any economic ideology. Neither capitalism nor socialism in their historical realizations differs in the way they view creation and humanity's relation to it. Both Adam Smith and Karl Marx had a strong bias toward instrumental rationality. At the same time, neither system should be dismissed as inevitably inhospitable to environmental concerns. Whether or not a sacramental vision of creation can take root in either approach remains to be seen. In both systems what must be addressed is the proper balance between the environment and economic development. Here the magisterium's theme of true development is a reminder that economic growth must be based on a model that is ecologically sustainable. In this regard the World Council of Churches' call for a criterion of sustainable efficiency strikes an important note for future decision making.

In addition, the criterion of social justice cannot be lost in the struggle for ecological responsibility. A simple disavowal of economic growth may perpetuate injustice to humans in the name of nonhumans. Ecology has to do with the relationship of organisms to the total environment, including other organisms of the same or different species. Ecological balance has unquestionably been lost in the way that human beings have treated nonhuman nature. Righting the imbalance, however, cannot entail injustice to fellow human beings for the sake of other species. Poorer nations will not be willing to forego economic development at the behest of wealthier nations, who have belatedly seen the results of their own assaults on nature in the quest for more and more expansion. To avoid a new imbalance, an environmental ethic must be informed by a careful analysis of the demands of economic justice.

Justice in economic development, economic growth premised on sustainable efficiency, and a heightened role for the environment in our understanding of the common good are three vital elements in any environmental ethic. But seeing the world rightly precedes our ability to act wisely and justly. The first task before us, that which theology can assist, is to revision all beings as united in their createdness, given to one another as companions, sacraments of "the love that moves the sun and other stars."

Get Him Out of the Birdbath! What does it mean to have a Patron Saint of Ecology?

Keith Douglass Warner, OFM[*]

On Easter Sunday, 1980, Pope John Paul II named Francis of Assisi the patron saint of Ecology. Now that we have passed the twentieth anniversary of this event I would like to reflect on the implications of having a patron saint of ecology in the Catholic Church. I would like to believe that he would inspire us to address environmental issues seriously, to reflect on what it means to be people of faith in an age of ecological crisis. In this essay I would like to frame environmental problems through the lens of Christian Franciscan spirituality, and to offer some ideas on how we might want to address them. This essay does not pretend to be scholarly nor comprehensive. Rather, I wish to invite any person inspired by Francis to consider the spiritual and religious implications of being part of a Church having a patron saint of ecology. I have a formal relationship to St. Francis: as a vowed member of the religious fraternity that he started, I have a particular responsibility to manifest his spirituality and that includes giving witness to the love he had for all creatures. But one need not be a Franciscan friar or sister to be a Franciscan. The vast majority of Franciscans have always been and will continue to be ordinary men and women, inspired by the witness of the poor man of Assisi. Some lay men and women formally affiliate by

* This article originally appeared as: "Out of the Birdbath!! Following the Patron Saint of Ecology" in *The Cord* 48/2 (April 1998):74–85.This revised version of the work is reprinted with the author's permission.

becoming Secular Franciscans (formerly: the Third Order), but most simply look to him as an example. These are sometimes called "the fourth order." Anyone can become a Franciscan simply by following Francis' way of following Jesus; one need not join a vowed community to express his ecological vision of spirituality. Francis is perhaps Christianity's most famous nature mystic, and his experiences can inspire us to act on behalf of God's Creation.

I have noticed an odd disconnection between the difficult and practical struggle to defend the integrity of Creation and the majority of discussions that I have had with other Franciscans about these matters. When I listen to other Franciscans talk about nature, I often feel like I am looking at one of the nineteenth century paintings from the "American Romantic period." These painters created quasi-fantastic landscapes inspired by the Western frontier. It is this kind of desire to "feel good" about nature that has led to so many insipid garden statues of Francis, inanely presenting a birdbath. While I certainly prefer a beauty ethic to a perspective on nature that sees it only in terms of economic profit, I would like to invite anyone inspired by Francis to move beyond nature as something to look at and "feel good." As a nature mystic, Francis savored his relationship with earth, moon, fire, water and living creatures, but to emotion he added solidarity, compassion, and action. I understand how overwhelmingly complex environmental issues can be, especially when science, statistics, and future projections are involved. I am not, however, content that Franciscans tend to see nature exclusively as a gift of beauty. I feel that we need to be able to face the distressing facts of our environmental crises and hold Creation's beauty and the threats it faces in tension. The threat of tremendous human and non-human suffering is unprecedented, and yet Franciscans seem reluctant to commit time or resources to these concerns.

My question is: where are the Franciscans in the debate about the environment? Have there been any efforts to address environmental issues from a Franciscan perspective? Why have so few Franciscans, lay or religious, involved themselves in environmental issues? Whenever I tell non-Catholics that I am a Franciscan interested in promoting concern for Creation, I get strong responses along the lines of: "where have you been all these years? We've been waiting for the Franciscans to address these issues!" As a follower of the patron saint of ecology, I feel I have a responsibility to devote part of my life's effort to following his example of loving Creation. I hope others would feel called to this ministry as well. I would like to use this essay to explore some ideas about how Francis might serve as a model for doing this.

INCARNATIONAL SPIRITUALITY

The two major components of our task at hand are to construct a different theological lens for viewing nature and environmental problems, hopefully one that is authentically Franciscan, and to help those around us to realize that our environmental behavior is an expression of our spirituality. The first is perhaps an assignment of a more specialized nature, but it cannot stand alone. I will only be able to suggest a new direction we might want to move in this essay. In Francis' writings and the historical sources of his life, we have evidence of his spirituality of nature. In addition, Bonaventure and Scotus developed the Franciscan theological tradition which emerged from their perspective and experience as Franciscans. As early Franciscans who built on Francis' nature mysticism and mystical insight, they have provided important theological tools for helping us with this first task. A rationale helps provide a response to our crises that is both consistent and faithful.

Until the industrial revolution, the relationship between humanity and nature was much more simple, and inherited Biblical attitudes toward nature were sufficient to provide guidance in this area. The human-nature relationship is now far more strained and problematic than it ever has been, thanks in large part to the unprecedented power humans now have through technology. We need a theology or rationale for a more positive view of nature, one that assigns non-human Creation value and reins in the power of our technology. Until there is a broader awareness of the consequences of indifference toward the environment and there is consensus to value the survival of non-human creation over human convenience and greater consumption, we will not see noticeable improvement in the well-being of the earth's natural systems. I believe that the Franciscan theological tradition can provide this.

I do not intend to articulate this theological vision here; I merely hope to point toward a direction that could help, and to challenge you, the reader, to reflect on the intersection of your spiritual practice and our ecological crisis. For many, Creation spirituality has provided a refreshing change from Christian theologies concerned exclusively with humans. Writers such as Thomas Berry, Matt Fox and Brian Swimme have argued for a reinterpretation of the creation story, one more positive and centered on the inherent goodness of creation. While there is much that I like about Creation spirituality, to me it seems a bit utopian, short on specific suggestions for how to address our problems. It is a vision for how human/non-human and human-divine relationships ought to be, yet it fails to adequately explain how to move in that direction. At times, Creation spirituality seems to be more concerned with rejecting major pieces of Christian theology than renewing it in a way relevant to the social and ecological problems we currently face.

I certainly appreciate Creation spirituality and I agree with many of its tenets. Yet as a person trained in Franciscan theology, I cannot accept Creation spirituality uncritically. While both Franciscan spirituality and Creation spirituality advocate a deep sense of relationship with nature, there are points of conflict between them, at least as these three men have articulated Creation spirituality. Two of the conflicts are over the person of Christ, and the means of reforming human behavior (which is based on our theological anthropology). I believe the Franciscan theological tradition has the insight and tools that can help connect the faith of ordinary Christians with the need to see the well-being of all of Creation as something in which God takes great interest. The increased importance placed on the incarnation of Christ unites Christocentric and Creation-oriented theologies.

Christocentrism has been a defining characteristic of Franciscan theology since Francis himself. By Christocentrism, I mean that Jesus Christ is the center of our theological understanding of the world. As Paul wrote in Colossians, "for in (Jesus) all things were created, in heaven and on earth, visible and invisible, whether thrones or dominions or principalities or authorities—all things were created through him and for him" (Colossians 2:16). Francis opened the rule of life for his first followers insisting on the principle of "the teaching and footprints of our Lord Jesus Christ," and this captures the essence of Franciscan spirituality. While I certainly agree with the need to broaden the focus of God's saving activity beyond just the human species, I grow uneasy when I read theologies that fail to make any connection between Jesus and our relationship with nature or the material world. And I know that the majority of Catholic and Protestant Christians would be more open to an ecological theology if it were more clearly connected to the Jesus Christ they worship on Sunday morning.

FRANCISCAN CHRISTOCENTRISM, REDEMPTIVE COMPLETION, AND THE COSMIC, ECOLOGICAL CHRIST

In some ways it is remarkable how succinctly the theology of the cosmic Christ in the Franciscan tradition addresses the need for an understanding of Jesus that lays a foundation for a greater valuation of the natural world. Through a Franciscan understanding of Jesus' life and person, as interpreted by Bonaventure and Scotus, we can connect the Jesus-story with our contemporary needs to revalue nature. Their reflection on the mystery of the incarnation of Christ serves a portal into a more sophisticated understanding of God's belief in the goodness of the created world. The incarnation marked a threshold in the relationship between God and humanity, and God and the whole created world. God chose to sacramentalize the world in a more profound and unprecedented way, to make the entire material world a vehicle for communion with God. This belief in the goodness of Creation has been present in the Franciscan tradition since Francis, but we now find ourselves in a social situation in which we need to give this belief even greater emphasis.

I am neither a philosopher nor a sophisticated theologian. Thankfully, we have two fine Franciscan systematic theologians who can help us. In his succinct essay on John Duns Scotus, *Incarnation, Individuality, and Diversity*, Kenan Osborne writes:

> ...Jesus, in his humanity, indeed sacramentalizes the finality of God's whole world, a world in which human freedom and mis-freedom (sin) exist. The whole world is sacramentalized, not just the "nice" part of it. The incarnation then begins, one might say, with the very first act of God *ad extra*—the first creative moment of our world. The incarnation is a process moving through the history of our created world, and with each subsequent step the meaning of the world, the finality of the world, the "why" of the world emerges to some degree in a clearer way. We are finding out more about the incarnation than ever before. It is an ascending experience. Like climbing a mountain, the higher one goes, the wider and broader one's perspective. In the Jesus-event, a major revelation of the meaning of creation, the "why" of creation, takes place. This is what the world and its history are all about.[1]

This understanding of Incarnation is both deeply Christocentric and at the same time embraces material Creation as good. Creation is sacramentalized in an even more profound way by the incarnation of Christ. God's generosity is expressed to us through Creation, and the incarnation of Christ builds on this.

Zachary Hayes has written very helpful works on Christology in the Franciscan tradition. In an article for *The Cord*, a Franciscan journal, he writes:

> The cosmos, as Bonaventure writes, is the primal book of divine self-revelation. And the meaning of the cosmos is concentrated in humanity and radicalized in the person of Jesus Christ. Thus, the doctrine of the primacy of Christ points the believer to an understanding of the inherent meaning of the cosmos. There has probably been no period in history when this doctrine of the cosmic Christ was as important as it is right now....[2]

In Hayes' explanation of Franciscan Christocentrism, we are freed from the dilemma of being forced to choose between a creational theology and a redemption theology. Creation spirituality, as it has been commonly articulated, has been set in opposition to the need for human redemption. Hayes proposes Bonaventure's theory of redemptive completion as a way to integrate a positive appreciation of Creation and humanity's need for redemption.

> Completion refers to the process of bringing creation to its God-intended end which is anticipated already in the destiny of Christ. Redemption refers to the necessary process of dealing with all the obstacles that stand in the way. Such a model could be easily related to the sense of an emerging cosmos as it appears to us today in the light of the sciences. This would allow us to create a larger framework of spirituality and theology which would have some resonance with the cultural images that have such a pervasive impact on the minds of our people.[3]

Thanks to these two contemporary theologians, among others, we can see that Jesus Christ is not irrelevant to our environmental problems. Although he was not a trained theologian, Francis had a profound insight into the love of God expressed through Creation. Francis, Bonaventure, Scotus and many others have preached a theology broad enough to embrace Jesus Christ of the Scriptures, our Christian tradition, and a theology of nature as inherently valuable and good.

PENANCE IN AN ECOLOGICAL AGE

Francis also understood the human heart, and his prescription for its change was to do penance. He identified himself as penitent and chose to follow Jesus in this way. While our ecological situation may be quite different today, there are several key penitential values that point us toward what I believe would be a Franciscan response to environmental problems. Some of these values are: humility, expressed through poverty and simplicity; refraining from the excesses of technology; service to the poor, vulnerable, and marginalized; participation in the mystery of the Eucharist; and peacemaking.

Here again we see a clear contrast with Creation spirituality. Fox and Berry have both been criticized because they fail to take into account the difficulty of changing human behavior. Berry writes beautifully of the mystery and celebration of the vitality of life on our planet, and his prose is truly inspiring. Fox, like most Creation spirituality writers, is uncomfortable with the idea that human beings are fallen and in need of redemption, and he prefers an emphasis on "original grace." He suggests that the release of the "mystic child" within us will lead us to want to share our wealth and develop a respect for the Earth.

One of the major problems I have with Creation spirituality is that it fails to take into account the real brokenness and darkness in human nature due to sin. Compulsive greed and chronic indifference are the two greatest obstacles to a healthy relationship with Creation. I fault mainstream Christianity and Creation spirituality for failing to acknowledge that sin has an ecological dimension. We North Americans are grasping for so much wealth that it cannot possibly be sustained. Our society's lifestyle is robbing from the underdeveloped world and from nature's ability to restore herself. We are refusing to accept our place, and this is a classic definition of sin. I agree with the overall direction of Creation spirituality, emphasizing mystical imagination, but without including repentance, or life-changing *metanoia*, I fear that it will remain a utopian vision, or an eschatological vision, if you prefer.[4]

I am, however, appreciative to Creation spirituality because it has provoked me to reflect on what the human-nature relationship could be. The more I have reflected on Francis' writings and spirituality, the more I am convinced that his model for all the relationships in which humans participate is the human family. Two of his texts which provide the clearest indication of this are *The Canticle of the Creatures* and the *First*

Letter to the Faithful. In the latter, Francis writes to his lay followers of how our decision to do penance places us in relationship with Jesus. When we do penance we become the spouse, brother or sister, mother, and parent of Jesus. The strongest theme to emerge from the first part of the First Letter to the Faithful is that we become related to Jesus when we become penitents. Francis assumes this same underlying grid of familial relationship when he writes the capstone of his theological vision, *The Canticle of the Creatures.* He wrote this poem at the end of his life, and it captures his mystical relationship with God through the created world. This poem expresses through powerful symbolic language how the elements of nature are praiseworthy and related to both God and humanity. Francis praised the diversity and beauty of the plant kingdom ("Praised by You, my Lord, by our Sister Mother Earth, who sustains and governs us, and who produces varied fruits with colored flowers and herbs"). He admitted that we humans are subject to sin and in need of forgiveness, but he affirmed an even more fundamental truth that we are all related. The work seems to capture the sense of peace and reconciliation he achieved with the various elements of himself at the end of his life. I believe that Francis was named the patron saint of ecology because he loved nature but also because he articulated a mystical vision of the interrelatedness of all Creation in his life and in this poem.

Francis' vision of the goodness of the world is most evident in this poem, and with its lyrics it presents a vision in clear contrast to the pessimism of the heretical Cathars of his time. Raoul Manselli, an Italian social historian, has written a biography of St. Francis that is most helpful because it helps us understand him in the context of the popular religious currents of his era. He wrote:

> Francis' repeated affirmation of deep devotion to the Eucharist and to the permanent presence of Christ on earth that it signified was directed in turn against the Cathars. Similarly, the *Canticle's* praise of God as Creator and for what he created strikes at the heart of one of the basic tenets of Catharism, according to which the Creator, or at least the ruler, of the physical world is Satan, as portrayed in the heresy's many and varying myths.
>
> Against these ideas Francis did not resort to theological argumentation that would have been foreign to his temperament and, frankly, to his level of education. Rather, he brings out two aspects

of the world: the omnipotence of God and the positive quality of creation as a work of beauty, implying as well its goodness... The universe, therefore, cannot be evil: this is the conclusion contained in Francis' *Canticle*. Nor is it hell within which angels are imprisoned. Rather, it is the work and the result of an extraordinary, almighty goodness that, in the creation of the universe, reveals itself to be beauty as well.[5]

In *The Canticle of the Creatures*, therefore, we apprehend Francis' view of nature as a sacramental expression of God's generous love, a love which binds us to interdependent relationship. As in Francis' era, we live in a time that devalues nature's inherent goodness. The Cathars rejected this notion on religious grounds, while today our society strips, beats and pollutes nature for economic profit. Both stances are fundamental rejections of the incarnation.

BEYOND THE STEWARDSHIP MODEL: NATURE AS FAMILY

In the past thirty years, Christian theologians have tentatively begun to address the abuse of nature, generally by asserting that the Genesis story has been misunderstood and appropriated to justify profit at the expense of ecological wholeness. Christians and Jews have pointed to the early chapters in Genesis as a model for environmental stewardship. I certainly agree that stewardship is a good idea, and as a species we definitely need to embrace this as a model for caring for Creation. But the Franciscan theological tradition presents an additional model. I believe Francis left us a *familial* model of relating to Creation. In the stewardship model, humans care for the earth because we want to take care of ourselves and future generations; God "put us in charge" of the beauty and bounty of Earth. We are to care "on behalf of." The familial model values relationship with the beauty and diversity of Creation, celebrating the interaction between ourselves and Earth's many creatures. We are called to care for, as a member of God's family of creatures. We exist by God's grace, together, side by side. We can marvel at the miracle of life's diversity, and humbly acknowledge our simple membership, and at the same time recognize that there are certain responsibilities that we have as a species. I believe both of these spiritual traditions, stewardship as majority tradition and familial as minority, have co-existed from the beginnings of human religious practice.

Obviously we cannot live without objectifying parts of nature and using them for our food and well-being, but at the same time, I believe we are called to reflect on God's generosity to us expressed in the diverse colors, shapes, power, smells, textures, intricacy and magnificence of Creation. Agriculture necessarily operates out of the stewardship model, but I believe that we all need to practice some appreciation of nature for its own sake, whether it be bird-watching, flower planting, or camping. Creation has intrinsic value, and we do well to remind ourselves of this through regular activities. This was Francis' joy, and I became a Franciscan in part because that was my passion too, and his spirituality helped validate my own experience. I consider nature observation a spiritual discipline.

Francis is perhaps most original when he extends his notion of chivalric courtesy to non-human creatures. He was, of course, deeply influenced by the ideals of the troubadour and courtly love. He "spiritualized" the notion of *cortesia*, an Italian word far stronger than the English word "courtesy." It implies the notion of honorable deference, respect, largesse, special and personal consideration of the needs of others, especially the poor and vulnerable. Francis embodied a joyous humility in his respect for the good of Creation.[6]

I return to what I believe to be three essential themes of the Franciscan world view: a profound concern for relationship, a life of penance, and concern for the marginalized. Throughout history elements of this world view have been re-interpreted by followers of Francis to address the social, ecclesial and political challenges of their day, and I propose we simply do the same in our ecological age.

Based on Francis' approach to nature, I believe there are three attitudes most appropriate to followers of Francis today: the celebration of relationship, the promotion of courtesy and the practice of penance. What form might these attitudes, so fully embodied by Francis in the Middle Ages, take among us today? Celebrating our relationship with Brother Wind, Sister Water, Brother Fire, and our Sister Mother Earth must serve as the foundation for all of this, but for many, this must be preceded by acknowledging the existence of interdependent relationship. We in the industrialized West have forgotten how dependent our bodies are on safe and pure air, water, and food; these are fundamental to life, yet we take them for granted. Franciscans can provide a tremendous service to the Church and world by reminding our brothers and sisters to be grateful for the gifts of each day, and Francis left us an example of celebrating the simple elements of life which most take for granted. Like Creation spirituality, a Franciscan Incarnational spirituality will begin by changing our internal focus, or consciousness. Personal, familial and communal celebrations can help this immensely.

The courtesy of Francis charms us even today. Generosity, respect and honor, all pillars of courtesy, are much-needed virtues throughout our world today, especially in areas of conflict over environmental issues. If one can sort through heated arguments, at stake are the well-being of plants, animals, and humans. All forms of life have an inherent right to exist, and elementary courtesy requires that we acknowledge this. Proclaiming peace and reconciliation was an expression of Francis' courtesy. We can imitate him by being environmental peacemakers. Just as Francis built peace in the relationship between the bishop and mayor by singing *The Canticle of the Creatures*, we can bring reconciliation to the conflicts around us by practicing and promoting respect for the existence and well-being of others. By honoring both parties in a conflictual situation we invite others to adopt a stance of respect and to acknowledge the right of others to exist. Direct confrontation of personal and corporate greed can be ineffectual. I believe that by encouraging others to acknowledge, respect and enjoy the relationships they have with others, that greed can be replaced with courtesy, and this seems fully consistent with Francis' approach.

ECO-PENANCE

In the face of the global scale of environmental problems, I have often felt paralysis and despair. So many people making so many choices that cumulatively damage the earth's oceans, forests, food supply and atmosphere. Is there any reason to hope for a change of heart? I take great solace in being able to turn to the example of Francis. In the face of conflict, war, vice and violence, he practiced penance. More than simply manufactured feelings of regret, the Franciscan practice of penance is embodied humility. It consists of acknowledging our brokenness and sinfulness, our dependence on God's grace, and our need for conversion to the Gospel of Jesus. I firmly believe that in our age we can adopt Francis' stance of penance and humility in our relationship with the environment. We need to acknowledge that our environmental problems are not caused by any other species than ourselves. We need to admit that we are in need of God's grace to reform our behavior so that we might live in peace with Creation, which is God's plan. We need to practice greater humility as a species. We need to practice eco-penance.

Eco-penance is both an interior attitude and a praxis. It promotes consistency between the statement of values we make about Creation and our behavior toward it. The practice of eco-penance includes a sense of personal responsibility for the environmental impacts of our lifestyle, and that of our society, and will lead to efforts to reduce the harmful effects that we have on other forms of life and our planetary habitat that we all depend upon. We can call upon the Church and world to join us in adopting this stance and then taking action appropriate to our local area.

Eco-penance promotes a sense of connection with the earth and relationship with other creatures, but it can take various forms: political advocacy, local actions, and communal prayer. In many cases the most important action we can take on behalf of other forms of life takes place in the political realm, whether writing letters of advocacy on behalf of endangered species or speaking at public meetings to urge the clean up of abandoned toxic sites near families. Yet politics can be confusing and frustrating for all of us, so many times the best way to create and maintain a passion for Creation is through a local project which shows specific, observable results. Beach and creek clean-ups can generate great enthusiasm because people can see the fruits of their labors. This kind of activity is even more powerful if it is accompanied by reflection and social analysis. Transformation of individuals and structures is most possible when action is joined to reflection. How powerful it would be if a parish community had a period of theological reflection the week before a clean-up day and hosted a large celebration afterward! A community garden can provoke a neighborhood to a greater connection to their locale and foster a greater awareness of the need for clean air, soil and water.

Those inspired today by Francis could foster more of these good actions by participating in them but also by bringing concern for the earth into our prayer. We have the ability to influence our local faith communities by including concern for creation in our prayer and work. There is no reason that concern for other forms of life and our planet's health could not be made a major part of a parish penance services during Advent or Lent. If we did nothing else, simply practicing simplicity and spending more time with friends, family and nature would do wonders for those around us, and encourage those who work in the environmental movement as well.

A DISTINCTIVE FRANCISCAN CONTRIBUTION

One of the greatest strengths in the Franciscan tradition has been the diversity of responses to God's generous love. There are many ways in which Franciscans can begin to take action to address the threats to our Sister Mother Earth, and I would encourage everyone to engage themselves in more than one. Nonetheless, I would like to highlight two broad issues in particular. I hope that the efforts of many Franciscans can touch on either of these concerns.

Environmental justice is an issue that ties together two dimensions of our Franciscan world view—concern for Creation and option for the poor and marginalized—by stressing equal protections for those typically ignored in the pursuit of the environmental agenda, people of color and the poor. Environmental justice directly links environment concerns with social justice issues by addressing the disproportionate impact of pollution on people of color and the poor. Low-income neighborhoods suffer more than those with greater income because they cannot marshal the resources to defend themselves from those who have more political and social power. The appalling contrast between the obese bodies in the industrialized North and the distended bellies of starving children in the South is a powerful picture. On an international scale, addressing debt relief for "Third World" countries must be the highest priority for environmental justice. Environmental racism can take many forms. Recent immigrants from Mexico working in agriculture may suffer from the harmful effects of pesticides. Powerful agribusiness corporations have resisted efforts to restrict the use of these chemicals, but when there is an incident in the fields, media don't report it because it doesn't concern "their audience." There are some who do not yet feel comfortable embracing concern for Creation, or who do not yet see any connection between their religious faith and environmental concern. Environmental justice is a perfect "starter issue," because the anyone with an awareness of God's justice can see the harmful effects of environmental injustice in the U.S. Concern for environmental justice is of course more than a "starter issue." We can express our solidarity with suffering human and nonhuman communities by taking action to defend their well-being. Hopefully this issue can help all of us see that God's concern for the well-being of Creation extends to more than human beings.

Biological diversity is the variety of different plant, animal and insect species on our planet. Diversity is important ecologically because many forms of life depend on each other, and when human activities injure one species, its loss may impact many other forms of life. Our ecosystems need all their "pieces," all their species; human disruption is now ripping off large parts of the fabric of life, and the whole cloth is at risk of unraveling. Biological diversity is not simply an abstract concept removed from our everyday existence. Many medicines are based on new chemical compounds discovered in rare species in the tropics. People in the United States used to consume a far more diverse diet than they do today; industrial agriculture finds it far easier to manage a small number of crops. Biological diversity is needed even more today because of human-caused disruption to our planet's climate; diversity between species and within species provides more flexibility for responding to environmental change. Endangered species are truly the most vulnerable and threatened forms of life today.

Diversity is an important principle in Christian spirituality as well. Psalm 148 and the canticle of the three young men in the fiery furnace (Daniel 3:56–88) are the Scripture passages which are the clearest influences on Francis' *The Canticle of the Creatures*, and both speak of the value of diversity, fishes, sea monsters, different kinds of trees, beasts, creeping things, flying birds, all things growing from the earth. God loves all kinds of diversity and individuality; otherwise, God wouldn't have made it so! Christianity has celebrated the goodness of this diversity, but we Christians have never had to confront the threats to its diversity that we do today. Because Scripture and Francis speak so eloquently of diversity, indeed because they treasure it, I believe that we are called to be its advocates today.

Few other Christians have the rich theological tradition of relationship with nonhuman creation and of valuing diversity and individuality. Followers of St. Francis are uniquely positioned because of this tradition to address issues of species diversity. Because we value these, I heartily urge all Franciscans, lay or religious, to consider how we can become better advocates for other forms of life. I honestly believe that if we don't speak up for nonhuman Creation, few others in Christianity will.

Followers of Francis are called in a special way to call all people to a healthy relationship with Creation. As followers of the patron saint of ecology we have a special responsibility to model a loving, familial relationship with all Creation, especially those members, human and nonhuman, who are threatened by actions of violence, greed and callousness.

We are called to be advocates for those who cannot speak of the suffering caused by human ignorance and indifference. We are heirs to a rich theological tradition that can provide a framework for incorporating environmental sensitivity into religious practice and activity. I pray that those more skilled than I can articulate a contemporary theology of nature in the Franciscan tradition that can spur us on to more radical prayer and action in relationship with nature. We have the tremendous resource of being leaders in the Church, and we are capable of embodying Francis' passionate love of Creation and preaching about it through our word and example.

Notes

1. Kenan Osborne OFM, *Incarnation, Individuality and Diversity*, The Cord (1995) 45:3, 23.
2. Zachary Hayes OFM, *Christ, Word of God and Exemplar of Humanity*, The Cord (1996) 46:1, 13–14.
3. *Ibid.*, 16.
4. For further critique of Creation spirituality, see Sallie McFague, *Body of God*, Minneapolis, MN: Fortress, 1993, 69–73.
5. Raoul Manselli, *St. Francis of Assisi*, trans. Paul Duggan, Chicago: Franciscan Herald Press, 1988, 316–317.
6. For a discussion of Francis' courtesy toward nature as innovation, see Roger Sorrell, *St. Francis of Assisi and Nature*, New York: Oxford University Press, 1988, 69–75. This work is the best treatment of Francis' attitudes toward nature.

How to Love a Worm? Biodiversity: Franciscan Spirituality and Praxis

James F. Edmiston, OFM[*]

Casual observation and common sense indicate that numerous and unique creatures live on the earth. Not only is there such diversity, but no two living organisms have ever been exactly alike or experienced the universe in exactly the same way. Individuality is normative!

The diversity of living organisms overwhelms the human senses and piques the imagination. Scientists attempt to describe and categorize the living diversity. Theologians and philosophers attempt to explain the implications of such a creation. Diversity and individuality influence our personal and corporate behaviors. To observe, explore, and attempt some understanding of this diversity and individuality as expressed through living creatures can enrich our lives.

The purpose of this work is to acknowledge our experiences of biodiversity, and look into the Franciscan tradition for some theological underpinnings to support the preservation of biodiversity. Ideas only take us so far, practical suggestions for actually experiencing and teaching others about biodiversity will be made.

---

[*] This article originally appeared as "How to Love a Worm? Biodiversity: Franciscan Spirituality and Praxis" in John E. Carroll and Keith Warner, eds. *Ecology and Religion: Scientists Speak*, (Quincy, IL: Franciscan Press, 1998), 289–301. Reprinted with permission.

BIODIVERSITY

Humans live on a planet containing at least 1 million and possibly as many as 10 to 100 million different, distinct life forms—species.[1] Scientists and philosophers struggle with the process of separating, categorizing, and identifying the "types" of life and how to distinguish between the distinctly different species. Regardless of how the taxonomists proceed to describe the differences in life forms, from molecular to organismal, through population and community levels of organization, the diversity of life on planet earth is rich. From the perspective of an individual human person—awareness of biodiversity is wonderfully overwhelming!

People of the twentieth-century who dedicate themselves to studying the diversity and distribution of life tell us the number of different species is drastically declining.[2] Much of the decline is related to activities of our human species. As our population grows, we occupy more space, and our activities destroy and consume resources other species need to survive.

Accepting that the diversity of earth's life forms is declining, why is this a concern and what is our response? Just asking the question implies that we have some interest, and that we are interconnected with other life forms. These interconnections influence what we eat, what we wear, what medicines we can develop, and even how we come to aesthetically appreciate the living earth.

Commercial and medical implications of declining biodiversity have been clearly established. The realization that many new human medicines come from endangered tropical plants has caused grave concern.[3] But, the question of declining biodiversity transcends our anthropocentric focus, as people begin to realize that personal human life decisions have implications for other life forms.

Books have recently been written that explore the large scale and subtle implications for finding answers to declining biodiversity. E. O. Wilson particularly addresses the interrelationship between biological processes, sociological systems and the reduction of biodiversity. Recommendations presented in Wilson's book involve soliciting support for national and international programs to inventory and preserve the remaining biodiversity.[4]

Beyond these sophisticated and succinctly written popular materials with their wide-ranging proposals for programs, the question remains to be experienced and understood from a personal context. To focus on people in the United States with Western philosophical and spiritual backgrounds who are engaging in a process of formulating responses to the issue of declining biodiversity, I would like to consider: How do people in the U.S. generally view their relationship to creation? How does the Franciscan tradition within Western spirituality inform us about biodiversity? What practical methodologies are available to us that can assist our understanding, and help us to build appropriate relationships with other species? While the effects of reducing biodiversity are seen globally, these questions face each human person, right now.

PERSONAL RELATIONSHIPS WITH CREATION

To appreciate someone or something, we must know them. We must enter into relationship with the person or creature, with the painting or the sunset. In some way, a person, event, creature, or concept must be experienced, our brains must be neurologically stimulated, if we are to develop a relationship that includes our effective and affective dimensions. To know is the first step to appreciation and love.

The air we breathe and the chemical components of our bodies are continuously cycled through the bodies of almost all living creatures. Such intimate connections often go unnoticed. Yet, even people whose lives are centered on industrial and technological pursuits seem to have an inner-longing for experiences of other living organisms. Notice how people pack up the hiking, camping, and fishing equipment, and clog the urban highways for weekend and vacation returns to nature. Even with these extensive personal, and often highly commercialized "return to nature" adventures—the typical lifestyle within the twentieth-century U.S. society is structured to continuously avoid a person's connections with creation.

Think about a typical day in urban America—most of our time is spent going from one temperature and humidity controlled space to another, rarely do our feet touch the soil, and the extent of our interaction with other living species is at best the recognition of trees in rows along the streets. Daily encounters with other living animals is limited to a glimpse of an urban squirrel or sparrow.

People living in the rural U.S. have similar encounters with other species. U.S. agriculture has become big business. Agricultural fields have become food factories. Natural landscapes have become backdrops for commercial enterprises, rather than integrated components of daily rural life.

Even when we are interacting with other species, our anthropocentric bias shows. The animals we like are "cute as a puppy" or "cuddly as a bear," demonstrating our vertebrate bias. Even the invertebrates which we respect reflect human qualities—"busy as a bee." Colorful butterflies and moths receive some attention, but only as they stimulate our emotions through the visual spectrum. Even colorful creatures are being commercially exploited as components of jewelry and other ornaments. From the perspective of our domesticated anthropocentric lifestyles, rain forests, ecological cycles, invertebrates, and biodiversity remain abstract concepts for most people.

Some efforts to construct artificial rain forests in special buildings, to present a sanitized version of nature through the television media, or to enhance ecological components of educational curriculum indicate that twentieth-century people of the U.S. have not totally ignored our relationships to other organisms. Every school age child has some exposure to concepts of animals and plants, or photosynthesis and respiration. However, environmental concepts often remain within the abstract realm of academic training and entertainment. Relationships with other organisms rarely become integrated conceptual components of daily life.

If our concern for other life forms is genuine, the need exists to create opportunities for each person to enter into relationships with other creatures, enabling us to experience the earth from another creatures perspective. To personally know other creatures that are not like us can enable us to appreciate how our life interconnects with millions of other life forms.

BIODIVERSITY AND FRANCISCAN SPIRITUALITY

Looking for people from our Western spiritual traditions who have modeled relationships with other creatures, the most frequently cited exemplar is Francis of Assisi. He was a thirteenth-century nature mystic, officially designated as patron of ecology by the Roman Catholic Church, and presented in Lynn White's publication on the relationship between culture and the environment as a source for such a model.[5] Unfortunately, the typical representation of Francis in the U.S. is as a plaster statue in the middle of a bird bath!

A recent collection of essays emphasizes the wide-ranging influence of the humble man from Assisi relating that, "As an enormously free and spontaneous person, he nevertheless adhered faithfully to the institutional church; a fully alive human being, he embraced suffering; a true lover, he chose celibacy; born into relative affluence, he chose poverty."[6] Such paradoxes have inspired people to look at the values behind religious communities, economics, and politics. Francis' life is an inspirational model of love and simplicity enshrined in an ultimate respect for each person, each relationship.

Millions of people throughout the last eight hundred years have resonated with his approach to life, to creation, and to the divine. A recent *Time* magazine article presents him as one of the ten most influential people in history.[7] Francis and his followers have quite possibly inspired more publications than any other spiritual traditions. Francis' spirituality has permeated the world.

With the late twentieth-century focus on environmental concerns, Francis has become an important source of inspiration about creation. Particularly, Francis' "Canticle of the Creatures" has been the source for personal reflections, and critical analysis.[8] Richard Rohr explores Francis' relationship with creation.[9] Keith Warner articulates a connection between Francis' and the philosophical movement of deep ecology.[10]

Declining biodiversity was not a concern for medieval people, but the significance of creatures is a continual theme in many of the early Franciscan writings. Nature themes in the medieval Franciscan sources are systematically explored by Edward Armstrong and Roger Sorrell. Their works clearly present the impression of Francis' contemporaries about his intimate relationships with many different creatures.[11]

Events in Francis' life indicate he not only aesthetically appreciated creation, but he entered into significant relationships with other life forms. Francis attempted to empathically know creation. A summary statement about Francis and his attitude toward creatures is found in the *Legend of Perugia* as,

> "He had so much love and sympathy for them [fire and creatures] that he was disturbed when they were treated without respect. He spoke to them with a great inner and exterior joy, as if they had been endowed by God with feeling, intelligence, and speech."[12]

A key example of Francis disposition is seen when Thomas of Celano tells that as Francis was walking, whenever he noticed a worm crawling across the road, he would gently lift the worm from harms' way. The biographer attributes Francis' action to the allegorical representation between Jesus Christ and the worm through an interpretation of Psalm 21:7, "I am a worm, not a man."[13]

Creatures stimulated Francis to reflect upon aspects of God's incarnation. This led Francis to a high level of regard for each creature. For Francis, each creature, regardless of status, commands respect, and elicits a spiritual relationship with people. Through the simple, yet profound act of lifting a worm from the road, Francis experienced incarnation, and became intimately involved with creation.

BIODIVERSITY AND THE FRANCISCAN INTELLECTUAL TRADITION

From Francis' spirituality, an intellectual tradition emerged through the medieval universities. Bonaventure (1221–1274) and John Duns Scotus (1266–1308) were Franciscan Friars and scholars who in their writings represent the philosophical and theological essence of the tradition.[14] The continuing development of the Franciscan intellectual tradition has been characterized by Philotheus Boehner, O.F.M. and reviewed by Zachary Hayes, O.F.M. as critical, scientific, progressive, and practical.[15] Philibert Hoebing, O.F.M. recently showed how the thought of Bonaventure and Scotus were rooted in Francis' intuitions and nature mysticism.[16]

John Duns Scotus developed his concept of "haecceity" which means "thisness" or individuation. "Haecceity" expresses what we already know through experience about the diversity of organisms and the individuality of each living organism. From the concept of individuation comes a further realization that due to complexity, historical progression, and diversity, each individual organism has a unique perspective in history that has never been, and never will be, like the perspective of any other living organism. Kenan Osborne, O.F.M. summarizes this when he wrote, "Scotus makes the claim that individuation must be based in the very substance of a thing or person, not in some accidental aspect of a thing or person."[17] Individuation is how the universe is constructed! And according to Hoebing, "it is this *haecceity* that gives each creature its special value and real worth in the eyes of God."[18] Hoebing quotes Wolter and O'Neill,

"If we reflect on this Scotistic conception of individuality in the context of what he believes God to be, we discover that it means that God's creative love wanted just this person or this creature to exist, rather than its twin or perfect copy."[19]

Hoebing clearly summarized the Franciscan perspective of creation as

"Scotus offers a theology and a cosmology according to which the very nature of beauty and order in the universe requires not only a multiplicity of species, but also a number of individuals within a species."[20]

While our experience and aesthetic appreciation of biodiversity provides ample reason for protecting and preserving the multitudinous expressions of life, Scotus and his Franciscan successors offer something more. Their concept of "thisness" would suggest that preserving many different life forms is a way to cooperate with the fundamental substance from which life expressed in the form of individual creatures operates. Here is a *Theology of Biodiversity* that needs to be individually and corporately realized, then we can draw each other into experiences of individuation, and allow this perspective to move us toward biodiversity preservation.

EXPERIENCING INVERTEBRATES

To begin the process of retrieving individuation from our spiritual heritage, each person needs to feel as though they have received a personal invitation to encounter the "thisness" represented in creatures that are not of our species. A role of scientists, and especially scientists who stand with professional feet in both the humanities and biological science disciplines, is to teach and preach about creatures.

A particular focus could be the most numerous creatures that share our world—the invertebrates. Enabling others to teach and to preach through the eyes of a worm or a fly brings us back to Francis' respect for creation melded with our zoological science. Such an "invertebrate" perspective on the world can provide an intriguing view that heightens sensitivity to creation.

A personal sensitivity to biodiversity reduction can emerge if scientists, teachers, and ministers enable people to build relationships with organisms that do not reflect our anthropocentric bias. Over the last 20 years, I have been engaged in those activities, and I offer you a personal perspective, and a few simple exercises that can change, indeed have already changed, the world views of students and parishioners.

HERBERT ZIM, PORCH LIGHTS, AND NOSTIMA

As a five year old boy, I knew already my life would somehow involve working with or studying insects. Introduced to the insect world through Herbert Zim's Golden Guide Series, I would spend my pre-school days filling jars and bottles with many creatures.[21] I fondly remember the thousands of creatures that would fly to our porch lights. I also came to sadly realize that in my lifetime the populations of these common North American species have been reduced because of habitat destruction.

I have been privileged to spend many hours with a group of species humans only know through their taxonomic names as members of the genus *Nostima*. The name *Nostima* is derived from the Greek word meaning "beautiful, elegant"! These minute shore flies have probably only been consciously known by several scores of humans throughout history. Few people have seen their small bodies (1 to 3mm long) bespectacled with golden and silver patches. They fly on their gossamer wings along the shores of streams and lakes feeding upon patches of blue-green algae. I entered their world, and had to build an intellectual, and even spiritual relationship with these organisms.

Entering their lives, I became personally aware that the entire universe for an individual *Nostima* fly larva is a several square centimeter patch of algae. It has been not only an intellectual curiosity, but a moment of grace and a privilege to see the world from another creature's viewpoint. Similar experiences have recently been published in a series of essays by prominent biologists who began their careers as children in their encounters with invertebrate creatures.[22]

After realizing the perspective of a fly, I was able to acknowledge that the smallest environmental disturbances affect individual living creatures. Such sensitivity led me to change the context from which I view my world. Providing opportunities for such experiences changes the way people think of their world, and other forms of life. To begin entering into a relationship with a creature, a person usually must know something about the creature, ideally through a direct and positive encounter.

NETS AND FUNNELS

I often ask groups of people to tell me some animals they know about, and the typical cat, dog, horse, cow examples come to mind. Then, I ask them to tell me some invertebrate animals they know. After a pause, people will begin to think of different insects, and then their favorite seafood will usually come to mind as they remember that crabs, shrimp, and clams are invertebrates. Probably most groups of people could only list several hundred, at most a thousand species they have encountered in their lives. Of the ten million or more different species, daily life in the U.S. would bring us into contact with very few different organisms.

In the most respectful, and least invasive way, people need to have the opportunity to experience the undetected creatures surrounding them. Three uncomplicated, yet effective methods of experiencing bio-diversity that can be elaborated in many ways for the pre-school child and adult are (1) yard sweeps, (2) soil extractions, and (3) stream walks.[23]

YARD SWEEPS

Obtain a net. If you don't have access to an educational institution, almost every toy store and department store in the U.S. sells them for less than $5. Go to a domestic "backyard" environment. If you're doing this with a group, ask them to identify any animals that are around them. Most groups will look for squirrels and birds. Take your net, lower the net to the ground in front of you, and begin a back and forth sweeping motion touching the tops of the grass plants with your net. Continue this sweeping motion, move forward through the yard about 10 steps, capture any "invisible" things that may be in the grass.

When people begin this activity for the first time, the usual response is, "He really has lost his marbles, let's get out of here!" But, those who don't run away after experiencing a grown person sweeping through the grass with a net are usually overwhelmed with the quantity and diversity of creatures that have been obtained. Even on the poorest days, the summer North American yard catch includes many (typically several hundred) organisms, including quite a few species of flies, leafhoppers, froghoppers, spiders, gnats, beetles, moths, caterpillars, and many more. The best part of the activity is to see the look on the faces of people, as many for the first time in their lives, experience biodiversity, and it's in their own back yard.

Depending on the reason for doing this activity, the catch can be released or taken back to the lab or kitchen table for further examination. The discussion of insect consciousness and trauma is beyond the scope of this essay. Killing the creatures or confining them for extended periods could defeat the purpose of exposing people to biodiversity. Likewise, be sensitive that many people have learned to fear insects and other small organisms. A discussion of why these harmless animals live in our backyards is a necessary component of exposing people to a new part of their world.

SOIL EXTRACTIONS

The soil under our feet, even in cities, is densely teeming with thousands of different macroscopic, and microscopic organisms. Similar to the yard sweep, an appreciation for the richness and quantity of soil organisms can change how people see their world.

Anyone can easily set up a device called a Berlese Funnel to extract and observe these organisms. Obtain a funnel (any size), a small piece of screen (about 1 square inch) that will fit inside the funnel, a 60 watt desk lamp, and a jar with some rubbing alcohol. Obtain enough soil from the yard to fit inside the funnel, and after putting the piece of screen inside the funnel, place the soil on top of the screen. Place the funnel over the jar with the alcohol, leaving a space between the spout of the funnel and the top of the alcohol. Place this jar and funnel with soil under the lamp. The heat from the lamp will dry the soil, and the organisms will move away from the drying area and eventually fall into the alcohol. Depending on the quantity and wetness of the soil, organisms such as springtails, centipedes, millipedes, diplurans, proturans, and many more will begin to appear in the alcohol, usually within hours after setting up the sampler.

As with the sweep activity, the quantity and quality of life found in the backyard can be overwhelming to people who have never considered that biodiversity is not just on television or in a rain forest.

STREAM WALK

Almost every person I ever met likes to play in water! Taking groups to a stream or pond in search of biodiversity is another overwhelmingly positive experience for those who have never been exposed to this part of their world. The setting will depend on the availability of access to a water body, but usually local park service personnel or environmental groups can help.

Aided with jars and bottles, and ideally white enamel pans, looking for organisms under stones and rocks and among the vegetation in a stream or a pond can produce a richly rewarding experience. Carefully done, the disturbance of the creatures and area can be even less than that caused by a heavy rainstorm. To see stoneflies, mayflies, dragonflies, damselflies, beetles, and worms face-to-face as they live in a stream can affect human thinking and behavior patterns.

Real-life experiences of biodiversity can part the veil of culture, and connect people with other life forms. To begin a relationship with the animals and plants that live with us is a first step to awareness of problems caused when habitats such as streams are destroyed. These few simple exercises, if engaged by those who care—parents, ministers, and teachers—can be an important first step in helping people to understand the need for building relationships with other creatures.

CONNECTIONS: SPIRITUALITY AND SCIENCE

Science and spirituality are mostly considered to be distinct and separate approaches used to construct meaning from our experiences of the world. However, these distinct approaches rarely come together in the lives of most twentieth-century U.S. people. Each day we are confronted with the systematic empirical observations collected through scientific methodology that describe the effects we have on the world and upon its life. Our biological sciences clearly inform us that many species are becoming extinct. Even as we are informed that biodiversity is declining, our actions to stop the destruction seem to be paralyzed.

Human action based solely upon response to information is empty, and does not engage the emotions. Even though our science has done a good job in providing the data, our hearts need to be moved toward acting on the data. Our science needs to connect with our spirit.

People of the U.S. culture are gradually moving from positions of reacting to information toward integrating our science with the human spirit. Responding to the decline in biodiversity is a situation where we can turn to our spiritual resources in order to engage with our science in an integrated way. We don't need to save species; we need to build relationships with other species. A rich resource for modeling the integration of our science with our spirit is found within the Franciscan spiritual and intellectual traditions.

The integration of our scientific method with our experiences of spirituality begins to be realized not at the level of institutional religion, but within the individual person. The voices of contemporary women and men who are involved with science, and who also have a deep sense of the underlying mystery expressed through the individuation of creation need to be heard. In my own case, the systematic and personal exploration of the lives of invertebrates has revealed to me a new perspective on creation that lifts up the important roles individual creatures play.

After I saw the world from the perspective of a fly larva, the world never looked the same. Each living creature becomes an instrument of creation that cries out to be respected for its role and for its individuality. Species no longer become abstractions, but realities to be lived through each unique life in each unique moment of time. Connecting with as many of these life forms as possible has changed me into a person who not only continues to explore the diversity of life, but also is able to reverence the creator through appreciation of the individuals who constitute the diversity.

Building relationships with other species can help rejoin information with the soul. Building relationships with other species can promote connecting our spirituality with our science. Building relationships with other species will promote receptivity to national and international policies that can reduce the reduction of biodiversity. And the people most important in this rejoining are the parents, teachers, and ministers who can skillfully articulate the connection between science and spirituality, and are able to preach from an "invertebrate" perspective. These facilitators will provide opportunities to help us begin making connections that will determine what life forms will survive!

Notes

1. Wilson, E. O., *The Diversity of Life* (New York: Penguin Books, 1992), p. 124.
2. Ibid, pp. 242–247.
3. Ibid, pp. 271–276.
4. Ibid, pp. 297–326.
5. White, Jr., L., "The Historic Roots of Our Ecological Crisis," *Science* (1967) 155: 1203–1207.
6. Dennis, M., J. Nangle, C. Moe-Lobeda, and S. Taylor, *St. Francis and the Foolishness of God* (Maryknoll, NY: Orbis Books, 1993), pp. 8.
7. List of the ten greatest people of the millennium in "Beyond the Year 2000," *Time* 140 Special Issue, Fall 1992.
8. Dennis, pp. 104–120.
9. Rohr, R., "Christianity and Creation A Franciscan Speaks," In *Embracing Earth Catholic Approaches to Ecology,* ed. A. J. La Chance and J. E. Carroll (Maryknoll, NY: Orbis Books, 1994), pp. 129–155.
10. Warner, K., "Was St. Francis a Deep Ecologist?" In *Embracing Earth Catholic Approaches to Ecology,* ed. A. J. La Chance and J. E. Carroll (Maryknoll, NY: Orbis Books, 1994), pp. 225–240.
11. Armstrong, E. A., *St. Francis: Nature Mystic the Derivation and Significance of the Nature Stories in the Franciscan Legend,* (Berkeley, CA: University of California Press, 1973); Sorrell, R. D., *St. Francis of Assisi and Nature Tradition and Innovation in Western Christian Attitudes toward the Environment,* (New York: Oxford University Press, 1988).
12. "Legend of Perugia," In *St. Francis of Assisi, Writings and Early Biographies,* ed. M. A. Habig, (Chicago: Franciscan Herald Press, 1972), p. 1027.
13. Thomas of Celano, "First Life of St. Francis," In *St. Francis of Assisi, Writings and Early Biographies,* ed. M. A. Habig, (Chicago: Franciscan Herald Press, 1972), p. 296.
14. Biographical dates for Bonaventure and Duns Scotus from the *New Catholic Encyclopedia,* (New York: McGraw Hill, 1967).
15. Hayes, Z., "In Search of an Identity: Franciscan Schools in a Changing World," In *Franciscan Charism and Higher Education,* Symposium Celebrating the 25th Anniversary of Neumann College, Aston, PA.
16. Hoebing, P., "St. Francis and the Environment," In *Divine Representation Post-modernism and Spirituality,* ed. A. W. Astelle, (Purdue Univeristy: Paulist Press, 1994), pp. 210–15.

17. Osborne, K. B., "Incarnation, Individuality, and Diversity," *The Cord* (1995) 45.3:25.

18. Hoebing, p. 209.

19. Wolter, A. B. and B. O'Neill, *John Duns Scotus: Mary's Architect* (Quincy, IL: Franciscan Press, 1993), p. 37.

20. Hoebing, p. 210.

21. Zim, H. S. and C. Cottam, *Insects: A Guide to Familiar American Insects*, revised edition (New York: Golden Press, 1961).

22. Wilson, E. O., "A Grassroots Jungle in a Vacant Lot," Rothschild, M., "Ages Five to Fifteen: Wildflowers, Butterflies, Frogs," Eisner, T., "The End of Superstition"; Pyle, R. M., "Butterflies in Winter," In *Wings* (1995) 18:3–21.

23. A clearly written popular source that includes technical methods and information about the invertebrates mentioned is the original or revised edition within the Peterson Field Guide Series by Borror, D. and R. E. White, *Insects of America North of Mexico* (Boston: Houghton Mifflin, 1970).

Care of Creation:
Working with
the United Nations

Margaret Pirkl, OSF*

That Franciscans should work in collaboration with the United
Nations to care for creation is right and fitting. Francis of Assisi
and his way cross not only religious, ethnic, cultural, political, and
philosophical boundaries, but historical periods as well. To translate his
attitude toward nature, toward the earth, for a world headed into the
twenty-first century is one of the challenges we Franciscans face today.
Many through the years have pointed to Francis as a cosmic person who
lived out of a belief in the unity of all that is and all who are, who considered himself to be simply part of creation, brother to all creatures, no
more, no less. His attitude toward nature was original: sensitive, affectionate, compassionate, fraternal, courteous, particular, and filled with
wonder.

One might argue that the large-scale approach of the United
Nations would be foreign to Francis. Obviously, though, Francis was
large-minded and large-hearted and inclusive (*omnia* or "all" appears
often in his writings).[1] In the Rule of 1221, he invited to faith and
penance "all peoples, races, tribes, and tongues, all nations and all peoples everywhere on earth who are and who will be...." (Reg NB 27, 7).[2] In
the "Canticle of Creatures" he celebrated everything and everybody:

* This article originally appeared as: "Care of Creation: Working with the United
Nations," *The Cord* 40/8 (September 1991): 238–48. Reprinted with permission.

"Praised be You, my Lord, with *all* creatures...." (CantSol 3) With today's almost instantaneous planetary communication, information about human pain and ecological devastation from anywhere on the globe is inescapable. It is difficult to imagine that, in the face of this knowledge, Francis would not seek every way possible to alleviate suffering, to reconcile, to heal the earth family everywhere. This is why I believe Franciscan's participation as an NGO (non-governmental organization) in the work of the United Nations has our founder's blessing.

Francis probably would have difficulty separating the three aims of this effort, concern for the poor, peacemaking, and care of the earth, for he might see them as three facets of the goodness to which God calls us. They might be for him implicit aspects of love for brother and sister whose needs one moves immediately to fulfill. In this discussion of care for creation, we shall see natural interconnections with peacemaking and concern for the poor. We shall find the three, in fact, integral to each other here as they were in Francis' heart.

The Franciscan familial model of the earth's functioning has much to offer our ecological age. Challenging a domineering attitude with respectful mutuality, replacing alienation with loving acceptance, eliminating dualism by work toward wholeness, excluding none, including all, reverencing each particular being—these are gifts from our heritage we can offer humbly in today's efforts to save the planet, gifts given by God to Francis for whom all creation, not only humankind, was family. One behaves sensitively toward ground water that is sister and animal that is brother, toward tree that is sister and air that is brother, toward earth that is sister-mother and political oppressor or victim who is brother or sister.

With and through the United Nations, Franciscans have tremendous increased potential for sharing, networking, and reaching out to meet urgent needs in their efforts to heal earth and to help earth heal herself. Even though UN values and Franciscan values seemingly have different sources, they are not only compatible but supportive of each other. For example, the "World Charter for Nature," promulgated in 1982 by the UN General Assembly and hailed as one of the most significant documents of our time, seems very close to Franciscan teaching. To demonstrate several aspects of such relatedness, we will consider here a small part of the Charter, namely the preliminary philosophy and rationale that give rise to the document's principles. Though all seven sections are interconnected, the first four will be treated individually and the last three as a group.[3]

1. [Humankind] is a part of nature, and life depends on the unin-
terrupted functioning of natural systems which ensure the supply of
energy nutrients....

We have already indicated that for Francis all of creation, including humans, was family and that its functioning was guided by mutuality. Members of this family were to meet each other as creatures belonging to the same Creator, not holding dominance over one another and over natural process but, like a sort of cosmic democracy, supporting the delicate balance that sustains all on earth. This attitude of Francis flowed from an insight Celano describes:

> [Francis] called all creatures brother [and sister], and in a most extraordinary manner, a manner never experienced by others, he discerned the hidden things of nature with his sensitive heart, as one who had already escaped into the freedom of the glory of the [children] of God. (1 Cel 81)[4]

If our planet and its inhabitants are to survive in a healthy state, the most basic "hidden thing of nature" grasped by Francis, after the revelation of God in all creatures, must also be recognized by us, that is, the call to live and think and love as members of the earth-family whose natural systems and processes support life itself. This truth permeates the teaching of Thomas Berry, which I believe is prophetic for our day. Better than any contemporary thinker, Berry has articulated the oneness of creation with life's dependence on healthy ecosystems. He once said in conversation, "Nothing can be itself without everything else," and, another time, "Humans are a dimension of the earth; these two are totally implicated each in the other." When the United Nations states in a rationale that "[Humankind] is a part of nature," it is naming this implication as fundamental to further thinking about and living on our planet.

From our heritage, we Franciscans can bring to the UN a familial dimension, a loving, emotional dimension, to humankind's relationship with earth. This way of thinking and being could be propagated throughout the world both by realizing in our own lives that we are but part of the earth-family and by networking with other groups who wish to bring humankind to the same awareness. It seems clear that a strong effective link with the UN is a highly desirable opportunity for us to strengthen in ourselves a sense of cosmic familiality and to share it with others over the entire planet.

> *2. Civilization is rooted in nature, which has shaped human culture and influenced all artistic and scientific achievement, and living in harmony with nature gives [human beings] the best opportunities for the development of [their] creativity, and for rest and recreation....*

As a process rooted profoundly in earth, our human development arises out of our experience of all we encounter during our lives. Thomas Berry says it beautifully:

> If we have a wonderful sense of the divine, it is because we live amid such awesome magnificence. If we have refinement of emotion and sensitivity, it is because of the delicacy, the fragrance, and the indescribable beauty of the delicacy, the fragrance, and the indescribable beauty of song and music and rhythmic movement in the world around us.... If we have powers of imagination, these are activated by the magic display of color and sound, of form and movement, such as we observe in the clouds of the sky, the trees and bushes and flowers, the waters and the wind... if we have words with which to speak and think and commune, words for the inner experience of the divine, words for the intimacies of life, if we have words for telling stories to our children, words with which we can sing, it is again because of the impressions we have received from the variety of beings about us.[5]

Francis knew this well. He sang, "Praised be You, my Lord, through our Sister Mother Earth who sustains and governs us and who produces varied fruits with colored flowers and herbs." (CantSol 9) The verse clearly reflects its author's experience of earth's influence in his life. In celebrating other creatures, Francis used adjectives like "precious," "beautiful," "cloudy and serene," "humble," and "playful" (CantSol), words that point to the saint's personal involvement with nature and evidence of the union of his inner and outer worlds.[6]

In the phenomenal order, earth with its creatures, including humans, is primary in the various aspects of human development. The richer this development in individuals, the healthier is the society formed by the individuals. On a large scale, nature determines to a great extent the livelihood and culture of a people. For example, the desert gives rise to a nomadic way of life, the mountains to an independent one; cultures in the plains are individualized by their soil and water supply as well as their locations in northern or southern areas.

The UN's assertion that "civilization is rooted in nature" and that "nature sustains our creativity and rest and recreation" implies society's dependence on its member's experience of nature. The statement also acknowledges implicitly that a society's health is contingent on the health of its environment. In the "World Charter for Nature," the UN seeks to foster consciousness of this truth. Our Franciscan tradition supports living in harmony with all creatures because Francis knew it was a way to God and fullness of life. As an NGO moving along UN channels in decision-making and education, we Franciscans, true to our charism, will become more aware of how nature forms us, and find opportunities to share that awareness with others. The more heightened our awareness, the greater will be our sense of urgency in work toward the planet's healing.

3. Every form of life is unique, warranting respect regardless of its worth to [human beings] and, to accord other organisms such recognition, [humans] must be guided by a moral code of action....

This statement by the UN is remarkable from a Franciscan vantage point for (1) it makes humans' behavior toward earth a matter of morality and (2) it could be pointing to the respect we owe each particular being ("every form of life"). According to the early sources, Francis believed that all creatures have rights and deserve our respect (even Brother Fire who was consuming his clothing! (LP 49). The narrator of the "Legend of Perugia" states:

> ...we who lived with [Francis] were witnesses of his affection and respect for [creatures] and of the pleasure they gave him. He had so much love and sympathy for them that he was disturbed when they were treated without respect. (LP 49)

In the stories coming down to us, we note another point. Francis was dealing with and fascinated by *particular* creatures: it was a particular rabbit he consoled and comforted and protected (I C 60); it was a particular cricket he urged to sing (LP 84); it was a particular nightingale he joined in antiphonal praise.[7] Francis' courteous attitude toward each one marked his life.

Franciscan theology, after John Duns Scotus, teaches that not only each species but each particular creature takes its design, its pattern, from the Incarnate Word and therefore radiates the light and beauty of Christ in an unique way, never to be repeated—every leaf, every blade of grass, every flower, every snowflake, every cloud, every newborn. This gives serious reason for respect.

I doubt that the ecological situation today will get better until humans begin to reverence every particular being and recognize its right, as a precious creature of God, to exist in sustainable balance with the rest of nature. If we lived consciously, in communion with God's beautiful earth and its members, I believe we would automatically honor every creature, regardless of its usefulness to us. Such respect is a hallmark of the Franciscan charism and a religious responsibility that might be shared with many through the UN. In turn, as we Franciscans network with other groups, we will learn a great deal about unique life systems over the entire earth and humans' interaction with them. Such knowledge will be both motivation and support for the conversion of our own attitude toward creatures other than ourselves.

> 4. *[Human beings] can alter nature and exhaust natural resources by [their] action or its consequences and, therefore, must fully recognize the urgency of maintaining the stability and quality of nature and of conserving natural resources....*

Never before has the planet experienced the effects of human activity to the extent we see today. Until relatively recently, human power over nature was limited; over the last 300 years that power has drastically increased. As Thomas Berry states:

> The power of our technologies is now such... that nature cannot prevent us from doing whatever we decide in diminishing the splendor and vigor and variety of life upon the earth.[8]

Soil, air, and water are poisoned so that they can no longer support life; species of plants and animals, tens and hundreds of millions of years old, many of which we do not know yet, are rapidly being extinguished; the planet is warming, very probably as the result of extra greenhouse gases emitted in fossil-fuel burning; the delicate balance of entire ecosystems and of the globe itself is being disrupted. Although earth damage in the thirteenth century was not nearly as extensive as it is now, it affected Francis' sympathetic heart. In the story describing the origins of the "Canticle of Creatures," Francis speaks these words:

> I want to compose a new "Praise of the Lord in His creatures" for we daily make use of them, and cannot live without them, and through them the human race greatly offends their Creator. (SP 100)

We may conclude that our founder not only paid attention to humans' effect on nature but that he was concerned about it. Eric Doyle argues:

> Even so long ago the ecological problem, manifestly in a milder form than we have it now, had its part in the composition of "The Canticle." This, therefore, is not only a beautiful piece of literature, it is also a protest against the misuse of creatures.[9]

If Francis in his day tried to address human activity harmful to nature, can we do less in our day when the magnitude of earth's wounds overwhelms us? Working with the United Nations will provide many channels for carrying out this mission.

> *5. Lasting benefits from nature depend upon the maintenance of essential ecological processes and life support systems, and upon the diversity of life forms, which are jeopardized through excessive exploitation and habitat destruction by [human beings]....*
> *6. The degradation of natural systems owing to excessive consumption and misuse of natural resources, as well as the failure to establish an appropriate economic order among peoples and among States, leads to the breakdown of the economic, social and political framework of civilization....*
> *7. Competition for scarce resources creates conflicts, whereas the conservation of nature and natural resources contributes to justice and*

the maintenance of peace and cannot be achieved until [humankind]
learns to live in peace and to forsake war and armaments....

Underlying these three statements from the "World Charter for Nature" is the truth that justice, peace, and earth wholeness are integral to each other and cannot be separated; they are three aspects of goodness, as we said earlier. Injustice, violence, and ecological damage also come together, never singly, as three manifestations of evil. Oppression and injustice lead to war; military spending takes funds from the poor; poverty causes damage to nature; the poor suffer disproportionately from environmental decline; tensions from environmental problems lead to violence and war; and war-making causes damage to the earth.

Probably the unfairness in which we individuals of this country are most implicated is our wasteful lifestyle, our over-consumption, and our participation in a throwaway society. Our clothes, our diets, our homes, our recreation, our transportation—practically all aspects of our lives—are energy-intensive, require fossil-fuel burning, and contribute ultimately to the greenhouse gases in the atmosphere. Our excessive per capita consumption cheats the world's poor of food, clothing, shelter, medicine. Our demand for "things," including certain foods, supports exploitation of poor workers and ecosystems abroad and encourages unfair land ownership practices and economic policies; these, in turn, cause intranational and international tensions. In a word, affluence in the United States is devastating in its effects on people and nature over the entire globe.

I believe that we Franciscans, working with the United Nations, can help to address this dreadful state of affairs (1) by renewing the gift of simplicity in ourselves and (2) by convincing others that eating lower on the food chain and having fewer things leads to both healthier and happier lives, to say nothing of helping the poor, abating violence and caring for the earth!

Selfish behavior of individuals harms others the world over, but larger systems also bear responsibility for the immense pain in people and nature everywhere. For example, UNICEF has blamed the death of half a million children per year on the debt burden of the eighties;[10] this tragedy may be intensified during the nineties. In most poor countries land ownership is unjustly concentrated in the hands of a few. Lakes and forests of some areas are dying because of acid rain resulting from coal burning in adjacent regions. Global military spending over four days, about $8 billion, would pay for five years of effort to save the world's rain forests; two days of this spending would cover the cost of a proposed UN program to halt desertification over twenty years.[11] In one year, the world's military spending comes to about $200 for each person on the planet, but governments cannot find the $5 per child needed to eradicate the simple diseases that killed 14 million children in 1988 alone.[12]

Since its establishment in 1946, the UN has sought to promote justice, peace and the care of nature at the international level. The basic premises undergirding its founding Charter are (1) that human beings have dignity and are to be treated justly and (2) that conflicts can be resolved peacefully. The "Convention on the Law of the Sea," the Decade of Women, the "Universal Declaration of Human Rights," the "Convention on Climate Change," and international meetings and negotiations on global warming and on depletion of the ozone layer are but a few efforts of the UN. The 1990 "Convention on the Rights of a Child" names a life-sustaining environment among the rights of today's and tomorrow's children. The annual Environmental Sabboth celebration originated with and is supported by the UN Environmental Program. By these endeavors and many others the United Nations seeks to make the world a better place.

Many within the Franciscan family by their work and preaching are already addressing abuses of people and nature by large systems. The effectiveness and scope of these healing efforts can only be increased by collaboration with the United Nations. Further, more Franciscans will be alerted to and convinced of the urgent need to work for systemic change as well as personal conversion for the sake of the entire earth-community. In the process, Franciscan hearts and minds will be encouraged to grow large enough to hold the planet, the cosmos even.

PRACTICAL PARTICIPATION

In the story of Noah and the flood, God puts a rainbow in the sky as a sign of covenant not only between God and humankind but between God and the earth! (Gn 9:17) I believe we human beings are beginning to understand that we must be part of the gift of that covenant. Might the rainbow with all its colors be an image of Franciscans coming together to collaborate with each other and with the United Nations in efforts toward a whole earth? What could the rainbow look like when translated into concrete works that care for the earth?

Last year, each Franciscan community was urged to plant trees in order partly to offset global deforestation activity. Franciscans in thirty-three countries responded by planting 20,844 trees. The invitation was renewed last January. Might the response result in hundreds of thousands, or even millions, of new trees?

Franciscans everywhere celebrated the UN Environmental Sabboth in June this year and joined concern for nature with concern for children. Many planted trees during the Sabbath weekend, dedicated the planting to children, and involved children in the event. In preparation for the Sabboth, a communication from the UN Environmental Program Office stated:

> Children—our most precious natural resource—will be the theme of this Environmental Sabboth.... The state of our children and the state of our environment say more than anything else about the state of our civilization and the prospects of our future as a species.[13]

June 1992 will see in Brazil a United Nations Conference on Environment and Development. Among the objectives are

> —the production of an earth Charter that will embody basic principles which must govern the economic and environmental behavior of peoples and nations to ensure 'our common future';
> —the production of Agenda 21, a blueprint for action in all major areas affecting the relationship between the environment and the economy—focusing on the period up to the year 2000 and extending into the 21st century.[14]

The Conference, intended for heads of state or governments, will be the largest Earth Summit ever held. Some consider that it will be one of the most significant conferences in history, for it will involve the most far-reaching global negotiations since the founding of the UN. It will bridge earth care and concern for the poor, and it will also embrace peacemaking; for, if we do justice to people and to the environment, we will reduce causes of violence, increase security, and therefore further peace. All Franciscans can stay in touch with the Conference, let themselves be "stretched" by it, and seek to act locally—and globally—in support of its work.

A year of education on the environment from June 1991 to June 1992 is a special project for Franciscans connected with the UN. Brother Kevin Smith, Executive Director of the Franciscans at the UN Project, expresses the hope that each local community will prepare a program for education. Working together, we are capable of accomplishing miracles! Schools and parishes are fertile ground for sowing education about earth's beauties and mysteries and gifts, her present travail and woundedness, and ways toward her healing. Environment can be incorporated not only into science classes but classes in religion, social science, mathematics, art, history, geography, language arts and literature, and adult education. In parishes, religious education programs, Confirmation classes, reflection days, and retreats provide avenues for teaching about earth. Liturgical celebrations, homilies, in particular, may educate even though that is not their primary purpose. Health care institutions can relate earth to human health and educate employees and patients by ensuring that their use of materials is friendly to the environment. Informal education can accompany every ministry, and each individual Franciscan can educate others by "living lightly" on the planet.

The movement has only begun; much work remains to be done. The challenge is great because the scope of caring for the earth is vast and the planet's systems, some large, some small, are complex and interconnected. The opportunity to work with the United Nations in order to effect changes in humanity's interaction with nature at both individual and systemic levels, as well as the conversion of our own attitudes toward the earth and the widening of our vision, is an opportunity I believe we are called to embrace, even though at times the goal of planetary well-being seems impossible.

We will find that pivotal in our collaborative effort with the UN to care for creation is the gift of simplicity, allowed to influence us and others through us. The gift challenged Francis, it challenges us; it promises healing and asks for total commitment, as the poet's lines declare:

> Quick now, here, now always—
> A condition of complete simplicity
> (Costing not less than everything)
> And all shall be well and
> All manner of thing shall be well....[15]

Notes

1. See Patricia A. Keefe, OSF, "Sisters and Brothers Throughout the World: Franciscan Response to Global Human Rights Issues," *Franciscan Global Perspectives* (Pittsburgh: Franciscan Federation, 1986) Vol.1, No.1, 15–17.

2. All references to the writings of Francis are from *Francis and Clare: Complete Works*, trans. Regis J. Armstrong, OFM Cap, and Ignatius Brady, OFM (Ramsey, New Jersey: Paulist Press, 1982).

3. "World Charter for Nature," Annex to UN Document A/37/L.4, October 1982. Excerpts used in this article are in bold print and numbered from "1" through "7."

4. All references to writings about Francis are from *St. Francis of Assisi: Writings and Early Biographies; English Omnibus of Sources for the Life of St. Francis*, ed. Marion Habig (Chicago: Franciscan Herald Press, 1972).

5. Thomas Berry, *The Dream of the Earth* (San Francisco: Sierra Club Books, 1988) 11.

6. Eloi Leclerc's discussion of this is fascinating. See Eloi Leclerc, OFM, *Canticle of Creatures: Symbols of Union*, trans. Matthew J. O'Connell (Chicago: Franciscan Herald Press, 1977).

7. Presented in E.A. Armstrong, *St. Francis: Nature Mystic* (Berkeley, CA: University of California Press, 1973) 63–70.

8. Berry 10–11.

9. Eric Doyle, *St. Francis and the Song of Brotherhood* (New York: The Seabury Press, 1981) 67.

10 Alan B. Durning, "Poverty and the Environment: Reversing the Downward Spiral," *Worldwatch Paper* 92 (Washington, D.C.: Worldwatch Institute, 1989) 6.

11. Michael Renner, "National Security: the Economic and Environmental Dimensions," *Worldwatch Paper* 89 (Washington, DC: Worldwatch Institute, 1989) 48.

12. Durning 6.

13. Quoted in *Newsletter of Franciscans: A Non-Governmental Organization at the United Nations* (Winter, 1990): 2.

14. *Newsletter of Franciscans: A Non-Governmental Organization at the United Nations* (April 1991): 2.

15. T.S. Eliot, "Little Gidding" in *T.S. Eliot: The Complete Poems and Plays, 1909–1950* (New York: Harcourt Brace Jovanovich, Publishers, 1980) 145.

Benedictine Responsibility and Franciscan Mutuality: Perspectives on the Relationship Between Humans and the Environment

Dawn M. Nothwehr, OSF

The Benedictine and Franciscan charisms[1] are among the most influential in the history of Christianity. Thus, my purpose here is to explore the role of the human being in relation to creation as explicated in these two traditions. To that end, I first, review sources Franciscans and Benedictines frequently cite as those most substantially representing the contribution of their particular charism to the modern conversation on ecology and the human person. I then set out my argument concerning the complementarity of two distinct perspectives presented by the two traditions. The sources concerning the human being in relation to nature most frequently cited by the Benedictines include segments of the *Rule of St. Benedict* and parts of the *Scivias* of Hildegard of Bingen.[2] Franciscan sources most authoritatively cited on this topic include selections from the writings of Francis of Assisi, Bonaventure, and John Duns Scotus. Conclusions concerning the human-environment relationship are drawn from the exploration and placed in conversation with the biblical text, Genesis 1:26.

WHAT DO THE SOURCES SAY?
The Rule of St. Benedict of Nursia (ca 480–ca 547)[3]

The Rule of St. Benedict[4] gives several hints about Benedict's attitude concerning the natural world by addressing the relationship of the monks with nature, (though animals are never mentioned). Yet, much affecting the human-nature relationship is implied within the Benedictine vow of stability.[5] The vow of stability concerns the commitment of the monks to stay long periods of time in the same place, utilizing the same space, buildings and tools, and ultimately passing something on to yet another generation. In his *Rule* Benedict also makes clear that God is present in every *place*, and therefore it is assumed that humans as creatures would maintain an attitude of worship in the *place* they reside.

Benedict is emphatic that what the monk is to avoid is *pride*, and thus must acknowledge with all *humility* the ontological (ultimate) status of his creaturehood before God, the Creator. Obedience is first to God, then to fellow monks, including the Abbot, who is to heed even the suggestions of the newest member.[6] That humble reverence, which holds everything in relationship with the Creator, also extends to care for one's physical body and for things, in order to not jeopardize the well being of others.[7]

More explicit in the *Rule* is the relationship between humility and service. The cellarer, for example, is not to exert managerial control over the monks and their guests, but rather, he must execute his duty in a timely and humble manner, never flaunting his authority.[8] Although Benedict did not require monks to take a vow of poverty, he clearly set a prohibition on superfluity, satiety, and overindulgence. Private ownership was not needed in a community where each monk worked at his assigned task and then was given what he needed.[9]

Indeed, the relationship with creation and the environment is most evidently implicit in Benedict's treatment of work and the monk as a worker. The monks were to earn a moderate living and be frugal with their resources, giving their excess wealth to those in need and for various building and evangelistic projects. Clothing was to be what was available at a reasonable cost.[10] The human vocation to work can be understood as participating in God's ongoing creation. Benedict states: "He will regard all tools of the monastery as the sacred vessels of the altar, aware that nothing is to be neglected."[11]

Though Benedict's was a high Christology, he regarded the poor, needy, sick, elderly, and the young guests and pilgrims as representing Christ in a particular way.[12] However, it is not too great a stretch of the imagination to suggest that one could also see Christ "in the helpless species and ecosystems that depend totally on human restraint and care for their survival."[13]

What Benedict did address were matters that if heeded, would form and shape a person who would be "user friendly" toward our planet. The ideal Benedictine monk would be frugal, reverent, humble, hard-working, kind, compassionate, quiet and thoughtful—the kind of person who would be alien to the ways of a world that valued and promoted powerful rule toward the end of ever greater consumption of natural resources and oppressive treatment of human persons.[14] The work of Hildegard of Bingen more fully illuminates Benedict's *Rule*.

The Scivias *of Hildegard of Bingen (1098–1179)*[15]

The first four visions of Book I of her work, the *Scivias*,[16] as well as the first vision of Book III provide us with Hildegard's fundamental understanding of creation and the relation of the human. In the first vision of Book I, God, seated upon an iron colored mountain, is seen as the mighty ruler over a strong and stable kingdom.[17] Yet, God embraces all of creation with wings of love. Humanity receives from God the "divine life," the ability to live in poverty of spirit and reverence.

In spite of God's love and reign, the poisonous form of Lucifer enters paradise and *adam* is seduced by the snake. This seduction is treated in the second vision of Book I. God is angered at this failure and the elements of the earth turn against *adam*. And, because *adam* is "of the earth," humans become imbalanced and fall into the chasm of Lucifer.

The third vision of Book I is of the great cosmic egg. God created all things visible and invisible. The visible elements show forth as manifestations of God's eternal and unseen majesty, so his name would be known and glorified and for the service of humanity.[18] Clearly, regardless of *Adam's* fall, God holds the universe together and humans are intimately related to God through belief and baptism. Christ restored virtue to humanity, particularly humility and charity. The human is now placed at the center of the cosmos and, supported by the four Empedoclaen elements (earth, air, water, fire), is charged with the task of returning the universe to a close relationship with God.

Numerous anthropological themes are illustrated in the fourth vision of Book I.[19] In language familiar to the *Rule of St. Benedict*, Hildegard likens the plight of humanity to that of someone who is ill and in need of a doctor to prescribe medication, or that of a laborer earning wages. Among these themes is the struggle of reason to overcome carnal desire, depression, anger, hatred and pride. It is in aligning themselves with God who is the one who ordains all that is right, that the human's soul conquers these vices.

That God knows all human acts thoroughly is discussed in the first vision of Book III.[20] The human stands in fear of the Lord, in humility gazing upon the Kingdom of God. Fear of the Lord is a difficult burden for humans to bear and ultimately in poverty of spirit, simplicity, and sobriety of mind, they must attribute all their good works to God.

In summary, for Hildegard the entire universe is a marvelous vestige of God, a means of God's self-revelation. As such, the universe calls forth praise of the Creator from all creatures, especially humans. While all creatures have their place in the order of creation, the human though vulnerable to sin, stands as the greatest creature. However, humans are inextricably bound to all other creatures, yet, one presides over them with a beneficent care. In return, the other creatures serve humanity. So humanity is at once one with, yet other than, the rest of creation.

For Benedict, spiritual emphasis on humility, frugality and stability created a framework for care of the land. To this Hildegard attached her theology of creation. As was seen in Hildegard's explanation of her first vision, her moral vision takes direction from her theology of creation. Concurring with Benedict, she holds that God is God and all else is "ashes of ashes."[21] Hildegard urges her readers to live reverently aware of the presence of the Creator, to contemplate God's realm, and to recognize that all humans are and have comes gratuitously from God.[22]

This understanding of the relationship of the human and creation proposed by Benedict and Hildegard is similar to, yet distinct from that of Francis of Assisi. Some, particularly the distinguished Nobel Prize winner, microbiologist Rene Dubos,[23] have discounted Francis as a sentimental romantic, in favor of the more pragmatic approach of Benedict. However, I contend that such an assessment is grossly misguided and it fails to probe the depths of the pan*en*theistic theology that has been recognized for centuries as orthodox by all of Christianity. This point is addressed later, but first the Franciscan theology of the environment and the relationship of the human with creation as understood by some early Franciscans needs to be reviewed.

Francis of Assisi (1181–1226)[24]

Standing before the crucified Christ, Francis was keenly aware of his creaturely status with all of its imperfections. Nonetheless, in his *Fifth Admonition*[25] Francis exhorts:

> Consider, O human being, in what great excellence the Lord God has placed you, for He created and formed you *to the image* of His beloved Son according to the body and to *His own likeness*, according to the Spirit.[26]

Humans have particular status insofar as they are related to the Incarnate Christ, and are bearers of the *imago Dei*.[27] Two moments of conversion in Francis' life were crucial toward forming his insights.[28]

First, Francis embraced radical poverty, rejecting the singular and egotistical possession of anything in any form.[29] Instead, he was able to recognize the common Source of All Creation, and know as well, the radical relatedness of the entire cosmos.[30] So, he was inspired to say:

> ...I want to write a new *praise of the Lord* for His creatures, which we use every day, and without which we cannot live. Through them the human race greatly offends the Creator, and every day we are ungrateful for such great graces, because we do not praise, as we should, our Creator and the Giver of all good.[31]

In his *Salutation to the Virtues*, Francis shows that the fitting relationship among all creatures is one of obedience:

> ...[the person who possesses holy Obedience] is subject and submissive to everyone in the world and not only to people but to every beast and wild animal as well that they may do whatever they want with it insofar as it *has been given* to them *from above* by the Lord.[32]

Francis' embrace of obedience included a conversion from understanding humans as superior to other creatures of creation to a view of humans as not only part of creation, but indeed, even indebted to the other creatures.

Roger D. Sorrell speaks of the relationship as "mutual deference." Just as in the relationship of chivalry between the medieval knights, who exercised the virtue of *noblesse oblige*, "a mutual regard and deference between brothers serving God together," so too Francis' view of the relationship among humans and the animals was one of "sisters" and "broth-

ers" serving the Creator. Humans do not hold a clear dictatorial power
over the animals. Rather, humans and animals are related to one another
in light of their commonness as creatures of God, the Creator. This
"deference" addresses the dynamics of power in a relationship which
have been defined as "cosmic mutuality,"[33] which we will address further
below.

The second moment of Francis' conversion occurred while he was
gazing upon the crucifix. It was then that he discovered that, not only is
God the glorious Creator, but that God loves to the extent that "the
Word of God became flesh," part of the material universe. This realiza-
tion served to deepen Francis' sense of the sacredness of creation.[34]
Through Jesus' materiality, humans are sisters and brothers to one
another and to rocks and worms, as well. We read from Thomas of
Celano's early biography of Francis, the *First Life*:

> ...he [Francis] used to call all the creatures by the name of "broth-
> er" and "sister" and in a wonderful way, unknown to others, he
> could discern the *secrets of the heart* of creatures like someone who
> had already passed *into the freedom of the glory of the Children of
> God*.[35]

Francis' union with nature is distinct from the parabolic associations of God with nature in the New Testament, the pantheistic
identification of God and Nature of the Renaissance, or the ecstatic joy
over Nature of the Greeks.[36] It is from Francis' deep faith in the crucified
and glorified Savior that the Christocentric theology of the Franciscan
school emerged.[37]

From the writings of Francis then, we can draw three distinct
aspects of Francis' charism that influence the relationship of humans
with all of creation. First (poverty): While not relinquishing the unique
role of humans as bearers of the *imago Dei*, Francis holds that all ownership, power, and authority belong only to God, the Creator and sustainer
of all life. Secondly (obedience): Just as Jesus took on humanity and
experienced life and death in the material world, so too humans must be
obedient to the lower creatures. Thirdly (kinship): All of creation is intimately related as siblings in one vast family. Pulsing through the veins
of all creation is the energy of the Creator in whom everything and
everyone has its origin. When there is a conflict in the family, a settlement must be negotiated through a process that involves *all* parties

affected and for the good of *all*, just as in the legend of the Wolf of Gubbio.[38] All of these notions are borne in the multifaceted *charism* of Francis which stands as a significant source for Bonaventure's theological reflection.[39] It is to the work of Bonaventure of Bagnoregio that we now turn our attention.

Bonaventure of Bagnoregio (1217 or 1221–1274)[40]

Bonaventure's point of departure was Christ as the self-communication of God.[41] Beginning with the Pseudo-Dionysian[42] tenet that the first name of God is *Good*, Bonaventure defines the perfect and complete self-diffusion as the first phase of the inner life of the Trinity. The Father is the *fontalis plenitudo* (font of all goodness). The Son is the primal diffusion of the Father, his self-knowledge, Word or Image. The Word expresses and represents the ideas of all created things. The inner life of the Trinity is consummated in the love between the Father and the Son which *is* the Holy Spirit. Thus the inner life of the Trinity represents a complete process of emanation, exemplarity, and consummation. The Word is the exemplar or the prototype of all that exists and God is expressed in all creatures. Therefore, all creatures participate in the life of the Trinity through Christ, Word, and Exemplar.[43]

Put another way, it is in the Johannine definition, "God is love," (I Jn.4: 8,16) that Bonaventure uncovers Christ, not human power, as the creative and sustaining principle of all created reality in which all things are grounded. This incarnational notion certainly limits the construal of human power and authority, especially in our relations with the nonhuman creation, to those forms in which power is not simply imposed, but negotiated and shared with an eye toward the flourishing of all involved. God, not humans, creates and sustains the cosmos; yet, God is present in each element of creation.

Indeed, in his *Disputed Questions on Evangelical Perfection*, Bonaventure shows how at the root of the Gospel mandate of poverty, there lies a recognition that all things, including human life, are pure gift from the loving creative power of God.[44] From the Uncreated Lover come an unlimited variety of ways in which love is communicated, namely all of creation, and in Christ Incarnate the entire cosmos is united and transformed.[45]

Just how widely and deeply are the various elements of creation related to one another? Bonaventure states:

All things are said to be transformed in the transfiguration of Christ. For as a human being, Christ has something in common with all creatures. With the stone he shares existence; with plants he shares life; with animals he shares sensation; and with the angels he shares intelligence. Therefore, all things are said to be transformed in Christ since—in his human nature—he embraces something of every creature.[46]

In *The Soul's Journey into God*, Bonaventure extends Francis' insight of cosmic union. Not only does Bonaventure see union with God reflected in the external world, but also in humans "in the inner act of sensation, in aesthetic experience, in the activities of memory, understanding, and will, and in the contemplation of Being and self-diffusive goodness."[47]

The human holds a central place in Bonaventure's conception of the universe in that humans are both creatures and bearers of the *imago Dei*. Indeed, the creation of the human formed the high point of the cosmic process.[48] From this Bonaventure concludes:

It is true without any doubt that we are the end of all existing things, and all bodily things exist to serve humanity by enkindling in human beings the fire of love and praise for the one who has made all things and by whose providence all things are governed. So this sensible machine of bodily beings has been formed as a sort of home for humanity by the supreme architect until such time as humanity should arrive at that "house not made by human hands ...in heaven."[49]

Bonaventure's theology is theoretically undergirded by Christian Neoplatonism.[50] Creation (emanation) was executed by God like an artist who conceives an idea in her imagination and then expresses it externally. Beginning with time, God created everything from nothing, setting the cosmos on a journey that moves forth from God and moves toward a return to God, revealing God-self along the way. The role of the material and natural world is to arouse the human consciousness to praise and love God, and in turn, humanity is to serve nature by giving it a voice that in the cosmos would not otherwise be heard.[51] God is the One Divine Idea which is given expression through the Word of God. The Word, Jesus Christ, is the exemplar of all external expressions of the Divine Idea, God.[52] All other elements of creation are an analogy of God insofar as each is made according to its pattern as found in God, the Divine Idea. Thus, through his doctrine of universal analogy Bonaventure shows how all of creation bears the mark of the Creator as shadow, vestige, or image of God through Christ.[53]

Bonaventure thus demonstrates how there is an intimate relationship between God and each creature of the cosmos, and of each of them with one another through Christ. If humans ignore this relationship, they fail to comprehend their position in the world and the cosmos. However, humans are created in the *imago Dei* and have been given the faculties of memory, intellect, and will. Through these, it is possible for humans to comprehend nature as revelation of the Creator and to value it as sacred in the pan*en*theistic sense. In so doing, humans find their role as the mediators between God and creation and as guardians of the multiple manifestations of God's self-revelation.[54]

John Duns Scotus (1266?–1308)[55]

One of finest minds to recognize the Creator through the study of creation was John Duns Scotus (1266–1308). In his work *A Treatise on God as First Principle*, the Subtle Doctor reviewed the vast array of creation and concluded that the primary efficient cause is God, the first principle.[56] For our purposes, and of the utmost importance for Scotus, is the fact that God did not *have to* create anything. Scotus understood God as absolutely free and absolutely necessary.

Creation and *Imago Dei*

According to Scotus, even though humans may come to realize that their source is God, they cannot naturally and fully grasp the image of God within the human soul. The limitations of human cognition allow humans to know only one aspect of the God/human relationship, from the human side. In addition to what philosophy can tell us, revelation about creation, such as the Genesis 2 account, is needed in order for us to grasp some notion of how we are related to God.[57] Scotus relies on revelation to further explicate that relationship between God and humans in his discussion of the divine creative action *ad extra*, specifically the Incarnation.

Haecceitas

In order for one subject to be related to another, it must first be known for what it is in itself. Scotus' principle of *haecceitas*[58] (individuation or "thisness") provides the philosophical foundation for all created reality being specified. *Haecceitas* makes a singular thing what it is and differentiates it from all other things (of common nature) to which it may be compared because of its commonality.[59]

For our purposes, *haecceitas* is important because it makes possible individuation, and mutuality is a relationship between or among distinct beings.[60] More will be said about the relationship of mutuality and individuation, below. For now, we simply note how Scotus draws attention to the sacredness of each cosmic element in particular. He held that everything and everyone, including the natural and the imperfect, are embraced by God. In God there is something incarnational about each particular being, human and nonhuman. *Haecceitas* affects human relating in general because it affects how one understands contingent reality, one's capacity for the beatific vision, God, freedom, and the value of all elements of the cosmos. Not only is each element of the cosmos different in its accidental characteristics, but each is distinct in its very essence. The implications of *haecceitas* for ecology are vast in that it requires humans to value each element of creation, in its particularity, as sacred—God's self-expression.

Incarnation

Scotus maintained that the Word would have become incarnate even if *adam* had not sinned.[61] He stressed the importance of the humanity of Jesus as preordained for the glory of union with the second person of the Trinity.[62] This foreordaining of Christ was part of the manifestation of divine glory and God's intent to raise human nature to the highest point of glory by uniting it with divine nature.[63] Understood in this way, the Incarnation is a paradigm for human beings as partners with God in the ongoing co-creation and co-redemption of the world.[64] Christ embodies the divine message that human persons and human actions are pleasing to God, and humans are loved by God. Scotus views God as a creative artist who selected the human nature as the "material" most fitting to receive the highest glory of subsisting in the person of the Word.[65]

One powerful implication for ecology suggested by this understanding of the Incarnation is that humans are both challenged and empowered to play a Christ-like role in the cosmos. That role is to love God in Godself and in the entire cosmos which is God's self-expression. Because the entire cosmos in some way resembles Christ, the "first born of all creation," we must cherish creation as we reverence Christ. This is the finest example of orthodox panentheism.

DISCUSSION AND CONCLUSIONS

In summary, contrary to Dubos' suggestion that the Franciscan view is simplistic and romantic, the Franciscan sources press several significant ideas that hold very practical implications for the ecological crisis of our day. First, as St. Francis of Assisi enjoins, we must relinquish any attitude of possession or exclusive ownership of the cosmos or its parts; it indeed is given to *all* who inhabit it. Second, we must be obedient to the other inhabitants of the cosmos, taking a long-term view of the broad vision of what is truly good for *all* involved, not *merely* our own *self-interest*. Third, we humans must recognize our familial bonds with *all* of creation and zealously seek the well-being of the entire family—as would a good "brother" or "sister." When there is conflict, we can draw wisdom from the negotiated settlement modeled in the legend of the Wolf of Gubbio.[66]

The theology of Bonaventure gives more systematic arguments to undergird Francis' intuited theology. If Christ is the creative and sustaining center of all reality, then human power and authority becomes eclipsed and is relegated proportionately. The human role then becomes that of the co-creative and co-redemptive partner, giving voice to the needs of the cosmic elements, having first responded to the call to honor God above all else. Human memory, understanding, and will are the instruments through which God cultivates, nurtures, and negotiates an exchange of power in the universe for the flourishing of the entire cosmos.

In Scotus' notion of *haecceitas* we find the basis for the unique form and function of all in the universe. This is significant because it is from many particularities that the possibility of the sharing of power that is mutuality takes shape. Also, Scotus' understanding of the primacy of Christ grounds the human as the creature empowered to play a Christ-like role in the cosmos. Just as Christ, "the first born of all creation" became one like us in order to redeem humankind, so too humans must join with other creatures and elements of the cosmos for the ongoing creation and redemption of the world.

Some critics of Franciscan cosmic mysticism, such as Dubos, erroneously ascribe to Francis an absolute identification of God with nature (*pan*theism) and thus write off any possible contribution by Francis to the modern conversation concerning the place of the human person in relation to the environment.[67] However, those who construe Francis of Assisi as a mere sentimental emotivistic nature worshiper are proven wrong on several counts. There is first no evidence that St. Francis was a *pan*theist, but he was certainly an orthodox pan*en*theist.[68] Further, there is no specific evidence that Francis would require absolute conservation of all resources. To the contrary, there is evidence that Francis taught an attitude of non-possession—all one has is a gift of God for one's use, while God remains the sole owner.[69]

Dubos' first erroneous assumption about Francis of Assisi contributes to a second mistaken argument. Dubos holds that there is only one relationship style that would allow humans to make use of the earth, specifically a hierarchical model in which power is imposed from the more powerful upon the less powerful. Contrary to Dubos, Francis promoted a kinship relationship with nature in which power and authority can be mutually beneficial (such as in the use of organic farming techniques). Use does not necessarily include abuse, nor does harmonious, respectful coexistence necessarily exclude use.

Francis' method of relating requires more than reverence. It, in fact, delimits the parameters of power and authority of the human in relation to God and in relationship with all of creation. As both Bonaventure and Scotus so clearly showed, the human is the mediating agent who, as co-creator and co-redeemer with God, must make decisions about nature based on concrete reality and toward the greater flourishing of all. The style and the dynamics of power engaged toward achieving any decision and its end are limited to 'power-with.'[70] The human is one creature among many with a distinct duty to include all creatures and earth elements and give them a voice in the destiny of the universe. In today's language, mutuality, "*the sharing of power-with by and among all parties in a relationship that recognizes the wholeness and particular experience of each participant toward the end of optimum flourishing of all*," most adequately describes the Franciscan notion of the relationship of the human with nature.[71]

In comparison, it seems that H. Richard Niebuhr's notion of *responsibility* most adequately describes the Benedictine understanding of the relationship of the human and nature:

> [t]he idea of an agent's action as response to an action upon him in accordance with his interpretation of the later action with his expectation of response to his response; and all of this in a continuing community of agents.[72]

While some similarity exists between Niebuhr's notion of responsibility and the "Franciscan" understanding of mutuality, the differences are significant for ecotheology and environmental ethics. The very fact the Benedict did not prohibit ownership of "places," i.e. monasteries, implies a very different understanding of the power of the human person in relationship with the earth, and a different sense of place. The power dynamics of responsibility defined as "stewardship or trusteeship *over* things" are and remain those of "power-over." Rather than serving maximum human thriving, the dynamics of "power-over" readily become oppressive. The monastery was "home," a place of tranquility and security. The Abbot and the monks controlled and thus were responsible for what went on in that place. Where the Benedictine is the entrepreneur and resident, the Franciscan is a mediator, sojourner and guest in the world.[73]

Benedict, indeed, held that ownership was to be open handed, somehow recognizing that the end of all human endeavor was worship. Nonetheless, he *did* recognize the notion of *ownership* of particular places for indefinite periods in history. For Francis, the view was more broadly and deeply focused. The whole creation was "the Lord's" and humans among all the other creatures were "sojourners and guests" in the realm of the Great King. Having been schooled in knightly chivalry, Francis understood that courtesy (in the Twelfth Century sense of the word) required that the guest do nothing to displease the host. In other words, the guest would extend the original courtesy of the host to all s/he encountered during her/his sojourn. Conspicuously absent from this kind of sharing of power and being empowered by the generosity of the Host is any sense of proprietary ownership. For the Franciscan, the vow of poverty focuses her/him and away from any sort of possession whatsoever. In turn, fidelity to poverty requires that s/he utilize the capacity that makes the human distinct among the creatures—memory, understanding, and will—to extend the courtesy of the Host to the cosmos, give voice to the various elements of the cosmos, mediating their needs to one another.

The ecological crisis poses questions of relationship and survival which are ultimately questions of power. Our response to these inquiries is dependent upon the meaning framework we bring to bear upon these issues and the assumptions that undergird that structure. As I have shown, the facticity and even the ontological status of mutuality is increasingly being recognized.[74] Christian feminists, particularly Rosemary Radford Ruether, Carter Heyward, Beverly Wildung Harrison, and Elizabeth A. Johnson give mutuality the status of a formal norm when shaping their ethical arguments. It is precisely in the consideration of what behavior constitutes "thriving" that the need arises for mutuality as a formal norm to complement and correct love and justice in the Christian social ethical framework. Traditionally, it was thought that love and justice function as the foundational norms which adequately measure human thriving. However, as I have shown elsewhere, love and justice do not always adequately measure what constitutes human thriving because neither norm necessarily requires the moral agent to consider issues pertaining to the dynamics of power in a relationship. When mutuality is considered as a foundational ethical norm along with love and justice, the conditions for optimum human flourishing are more adequately revealed and measured.[75] Mutuality (as defined above) is a necessary condition for genuine love and/or justice. When mutuality accompanies love and justice, a vast qualitative difference in each virtue is determined, namely, the dynamic of power becomes limited to "power-with."[76]

The Complexity of Mutuality

In its complexity, the notion of "mutuality" is comparable to the tripartite theory of "justice."[77] Similarly, mutuality[78] has four key loci of expression—cosmic, gender,[79] generative,[80] social.[81] All four loci are interrelated in a manner similar to the interrelationship of social, distributive, and commutative justice. Cosmic mutuality, which is the focus of our discussion here, is found in the relation between God and the whole

of creation, and in the fact that humans are mutually related to everything in the entire cosmos by virtue of their relationship with God. I
define cosmic mutuality as: *the sharing of "power-with" by and among the
Creator, human beings, all earth elements, and the entire cosmos in a way that
recognizes their interdependence and reverences all.*[82]

Evidence for cosmic mutuality is adduced from the natural sciences
including astrophysics, ecology, and quantum physics.[83] Also, eco-femi-
nist theory holds that the natural environment asserts itself as a living
aspect of "our bodies, ourselves"—it "answers back" when humans defile
nature.[84] The most effective social analysis takes into account how any
form of power impacts the most disadvantaged, not forgetting all elements of the ecosystem, in the interest of attaining the well being of all.
As expressed in the Franciscan charism, traditional Christian cosmology
is retrievable to the extent that the relatedness of the created order and
the social order is stressed in the light of the Hebrew and Christian
Testament witnesses. The deep relatedness represented by the phrase
"God in the world and the world in God" expresses the sort of pan*en*theism that has been recognized for centuries as orthodox. The fact that
God is known as Creator, Vivifier, or Redeemer only in relation to creation shows, in a certain analogous sense, need on God's part for relationship to the cosmos. If we acknowledge the kinship of all creation,
then the command to "love thy neighbor" must be extended to everything and everyone (although admittedly with varying degrees of
emphasis). In short, all of this points to a form of mutuality I call "cosmic mutuality" and which can be found at the heart of the Franciscan
understanding of the human-cosmos relationship. But how does this
notion of cosmic mutuality affect a proper understanding of the relationship humans have with nature?

Sources and the Hebrew Scriptures in Conversation

Without a doubt one can find support in the Hebrew Scriptures for
both the Benedictine and the Franciscan approaches to the relationship
of humans and nature. There is wide agreement among scripture scholars that the latter half of Gen. 1:26 must be read in light of the first half
of the verse.[85] Humans are set in a unique relationship with God which
is characterized by a greater intensity and intimacy than God's relationship with other parts of creation. From that stance, humans are to be for

creation what God is for them. Humans stand as "only God's representative, summoned to maintain and enforce God's claim to dominion over
the earth."[86] In addition, humans receive the same blessing as the creatures (v. 26), insuring their creaturely status. This reading of Gen. 1:26 is
consistent with the widely agreed upon reading of Gen. 2 where the
human is even more clearly called to be a servant, guardian, and preserv-
er of creation.[87] In Gen 3, *adam* sins and the relationship between
humanity, God, and creation becomes estranged. *Adam* fails to understand Godly matters, and nature becomes (at most) a cursed shadow of
its paradisal self. Only through God's constant fidelity to the Covenant
is the right relationship among *adam*, God, and nature restored.

In the Hebrew Testament, by the very fact that nature gives God
praise, it bears spiritual and aesthetic value. Since such value is part of
the Creator's intent, humans become servants to nature insofar as they
are called to serve God's interests. The human shares the status of *nefesh
chayah* ("living soul" or "living creature") with plants and animals (cf.
Gen. 1:20; Ps.42:2–3)[88] Indeed, nature has its own *mitzvot* (commandments
to do what is right and just) to fulfill (Gen. 1: 11,12,22; 5:4; 8:17; 9:3,7)[89] and
animals share in the Covenant (Gen. 8:21–22; 9:10–17).[90] Animals stand as
a witness to Israel's fulfillment of its *mitzvot* (Deut. 30:10).[91] Also evident
is God's promise of a new covenant with the animals in which they will
no longer need to fear destruction by humans or other beasts (Is. 11:6–9;
65:25; Hos. 2:20).[92]

It is not only animals and humans who worship God, but even the
hills, valleys, floods, trees—indeed, the whole world (Ps. 65:13–14; 66:1–4;
89:6; I Chron. 16:23–33).[93] In fact, nature recognizes God and trembles in
God's presence. (Ps. 68:9)[94]

The Hebrew Scriptures address both the dominion of humans over
nature and the dominion of nature over humans. While humans do use
plants and animals for their comfort, there is also ample evidence indi-
cating that various elements are created to serve one another (Ps.
104:14–20; Gen. 1:30; Ps. 145:16; 147:8–9; Job 38:39–41; 39:1–8,28).[95] Clarence
J. Glacken shows that the spirit of God's relationship with nature is not
utilitarian, so the human-nature relationship must not be so, either.[96] At
times human ability to comprehend, much less control, nature is even
mocked (Job 38:25–27; 39:9–12; Eccles. 11:5).[97] Nature's dominion over
humans is often a check on immorality (Jer. 15:3; 35:20; Hos. 13:8; Joel
1:4; I Kgs. 21:23–2; Is. 13:17–22; 14:11). In short, human dominion over
nature depends on human moral fitness.[98] The purposeful destruction of

nature is God's prerogative, and is not in the human's realm of discretion (Ps.29:5–6,9; Zech. 11:1–3; Hab. 3:5–8). It is idolatry to usurp God's role, and humans lose their authority as God's viceroys when they step out of line. As Kay points out, crimes against God or society are also crimes against nature (Gen. 4:10; Ezek. 12:19; Hos. 1:1–3).[99] Kay explains:

> The Bible prescribes not only reward and punishment, but *reciprocal* justice. This concept is crucial for understanding why the Bible threatens to punish misdemeanors in business or interpersonal relations with drought or eviction from the land. In the Bible, all moral and immoral deeds have positive or negative impacts on the land on which they were perpetrated, and the land responds accordingly.... Humans do not commit evil in isolation without repercussions in the community.... The belief that all human offenses potentially imperil nature is the Bible's strongest statement about human dominion over the environment.[100]

Thus we see that arguments from the Hebrew Scriptures could be made for the Benedictine approach to relations with nature—"stewardship and ownership," or the Franciscan approach, "mutuality and sojourning." However, the way of ownership and stewardship is more easily misunderstood and co-opted in today's dominant North American culture which is known for its worship of rugged individualism, its utilitarian manipulation of anything toward the blatant self-interest of making a profit, and for its gross neglect of the poor—even within its own borders. Perhaps it is the case that the language of Benedict can more easily bridge the gap that exists between the Utilitarian and the Steward, but I claim that it is the Poor Man of Assisi who holds the paradigm for the kind of power needed in the future.

Through the manifold particularities of God's self-revelation in nature, humans come to know God. In turn, the human creature uses its gift of reason (mind, intellect, and will) to engage in the great doxology of participating in sustaining creation. In our ecologically ravaged world, to believe that Christ is at the heart of every creature is to shift our understanding of power dynamics within the entire cosmos. Humans can no longer construe themselves as the sole brokers of power over all others. Rather, we must embrace the stance of cosmic mutuality:

> *The sharing of power-with by and among the Creator, human beings, all earth elements, and the entire cosmos in a way that recognizes their interdependence and reverences all.*[101]

Notes

1. Broadly defined, a charism is a gratuitous gift of the Holy Spirit given for the common good and toward the salvation of humankind. See s.v. "charism," Karl Rahner and Herbert Vorgrimler, *Theological Dictionary*, Cornelius Ernst, ed., New York: Herder and Herder, 1965, 72. Traditionally the Benedictines have been known for their gifts of moderation in all things, prayer, learning, and valuing common labor. The Franciscans are known for their gifts of poverty, penance, hospitality and joy. For a more complete treatment of the Benedictine and Franciscan charisms, respectively, see: Pierre-Marie Gy, s.v. "Benedictines," in Vol. 2, *Dictionary of the Middle Ages*, Joseph R. Strayer, ed., (New York: Charles Scribner's Sons, 1983), 171. See also Lester K. Little, s.v. "Franciscans," in Vol. 5, *Dictionary of the Middle Ages*, Joseph R. Strayer, ed., (New York: Charles Scribner's Sons, 1983).

2. Hugh Feiss, "Watch the Crows: Environmental Responsibility and the Benedictine Tradition," in Drew Christiansen and Walter Glazer, eds., *And God Saw That It Was Good: Catholic Theology and the Environment*, (Washington, DC: United States Catholic Conference, 1996), 147–61.

3. Benedict of Nursia was the founder of the Benedictine religious order. See Gy, "Benedictines," 171.

4. See Timothy Fry, ed., *The Rule of Benedict*, (Collegeville:Liturgical Press, 1981).

5. Feiss, "Watch the Crows, 147.

6. See Timothy Fry, ed., *The Rule of Benedict*, (Collegeville:Liturgical Press, 1981), the thematic index: *RB* 80, 62, 3.3, 5, 71.

7. Ibid., *RB* 72, 3, 60.

8. Ibid., *RB* 80, ch.31, 226–29.

9. Ibid., *RB* 55:11, 33, 34.

10. Ibid., *RB* 40.8, 55.7.

11. Ibid., *RB* 31.10–11.

12. Ibid., *RB* 53.7, also see 36.1–2, 8–9. The term "high Christology" here refers to Benedict's greater stress on the divinity of Christ, in contrast to the importance Francis of Assisi and his followers placed on Christ incarnate. Benedict focused on the worship of Jesus as the Christ, in contrast to Francis of Assisi who focused on the Christian's imitation of the poor human Jesus. See Karl Rahner, "The Two Types of Christology," in *Theological Investigations* 17, trans. Margaret Kohl, (New York: Crossroad,

1981), 212–23. See also Allan B. Wolter, "John Scotus on the Primacy of Christ and the Personality of Christ" in *Franciscan Christology: Selected Texts, Translations and Essays*, Franciscan Sources No. 1, Damian McElrath, ed., (St. Bonaventure, NY: Franciscan Institute Publications, 1980) 147–55.

13. Feiss, "Watch the Crows," 151.

14. Ibid., 151–52. See *RB* 72.9, 5, 3; 6; 4.20.

15. See Ernst H. Soudek, s.v. "St. Hildegard of Bingen," in Vol. 6, *Dictionary of the Middle Ages*, Joseph R. Strayer, ed., (New York: Charles Scribner's Sons, 1983), 228–29. Hildegard was a German nun, mystic, healer and physician, and scientist. She was Prioress of the Benedictine cloister at Disiboden (elected in 1136) and later at a newly formed cloister in Bingen (1147 until her death, September 17, 1179).

16. Ibid., 228–29. Among Hildegard's many writings was her *Scivias*, a work of Latin prose consisting of twenty-six highly allegorical and symbolic sections revolving around the central image of the Living Light (God).

17. See Hildegard of Bingen, *Scivias*, trans. Bruce Hozeski, (Sante Fe: Bear & Company, 1986), 8.

18. Ibid., 27.

19. Ibid., 39–57.

20. Ibid., 177–86.

21. Ibid., Sc. Prol. CC 1:9.

22. Feiss, "Watch the Crows," 157.

23. See Rene Dubos, *A Theology of the Earth*, October 2, 1969, lecture given at the Smithsonian Institution, Washington, DC, (Washington, DC: Smithsonian Institution Office of Public Affairs, 1969). See also Rene Dubos, *A God Within*, (New York: Charles Scribner's Sons, 1972), esp. 153–74.

24. Francis of Assisi was the founder of the Franciscan religious order. See Little, "Franciscans," 194.

25. See "The Admonitions," in Regis J. Armstrong, J. A. Wayne Hellman, and William J. Short, eds., *Francis of Assisi: Early Documents*, Volume I - The Saint, (New York: New City Press, 1999), 128–37. At 128: "A medieval admonition was more than a warning or a calling to mind; it had more of a religious sense in which a biblical passage or image was presented and, in light of it, a practical application was made." Some twenty-eight admonitions are among the undated writings of St. Francis of Assisi.

26. Francis of Assisi, in Ibid., 131.

27. See Karl Rahner and Herbert Vorgrimler, s.v. "Image and likeness of God," in *Theological Dictionary*, Cornelious Ernst, ed., trans. Richard Strachan, New York: Herder & Herder, 1965.

28. Zachary Hayes, "St. Francis of Assisi and Nature: A Model for a 21st Century Spirituality," Unpublished Manuscript, 8–16.

29. Bonaventure, *The Major Legend of St. Francis*, Chapter 2. 4, in Regis J. Armstrong, J. A. Wayne Hellmann, and William J. Short, eds., *Francis of*

Assisi: Early Documents, Volume II - The Founder, (New York: New City Press, 2000), at 538: "Until now I have called you father, but now I can say without reservation, *'Our Father who art in heaven,'* since I have placed all my treasure and all my hope in him."

30. Ibid., Chapter 8.6, at 590: "From a reflection on the primary source of all things, filled with ever more abundant piety, he would call creatures, no matter how small, by the name of 'brother' or 'sister,' because he knew they shared with him the same beginning."

31. Bonaventure, *The Assisi Compilation*, 83, in Armstrong, Hellmann, and Short, eds., *Francis of Assisi: Early Documents*, Volume I - The Saint, 186.

32. Francis of Assisi, *Salutation of the Virtues*, 14 in Ibid., 165.

33. Roger D. Sorrell, *St. Francis of Assisi and Nature*, (New York: Oxford University Press, 1988), 74. See also my *Mutuality: A Formal Norm For Christian Social Ethics* (San Francisco: Catholic Scholars Press, 1998), 233.

34. Francis of Assisi, *Earlier Exhortation to the Brothers and Sisters of Penance*, 13, in Armstrong, Hellmann, and Short, eds., *Francis of Assisi: Early Documents*, Volume I - The Saint, at 42: "Oh, how holy and how loving, gratifying, humbling, peace-giving, sweet, worthy of love, and above all things desirable: to have such a Brother and such a Son, our Lord Jesus Christ, Who laid down His life for His sheep (cf. Jn. 10:15)...."

35. Thomas of Celano, *The Life of St. Francis by Thomas of Celano*, Book 1, Chapter 29.81, in Ibid., 251.

36. Max Scheler, *The Nature of Symapthy*, trans. Peter Heath, (Hamden, CT: The Shoestring Press, Inc. 1970), 90.

37. Without discounting the divinity of Christ, the Franciscans' starting point in theology was the Christ incarnate. See Kenan B. Osborne, ed., *The History of Franciscan Theology*, St. Bonaventure, NY: The Franciscan Institute, 1994. See also Damian McElrath, ed., *Franciscan Christology: Selected Texts, Translations and Essays*, Franciscan Sources No. 1 (St. Bonaventure, NY: Franciscan Institute Publications, 1980). Many of the Franciscan theologians were also mystics, for example St. Anthony of Padua and St. Bonaventure. They had an intimate personal relationship with Christ as well as a fine command of the academic theology of their day.

38. See "Blessed Francis Leads a Wolf To Become Very Tame," in *The Deeds of Blessed Francis and His Companions by Ugolino Boniscambi of Montegiorgio (1328–37)*, in Regis J. Armstrong, J. A. Wayne Hellmann, and William J. Short, eds., *Francis of Assisi: Early Documents*, Volume III - The Prophet, (New York: New City Press, 2001), 482–85. In this legend, Francis negotiated a peace between the wolf who had been eating the livestock and the townspeople of Gubbio. Confronting the wolf, Francis recognized the need of the wolf to eat, and the need of the townspeople to live without fear of harm. The people agreed to supply the wolf with food, in turn, the wolf agreed to

not harm the people or their livestock. A peaceful and mutual relationship was achieved.

39. *The Works of Bonaventure: Collations on the Six Days*, I.10, Vol.V, trans. José de Vinck, (Paterson,NJ: St. Anthony Guild Press, 1970), 5–7. See Zachary Hayes, "Christ, Word of God and Exemplar of Humanity," *The Cord* 46/1, (1996): 6–7. Among the frequently cited texts in Bonaventure's Christological writings are: Jn. 1:1–15, I Jn. 1–3, Col. 1:15–20, Eph. 1:3–14, I Cor. 8:6, and Heb. 1:2–14. See also Zachary Hayes, *Bonaventure: Mystical Writings*, A Spiritual Legacy Book, (New York: Crossroad Publishing Company, 1999), at 116 Hayes quotes Bonaventure, *Collations on the Six Days of Creation*, 1:10–11[5: 330–31]: "It is necessary to begin at the center, that is, with Christ...".

40. Bonaventure of Bagnoregio was the first major Franciscan theologian following Alexander of Hales. See Zachary Hayes, "Bonaventure: Mystery of the Triune God," in Kenan B. Osborne, ed., *The History of Franciscan Theology*, St. Bonaventure, NY: The Franciscan Institute, 1994, 38–125.

41. Ewert Cousins, *Bonaventure and the Coincidence of Opposites*, Chicago: Franciscan Herald Press, 1978), 101–102. Cousins explains how Bonaventure joins theological and metaphysical notions to ground his understanding of Christ as the center in the Trinity: "...the root of Bonaventure's doctrine lies in his conception of the Father as dynamic, fecund source of the Trinitarian processions. In examining the Father, Bonaventure employs two principles: the principle of fecund primordiality and the principle of the self-diffusion of the good. Both of these principles he applies to the divinity in relation to creation and to the Father in the Trinity... For Bonaventure God's self-sufficiency and self-communication are so intimately united that his principle can be stated as follows: Because he is self-sufficient, he is absolutely self-communicating."

42. Dionysius the Areopagite (Acts 17:34) is the name that was attached to a corpus of nine texts that have survived antiquity. See John Farina, ed., *Pseudo-Dionysius: Complete Works*, Classic in Western Spirituality, Colm Luibheid, trans., (New York: Paulist Press, 1987). The true author of the texts is unknown to scholars. These writings were sources known to and used by Bonaventure. For a brief summary of the pseudo-Dionysian influence on Bonaventure's Christology, see J. Guy Bougerol, *Introduction to the Works of Bonaventure*, José de Venck, trans., (Paterson , NJ: St. Anthony Guild Press, 1964), 41.

43. Viktrizius Veith, "Jesus Christus-Der Weg, Die Wahrheit und Das Leben: Ein Beitrag zur Christologie und Christusverkundigung nach Bonaventura," *Laurentianum* 15 (1974): 54–55. See also Leonard J. Bowman, "The Cosmic Exemplarism of Bonaventure," *Journal of Religion* 55 (April 1975): 181–85.

44. Hayes, "Christ, Word of God and Exemplar of Humanity," 11.

45. Here we can see the influence of Pseudo-Dionysus on Bonaventure. See José de Vinck, *Introduction to the Works of Bonaventure*, J. Guy Bougerol, trans., (Paterson, NJ: St. Anthony Guild Press, 1972), 40.

46. Bonaventure, *Sermo I, Dom II*, in Quad. IX, 215–19, quoted in Hayes, "Christ, Word of God and Exemplar of Humanity," 13.

47. Ewert Cousins, *Christ of the 21st Century*, (Rockport,MA: Element, Inc., 1992), 151. See also Bonaventure, *Hexaem.* XII,14, quoted in Cousins, *Christ of the 21st Century*, at 152: "Bonaventure states: '..the entire world is a shadow, a road, a vestige, and it is also a book written without (Ex.2: 8; Ap.5:1). For in every creature there is a shining forth of the divine exemplar, but mixed with the darkness. Hence creatures are a kind of darkness mixed with light. Also, they are a road leading to the exemplar. Just as you see a ray of light entering through a window is colored in different ways according to the colors of the various parts, so the divine ray shines forth in each and every creature in different ways and in different properties; it is said in Wisdom: *In her ways she shows herself* (Wis.6: 17). Also creatures are a vestige of the wisdom of God. Hence creatures are a kind of representation and statue of the wisdom of God. And in view of all of this, they are a kind of book written without.'"

48. Bonaventure, *Brevil.* 2,4 (V,221), cited by Zachary Hayes, "Bonaventure: Mystery of the Triune God," 67–68: "The heavenly bodies influence human bodies which are disposed for the most noble form, the rational soul. The desire of the entire sentient, corporal nature is ordained to this form (the rational soul) and finds its end in this form. So it is that through this form, which is an existing, living, sentient, and intelligent form, the human body may be led back as if in the manner of an intelligible circle to its point of origin in which it is brought to perfection and beatified."

49. See Ibid., 68 where Hayes cites *Brevil.* 2,4 (V, 222).

50. See Cousins, *Christ of the 21st Century*, at 152 where he cites Bonaventure, *Hexaem.* I, 17: "This is our entire metaphysics: emanation, exemplarity, fulfillment, that is, to be illuminated by spiritual rays and led back to the highest reality." See also *Merriam Webster's Collegiate Dictionary*, Tenth Edition, 1994, s.v. "Neoplatonism," "Platonism modified in later antiquity to accord with Aristotelian, post-Aristotelian and oriental conceptions that conceives of a world as an emanation from an ultimate indivisible being with whom the soul is capable of being reunited in trance or ecstasy."

51. See Hayes, "Bonaventure: Mystery of the Triune God," 67–68. Hayes cites Bonaventure, *Brevil.* 2,4 (V, 221).

52. Phil Hoebing, "St. Bonaventure and Ecology," in *The Cord* 40 (1990):341–42: "God is the exemplary cause of all creatures and is at the very center of Bonaventure's metaphysics. Bonaventure reasoned this way: If God created the world he would act, not in a blind manner, but rather in an intelligent

way.... [Plato's Ideas] or patterns are in God and He acts according to them.... God is supremely intelligible to Himself and comprehends Himself in a single act, but in performing this act he equals Himself. This similitude, as a Christian knows, is the Divine Word, which is equal to God and expresses all His being, all His power, and all His knowledge (*Hex.* III, 4, p.343). It is in the understanding of the Uncreated Word that everything is known and understood."

53.   Hayes, in "Bonaventure: Mystery of the Triune God," 74.

54.   Cousins, *Christ of the 21st Century*, 152–55.

55.   Known as the "Subtle Doctor," he is among the great scholastic theologians who taught at the University of Paris, at Cambridge and at Cologne. See Richard Cross, *Duns Scotus*, Great Medieval Thinker Series, (New York: Oxford University Press, 1999), especially 3–6.

56.   Armond A. Mauer, *Medieval Philosophy*, The Etienne Gilson Series 4, Second Edition, (Toronto: Pontifical Institute of Medieval Studies, 1982), 223–24. To make the switch from that which is possible to that which is... Scotus uses the Anselmian notion: "That of which nothing greater can be conceived" is God.

57.   John Duns Scotus, Quodlibet 14.nn.23–24 (Alluntis 1:83) in *John Duns Scotus: God and Creatures - Quodlibetal Questions*, trans. Felix Alluntis and Allan B. Wolter (Princeton: Princeton University Press, 1975), 338–9.

58.   "Glossary," in Felix Alluntis and Allan B. Wolter, trans., *John Duns Scotus — God and Creatures: The Quodlibetal Questions*, Paperback Edition, (Washington, DC: Catholic University of America Press, 1981), at 511: *"haecceitas*, (from the Latin *haec*, this): The term means literally, 'thisness.' It designates the unique formal principle of individuation that makes the nature, which all individuals of the same species have in common, to be just this or that individual and no other. Scotus regards it as a distinct positive formality over and above the common nature of the individual (*natura communis*)."

59.   Eric Doyle, "Duns Scotus and Ecumenism," *De Doctrina I. Duns Scoti*, vol. III, Acta Congressus Scotistici Internationalis Oxonii et Edimburgi, 11–17 September 1966 celebrati, Camille Bérubé, ed., (Roma: Cura Commissionis Scotisticae, 1968), at 460: "The uniqueness, the unrepeatable something of all things, is what gives them their intrinsic and eternal value. There is about everything, every person, an originality that gives new insight into reality, another aspect that has never been seen before. Each person enters into a new enriching relationship of knowledge and love with every new person met, with every new thing encountered."

60.   Mary Beth Ingham, "Integrated Vision," in Kenan B. Osborne, ed., *The History of Franciscan Theology*, (St. Bonaventure, NY: Franciscan Institute, 1994), 210. As Ingham concludes, Scotus' concept of haecceitas sheds light on his thinking in several ways, including, "...it suggests that each being possesses a dimension which it alone can reveal...."

61. See Robert North, "The Scotist Cosmic Christ," in *De Doctrina Ioannis Duns Scoti*, vol. III, 194–198. Positions of key Franciscans concerning the reason for the Incarnation are: Alexander of Hales (1200)—it would have been suitable had there been no sin; Matthew of Aquasparta (1282)—it was supposed for the perfection of the natural order; Raymond of Lull (1289)—its primary aim was to show forth the love of God; Roger Marston and William of Ware both believed it would have taken place "apart from sin"; Bonaventure affirmed that either position was orthodox, but he opted for the traditional Anselmian solution which held sin as the cause.

62. Scotus' position on the Incarnation is articulated in his *Reportatio* and *Ordinatio* III.7.3. See Allan B. Wolter, "John Duns Scotus on the Primacy and Personality of Christ," in *Franciscan Christology: Selected Texts, Translations and Essays*, Franciscan Sources No. 1, ed. Damian McElrath (St. Bonaventure, NY: Franciscan Institute Publications, 1980), 147–55. At 151: "Now the sequence in which the creative artist evolves his plan is the very opposite of the way he puts it into execution. One can say, however, that in the order of execution, God's union with a human nature is really prior to his granting it the greatest grace and glory. We could presume, then, that it was in the reverse order that he intended them, so that God would first intend that some nature, not the highest, should receive the highest glory, as he bestowed natural perfection. Then secondly, as it were, he willed that this nature should subsist in the Person of the Word, so that the angel might not be subject to a [mere] man."

    See also Antonio Aranda, "La Cuestión Teológica de la Encarnatión del Verbo: Relectura de Tres Posiciones Características," *Scripta Theologica* 25 (1993): 49–94.

63. Franciscans frequently cite these biblical texts to illustrate this point: Jn. 1:1–15, I Jn. 1–3, Col. 1:15–20, Eph. 1:3–14, I Cor. 8:6, and Heb. 1:2–14.

64. Ingham, "Integrated Vision," 222: "Mutuality between God and humanity was foreseen from eternity, begun in the Incarnation and is to be fully realized in the future when Christ will be 'all in all.' The summit of creation is the communion of all persons with one another and with God. Christ is the very person in whom the human and divine achieve mutuality."

65. See note 62, above.

66. See note 38, above.

67. Dubos, *God Within*, 167.

68. See Karl Rahner and Herbert Vorgrimler, ed., Cornelius Ernst, trans., Richard Strachan, *Theological Dictionary*, (New York: Herder and Herder, 1965), s.v. "Panentheism" at 333–34: "This form of pantheism does not simply identify the world with God in a monistic fashion (God, the 'All') but sees the 'All' of the world 'within' God as an interior modification and manifestation of God, although God is not absorbed in the world." See also Dubos, *God Within*, 158.

69. This is similar to Benedict. However, Benedict allowed ownership.

70. Beverly Wildung Harrison, "The Politics of Energy Policy," in *Making the Connections: Essays in Feminist Social Ethics*, ed. Carol S. Robb, (Boston: Beacon Press, 1983) 175 and Carter Heyward, *Touching Our Strength: Erotic as Power and the Love of God*, (San Francisco: Harper & Row, 1989), 191. The term, "power-with" appears early in feminist literature. See Mary Parker Follett, *Creative Experience* (New York: Longman, Green & Company, 1924) and her *Dynamic Administration* (New York: Harper and Brothers, 1942). As early as 1924, Mary Parker Follett distinguished "power-with" and "power-over." "Power-with" is the capacity for being acted upon or for undergoing an effect, in a side by side relationship with others. "Power-over" indicates a possession of control, authority, or influence over others from a hierarchical stance.

71. See my *Mutuality: A Formal Norm*, esp. Chapter 2.

72. H. Richard Niebuhr, *The Responsible Self: Essays in Christian Moral Philosophy*, paperback edition, ed., Richard H. Niebuhr, (New York: Harper & Row publishers, 1978), 65. See also my *Mutuality: A Formal Norm*, 197, where I show how Niebuhr's notion of responsibility is only an antecedent of the idea of mutuality.

73. Francis of Assisi, "The Earlier Rule," Chapters 1, 6, 7, 8, 9, 15, in Armstrong, Hellmann, and Short, eds., *Francis of Assisi: Early Documents*, Volume I - The Saint, 63–73.

74. See my *Mutuality: A Formal Norm*, at 1, n.1: "For a small sample of this huge literature see the following: In the natural sciences—Fritjof Capra, *The Turning Point: Science, Society, and the Rising Culture* (New York: Simon and Schuster, 1982); Fritjof Capra, *The Tao of Physics: An Exploration of the Parallels Between Modern Physics and Eastern Mysticism* (New York: Bantam, 1977); Nigal Calder, *The Key to the Universe: A Report on the New Physics* (New York: Viking, 1977); Steven Weinberg, *The First Three Minutes* (New York: Basic Books, 1977); John Boslough, *Stephen Hawking's Universe* (New York: Avon, 1985); Anne H. Ehrlich and Paul R. Ehrlich, *Earth* (New York: Franklin Watts, 1987); Thomas Berry, *Dream of the Earth* (San Francisco: Sierra Club Books, 1988); Anne H. Ehrlich, Paul R. Ehrlich, and John P. Holdren, *Human Ecology: Problems and Solutions* (San Francisco: W.H. Freeman, 1973); Brian Swimme, *The Universe is a Green Dragon: A Cosmic Creation Story* (Santa Fe, NM: Bear and Company, 1985); Brian Swimme, "How To Heal a Lobotomy," in Irene Diamond and Gloria Orenstein, eds., *Reweaving the World: The Emergence of Ecofeminism* (San Francisco: Sierra Club Books: 1989); In law—Roderick F. Nash, *The Rights of Nature: A History of Environmental Ethics* (Madison: University of Wisconsin Press, 1989); Christopher Stone, *Should Trees Have Standing?: Toward Legal Rights For Natural Objects* (Los Altos, CA: Sierra Club Books, 1974); In psychology—James Serpell, *In the Company of Animals: A Study of Human-Animal*

Relationships (London: Basil Blackwell, 1986); In philosophy—David Rothenberg, "The Individual and the Community: Two Approaches to Ecophilosophy in Practice," a paper presented at the Fifth Annual Casassa Conference, March 14–15, 1991, Loyola Marymount University, Los Angeles, CA; Erazim Kohak, *The Embers and the Stars: A Philosophical Inquiry into the Moral Sense of Nature* (Chicago: The University of Chicago Press, 1984); In urban planning—Marcia D. Lowe, "Rethinking Urban Transport," in *State of the World, 1991* (New York: Norton, 1991); In political science—Jeremy Rafkin, *Biosphere Politics: A New Consciousness for a New Century* (New York: Crown Publishing, 1991); In agriculture—Wes Jackson, *New Roots For Agriculture* (Lincoln: University of Nebraska, 1987); In economics—Michael Renner, "Converting to a Peaceful Economy," in *State of the World, 1990* (New York: Norton, 1990)."

75. Needless to say, the historical examples one might raise— slavery, the early Canonical status of women, lack of involvement of the Vatican in preventing the Holocaust, etc., are each complex. I do not claim that a lack of mutuality alone would detract from their proper resolution, nor do I claim that consideration of mutuality alone would insure moral integrity. Any such claims would take much greater development than is possible here. The point here is to merely suggest in some situations many would agree moral failure would include this dereliction occurred, and to invite the reader into the process of reflection, as I do in the Introduction of my *Mutuality: A Formal Norm*. In Chapters 4 and 5 of that work, I have shown that mutuality has probative value in that it illuminates and delimits loving and just behavior.

76. Cf. my Introduction, *Mutuality: A Formal Norm*. Mutuality requires a more critical view of hierarchy than is commonly found in natural law traditions. Mutuality shifts the criterion for justice from pure legalism to include the concrete and dynamic needs of the other as basic to thriving, and requires consideration of the good/needs of all beings and elements of the universe in relation to one another, not merely the greatest good for the greatest number. Thus, any construal of justice that fails to include the participation of all parties in deciding its limits or any interpretation of sacrificial love that is morally destructive to any party is excluded. Real love is not exclusively sacrificial. Any sacrifice must be chosen in freedom, cognizant of its consequences, with full integrity of a person and toward the goal of a greater mutuality in the relationship.

See *Encyclopedia of Philosophy*, sv. "justice." This article presents a discussion of major theories of justice. Generally theories of justice can be categorized in three classifications: Rationalist and natural law theories, analytical and positivist theories, and utilitarian and other theories.

See also Peter A. Angeles, *Dictionary of Philosophy*, sv. "rationalism." "In general, the philosophic approach which emphasizes reason as the primary source of knowledge, prior or superior to, and independent of sense knowledge." Key rationalists are Plato, Aristotle, and Descartes.

Ibid., s.v. "law, natural." "The set of obligations or principles (laws, maxims, duties, codes, commands, etc.) binding upon one's conduct which are obtained by reason from examination of the universe (nature) in contrast to those obtained by revelation, intuition, innate moral conscience, authority, feelings, inclinations." Key figures are Thomas Aquinas, Cicero, Ulpian.

Ibid., s.v. "analytic philosophy." "A twentieth-century philosophic movement... that concentrates on language and the attempt to analyze statements (or concepts, or linguistic expressions, or logical forms) in order to find those with the best and most concise logical form which fits the facts or meaning to be presented. Central to analytic philosophy is the forming of definitions—linguistic or non-linguistic, real or contextual." Key figures are Bretrand Russell, G.E. Moore, Ludwig Wittgenstein.

Ibid., s.v. "positivism, logical." "...The acceptance of the verifiability principle, which is a criterion for determining that a statement has cognitive meaning. The cognitive meaning of a statement (as opposed to its emotive or other levels of meaning) is dependent upon its being verified. A statement is meaningful if-and-only-if it is, at least in principle, empirically verifiable. Some rock-bottom sense experience (positive knowledge) must be reached before a statement can have cognitive meaning." Two key figures are Thomas Hobbes and Chiam Perelman.

Ibid., s.v. "utilitarianism." "...One should act so as to promote the greatest happiness (pleasure) of the greatest number of people." Key figures are Jeremy Bentham, John Stuart Mill, and John Rawls.

77. A thorough discussion of the nature of justice is found in Daniel C. Maguire, *A New American Justice* (Minneapolis: Winston Press, 1980), especially 55–84. Maguire notes (page 194, n.4) an excellent treatment of the tripartite nature of justice found in Joseph Pieper, *Justice* (New York: Pantheon Books, 1955), 48–55. See especially page 50, where Pieper refers to Thomas Aquinas' explanation of the forms of justice: "...Justice rules in a community or state whenever the three basic relations, the three fundamental structures of communal life, are disposed in their proper order: firstly, the relations of individuals to one another (*ordo partium ad partes*); secondly, the relations of the social whole to the individuals (*ordo totius ad partes*); thirdly, the relations of individuals to the social whole (*ordo partium ad totum*). These three basic relationships correspond to the three basic forms of justice: reciprocal, or mutually exchanged justice (*iustitia commutativa*), which orders the relation of individual to partner; ministering justice (*iustitia distributiva*), which brings order to the relations between the community as such and the individuals who are its members; legal or general justice (*iustitia legalis, iustitia generalis*), which orders the members' relations to the social whole." See also Aristotle, *Nicomachean Ethics* Book

V:1129a3 –1138b14 where he describes and defines the scope and external nature of justice, as well as its internal nature. For Thomas Aquinas' treatment of justice, see his *ST* II–II.57–122, especially Questions 58, 61, 79, 80, and 122.

78. See my *Mutuality: A Formal Norm*, at 98: "The basic definition: *Mutuality is the sharing of 'power-with' by and among all parties in a relationship in a way that recognizes the wholeness and particular experience of each participant toward the end of optimum flourishing of all.*"

79. Ibid., at 95: "*Gender Mutuality - the sharing of 'power-with' by and among women and men in a way that recognizes the full participation of each in the imago Dei, embodied in daily life and through egalitarian relationships.*"

80. Ibid., at 96: "*Generative Mutuality - the sharing of 'power-with' by and among the Divine, human persons, and all creation in the on-going co-creation and redemption of the world.*"

81. Ibid., at 96: "*Social Mutuality - the sharing of 'power-with' by and among members of society in a way that recognizes the fundamental dignity of each and the obligation to attain and maintain for each what is necessary to sustain that dignity.*"

82. See my *Mutuality: A Formal Norm*, 233.

83. See for example Elizabeth A. Johnson, *Woman, Earth, Creator Spirit*, 1993, Madeleva Lecture in Spirituality, (Mahwah, NJ: Paulist Press, 1993), 32.

84. Rosemary Radford Ruether, *Gaia and God: An Ecofeminist Theology of Earth Healing* (San Francisco,: Harper, 1992), 2–3.

85. Susan Power Bratton, "Christian Ecotheology and the Old Testament," *Environmental Ethics* 6 (Fall 1984): 202–03.

86. Bratton, "Christian Ecotheology," 204. Most scholars agree the Gen. 2 creation story is a combination of the Gen. 1 story with a second separate story.

87. Gerhard Von Rad, *Genesis*, 57–58, cited by Bratton in Ibid., 203.

88. Jeanne Kay, "Concepts of Nature in the Hebrew Bible," *Environmental Ethics* 10 (Winter 1988): 313.

89. Ibid., 314.

90. Ibid.

91. Ibid.

92. Ibid.

93. Ibid.

94. Ibid.

95. Ibid., 315.

96. Clarence J. Glacken, *Traces on the Rhodian Shore: Nature and Culture in Western Thought from Ancient Times to the End of the Eighteenth Century* (Berkeley: University of California Press, 1967), 166, cited in Ibid., 311.

97. Yi-Fu Tuan, "Treatment of the Environment in Ideal and Actuality," *American Scientist* 58 (1970):244–49, cited in Kay, "Concepts of Nature," 311.

98. Kay, "Concepts of Nature," 317–19.
99. Ibid., 320.
100. Ibid., 320–21.
101. See my *Mutuality: A Formal Norm*, 233.

Discussion Questions

1. Discuss your understanding of the notion that creation is "sacramental." How does this understanding of creation give direction to Christians in an ecologically threatened age?

2. Given the "elements of a new ethic" suggested by Ken and Michael Himes, assess the possibility of this approach to environmental ethics.

3. Based on your knowledge of St. Francis, do you agree with Warner's assessment of him? Explain. What difference does it make whether we understand Francis one way or another?

4. Does the story of the "Wolf of Gubbio" hold any lessons for present day seekers of environmental integrity? Discuss.

5. How does a person of the twenty-first century "love a worm"? Discuss.

6. What organizations and/or resources do you think effectively employ a "Franciscan" approach to resolving environmental issues? What is it about the approach or the group that you identify as "Franciscan?"

7. Do you agree with Nothwehr's assessment of the particular contributions of the Franciscan and Benedictine charisms, respectively, to our present efforts to resolve the environmental crisis? Discuss.

Resources and
Action Organizations

FRANCISCAN ORGANIZATIONS AND RESOURCES

The Franciscan Federation
www.franfed.org

This is the umbrella organization for Franciscan communities in the US,

435

with connections to the global Franciscan family. Numerous resources are available on a variety of topics.

Franciscans International
www.franciscansinternational.org
Franciscans International operates under the sponsorship of the Conference of the Franciscan Family (CFF) and serves all Franciscans in the world community by bringing spiritual, ethical, and Franciscan principles and values to the various United Nations forums.

Justice, Peace and the Integrity of Creation
www.ofm.org/3/just/JUSmain.html
This site is connected to the General Curia in Rome, Italy.

Franciscan Web Page
wwwwtu.edu/franciscan
Click on ecology for numerous resources connected to the Franciscan Orders around the globe.

Franciscan Custody of the Holyland
See:www.christusrex.org/www1/ofm/fra/FRAht01.html for a brief, yet quite comprehensive history of the Franciscan movement

CATHOLIC ORGANIZATIONS AND RESOURCES

Catholic Committee of Appalachia
www.cathcomappalachia.org/index.htm
Committed to the faith, traditions, environmental treasures of the people and resources of the Appalachian region of the US. Excellent resources available.

Catholic Social Teaching
www.osjspm.org/cst/doclist.htm
Several major ecojustice documents are available on this site. Click on Themes.

Columbia River Pastoral Letter Project
www.columbiariver.org/index1.html
Bishops' Pastoral letter; "The Columbia River Watershed: Caring for Creation and the Common Good," in English, Spanish and French. Excellent study materials available.

National Catholic Rural Life Conference
www.ncrlc.com

The premier Catholic organization dealing with rural ministry and land issues in the U.S. with numerous links to resources and organizations.

Theology Library
www.shc.edu/theolibrary/index.htm

Various documents, articles, and ecojustice & peacemaking organizations. Click on Environment.

U.S. Conference of Catholic Bishops - Office of Social Development and World Peace
www.nccbuscc.org/sdwp

The U.S. Bishops' site has a variety of links to organizations, resources, publications, and activities currently sponsored by this office. Click on environmental project.

Vatican Website
www.vatican.va/

The official Vatican homepage. Numerous documents and various kinds of information are available here.

ECUMENICAL ORGANIZATIONS AND RESOURCES

Coalition on the Environment and Jewish Life
www.coejl.org/home.shtml

Earth Ministry, Connecting People with Creation
www.earthministry.org

Connects Christian faith and care for the environment through environmental ethics, simple living and environmental justice.

Evangelical Lutheran Church of America
elcasco.elca.org/dcs/creation.html

Statement Caring for Creation

National Religious Partnership for the Environment
www.nrpe.org/

1047 Amsterdam Avenue, New York, NY 10025, 212-316-7441, Fax. 212-316-7547.

World Council of Churches
www.wcc-coe.org/wcc/what/jpc/ecology.html
Justice, Peace & Creation Concerns Ecumenical Earth section.

INTERNATIONAL ORGANIZATIONS AND RESOURCES

Earth Action
www.oneworld.org/earthaction/
A global network of about 1,500 citizen groups in 142 countries. Focuses on integrating organizing efforts in areas of environmental and peace and justice issues. Great resources.

Earth Charter
www.earthcharter.org
The mission of the Earth charter is the promotion of "a world-wide dialogue on common values and to craft and implement a People's Earth Charter to secure a sustainable future based on justice, equity, peace, and ecological security." The document has emerged from the 1992 Earth Summit and formed an ethical foundation for Agenda 21.

Friends of the Earth
www.foe.org/
A multinational environmental organization that focuses on public policy, advocacy on behalf of the environment and sustainable development. Excellent resources & links.

United Nations Environment Program (UNEP)
www.unep.ch/
New York Office - DC2-803, United Nations, New York, NY 10017, Phone: 212 - 963 - 8210, Fax: 212-963-7341. Email: uneprona@un.org

SCIENCE AND RELIGION ORGANIZATIONS AND RESOURCES

Center for Neighborhood Technology
www.cnt.org/
A Chicago based group that has done excellent creative re-thinking concerning issues that affect major cities around the globe. Many of their innovative studies can be downloaded from their website. The city is viewed as a resource toward sustainability.

Earth Communications
forests.org/ric/deep-eco/niznik.htm
A gold mine of educational media resources for purchase or for rent on a wide variety of ecological issues.

Harvard University Forum on Religion and Ecology
environment.harvard.edu/religion/
Brings together the world's most renowned experts in science and religion. Fantastic forums and resources.

Orbis Books - Ecology and Justice:A Series on Global Ecology
www.orbisbooks.com/
An excellent series that integrates social justice and peace perspectives with the effort to create a sustainable and healthy world environment.

Zygon Center for Religion and Science
zygoncenter.org/
An excellent Chicago-based resource on the conversation between science & religion.

GENERAL ORGANIZATIONS AND RESOURCES

EcoCompass
www.islandpress.com/ecocompass/BeSciRes/BSRec.html
A guide to multiple ecology links.

Environmental Education Resources on the Internet
www.eelink.net/

Greenpeace (USA)
www.greenpeaceusa.org/
Educates, organizes, lobbies, and engages in nonviolent direct action on behalf of environmental and disarmament issues throughout the world. Has great resources.

The National Audubon Society
www.audubon.org/
Maintains seventy wildlife preserves in the US, has local clubs throughout the US, and has fine resources and publications. A superb set of links to other websites.

The Union of Concerned Scientists

www.ucsusa.org/

A fellowship of distinguished academics who provide excellent material on global warming, toxins, biodiversity and more.

Worldwatch Institute

wwwworldwatch.org/

Publishes an annual on the world, *State of the World*. They have a companion piece, *Vital Signs*. A good place for current statistics and sustainable insights.

Weekly Journal Exercises[*]

adapted by

Dawn M. Nothwehr, OSF

The purpose of these exercises is to challenge yourself to perceive the world with "spiritual eyes." Let the perspective of utilitarianism and technological explanation for things drop from you as the old skin of a molting snake. Allow yourself to experience yourself as one with the Earth, Earthcreatures, and your Creator. Permit yourself enter into the world of wonder; view the world as a young child who is touching the Earth for the first time.

EXERCISE A

(1) For several days, at approximately the same time of day or night, go to the same spot (*Examples:* a certain tree, a place along the river, the sky) and make the following observations:
- Spend at least 15 minutes watching, tasting, smelling, feeling and listening at "your spot."
- Begin by describing your spot in as great a detail as possible, using the information you consciously draw in from use of your various senses.
- Why did you choose the particular spot? (Note any changes in this reason from day to day).
- How do you feel or experience yourself in this spot? How is this different from how you feel when you are "at home"?

[*] In his video *The Hidden Heart of the Cosmos* [Mill Valley, CA: Center for the Story of the Universe, 1996} Brian Swimme makes several suggestions of exercises to assist modern urban humans in getting in touch with their relatedness with the natural world and the cosmos. These exercises have been adapted here.

• If "your spot" could speak to you, what would it say?

(2) Take time to reflect on the questions (above) and then write and draw (color) in your journal to express your experience.

EXERCISE B

(1) Go outside after dark.

(2) Lie down on your back with your face toward the night sky.

(3) Imagine you are lying at the south pole looking downward and out into space. *Spend at least 15 minuets looking this way.*

(4) Be aware of your relationship to space, the members of the wider cosmos, the Earth, the spot where you are lying and your own inner feelings.

(5) In your journal, record your feelings and insights from this experience.

EXERCISE C

(1) Become aware of the proportionate size of the Earth in relation to the Sun and the vast distance light travels to reach us.

(2) Look at the Sun and place your hand between you and the sunlight such that you can no longer see the Sun. Recall that the Sun could contain a million Earth's—yet, you can block the Sun from view by a mere movement of your hand.

(3) Record your thoughts and feelings in your journal.

EXERCISE D

(1) Experience the Dusk or the Dawn: Position yourself outside in a place where you have a view of the broad horizon. Then be prepared for the ride of a lifetime!

(2) As the light at the horizon decreases or increases, make yourself fully aware that it is *the Earth that is moving on its axis*, not the Sun going down or coming up!

(3) In one split second, you will swing from total darkness into light or from light into total darkness.... Did you see it!?

(4) In your journal, record your feelings about this Earth ride.

Suggestions for Reflection

ECOTHEOLOGY EXPLORATION PAPERS - OPTION 1

Read a book and write a critical book review of 3–5 pages for the journal, *Theological Studies.*

CRITERIA

- Give full bibliographic information about the book
- Review the content of the book, focusing on the author's central thesis and four or five themes that support it
- Explain how the author's thesis supports or detracts from the Franciscan theology of the environment, making reference to our study of St. Francis, St. Bonaventure or Bl. John Duns Scotus
- Select a quote of about a paragraph length that illustrates the central theme of the book and its relationship to Franciscan theology
- Conclude by providing your recommendation of the work based upon the book's strengths and weaknesses as a work for an undergraduate readership

ECOTHEOLOGY EXPLORATION PAPERS - OPTION 2

Research a major figure in ecology or eco-theology. Write a 3–5 page article for the Franciscan spirituality journal, *The Cord*, in which you examine the person's understanding of spirituality and theology.

CRITERIA

- Provide the full name, date and place of birth, religious affiliation of the figure
- Provide a brief biographical sketch of the figure
- Describe her/his major contributions to ecology, including any publications and their significance
- Provide an interesting anecdote and "quotable quote" that illustrates

the person's understanding of the relationship of central themes of Christian theology and observations from ecological science

- Indicate clearly what part of the "Christian story" is most significant for this figure

ECOTHEOLOGY EXPLORATION PAPERS - OPTION 3

Prepare a report (3–5 pages) for public radio in which you compare and contrast the content of a major doctrinal or policy statement by the leadership of two Christian traditions concerning the ecological crisis facing us today.

CRITERIA

- Indicate why you chose these particular documents
- Explain the historical circumstances—social, political, ecological, economic conditions—of the period in which each document was written
- Indicate the significance of the authors of each document
- Summarize the content of each of the documents
- Compare and contrast the content
- Research how each of the documents was received by the general public as well as the parishioners of the particular religious tradition
- Explain the strengths and weakness of each document based on principles of Franciscan theology
- Conclude by providing a "Quotable quote" that captures a significant message common to both documents

ECOTHEOLOGY EXPLORATION PAPERS - OPTION 4

Select a work from any art form (painting, sculpture, film, dance theater, literature, etc.). Research the piece you have selected. Then write an article for the Arts Section of the *Chicago Tribune* in which you explain how the work of art expresses a Franciscan theology of the environment.

CRITERIA

- Describe the work of art including its cultural and historical context
- Explain the religious significance of the work in light of Franciscan theology
- Explain the environmental significance of the work in light of Franciscan values
- Offer your personal aesthetic response to the work of art
- Research the artist and offer basic biographical information about her/him
- What has the artist her/himself told us about the significance of the work to her/him ?
- Compare and contrast the artist's view of the work and your own response to it in light of Franciscan theology of the environment

Paper About Family Traditions and Values: Relating to the Earth

Why not explore the relationship with the earth and the values relating to the earth that have been passed on within your family? You are encouraged to go back into the family history as far as possible. Very likely most of the material for the paper will come from the personal interviews you have with family members. It will be important to research any issues that arise in your conversations *(Example:* You find out that your grandparents were forced off their farm in South Dakota during the Great Depression and they lived in a region known as the "Dust Bowl." You will need to include some explanation of the "Great Depression" and "the Dust Bowl" and explain the significance of each.).

CRITERIA

- Introduce your family focusing on where they have lived and why they have moved from one place to the other—if that is the case
- Were your forbearers involved with the land directly and dependent on it directly for their livelihood? Explain their circumstances in relationship to this question.
- Summarize the basic beliefs about their relationship to the land held by each person you interview

- How has each person been influenced in their beliefs about the land—was moving from one place to another an influence?
- Explain what methods, rituals, or aesthetic experiences were utilized in your family to hand on beliefs and values concerning the land
- Conclude by articulating your own ecotheological beliefs in a paragraph or so and explain how and why you hope to pass these beliefs on to the next generations

Contributors

Philotheus Boehner, OFM (d. 1955) was a Friar of the Holy Name Province. He was co-founder and first director of The Franciscan Institute, St. Bonaventure, NY. A professor of philosophy, he was also founder of *The Cord*, a Franciscan spirituality journal.

Eric Doyle, OFM (d.1984) was a member of the Immaculate Conception Province of the Friars Minor (England). He was a scholar, teacher, mentor, and brother.

Elizabeth A. Dreyer is professor of theology in the Department of Religious Studies, Fairfield University, Fairfield, CT.

James F. Edmiston, OFM is a member of the Sacred Heart Province of the Friars Minor. A nationally known entomologist, in 2000 he was credited with the discovery of two species of *Lemnaphilia*, shore flies. Currently he is on assignment from the Franciscans Minister General (Rome) working to renew Franciscan life and ministry in Russia and Kazakhstan.

Zachary Hayes, OFM is a member of the Sacred Heart Province of the Friars Minor and chair of the Department of Historical and Doctrinal Studies at Catholic Theological Union at Chicago. He is the premier Bonaventure scholar of the English speaking world.

Kenneth R. Himes, OFM is professor of Moral Theology at Washington Theological Union.

Michael J. Himes is professor of theology at the University of Notre Dame.

Phil Hoebing, OFM is a member of the Sacred Heart Province of the Friars Minor and Professor Emeritus of Philosophy at Quincy University, Quincy, IL.

Mary Elizabeth Ingham, CSJ is a Sister of St. Joseph of Orange, CA. She is professor of Philosophy at Marymount College in Los Angeles. Her work centers on medical ethics and the thought of John Duns Scotus.

Robert J. Karris, OFM is a member of the Sacred Heart Province of the Friars Minor. He teaches in the School of Franciscan Studies at St. Bonaventure University and is researcher in residence at The Franciscan Institute, St. Bonaventure, NY.

Jeanne Kay Guelke is currently Professor of Geography at the University of Waterloo, Waterloo, Ontario, Canada. When the present article was written she was in the Department of Geography, University of Utah, Salt Lake City, UT 84112. Kay was then coeditor of *The Professional Geographer*, forum and journal of the Association of American Geographers. Her current research interests included the historical geography of American Indians and biblical attitudes toward wilderness.

Séamus Mulholland, OFM is a member of the English Province of the Friars Minor and a poet. He has done research and writing at the Franciscan Study Center in Canterbury.

Thomas Murtagh, OFM is a member of the Australian Province of the Friars Minor. He has taught at The Franciscan Institute at St. Bonaventure, NY.

Thomas A. Nairn, OFM is a member of the Sacred Heart Province of the Friars Minor and Associate Professor of Ethics at Catholic Theological Union at Chicago.

Dawn M. Nothwehr, OSF is a member of the Sisters of St. Francis, Congregation of Our Lady of Lourdes, Rochester, MN. She is Assistant Professor of Ethics at Catholic Theological Union at Chicago.

Kenan B. Osborne, OFM is a Friar of the Santa Barbara Province and Professor of Systematic Theology at the Franciscan School of Theology, Berkeley, CA.

Margaret Pirkl, OSF a member of the Sisters of St. Francis, Congregation of Our Lady of Lourdes, Rochester, MN. She taught Earth Sciences at the College of St. Teresa, Winona, MN, and has been a lecturer in Franciscan Studies and the Franciscan Sabbatical Program at Tau Center, Winona, MN. She has worked on many special projects for the wider Franciscan Family, especially advocating for the participation of Franciscans at the United Nations.

Susan Power Bratton is currently chair of the Environmental Studies Program at Baylor University, Waco, TX. The article was originally published when the author was at the Institute of Ecology, The University of Georgia, Athens, GA 30602.

William Short, OFM is a Friar of the Santa Barbara Province and Professor of Franciscan Spirituality at the Franciscan School of Theology, Berkeley, CA. His work centers on Franciscan spirituality in the Middle Ages. He is co-editor of the three volume 1999-2001 critical edition of Franciscan sources, *Francis of Assisi: Early Documents.*

Keith Warner, OFM is a Friar of the Santa Barbara Province and a doctoral student in environmental studies at the University of California at Santa Cruz. He is a geographer, writer, environmental advocate and native plant lover.

Abbreviations

Adm	Admonitions
BenLeo	Blessing for Brother Leo
CantSol	Canticle of Brother Sun
EpAnt	Letter to St. Anthony
EpCler	Letter to the Clergy
EpCust	Letter to the Custodians
lEpFid	First Letter to the Faithful
2EpFid	Second Letter to the Faithful
EpLeo	Letter to Brother Leo
EpMin	Letter to a Minister
EpOrd	Letter to the Entire Order
EpRect	Letter to the Rulers of the Peoples
ExhLD	Exhortation to the Praise of God
ExhPD	Exhortation to Poor Ladies
ExpPat	Prayer Inspired by the Our Father
Form Viv	Form of Life for St. Clare
lFragm	Fragment of other Rule I
2Fragm	Fragment of other Rule II
LaudDei	Praises of God
LaudHor	Praises to be said at all the Hours
OffPass	Office of the Passion
OrCruc	Prayer before the Crucifix
RegB	Later Rule
RegNB	Earlier Rule
RegEr	Rule for Hermitages
SalBMV	Salutation of the Blessed Virgin Mary
SalVirt	Salutation of the Virtues
Test	Testament

TestS	Testament written in Siena
UltVol	Last Will written for St. Clare
VPLaet	Dictate on True and Perfect Joy

WRITINGS OF SAINT CLARE

BCl	Blessing of Clare
1LAg	First Letter to Agnes of Prague
2LAg	Second Letter to Agnes of Prague
3LAg	Third Letter to Agnes of Prague
4LAg	Fourth Letter to Agnes of Prague
LEr	Letter to Ermentrude of Bruges
RCl	Rule of Clare
TestCl	Testament of Clare

EARLY FRANCISCAN SOURCES

1 Cel	First Life of St. Francis by Thomas of Celano
2 Cel	Second Life of St. Francis by Thomas of Celano
3 Cel	Treatise on the Miracles by Thomas of Celano
AP	Anonymous of Perugia
CL	Legend of Clare
CSD	Consideration of the Stigmata
Fior	Fioretti
JdV	Witness of Jacque de Vitry
LM	Major Life of St. Francis by Bonaventure
LMin	Minor Life of St. Francis by Bonaventure
LP	Legend of Perugia
L3S	Legend of the Three Companions
Proc	Acts of the Process of Canonization of St. Clare
SC	Sacrum Commercium
SP	Mirror of Perfection

Glossary

Abbess A woman who is the Canonical superior of a convent of nuns.

Acts of the Process of Canonization The official Church record of all evidence and testimony of witnesses in the process of deciding if a person should be listed among the canonized saints of the Church.

ad extra outside of; The life of God *ad extra* includes all of God's self-expression and revelation such as God's creation of the world, acts of love, or saving acts toward humankind.

ad intra inside of; The life of God *ad intra* involves the relationships of the persons of the Trinity—Father, Son, and Holy Spirit—in relation with one another.

Agnes of Prague Sister to Clare of Assisi. She joined Clare as a Poor Lady in 1236. Clare sent her to found a Poor Clare convent in Prague with the aid of five nuns, and she became its abbess. Born in 1205 in Prague, Bohemia, she died in 1282, was beatified in 1874, and was canonized November 12 ,1989, by Pope John Paul II.

Albert the Great A Dominican scholar (1206–1280) and teacher of Bonaventure and Thomas Aquinas. He earned his Doctorate in 1245 from the University of Paris and he later taught there. He was known for his work in scripture and theology but also in biology, chemistry, physics, astronomy, geography, metaphysics and mathematics.

Albigensians Cathars or Albigensians was a heretical sect which flourished in the 12th and 13th centuries in Italy and southern France. They were dualists, believing in both 'good' and 'evil' realms. The spiritual, intangible, and metaphysical was 'good'; the material and tangible was 'evil.' They led ascetic lifestyles, acknowledged no sacraments, and rejected the Incarnation.

Alexander of Hales A scholar born about 1185, he died in 1245. He studied in Paris from before 1210. From 1225 until his death, he was a master of theology at Paris. In 1236/1237, he joined the Franciscan order, thus giving the Franciscans their first chair in theology at Paris.

Allegri's *Miserere* This work was written sometime before 1638 for the annual celebration of the matins during Holy Week (the Easter celebration). For more details see: http://www.classical.net/music/comp.lst/works/allegri/miserere.html.

Anselm He is recognized as the father of medieval scholasticism. He was born at Aost Piedmont in 1033 and died at Canterbury, England, on April 21, 1109. He was canonized in 1494. For details about his theology and philosophy see: http://www.utm.edu/research/iep/a/anselm.htm.

Aristotelian hylomorphism (from Greek hyle, "matter"; morphe, "form"), in philosophy, a metaphysical view according to which every natural body consists of two intrinsic principles, one potential, namely, primary matter, and one actual, namely, substantial form. It was the central doctrine of Aristotle's philosophy of nature. Many medieval scholars, including Avicebron and Bonaventure, extended hylomorphism to all beings in creation.

Aristotle Greek philosopher 384-322 B.C.E. See this website for more details: http://www.ucmp.berkeley.edu/history/aristotle.html.

Augustine of Hippo Considered to be one of the most outstanding theologians in the history of the Catholic Church, Augustine was born in North Africa in 354 A.D. and died there in 430. For more see: http://www.geocities.com/Athens/1534/august.html

Averroists Western Christian philosophers who, in the later Middle Ages and during the Renaissance, drew inspiration from the interpretation of Aristotle put forward by Averroës, a Muslim philosopher. The basic tenet of Latin Averroism was the assertion that reason and philosophy are superior to faith and knowledge founded on faith. See http://www.britannica.com/seo/l/latin-averroism/ for more.

Avicebron Avicebron was a Jewish religious poet, moralist, and philosopher. He was born at Malaga in 1020 or 1021, and died at Saragossa in 1070. He was educated at Saragossa, where he spent the remainder of his life, devoting himself to moral and intellectual philosophy, and writing religious poetry. See this website for more details: http://www.newadvent.org/cathen/02156a.htm.

Avicenna Arabian physician and philosopher, born at Kharmaithen, in the province of Bokhara, 980; died at Hamadan, in Northern Persia, 1037. See this website for more details on this physician and philosopher: http://www.newadvent.org/cathen/02157a.htm.

Bach's *St. Matthew's Passion* "Passion setting" is a musical/dramatic treatment of the events of the Last Supper, Betrayal, Arrest, Trial, and Crucifixion of Jesus, as related in the New Testament. "Passion" means "suffering," from the Latin, *patior,* "I suffer." The title of the work is correctly stated as: *The Passion according to St. Matthew* by J. S. Bach or Bach's *St. Matthew Passion.* See more details at this website: http://www.bachfaq.org/passion.html.

biblical revelation God's self-revelation known through the texts of the Bible.

biblical exegetical methodology Various ways used by scripture scholars to interpret biblical texts such as literary criticism, historical criticism, social science criticism. For an example of an exegetical research strategy see http://divinity.lib.vanderbilt.edu/otexeg.html.

Book of Sentences An admirable compendium of theological knowledge by Peter Lombard. Nearly every medieval philosopher and theologian studied it, commented on it, and/or referenced it in their major treatises. See this website for more details: http://www.utm.edu/research/iep/l/lombard.htm.

Breviloquium A theological synthesis written by Bonaventure of Bagnoregio at the University of Paris in 1257.

Brothers and Sisters of Penance The Third Order of St. Francis of Assisi was for people who wanted to follow Jesus and live the Gospels according to the style of Francis and Clare—but who were unable to live as consecrated celibates. Later some members came to live together in convents, took vows, and became the Third Order Regular. Some stayed "in the world" and are today's Secular Franciscan Order.

canonical title A title given in Canon Law for one who holds an office in the Church such as a leader of a convent of women known as an "Abbess."

Canticle of the Creatures; Canticle of Brother Sun A *laude* (Italian: "canticle, hymn of praise") is a type of Italian poetry or a nonliturgical devotional song in praise of the Virgin Mary, Christ, or the saints. The first lauda in Italian was St. Francis' moving canticle in praise. For more details on the *Canticle* see: http://www.britannica.com/seo/l/lauda/.

capax Dei Capable of receiving, bearing, and symbolizing the divine.

cause for canonization The official process in the Roman Catholic Church whereby evidence is gathered toward proving a person worthy to be upheld as a universal model of faith.

Christ Incarnate Incarnation comes from a Latin term meaning enfleshment. In Christ, God made manifest in human flesh.

Christocentric Focused on Christ.

Christology The area of theology that deals with the person of Jesus Christ.

Collations on the Hexaemeron This work, left incomplete at his death, is the final and highest synthesis of Bonaventure's thought and his response to the controversy over the Latin Averroism at the University of Paris. He used the six days of creation as a literary and symbolic framework.

cosmic revelation The disclosure of the divine Creator through the created elements of the cosmos.

covenant The relationship established at God's initiative between God and the people of Israel

David Tracy A Roman Catholic theologian who teaches at the University of Chicago. He is the Andrew Thomas Greeley and Grace McNichols Greeley Distinguished Service Professor of Catholic Studies and Professor of Theology and of the Philosophy of Religion. He received his S.T.L. and S.T.D. from the Gregorian University, Rome.

deference Respect, esteem, affected and ingratiating regard for another, usually an elder person or one's superior.

dialectical relationship Discussion and reasoning by dialogue as a method of intellectual investigation.

Divine Ideas See http://www.humanities.mq.edu.au/Ockham/ x52t01.html

Doctrine of the Trinity In Christian doctrine, the tenet that God is the unity of Father, Son, and Holy Spirit as three persons in one Godhead. See http://www.britannica.com/seo/t/trinity/ for more.

ecclesiology The area of theology that deals with the Church.

ecstatic love Love beyond one's control. See this website for more on Bonaventure's use of the term: http://www.dal.ca/~claswww/BO-VENT.htm.

efficiency The way something is brought about.

eminence The position of prominence or of superiority.

escapism The habitual diversion of the mind to distract one from reality or routine.

Fathers of the Church The great bishops, doctors and other eminent Christian teachers of the early centuries whose writings remained as a court of appeal for their successors, especially in reference to controverted points of faith or practice.

Fermilab Fermi National Accelerator Laboratory advances the understanding of the fundamental nature of matter and energy by providing leadership and resources for qualified researchers to conduct basic research at the frontiers of high energy physics and related disciplines. See this website for more details: http://www.fnal.gov/pub/about/whatis/mission.html.

Fonte Colombo The place on a hill of evergreen oaks, five km far from Rieti, Italy where St. Francis lived for forty days and received from Jesus the *Rule for the Friars Minor.*

Franciscan Family The term refers to all members of the first, second and third orders founded by St. Francis and St. Clare of Assisi.

Golden Sayings of Brother Giles Bl. Aegidius of Assisi, better known as Br. Giles, was one of the original companions of St. Francis. Not a theologian, he was known for giving counsel to all sorts of people. His collected wisdom forms the "Sayings" of Aegidius. St. Bonaventure held these "Sayings" in high esteem. See also http://www.newadvent.org/cathen/01170d.htm.

Greek Fathers Eusebius, Athanasius, Basil the Great, Gregory Nazianzenus, Gregory of Nyssa, Cyril of Jerusalem, Chrysostoma, Epiphanius, Cyril of Alexandria, and Ephraim, deacon of Edessa. See this website for more details: http://www.newadvent.org/fathers/.

Hebrew Bible (Hebrew Scriptures or Hebrew Testament) The *Old Testament*.See also http://wwwwsu.edu:8080/~wldciv/world_civ_reader/world_civ_reader_1/hebrew_bible.html.

hermitage A place set apart for prayer. At the time of Francis' reconstruction of San Damiano he dressed as a hermit. Throughout his life, he sought solitude, even when traveling. There is evidence such as in the *Regula Non Bullata* 7,13 (Rule of 1209-21) that friars lived in hermitages or other places. For more details see this website: http://www.capuchinfriars.org.au/hermitag.htm#10t

Holmes Rolston III is University Distinguished Professor of philosophy at Colorado State University. His more recent books are: *Genes, Genesis and God; Science and Religion: A Critical Survey; Philosophy Gone Wild; Environmental Ethics;* and *Conserving Natural Value.* He edited *Biology, Ethics, and the Origins of Life* .

Image of God A concept known from revelation that humans are in a unique relationship with God. The whole person is created in God's image as a partner with God in caring for the world (Gen 1:26ff).

Incarnation The process by which the Word of God became flesh.

instrumental value The value of something based on its perceived usefulness.

intrinsic value The value of something for its own sake.

Itinerarium mentis in Deum Bonaventure's 1259 work, follows Augustine's path of the soul to God, from the external world to the interior world of the mind, and then above the mind from the temporal to the eternal. Throughout this journey, the person is aided by a moral and intellectual divine illumination.

J.Baird Callicott Professor in the Department of Philosophy and Religion Studies, University of North Texas. His books include: *Beyond the Land Ethic: More Essays in Environmental Philosophy; Earth's Insights: A Survey of Ecological Ethics from the Mediterranean*

Basin to the Australian Outback; and In Defense of the Land Ethic: Essays in Environmental Philosophy.

Joachim of Fiore Born about 1130 and died about 1202 in Fiore, Italy. He was a mystic, theologian, biblical commentator, philosopher of history. His philosophy of history maintains that history develops in three ages of increasing spirituality: the ages of the Father, the Son, and the Holy Spirit. See this website for more details: http://www.britannica.com/seo/j/joachim-of-fiore/.

Johannine literature The *Gospel of John* and the three *Letters of John* in the *New Testament*. See this website for more: http://bellarmine.lmu.edu/faculty/fjust/John.htm.

John of Rochelle A master of theology and friar at the University of Paris. He worked closely with Alexander of Hales as his student and their works are closely linked. His works include a commentary on the *Rule of St. Francis* and book one (on God) and book three (on the incarnation and passion) of the *Summa Alexandri*. He was also well-known as a preacher.

Jordan of Giano An early Franciscan who chronicled the friars' mission in Germany around 1262.

La Verna, Italy The place where Francis received the Stigmata.

Legend of Perugia An oral source of the life of St. Francis as told by: "we, who lived with him."

literal sense Literal interpretation of a text means that a biblical text is to be understood according to the "plain meaning" conveyed by its grammatical construction and historical context. The literal meaning is held to correspond to the intention of the authors.

literary device An indirect way of stating an idea for persuasive or artistic effect.

macrocosm The universe or the entire world considered in its totality.

materiality Physical characteristics of an object such as position, size, shape, structure as it exists in time and space, inertia, movement, color, texture, etc.

metaphorical language A figure of speech in which word or phrase denotes one thing as applied to another thing to suggest a likeness between them.

metaphysics (metaphysical) For Aristotle it was the study of being-as-such as distinct from the study of particular beings that exist in the universe.

microcosm A philosophical term designating the human as being a "little world" in which the macrocosm, or universe, is reflected. Plato's "world soul" which animated the universe had as a corollary the idea of the human body as a miniature universe animated by its own soul. Find more details on this concept at this website: http://www.britannica.com/seo/m/microcosm/.

Minister General of the Order The international head of the Franciscan friars.

Mirror of Perfection In 1899 Paul Sabatier, a French religious historian, claimed he had discovered the oldest manuscript of the life of St. Francis. This was the start of a heated debate regarding the Franciscan question that continued for years. Today, the question is definitely solved, and the *Mirror of Perfection* is dated 1318.

moral imagination The human capacity to envision what is good and what is right based on the facts of a situation and on an understanding of intent, act, and circumstances.

Mozart's *Ave Verum* Mozart wrote a number of shorter works for church use. These include the simple four-part setting of the Ave Verum, written to oblige a priest in Baden in June 1791. Hear this work at this website: http://www.ask.com/main/meta-answer.asp?metaEngine=directhit&origin=7039&MetaURL=http%3A%2F%2Fask%2Edirecthit%2Ecom%2Ffcgi%2Dbin%2FRedirURL%2Efcg%3Furl%3Dhttp%3A%2F%2Fwww%2Emegsinet%2Enet%2F%7Efigueroa%2Faveverum%2Ehtm%26qry%3DAve%2BVerum%2BCorpus%26rnk%3D3%26cz%3Dfd72a664bc35b3c9%26src%3DDDH%5FAsk%5FSRCH&qCategory=jeeves&metaTopic=aveverum%2EHTM&ItemOrdinal=2&logQID=376807390D1AA44E98B03902E505228A&sv=206&back=http%3A%2F%2Fwww%2Eask%2Ecom%2Fmain%2Faskjeeves%2Easp%3Fmetasearch%3Dyes%26site%5Fname%3DJeeves%26origin%3D7039%26ask%3DAve%2BVerum%2BCorpus%26qsource%3D56%26meta%3Drs&ask=Ave+Verum+Corpus

natural philosophy The study of nature in general, or in modern times, the study of physics.

nature mystic One who experiences God through the natural world.

neoplatonism Neo-Platonism is a modern term used to designate the period of Platonic philosophy beginning with the work of Plotinus and ending with the closing of the Platonic Academy by the Emperor Justinian in 529 CE. See this website for more: http://www.utm.edu/research/iep/n/neoplato.htm.

ontological Concerning being or existence.

Oxford Franciscans Early Franciscans at Oxford included Adam Marsh, Roger Bacon, and Alexander of Hales. See http://www.bartleby.com/211/1017.html for more details.

panentheism The belief that all things are imbued with God's being in the sense that all things are *in* God. God is more than all that is and is a consciousness and the highest unity possible.

Patristic commentaries Works by the Fathers of the Church.

Pauline literature New Testament books ether written by Paul the Apostle or attributed to him.

Peter Singer Peter Singer is the Ira W. DeCamp Professor of Bioethics in the University Center for Human Values at Princeton University. He first became well-known internationally after the publication of *Animal Liberation.* For more see: http://icarus.uic.edu/~strian1/whoissinger.htm.

Peter Lombard An Italian theologian, born about 1100 and died in 1160. He studied at Bologna, Reims, and Paris, where he later taught. His most significant work was the *Sentences.* By the 13th century, the *Sentences* was the premier university theological text and was commented on by the likes of Bonaventure and Aquinas.

Plato Born about 428 BC, and died about 347. Considered the second of the great trio of ancient Greek philosophers—Socrates, Plato, and Aristotle—who between them laid the philosophical foundations of Western culture.

Portiuncula The Franciscan Order (Friars Minor) was founded by Francis of Assisi (1182-1226) in the little church of Portiuncula in 1209.

In 1212 Clare of Assisi joined the brothers there and later founded the Poor Ladies or Poor Clare order.

Primacy and Predestination of Christ See the *Catholic Update* (Jan. 2001) at this website:: http://www.americancatholic.org/Newsletters/CU/ac0101.asp.

Pseudo-Dionesius lived in the late-fifth century, and was probably a Syrian monk. He wrote a series of treatises and letters uniting Neoplatonic philosophy with Christian theology and mystical experience, and established a definite Neoplatonic trend in medieval Christian doctrine in the Western Latin Church that influences it still today.

Richard of St. Victor A Scottish monk, mystic and prior of the Abbey of St. Victor, Paris. His principal importance for our purposes is his work on the Blessed Trinity and on the Incarnate Word.

Robert Grosseteste An English bishop and scholar, born in 1175 and died in 1253. His was known for his translations of, and commentaries on, Aristotle—a major contributor to thirteenth-century Scholastic philosophy. He studied and taught at the University of Oxford, where he later lectured to Franciscans there until 1235.

Rublev's icon of the Trinity Rublev was a monk in the Trinity-St. Sergius Monastery. St. Sergius (1314–1392), the founder of the monastery emphasized a life of "fraternity, calm, love (toward) God and spiritual self-improvement." See Russian iconographer Andrey Rublev's famous icon Holy Trinity at this website: http://webl.duc.auburn.edu/academic/liberal_arts/foreign/russian/icons/trinity-rublev.html

Rule A way of life. For St. Francis the way was to follow in the footprints of Jesus.

Stephen Hawking Born on Jan. 8, 1942, attended University College at Oxford. He subsequently received a Ph.D. in physics. Hawking's most important discovery so far is that black holes emit X-rays and gamma-rays that can be detected by special scientific instruments. His best known works are: *A Brief History of Time* and *Black Holes and Baby Universes and Other Essays*.

S.J. Gould Stephen Jay Gould (Sept. 10, 1941–May 20, 2002) received his Ph.D. from Columbia University in 1967. He was Professor of Geology and Zoology at Harvard University. Primarily a paleontologist and an evolutionary biologist, he taught geology and the history of science as well.

San Damiano The church in the valley below Assisi that Francis restored, and where Clare and the first Poor Ladies lived. See this church at: http://listserv.american.edu/catholic/franciscan/tour/sd05.html.

Scholastics Philosophers and theologians who attempted to use natural human reason, particularly the philosophy and science of Aristotle, to understand the supernatural content of Christian revelation. They taught in universities of Europe between the mid-eleventh to mid-fifteenth century.

self-diffusive From "diffuse" which is to pour out and to permit or cause something to spread out. Goodness is not self contained, but rather by its very nature, causes itself to move outward toward others.

Sentence Commentary It was a standard exercise for theology students at the Master's degree level in medieval universities to write a book-length work presenting their criticisms and interpretation of Peter Lombard's *Sentences*. Bonaventure's *Commentary on the Sentences* is significant for understanding his theology.

St. Martin's Church in Canterbury Go to this website to see a photo of this church and learn about its history: http://members.aol.com/butrousch/augustine/stmartin.htm.

St. Prian's Oratory in Cornwall Legend has it that St Prian came to Cornwall on a millstone. A gang of heathen Irishmen had tied him to the stone, rolling it over the edge of the cliff into a stormy sea, which thereupon was stilled, and the saint floated calmly over the water to the sandy beach of Perranzabuloe. Today the ruins of a little oratory built in the manner of the Celtic chapels of Ireland in the sixth to eighth century remains near Cornwall.

Summa Halensis A major collection of theological treatises attributed to Alexander of Hales (1170/85-1245). Hales theological and philosophical thought influenced the teachings of St. Bonaventure and John of La Rochelle. The *Summa theologica*, for centuries thought to be Hale's, is now considered to be largely the work of followers.

Synoptics The Gospels of Matthew, Mark, and Luke in the Christian Testament.

Testament of Clare of Assisi (1193–1253) Somewhat controversial as to its authenticity because the manuscript tradition is not strong, this document is Clare's dying expression of her desire for the life of the Poor Ladies and their relationship to the Friars Minor.

Testament of Francis of Assisi Just before Francis died on October 3, 1226, he dictated what came to be known as his *Testament*. In it he addresses the future of his order and states his position one more time as forcefully as possible. For the full text, see this website: http://www.fordham.edu/halsall/source/stfran-test.html.

The Little Prince A book written by the French author, journalist, and pilot, Antoine de Saint- Exupéry in 1943. From the outside it appears to be a simple children's tale, but actually it is a profound book, written in riddles and laced with philosophy and poetic metaphors. For more details about this famous work see: http://www.CNR.Berkeley.EDU/~gsposito/LittlePrince/.

The Fioretti Also known as the *Little Flowers of Francis of Assisi*, a classic collection of popular legends about the life of St. Francis of Assisi and his early companions as they appeared to the Italian people at the beginning of the fourteenth century. For the full texts see: http://www.ccel.org/u/ugolino/flowers/flow.htm.

The Father of Lies Speaking of the devil, whose name is Satan, Jesus said, "When he lies, he speaks his native language, for he is a liar and the father of lies." (Jn 8:44b NIV)

Theodosius Dobzhansky (1900–1975), American geneticist and zoologist, who, through his research, made important contributions to the field of genetics. His works include: *Genetics and the Origin of Species; Evolution,Genetics, and Man*, and *Mankind Evolving*

theophany A visible manifestation of the divine.

Thomas of Celano A poet, and hagiographical writer who was born about 1200; died about 1255. He was one of the first to join St. Francis of Assisi, probably in 1215. He wrote numerous works about St. Francis and St. Clare and the early Franciscans including: "First Life" of St. Francis of Assisi (after 1228), "Second Life" of St. Francis (1244-

47), the Miracles of St. Francis (1257). He is also credited by many as the author of: two sequences honoring Francis: "Fregit victor victuals" and "Sanctitatis nova signâ," and, the "Life of St. Clare of Assisi" (1255-62).

Timothy Ferris An astronomer and journalist who teaches at the University of California, Berkeley. His works include: *Coming of Age in the Milky Way, Galaxies, The Red Limit*. He has received the American Institute of Physics Prize, the American Association for the Advancement of Science Prize, the Klumpke-Roberts Prize, and a Guggenheim Fellowship.

Tom Reagan An American philosopher who takes the expression "animal rights," literally and argues that the key moral rights of higher animals are the same as those moral rights of humans. Two important works are: *The Case for Animal Rights* and *All That Dwell Therein: Animal Rights and Environmental Ethics*.

transcendent love The love of God.

triadic relation The inner relations of the three persons of the Trinity.

Trinitarian life of God The relationships between the Father, Son, and Holy Spirit.

univocity of being A term is used univocally when it is used in only in the one sense For example, horse and dog are both animals in the same sense of animal as, "living material beings" (or whatever the sense is). A word is used equivocally when it shifts from one sense to another: for example, "book" as applied to some written work one can read and as a process of scheduling a flight.

Victorines William of Champeaux founded the Victorine order around 1113 in Paris. Under Guildin, the second abbot, the Victorine school of theology developed; among its proponents were Hugh of St. Victor, Richard of St. Victor, and Walter of St. Victor. The Victorines were a small order with great intellectual influence and many students, and in the thirteenth Century, the school of theology became a college within the University of Paris.

wisdom theology Central to this understanding of God and God's actions in history is the practical, unpretentious song of faith in a sovereign, good, and caring God. The God who creates is also the God who sustains the people—whether in the face of suffering or blessing, defeat or victory. Faith in God brings reward and restores all inequity. "Love the Lord and do what is right" is the byword of wisdom.